DOING INTERNATIONAL RESEARCH

DOING INTERNATIONAL RESEARCH

Global and Local Methods

CHRISTOPHER WILLIAMS

SAGE

Los Angeles | London | New Delhi
Singapore | Washington DC | Boston

SAGE

Los Angeles | London | New Delhi
Singapore | Washington DC | Boston

SAGE Publications Ltd
1 Oliver's Yard
55 City Road
London EC1Y 1SP

SAGE Publications Inc.
2455 Teller Road
Thousand Oaks, California 91320

SAGE Publications India Pvt Ltd
B 1/I 1 Mohan Cooperative Industrial Area
Mathura Road
New Delhi 110 044

SAGE Publications Asia-Pacific Pte Ltd
3 Church Street
#10-04 Samsung Hub
Singapore 049483

Editor: Jai Seaman
Assistant editor: Lily Mehrbod
Production editor: Victoria Nicholas
Copyeditor: Jane Fricker
Proofreader: Kate Campbell
Marketing manager: Sally Ransom
Cover design: Shaun Mercier
Typeset by: C&M Digitals (P) Ltd, Chennai, India
Printed and bound by CPI Group (UK) Ltd, Croydon, CR0 4YY

MIX
Paper from responsible sources
FSC www.fsc.org FSC® C013604

The picture on p.1, 'Even without Borders'. فكري نيايش is by Nia Fekri, International Student Advisor. (Based on the hadith, 'Seek knowledge, even as far as China'.)

First published 2015

Library of Congress Control Number: 2014954026

British Library Cataloguing in Publication data

A catalogue record for this book is available from the British Library

ISBN 978-1-4462-7348-7
ISBN 978-1-4462-7349-4 (pbk)

Contents

Full contents

List of figures

List of boxes

List of thinking zones

Additional thinking zones are on the accompanying website

Acknowledgements

Thanks to people who have shared their experience and insights, and organizations that facilitated forums for discussion, including:

Afghan ministries, EC and NGOs (*Afghanistan Demain, Aschiana, Enfants du Monde/ Droits de l'homme, Terre des Hommes*).

Belarusian students, academics, Irina Panteleev and others at *Magna Carta College, Belarusian State University of Informatics and Radioelectronics, Minsk State Linguistic University*, and the *British Embassy*.

Bosnian educationalists (Sarajevo schools, *WCCES*).

British criminologists, INGO staff, education and health students, politicians, and others. *International State Crime Initiative* Queen Mary University of London, UCL Institute of Education, *Oxford Brookes University, Royal Central School of Speech and Drama* (AHRC project, 'Bodies of Planned Obsolescence: Digital performance and the global politics of electronic waste.) Research Support Unit *Amnesty International*, and Kirt Holmes, jewellery maker, for explaining the significance of the Taforalt beads.

Bulgarian disability rights groups (*Karin Dom*).

Chinese heritage projects and tourism students (UNESCO Suzhou, *Sichuan University*). Toxicologists, School of Biological Sciences, *The University of Hong Kong*.

Croatian human rights activists and academics (*Zagreb University*).

European Union and international teachers (EU Parliament, *International School, Brussels*).

Gambian democracy experts (*Alliance for Democracy in Africa*).

Geneva Press Club, Geneva Institute for Water, Environment and Health and Eli Fumoto of *Polaris* project management.

Greek NGOs and officials (Ministry of Education/Welfare).

Hungarian curators (*Memento Park*, Budapest).

Indian MPs, academics and human rights activists (*Centre for Policy Studies, Parisar Asha*).

Japanese sustainable development students and academics (*Nagoya University, Asia Pacific University*, Chubu Institute for Advanced Studies). Environmental activists and the *Minamata Victims Museum* (Minamata Bay).

Jordanian health professionals (*Jordan University*).

Kazakh and Russian arts and Bologna Process experts (*Almaty National Academy of Arts*).

Korean 'international understanding' and global citizenship organizations (APCEIU, YWCA). Sun-young Park (*Seoul University*). Educationists and civil servants (Gyeonggi Province Governorate). Arts and youth-work academics (Seoul, Hongik, Ajou, Suwon and Donseo Universities). Yunjoo Lee UN-WIPO. Yujin Lee (Founding Director, *HANA Communications*).

Lebanese officials, NGOs and UN agencies (Ministries of Education / Labour / Social Affairs, AMIDEAST, CHF, ILO, IPEC, OCFT, UNESCO, USDoL, Rene Moawad Foundation).

Liberian NGOs (Oxfam).

Mexican environmentalists (*Yucatan Centre for Scientific Investigation*).

Nigerian performance artists, centre for Contemporary Art, University of Lagos.

New Zealand Centre for Global Studies – members and 'Global Citizenship' students.

Palestinian NGOs and UN staff (UNWRA, UNESCO).

Romanian educationalists and students (*Târgovişte School*).

Turkish NGOs and officials (Ministry of Welfare).

UN staff (ILO, UNEP, UNESCO, UNICEF, UNU, WHO, WIPO, WTO, Geneva).

Staff at the UK Foreign and Commonwealth Office, British Ambassadors, British Council, and many others who have assisted and responded to calls for information.

The International Student Advisors for inspiration, ongoing insights and reality checks. LIU Shujing, TONG Ning, Raghda Kawass, and Niayesh Fekri for Chinese and Arabic scripts.

Staff at Sage Publications who provided pertinent professional advice, editorial work and production support: Jai Seaman, Lily Mehrbod, Anna Horvai, Patrick Brindle, Victoria Nicholas, Jane Fricker, Sally Ransom and Shaun Mercier.

List of abbreviations

ADB	Asia Development Bank
AERE	Association of Environmental and Resource Economists
AI	Amnesty International
AMIDEAST	America-MidEast Educational and Training Services
APCEIU	Asia Pacific Centre for Education for International Understanding
ASEAN	Association of Southeast Asian Nations
AU	African Union
BAP	Balloon Aerial Photography
BC	Before Christianity
BL	British Library
BLDS	British Library for Development Studies
BP	British Petroleum
BRAC	Bangladesh Rural Advancement Committee
BRICS	Brazil, Russia, India, China and South Africa
C	Chapter in this book
CAN	Andean Community of Nations
CCTV	Closed Circuit Television
CDA	Critical Discourse Analysis
CEN-SAD	Community of the Sahel-Sahara States
CEO	Chief Executive Officer
CIS	Commonwealth of Independent States (Содружество Независимых Государств, СНГ)
CHF	Cooperative Housing Foundation
CPA	Critical Process Analysis
CPI	Corruption Perceptions Index
CS	Crowdsourcing
CSTO	Collective Security Treaty Organization (Организация Договора о Коллективной Безопасности Organizatsiya Dogovora o Kollektivnoy Bezopasnosti)
DAC	Development Assistance Committee
DHN	Digital Humanitarian Network
EARN	European Artistic Research Network
ECHR	European Court of Human Rights
ECJ	European Court of Justice
EEA	European Environmental Agency
EFA	Education for All
EIA	Environmental Impact Assessment
ELA	Error Level Analysis

EPA	Environmental Protection Agency
ESRC	Economic and Social Research Council
EU	European Union
FAO	(UN) Food and Agriculture Organization
FCO	Foreign and Commonwealth Office (UK)
GATT	General Agreement on Tariffs and Trade
GDELT	Global Database of Events, Language, and Tone
GDP	Gross Domestic Product
GIS	Geographical Information Systems
GM	Genetically Modified
GMO	Genetically Modified Organism
GPS	Global Positioning System
GWP	Gross World Product
HQ	Headquarters
HRW	Human Rights Watch
IACHR	Inter-American Court of Human Rights
IATA	International Air Transport Association
IATIS	International Association for Translation and Intercultural Studies
ICC	International Criminal Court
ICJ	International Court of Justice
ICPSR	Inter-University Consortium for Political and Social Research
ICRC	International Committee of the Red Cross
ICT	Information and Communications Technology
IDEA	International Institute for Democracy and Electoral Assistance
IGO	Inter-Government Organization
ILO	International Labour Organization
IMF	International Monetary Fund
INGO	International Non-Government Organization
IPCC	International Panel on Climate Change
IPEC	International Programme on the Elimination of Child Labour
IR	International Relations
ISCI	International State Crime Initiative, King's College, London
ISEE	International Society for Ecological Economics
ISIL	Islamic State of Iraq and the Levant
ISIS	Islamic State of Iraq and Syria
IT	Information Technology
KAP	Kite Aerial Photography
LAR	Lethal Autonomous Robots
LETS	Local Exchange Trading Systems
LiDAR	Airborne Light Detection and Ranging
MDG	Millennium Development Goals
MENA	Middle East North Africa
MINT	Mexico, Indonesia, Nigeria and Turkey
MNC	Multinational Company
MOOCs	Massive Open Online Courses
MoU	Memorandum of Understanding
MSE	Multiple Systems Estimation
MSF	Médecins Sans Frontières
NATO	North Atlantic Treaty Organization
NAWA	North Africa-West Asia
NCRM	National Centre for Research Methods
NGO	Non-Government Organization
OCFT	Office of Child Labor, Forced Labor, and Human Trafficking
OCHA	UN Office for the Coordination of Humanitarian Affairs
OCLC	Online Computer Library Centre
ODA	Overseas Development Assistance

OECD	Organisation for Economic Co-operation and Development
OED	Oxford English Dictionary
OS	Operating Systems
OSCE	Organization for Security and Co-operation in Europe
PA	Personal Assistant
PLOTS	Public Laboratory for Open Technology and Science
PRA	Participatory Rural Appraisal
PRIO	Peace Research Institute Oslo
R4D	Results for Development
RFI	Radio Frequency Identification
RMF	Rene Moawad Foundation
RRA	Rapid Rural Appraisal
SA	Situation Analysis
SAS	Sense About Science
SCO	Shanghai Cooperation Organization (上海合作组织)
SMS	Short Message Service
TdH	Terre des Hommes
TI	Transparency International
TIAR	Tratado Interamericano de Asistencia Recíproca (Inter-American Treaty of Reciprocal Assistance)
TCK / 3KC	Third Culture Kid
TNC	Transnational Corporation
UAV	Unmanned Aerial Vehicle
UCAV	Unmanned Combat Aerial Vehicle
UN	United Nations
UNASUR	Union of South American Nations
UNEP/DELC	United Nations Environment Programme / Division of Environmental Law & Conventions.
UNDESA-PD	United Nations Department of Economic and Social Affairs, Population Division
UNDP	United Nations Development Programme
UNEP	United Nations Environment Programme
UNESCO	United Nations Educational, Scientific and Cultural Organization
UNFCCC	United Nations Framework Convention on Climate Change
UNFPA	United Nations Population Fund
UNIDO	United Nations-Industrial Development Organization
UNSTATS	United Nations Statistics Division
UNU	United Nations University
UNU – CRIS	United Nations University Institute on Comparative Regional Integration Studies
UNWRA	United Nations Relief and Works Agency for Palestine Refugees in the Near East
USDoL	United States Department of Labor
VGI	Volunteered Geographic Information
VOI	Voice Over Internet
VRI	Video Remote Interpreting
WANA	West Asia and North Africa
WCCES	World Congress of Comparative Education Societies
WCED	World Commission on Environment and Development
WEF	World Economic Forum
WHO	World Health Organization
WIPO	World Intellectual Property Organization
WMD	Weapons of Mass Destruction
WMO	World Meteorological Organization
WTO	World Trade Organization
YWCA	Young Women's Church Association

International student advisors

	profiles time zone	research interests	*methods messages*
	**Alicia DE LA COUR VENNING** +12 **New Zealand**. UK, Vienna. LLM (Criminal Justice, Criminal Law, Criminol.), LLB. Bcom. *International State Crime Initiative.*	Civil society resistance to state violence and corruption. International law and state crime. Border and immigration policies as state crime.	*For ethnographic research, keep an open mind about meeting people. Contextual data allows you to approach your research holistically, and opportunities which seem irrelevant at first may prove immensely rich.*
	허윤진 +9 **Yoon-jin HUH** (Ginni) **Republic of Korea.** UK, Japan. BA (Politics and European Studies)	EU international political and economic cooperation (states and organizations). International diplomacy in post-crisis contexts.	*Being 'economical' in research is not always practical. Recognize when you need 'colour' and when you need 'black and white'.* *Researching is not only about searching for 'truth' and facts. It's also about studying values.*
	童宁 – 童甯 +8 **TONG Ning** (Rachel) **China.** Britain. BAs (English/Chinese Language and Literature). MA Education and International Development	Rural community development, through arts and culture. Youth leaders. Social entrepreneurship. Corporate social responsibility.	*Ethnographic research may be biased through not understanding local cultural or social norms. An emic/etic approach helps by identifying and balancing the identity of the local people and the status of a researcher.*

	သီရိဆု (+6½) **SU Thiri** (Iris) **Myanmar** (Burma). England, Barcelona. BA (English). MA (TEFL). MA International Studies in Education	Education and transformation before and after the dictatorship in Myanmar. Spanish and Myanmar education in eras of dictatorship and transition.	*Timelines are very useful for making comparisons, especially when countries are very different, like Myanmar and Spain. They can be compared 'asynchronously' – not by comparing the same things in the same time period, but by comparing key events such as when a regime changes.*
	Закия Сапенова **Zakiya SAPPENOVA** (+6) **Kazakhstan**. UK, Moldova, Russia, Kyrgyzstan. Musicology. MEd (International Education)	Culture. Archaeology. Yoga. Learning English through pop music. Comparative musicology. Kazakh traditions in western music.	*Comparative musicology helps to better understand the cultural context, and how and why people make music.* *Explore how people learn their other languages, and find global patterns and trends.*
	فكري نيايش (+3) **Niayesh FEKRI** (Nia) **Iran.** Jordan, England. Secondary school student. Philosophy. Art. Literature. Spanish. Arabic.	Immigration and open borders. Ethical trading. How to involve young people in global citizenship. Art and wellbeing.	*Mirroring and mediating the energy level of the person you are talking with creates a balanced flow of thoughts, without domination or withdrawal.* [Artist: *Even Without Borders* illustration on page 1]
	هبة خليف (+2) **Heba KHOLEIF** **Egypt.** Sweden, USA, UK. MA (Management of Special Education in Developing Countries). Principal Specialist Librarian at Bibliotheca Alexandrina	Social impacts on females with disabilities. Cultural stereotypes about disability. Family expectations and the psychological wellbeing of females with visual impairment.	*Facial expressions and body language contribute to understanding interview responses. And with people with visual impairment, I can detect if they are saying everything or hiding something, are at ease or stressed, want to skip a question or will elaborate.*
	Olúgbénga Awólaràn (+1) **Olugbenga AWOLARAN** **Nigeria**. UK. MBBS, MSc (Cancer Studies)	Health care organization. Cancer research. Clinical surgery.	*The goal of a quality research is to question old assumptions, discover new associations and deliver relevant applications.* *Africa must be understood through the almost inseparable mix of culture and religion.*

	**Sébastien HINE** (0) **UK**. France, Italy, Egypt, Japan, North Korea. MA (Educ. Planning, Econ., and International Development). Postgrad. Dip. (Arab World Studies)	Education. Equity, inclusion, quality and emergencies. Systematic literature reviews. Arab world.	*Given the exponential advances in technology, international research methods should be adapting and taking advantage of technological developments faster than ever.*
	Juliana Golin Vianna (–4) **Juliana VIANNA** **Brazil.** UK, Italy. History teacher. MA (Educ. and International Development)	Internationalization of higher education. Latin America. History of education. International event research.	*When doing 'international' research in your home country, think about your identity and how others will see you. If you say you are a student abroad, you may be seen as an outsider.*
	**Angela LATORRE** (–5) **Colombia. UK, USA.** MA (Educ. and International Development)	Education and conflict. Inclusive education. Education in emergencies. Situation analysis.	*With large projects, you need a large number of well-trained and efficient assistants to ensure that surveys and interviews are done during a well-focused time period.*
	Alvaro Fortin Morales (–6) **Alvaro MORALES** **Guatemala.** Nicaragua, USA, Pakistan, Thailand, Angola, Swaziland. PhD (Cross-Cultural Psych.). MA (Education & International Dev.). BA (Clinical Psych.)	Bias and fairness in cross-cultural comparative assessment. Education in heterogeneous populations. Effects of bilingualism in rural schools.	*Understanding how we are different, helps us understand how we are similar.* *In Tajikistan almost 100% of the population is Muslim, but because of the Soviet period, they are quite liberal. It creates an unusual combination.*

New Zealand Centre for Global Studies (+12)

Isabella Brown, Tremayne Reid, Katrina Seno, Sedef Dudder-Ozyurt, Amada Ngo, Benjamin Huxford, Nardos Tilahun, Isabella Lenihan-Ikin

We are a group of young New Zealanders, 15–18, with a common interest in global citizenship. Our questions for the future are:

What would a global world look like?

To what extent is our world global? Do we live in a global age?

Should there be a global sovereign? If so, who or what should it be?

In your lifetime, do you expect the world to unite politically?

Under what conditions do you see this happening?

Do you identify with all of humanity? Do you want a global passport?

Would you die for the UN?

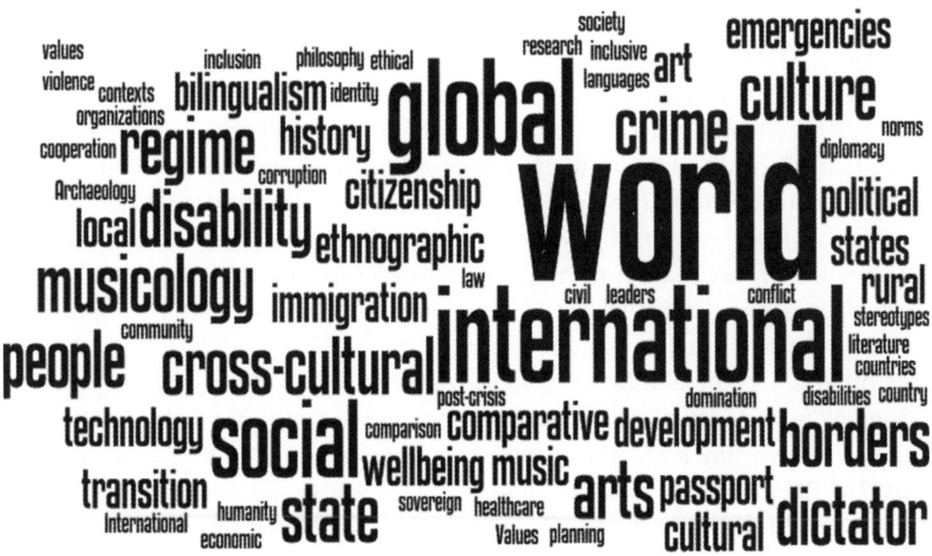

Student words. Thanks to Wordle.net

About the author

Christopher Williams (AGSM, PhD, FRSA) is an independent academic, visiting fellow at the University of London (UCL Institute of Education), and visiting professor at Chuba Institute of Advanced Studies (Chuba University, Japan). He has also held posts at the universities of Bristol (Medical School), Birmingham (College of Social Science), Cairo (Conservatoire of Music), Cambridge (Global Security Programme), and the United Nations (Leadership Academy).

Originally a professional trumpeter from London, his international interests started with a student visit to USSR in 1972 (without his parents' knowledge), across the Berlin Wall to Warsaw Pact countries in 1973, and then to Communist China. From 1980, he worked at *Cairo University* with Soviet colleagues, and experienced the assassination of Sadat and dictatorship of Mubarak. He then broke boycotts to work in apartheid South Africa, setting up projects for street children. Later he joined the *United Nations Leadership Academy* in Jordan, but had to leave during the build-up to the US/UK occupation of Iraq. His research includes studies for the *European Commission* (Afghanistan), UNESCO (Palestine), US Dept. of Labor (Lebanon and Jordan), and INGOs such as Oxfam (Liberia).

His other books include *Researching Power, Elites and Leadership* (Sage); *Leadership Accountability in a Globalizing World*; *Environmental Victims: New Risks, New Injustice*; *Invisible Victims: Crime and Abuse against People with Learning Disabilities*; and *Terminus Brain: The Environmental Threat to Human Intelligence*. He has written for the *Times Higher*, *Korea Herald* and *China Daily*, and has discussed his research on BBC TV and radio, and government TV in Kazakhstan and Korea. He has advised ministers and civil servants at the British House of Commons, Cabinet Office, and Foreign Office, and has presented on a range of topics for the UN at the Palais des Nations, UNEP, WHO, UNU (Jordan), and UNESCO (China & Korea).

Author contact: chrisunula@yahoo.com

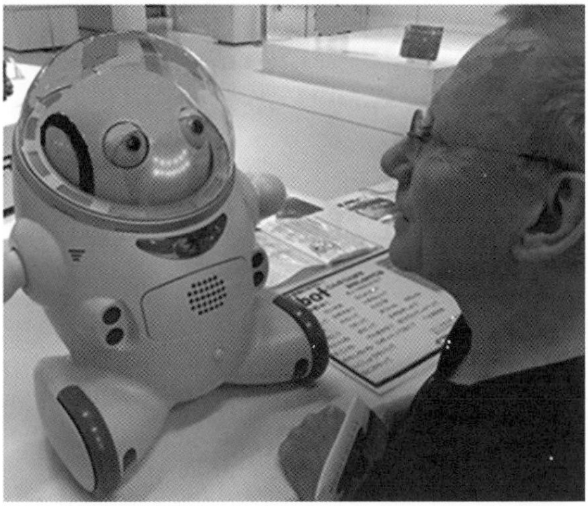

A Japanese robot interviewing the author

Author: "Good morning." (*Ohayo*)
Robot: "That's nice, but it's already afternoon. Have you had your lunch yet?"

How to use this book

The point of a methods book is to do better research and save time. Many people do similar research, and discover what works and what doesn't. There's no need to repeat the same mistakes. Researchers are also constantly developing new ideas and technologies, and it is vital to be aware of state-of-the art techniques. But some people think methods books are a waste of time. If you are one of them, think about search engines. They use research based on countless innovative methodologies – linguistics, informatics, programming. So if you "don't believe in methodology", don't use *Google*.

A method is a way of doing something according to a plan (Part Two), which is based on a research design (C4). This book explains how to:

- critically review world knowledge (C1) and literature (C3),
- use and develop diverse concepts and theories (C2),
- plan international studies globally and locally (C4),
- apply research ethics cross-culturally (C5),
- use a wide range of world research frameworks (C6),
- manage international data (C7),
- carry out innovative mixed-methods data collection (Part Three),
- do holistic local-global analyses (C14), and
- report and use research findings on a world scale (C15).

E.O. Wilson proposes the need for 'consilience' – a 'jumping together' of methods to create a 'unity of knowledge'.[1] New electronic devices make this increasingly easy through an instant 'iterative' use of quantitative and qualitative methods, data management (C7) and analysis (Box 4.1).

Throughout the book, and on the website, *thinking zones* provide the bases for creative (and entertaining) group exercises, using mobile devices to discover relevant facts, to encourage 'thinking without borders'. And a team of *International Student Advisors* have provided a reality check, reviewed drafts, and contributed innovative ideas and materials (see pp. xxii).

No textbook about world research can cover everything in depth, and so this book does not repeat detailed discussions that are easily available in standard methods books. The chapters provide basic explanations of relevant methodologies, introduce new or interesting ideas, and link these to international sources. It is therefore very important to follow up the references, indicated by superscript numbers – e.g.[95, 68] – when they relate to something that seems relevant. This referencing system also creates a "library shelf" of related sources in the references section, from which reading lists about each topic can easily be created by cut-and-paste from the reference lists on the website that accompanies the book.

Each chapter ends with a summary of ***main ideas***, ***key reading*** and a brief list of ***online resources*** which are elaborated on the accompanying website. Throughout, the key concepts are in **bold**, and the ***Glossary*** (p. 243) defines these and other relevant terms. These terms are also helpful keywords for making online or database searches. ***Bold italics*** indicate subsections, to make navigating the book easier. *Italics* are used in four ways: to show that certain words are technical terms (*others*), for the phonetic version of words not originally written in roman script (*ohayo*), for emphasis (*counter*-intuitive ideas), and for the names of organizations (*World Trade Organization*). (Further information can usually be found by an internet search on these organization names.) Explanations and examples are usually presented directly, or indicated by parentheses ( ) or dashes – . Double "quote marks" show illustrative words and phrases, examples, and terms that should be understood very critically such as "savages". References to other chapters or subsections in the book are shown in parentheses – (C5.6). The ***accompanying website*** provides many of the diagrams in the book, elaborations, handouts, more *thinking zones*, and other material shown by the cursor icon in text icon, including *PowerPoint* presentations to introduce each chapter and inspire creative discussions.

What are 'international','global' and 'world' studies?

What does **international**, **global** or **world** social research cover? In a globalizing world, the defining factors are no longer simply where a study is done, or who does it.

International (between nations) usually means that whole nations are the units of analysis, and the study concerns national systems – government, law, education, health (C12.1). **Global** (worldwide) describes systems that affect sectors of the world, but are neither total, nor entirely nation-based – communications, economics, health, fashion. In this book, **world** (the Earth with its peoples, places and systems) is used to encompass both international and global work. *Area studies* or *country case studies* are also an aspect of world research, if they make comparisons possible (C6.2). A study is therefore likely to be **international**, **global** or **world** if it is:

- about *more than one country or people* ("A comparison of divorce law in Iran and Ireland" – "The ethics of global social networking").
- based on *data in two or more national languages* ("Media discourses of crime in Farsi and Arabic" – "Global internet terminology").
- a *case/area study* structured so that it can be compared with other countries ("Human development indicators in Liberia" – "Pilot training in South Korea").
- related to *international or global theories/concepts* ("Human capital in small island states" – "Global civil society and fishing communities").
- concerns an issue that is related to *international codes* or *global ethics* ("The implementation of the UN Torture Convention in America" – "Teaching global citizenship in New Zealand").
- about *people* who are significant in the world[2] ("A history of the directors of UN-WIPO" – "Global elites in Brazil").
- investigating *methods* for researching across borders (online research, satellite photography, drones).
- about a place or topic where *local researchers may not be able to do proper research,* and outsiders can contribute ("The military power of *Imams* in Islamic states" – "*Wikileaks* and US global military power").

The important thing is that the *purposes* of the study, and how those purposes are evident in its *research design* (C4), have world dimensions. The word *glocal* is often used by NGOs to encourage people to, "think global and act local". This reflects the reality of how we do world studies.

Three cumulative categories provide the conceptual framework of this book, and have traditionally been associated with particular types of research (Figure 1):

- **peoples** and the *universal* aspects of *humanity* and civilizations (history, anthropology, linguistics, evolutionary theory), including ***population*** studies.
- **places** that *peoples* inhabit – their regions, nations, localities (geography, cartography, demography), including ***mapping***.
- **systems** that *peoples* use to run their lives and the *places* they live in (history, trade, economic, international organizations), which are recorded in ***formal documents***.

Useful distinctions can be made between systems that are:

- *natural* which exist independently of humans and are not an aspect of social science but are understood through human knowledge (astrophysics, mathematical and physical laws),
- *human-influenced* (climate, oceans), and
- *human-dominated* (government, religions).[3]

Social science is mostly concerned with *influenced* and *dominated* systems, but *natural* systems, such as weather, shape human existence. The obvious difficulty for researchers is that they are part of the world they are studying. We need to "sit outside" and be *reflexive* in order to achieve a greater *objectivity*, or at least recognize the ways in which world research is often not objective (C1.2).

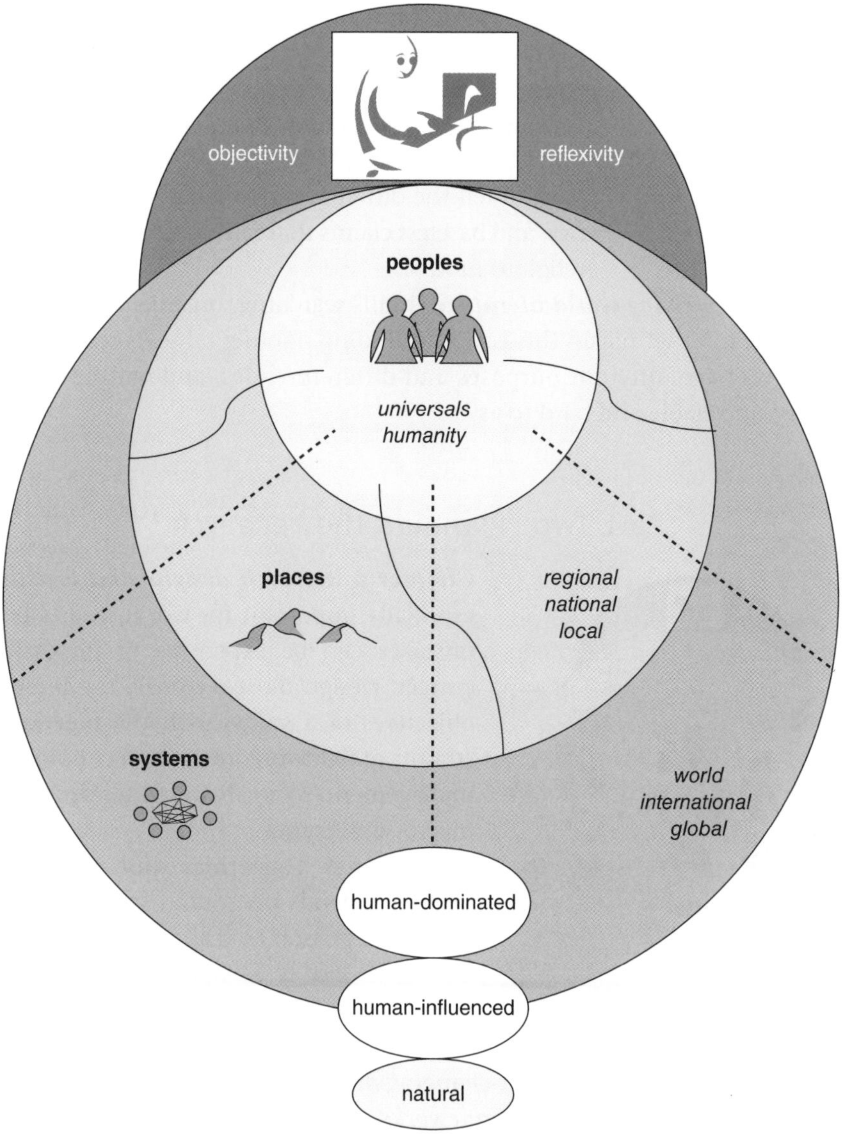

Figure 1 A conceptual framework for world research

The chapters

Part One: Understanding world research

Chapter 1 What is ***world knowledge***? *Ontology* helps to establish if and why international or global things exist and, if they exist, *epistemology* identifies how we know about them. World perspectives often reflect biased worldviews, and so a *reflexive* approach to international research and knowledge creation is crucial.

Chapter 2 ***Theories and concepts*** are discussed in relation to world *peoples, places* and *systems*. But it is often hard to tell the difference between evidence-based theories, and baseless claims that reflect nationalistic, racist or religious motives.

Chapter 3 ***Reviewing world literature*** entails searching, organizing and checking material. The internet makes this easy, but finding non-digital texts remains important. Reviews have different purposes and different styles, and world literature is often very unreliable and hard to assess.

Part Two: Planning the research

Chapter 4 ***Research designs and logistics*** are especially important for world studies because mistakes can be expensive or impossible to correct. Design must reconcile the intellectual objectives of a study, with the practical constraints of fieldwork, research technologies and management, to create micro-research that has macro-significance.

Chapter 5 The ***ethics and integrity*** of a project depends on sound, workable research ethics and an unbiased approach. International and local law is a significant consideration, because small mistakes can have big consequences. Consideration for 'others' is vital to avoid the unethical practices of past colonially-minded researchers. Remote and online research raises new and fast-changing dilemmas.

Chapter 6 Choosing research ***frameworks*** – the overall approaches – reflect the level of the study – *peoples, places, systems*. They also include cross-cutting frameworks – *cross-sectional analysis, crowdsourcing research* and *online research*.

Part Three: Doing the research

Chapter 7 The obvious problem about world data is that the world is a big place, and so good systems and technologies are vital for efficient ***data management***. Plans for *finding, selecting, testing* and *transferring* relevant data need to be considered before starting to *collect* data.

The subsequent chapters then explain the techniques for getting data from the main *sources*, in relation to the conceptual framework of the book. **Chapter 8** concerns ***people*** – identifiable individuals and groups (interviews, observation), and **Chapter 9** explains data collection from large groups of people – ***populations*** (surveys, big data). **Chapter 10** is about researching ***places*** – streets, urban, rural and coastal regions, and global commons (texts, objects, buildings, environment), and **Chapter 11** covers ***mapping*** research sites. **Chapter 12** discusses analysing ***world systems,*** and **Chapter 13** covers the related ***formal documents***.

Part Four: Using the findings

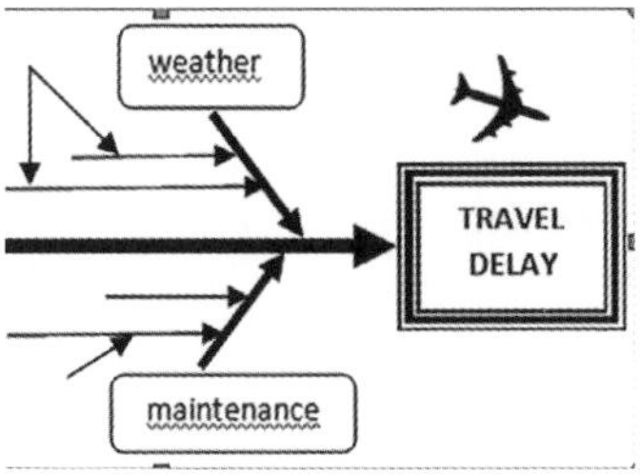

Chapter 14 ***Further analysis*** tries to "see what others see, but think what others have *not* thought" through *analysis* based on *comparisons*, establishing *causation*, *predictive* evidence, creating *indexes*, and *generalisation*.

Chapter 15 then outlines ***reporting research*** effectively using *international style*, for *academic*, *professional* and *public* audiences, to achieve *change* across the world, whilst being aware of scams.

Companion website

Doing International Research is supported by a wealth of online resources to aid your study/support your teaching, which are available at https://study.sagepub.com/williams.

For students:

- weblinks for each chapter
- examples/summaries/templates related to text marked with
- additional thinking zones
- an overview of data capture technologies.

For lecturers:

- copies of all the figures and thinking zones for use in teaching material.

Introduction

Seek knowledge, even as far as China. This Islamic *hadith* reveals the dynamics of world research. It encourages study in distant lands, yet it locates the researcher in the middle of the world, and suggests surprise that there is something worth learning elsewhere. Some Muslims argue the *hadith* is false, and Sufis say that 'China' really means 'meditation'.[1] And anyway, by this time China had already enshrined *its* claim to be centre of the world in the calligraphy naming its lands – central state – 中国.

Researchers would point out that peoples from West and East Asia had knowledge of one another well before this *hadith*. Eight centuries earlier, the Greeks 'extended their empire even as far as the Seres' (the Chinese).[2] Ptolemy's world map (150AD) includes *Sinae*. Rome had emissaries in China from 166AD. And earlier, China had been seeking knowledge in West Asia – in 97AD, the Chinese envoy, Gan Ying (甘英), reached the 'western sea'. In the light of this knowledge, the *hadith* might have added, "...and while you are there, find out what the Chinese know about us Arabs".

So world knowledge is often uncertain, contested, indirect, ethnocentric, lost, or overlooked. But the bigger lesson is that the world changes. Now, a *Google* search on 'research China' gets 1.5 billion hits, in Arabic (بحث الصين) 3.5 million. Around 90% of present-day world data was produced in the previous two years, and much can be accessed from almost anywhere. State level data is no longer controlled entirely by states, thanks to *big data* and *crowdsourced research*. We are in a new era of seeking world knowledge.

The aim of this book is to explain how to do world research – about *peoples, places* and *systems* – with these dynamics in mind. 'World' must integrate everyone, as research partners and as researchers – an inclusive world of diverse abilities and disabilities, wealth, sexualities, ages, peoples and cultures. Research design should encourage:

- thinking *without* borders[3]
- seeing the world through the eyes of *others,*[4] and
- seeing what other people see, but thinking what they have *not* thought.[5]

World researchers now need to use multi-methods, and diverse theoretical frameworks. This entails linking old and new – from the stones and bones studied by archaeologists and anthropologists, to crowdmaps and robots created by students. We now research the world at all levels from neurons to nations.

A brief history of world research

What can the history of world research tell us about doing world research now?

We started researching our world when *Homo sapiens* wandered out of Africa around 70,000 years ago, and new methods help us to understand that era. Thanks to modern mass spectrometry, we now know that perforated sea-shells found in Taforalt (Morocco) appear to be 82,000-year-old beads.[6] Similar shells have been found in South Africa,[7] Algeria, Israel and Turkey. These all provide evidence of 'cultural modernity',[8] and of the transfer of skills and information among peoples and places.

But *sapiens* acquired a skill that other animals do not have. Yuval Harari explains that by using language we could create 'imagined realities' – fictitious knowledge – about things that do not objectively exist. The resultant invention of gods, cults and belief systems created large social networks for sharing myths and ideologies around the world, but also for transferring tangible knowledge. We don't know who wrote the disparate texts that became known as 'the Bible', but they record that Lebanese cedar trees from Byblos apparently provided Hebrew priests with bark for curing leprosy.[9] In the present-day, these imagined realities, which do not really exist, do exist in the form of the religions, nations, human rights, financial systems and companies that dominate our world.[10] That is why questioning the existence of things that we think are real – ***ontology*** (C1.1) – is very important in world research.

Early texts (C10.6) – inscriptions on buildings and objects – provide evidence that early invaders and traders shared their problems and solutions, mysteries and myths, fashions and foods, diseases and cures. The garlic plant found its way from Central Asia to Greece, India and Egypt around 3000BC. The Silk Roads carried techniques for glass production and copper-smelting from west to east, and for silk production and iron-making east to west. The voyages of Chinese Admiral Zheng He predated the European explorers. In 1409 he erected a trilingual stella in Sri Lanka, and he reached India, Arabia and Africa, returning with a giraffe from (now) Somalia.[11] If you look carefully, museums and archaeological sites have a wealth of data about early researchers. Assyrian friezes, from Lachish around 700BC, show soldiers acquiring objects for the king to study – booty, including weapons, furniture, ornaments and chariots – and prisoners to interrogate (interview) to learn their skills and languages.[12]

So, world research was *not*, as some Europeans and Americans claim, invented during the 16th century Age of Discovery.[13] And Christopher Columbus was *not* the first world explorer because he "discovered America" in 1492. Not least, it seems that he mistakenly landed in the Bahamas while trying to find Japan, tried to cover up his mistake, and was then imprisoned for torturing indigenous peoples. The significant discovery of the Europeans was 'the discovery of ignorance' – they realized there were places and things they did not know, and they created large-scale systematic methods to explore and investigate these unknowns.[14]

But scholars and explorers, from many earlier civilizations, created the bases for the methods we now use. Few Europeans know of Abū Rayhān al-Bīrūnī (973–1048AD) (أبو ريحان بن محمد البيروني),[15] who wrote a book on cartography when he was 22, followed by a *Chronology of Ancient Nations*. Born in Khwarezm (now in Uzbekistan), he learned languages and made translations, compared law, and developed bases for diplomacy. His book *India* (circa 1030AD) was written while he was, what journalists would now call, 'embedded' with an army, but his aim was to facilitate understanding between the warring Hindus and Muslims. Recent postage stamps indicate his continuing significance in many countries – Iran, Egypt, Afghanistan, Syria, Pakistan, Turkey, Algeria and Guinea-Bissau. His ideas remain relevant, and are used throughout this book (Figure 0.1).

> How could we know the history of nations but for the everlasting monuments of the pen?
>
> Abū Rayhān al-Bīrūnī, *India* (circa 1030)

Figure 0.1 The history of nations (al-Bīrūnī)

An important lesson from history is that the interest has usually been about ***peoples** and **populations**, **places** and **mapping***, and ***systems** and **official documents***. And it is helpful to develop a research design in relation to one or more of those areas, which form the structure of this book.

Peoples (C2.1; C8) were often studied by missionaries. In 1543, Portuguese traders landed in Japan and taught the locals how to make guns, and in 1549 Jesuit missionaries arrived and taught them how to make peace. But they also documented women's hair-styles and fashions.[16] These books became best-sellers in Europe, and Europeans have researched and traded Eastern style ever since. Inevitably, world research started to create views, and sometimes stereotypes, about **others** (C2.1). The Jesuits also taught the Japanese to paint in the European style. Local Japanese artists then painted these *Namban* ('Southern barbarians') visitors,[17] and these images now appear on Portuguese coins and stamps.

The *ethics* of researching peoples has a difficult history, and present-day researchers need to be aware of past mistakes (C5.3). Five hundred years ago, powerful Europeans wanted to acquire human data for their 'human zoos' and World Fairs.[18] In 1582, those Jesuits shipped four Japanese boys to Europe, for kings and popes to study, and to raise funds for their travels.[19] But unethical practice is not confined to the past. A *Khoe* woman from Southern Africa, Saartjie Baartman (The 'Hottentot Venus'), was exhibited in London and Paris between 1810 and 1815. On her death, her brains and genitals were removed and displayed in the *Musée de l'Homme*, until 1974.[20] This sort of thing continues on the internet (C5.3).

Colonial administrators wanted to know more about larger ***populations*** of people (C9). They collected statistics, and photos. Among countless, often forgotten, women explorers, Gertrude Bell (1869–1916) – British colonial administrator, archaeologist, and spy – helped to establish modern Iraq and Jordan. She was considered, 'one of the few representatives of His Majesty's Government remembered by the Arabs with anything resembling affection'.[21] Population research is now central to diplomatic and commercial intelligence – understanding national politics, commercial markets, and how to deliver development assistance.

The press also wanted to know what populations thought about world events, and Gallup's sampling methodologies created scientific opinion polls in 1935 (C9.1). One outcome is *indexes* (C14.4) and ranking nations. But rankings often reflect the power of nations to control the methods. Why are the 'winning' countries in the Olympic Games ranked simply by the number of gold medals their athletes win? Surely that does little more than rank countries according to their size, and the wealth available to train their athletes. Blogger Simon Forthsyth shows that when the rankings are adjusted for population size and GDP, the outcomes are very different (Figure 0.2).[22] All indexes must be viewed very critically.

2012 Olympics			
Rank	**Number of gold medals**	**Number of gold medals in relation to population size**	**Number of gold medals in relation to GDP**
1	US	Grenada	Grenada
2	China	Bahamas	Jamaica
3	Britain	New Zealand	South Korea

Figure 0.2 Olympic rankings
Source: Forthsyth, S. (2012) London 2012 Olympic medal tally.

Places where people live have been the interest of geographers, architects, designers and engineers (C2.2; C10). If data could not be transported, it had to be recorded. Botanical artists perfected 'scientific drawing', which was then applied to buildings and people.[23] But this is also not a European invention. In the 15th century BC, Egyptians accurately recorded 275 plants they found in Syria, on a stone frieze in the tomb of Thutmose III in Karnak. Nowdays, anything, large or small, can be scanned, the information sent anywhere by the internet, and the item replicated by 3-D printing.

Cartographers studied and ***mapped*** places (C11), often for military purposes. Around 525BC the Persian king, Darius, 'wanted to know where [the Indus] river runs out into the sea, and sent with his ships...Scylax, a man of Caryanda'.[24] The *Royal Library of Alexandria* (3rd century BC) copied maps, books, logs and letters, which arrived on ships. Copies were returned, and the library acquired the originals.[25] The aim was to collect all the books in the world, much like *Google Books*. In 1900, aerial photography was first used for mapping during the Boer War, and the basic methods now used by *Google Earth* and crowdmaps are very similar. Mapping is often overlooked as a quick and simple method for initial research in a new place (C11).

Systems were the concern of historians (C2.3; C12). The research was used by governments to control and build their nations and civilizations, and information about other lands became a valuable tool of state power. When Francis Drake returned to England from his world travels, in 1581, Queen Elizabeth I decreed that his findings were 'secrets of the realm'. She had regularized TOP SECRET, the penalty for 'leaks' was death, as in the US today. A network of 'intelligenciers' – spies – enforced the system. The study of how and why governments continually try, and fail, to keep secrets can start by analysing the views of leakers. *Wikileaks* founder, Julian Assange, argues that, 'Secrecy is important for particular people at particular times.'[26]

Governments wanted to keep things secret, but traders needed good international information. The 17th and 18th century coffee houses in London became 'penny universities' where ship owners and traders, philosophers and explorers could exchange news and views.[27] The broadsheet newspapers, prints and poems provide fascinating data about this international cafe society. Shippers, traders and colonial administrators were also collectors, and created the world museums, such as Scotland's *Burrell Collection*, which are now significant sources of world data. Cafes and bars remain good places to find local data.

The press challenged government secrecy. In 1690, an American newspaper – *Publick Occurrences, both Forreign and Domestick* – was closed down after one issue, by the British colonial rulers. It included reports of acts that would now be seen as war crimes. In 1846 *Associated Press* transmitted news of the Mexican–American war by telegraphy, boat and horse, which bypassed political control. In 1851, P.J. Reuter used carrier pigeons to provide London's financial organizations with world news. The first daily press coverage of a war came from Crimea.[28] By 1855, a new underwater telegraph cable permitted news to reach Britain in two hours, which brought down the government. The creation of cell phone cameras, from 1997, empowered *citizen journalists*, who continue the tradition of discovering and communicating inconvenient international truths, often from crowdsourced research (C6.4).

But the realization that there was a world led to the concept of **others** (C2.1) and, to affirm their power, elites created the belief that other peoples must be hostile or inferior – **exceptionalism**. These ideas became embodied within language. The ancient Egyptians had a hieroglyph for the 'nine foreign lands', beyond the Nile valley hills.[29] An early Chinese world map is called *The World Diagram of Chinese and Barbarian Lands within the Four Seas* (四海華夷總圖). The Greek word 'barbarian' (βάρβαρος) described those who were not Greek citizens, and the sound of the word mimics the supposed 'babble' of other languages. Europeans still talk of the 'Far East' – *Extrême-Orient, Ferner Osten, Daleki Wschód* – yet this describes somewhere that is not 'far' if you live in Beijing, or Australia. In 1939, Robert Menzies, then prime minister of Australia, reminded the war-threatened world, 'What Great Britain calls the Far East is to us the near north.'[30] These **worldviews** are an interesting aspect of international linguistics. The early missionary anthropologists compiled dictionaries, which sometimes provided insights into how they viewed **others**, and we can now study international texting and emoticons similarly.

World research has often fuelled **nationalistic** and **ethnocentric worldviews**, and abuses of power (C2.1; C5.3). Progressive present-day approaches therefore aim to develop 'indigenous methodologies'[31] to 'decolonize' world research.[32] This book encourages a *reflexive* approach throughout (C1.2) so that researchers constantly question how worldviews affect their studies. The aim is to encourage the practical development of innovative methodologies to do research across borders, while thinking as if in a world without borders.

The history of world research can inform present-day studies, but also warns that world studies can be done in bad ways for bad purposes. So we need to turn the 'bads' into 'goods'. For example, the useful outcome from state spying, commercial espionage, and unethical journalism is an ever-increasing range of cheap technologies for researchers. Innovations that were state secrets a few years ago are now available through online spyware sites and toy shops. Developing innovative technologies for data collection is a central theme of this book. Old ideas can inspire new ideas, from the bugging devise used by the KGB, to robot *iFish* that film under the seas (Figure 10.2), and homing-pigeons carrying cameras to robot bats carrying pollution sensors. What next? We are told that China has even been testing electrical brain implants to steer pigeons.[33]

key reading

Chomsky, N. (2011) *How the World Works*. London: Hamish Hamilton.

Lonely Planet (2012) *The Book of Everything: A Visual Guide to Travel and the World*. London: Lonely Planet.

Therborn, G. (2010) *The World*. Cambridge: Polity.

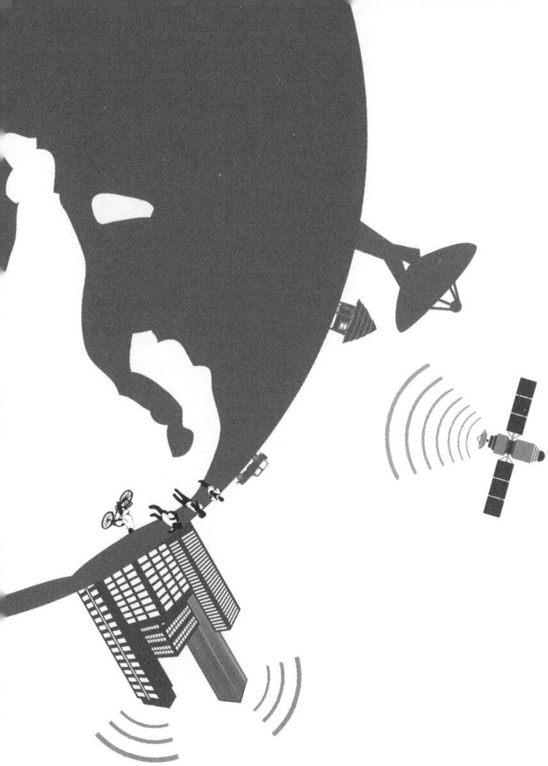

PART I

Understanding world research

Chapter 1 – What is 'world knowledge' and how is it created? *Ontology* helps to question if and why international or global things exist, and *epistemology* explains how we know about these things. World perspectives often reflect biased worldviews, and so a *reflexive* approach to international research and knowledge creation is crucial.

Chapter 2 – World theories are based around *peoples*, the *places* people live, and the *systems* created by peoples to run those places. But it is often hard to tell the difference between sound, evidence-based theories, and baseless claims that reflect nationalistic, racist or religious ideologies.

Chapter 3 – World literature, including audio and video material, is increasingly easy to access online, though finding non-digital texts remains important. But world studies are often very unreliable and hard to assess.

ONE
Understanding world knowledge

'Those who cannot remember the past are condemned to repeat it.' This idea often justifies the historical bases of international studies. The Spanish-American philosopher George Santayana wrote the phrase in his *Life of Reason* in 1905. But his preceding sentence is now forgotten: 'when experience is not retained, as among savages, infancy is perpetual'.[1] Colonial ideologies still influence the Euro-American **worldviews** that dominate present-day international 'knowledge'.[2] We should also 'remember the past' through the histories of the world written by Arab, Chinese, Greek, Persian, Hindu, Slavic, Roman and other non-European scholars.

Knowledge comes from the intellectualization of facts or opinion, usually by comparison (C14.1). The first part of this chapter outlines how we question the existence of things that we take for granted – *ontology* – and then how we come to know about these things – *epistemology*. This is particularly important within international studies, because the scale of knowledge is very large, and this creates endless possibilities for grand claims based on nothing more than 'authority'. For the researcher, this questioning starts from a *reflexive* approach to all aspects of a study – an ongoing personal assessment of "where we are coming from", and how our own, and other, worldviews, may affect the objectivity of a study. Because the world is a big place, most world knowledge arrives through intermediaries, and that is a problem as al-Bīrūnī noted a thousand years ago (Figure 1.1).[3]

> The tradition regarding an event...will invariably depend for its character as true or false upon the character of the reporters, who are influenced by the divergency of interests and all kinds of animosities and antipathies between the various nations.
>
> Abū Rayhān al-Bīrūnī, *India* (circa 1030)

Figure 1.1 Reporters

1.1 Ontology and epistemology

Are we just avatars in a virtual reality game played by higher beings – just objects in a massive computer simulation? And if not, how can we prove it?4 ***Ontology***[5] – the study of how we know that something exists – can help to explore questions like this. How did something (an *entity*) come into existence, how do we prove it *is*, in what way does it *be*, how do we know it is *real*, and how can we *categorize* it?

Ontological questions can be posed in simple forms – What makes this event **international**? Could 'international' situations occur without the political construction of **nations**? Is this phenomenon truly **universal**? How do we demonstrate **global** impacts? Questions can also be framed as a *null ontological hypothesis*, a default assumption that something does *not* exist until we can show that it *does* – that nothing is universal, global, international or human, until we explain why it is. Broadly, philosophers take a stance between accepting that anything that is a noun exists (**realism**), or arguing that existence comes from a subtle interplay of experiences and mental events (**nominalism**). Some argue that nothing exists (**nihilism**).

Philip Dick proposes a basic test of existence, 'Reality is that which, when you stop believing in it, doesn't go away.'[6] And John Searle makes a useful distinction:

- some things are '*observer independent*' – 'brute facts' that 'exist independently of us' (earthquakes, tides, weather);
- others are '*observer-relative*' – 'institutional facts' that 'depend on us for their existence' (citizenship, laws, moral values).[7]

The Earth clearly exists 'independently', but nations only exist because of us. What about the 'world'? To decide, we first need to define 'world' – is it the physical planet drifting aimlessly in space, is it the planet with its peoples, places and systems, or is it a geopolitical region as delineated by the UN? (Figure 2.6)

As mentioned in the Introduction, Yuval Harari's lucid argument that 'sapiens' are the only animals that can create *imagined realities* – religions, financial systems, companies – is very significant when analysing the social world. Money is clearly an 'imagined reality' and this is very evident in currencies from cowry shells and paper dollar bills to *Bitcoin*. Around 97% of world money now only exists in cyberspace. Throughout this book, keep in mind that *people* exist objectively as a type of animal, but when described in terms of 'nationality', 'race', 'religion' or 'ethnic group', these are imagined distinctions. *Places*, if described as a valley or sea exist objectively, but when a valley is a 'border', or seas become 'territorial waters', these are imagined places. The construction of these imagined things happens within social *systems* and related international institutions, which only exist in the human mind. These are constructed through the imagined knowledge in *documents* (C13), and now determine the future of the whole of our planet. Our Earth's climate, seas and ecosystems exist objectively, but their fate is now controlled by our imagined realities.[8]

Ontology can also help to address other fundamental questions: is something real or ideal (is or ought), actual or abstract, fact or opinion, empirical or reasoned, known or believed? What are the *relationships* (ties, causal chains, reasoned links – "if this then that") between *entities*, and what is the relationship and how do we know it exists?[9] How do we justify the existence of *categories*, which are often a European invention? Until the 19th century, East Asian countries had no direct equivalents for distinctions such as science, religion and philosophy.[10]

International discourse is often based on supposedly obvious facts that are very questionable and can fuel conflict.[11] Development theories assume that improved development can come into existence through external intervention. But how do we know that countries would not develop, perhaps better, without that intervention? Within environmental economics, the idea of 'green growth' assumes that environmental constraints can be reconciled with economic demands. But is green growth just an alliterative oxymoron – can growth continue infinitely or are there limits and, if limited, how do we know when the limits are reached? The word 'uncertainty' is commonly used to describe our *risk society* era. Technology may have created new risks, but does that mean that our certainty about risk has declined? Arguably science has made human knowledge considerably more certain about world risks than in any previous generation. Are we certain that uncertainty is now less (or should that be more) uncertain? Within international relations, many mainstream theories depend on the idea that humanity is intrinsically chaotic, and this must be prevented by strong laws and aggressive policy. But how can we prove this 'ontology of anarchy'?[12] Creating fear, without evidence, is an old political trick, but politicians with an academic background challenge it (Figure 1.2).

Cross-cultural ontology has distinct considerations,[13] such as the cross-cultural aspects of *relational* ontology?[14] Ontology is associated with the affirmation of identity through interpersonal communication, particularly when identity is in question, as among Palestinians.[15] International dimensions often demand a logical questioning of seemingly illogical claims. Logically, countries such as Iran and Saudi Arabia must still have witches and sorcerers, because they have laws against witchcraft and sorcery, sometimes resulting in execution.[16] But to what degree is the ontology of witchcraft just being used for social control, as throughout Europe until recently? Similarly, sexuality is accompanied by ontological claims, which are contested cross-culturally.[17] When, in 2012, the Iranian president,

> The stated purpose [of the Immigration Bill] is to enhance the ability to deter people-smuggling to New Zealand...
>
> ...the Minister of Immigration was requested to provide the annual figures for the last 10 years showing the number of people listed in prosecutions confirmed to have been smuggled into New Zealand.
>
> The Minister replied that 'The department's prosecution records do not record the number of people confirmed to have been smuggled into New Zealand...'
>
> This bill rests on a fear based on complete ignorance of the facts. But whatever they might be, the numbers will have been minuscule, and so the only real significance of this bill has to be in its symbolism.
>
> Let us look at the symbolism. It is based on a misperceived fear, it succumbs to the temptation to dog whistle to certain segments of the population...
>
> Kennedy Graham MP, Green Party.
> Speech on the Immigration Amendment Bill.
> New Zealand Parliament, 17 April 2013

Figure 1.2 Challenging the ontology of anarchy

With permission: K. Graham

Mahmoud Ahmadinejad, claimed, 'In Iran we don't have homosexuals like in your country...In Iran we do not have this phenomenon.' He was discounting the fact that Iranian law formally addresses homosexual acts by men (*lavat* – sodomy) and women (*mosahegheh*). His courts executed people for breaking these laws.[18] If there were no homosexuals in Iran, why would there be a need for laws and punishments to deal with homosexual behaviour?

Philosophers have now moved on from the age-old questions about whether gods exist independently of human existence, and whether the human mind exists independently of its body.[19] But the increasing global influence of violent religious or quasi-religious ideologies should prompt new discussions, because the problems are rooted in persuading people to believe that certain things exist, without objective evidence. Once people accept, on the basis of belief but not evidence, that a god and a heaven exist, it becomes easy to persuade them that this god wants them to kill non-believers and the reward will be anything they desire in another imagined world. Scriptures can be misused to support this. Evangelical churches teach that the Old Testament is the word of their God and is literally true. It therefore supports the killing and torture of animals and humans,[20] killing people who hold different views including family members who try to challenge religious views,[21] rewarding victorious soldiers with virgins from the defeated enemy to rape,[22] and the ethic that children can be punished for the sins of their grandparents.[23]

Quasi-religious ideologies are very similar. The idea that children can be punished for the sins of their parents pertains in North Korea, where the late Kim Il-sung now exists as the 'eternal president'. (Should new ambassadors therefore present their credentials to a corpse?) All ideologies are open to ontological questioning, including familiar grand world theories. Environmentalist Barbara Ward provides a realistic take on Marx's rhetoric:

> Karl Marx derives his critique entirely from Western ideas and sources...Dialectical materialism, the scientific secret of man's history,...has the grandeur and excitement of a great work of art – the somber force of a Verdi opera, the flashing vision of Goethe's *Faust*. But like them, it belongs to the world of imagination, not of fact...
>
> The Marxist vision of history, with its cosmic sweeps from slavery to feudalism to capitalism to communism, is not true in the sense that a scientific experiment or a plain record of dates and happenings is true. It cannot be tested. No predictions can be based on it. And it is contradicted by a large variety of facts.[24]

Comparing the ontological bases of religious doctrine and quasi-religious ideologies provides a way to question and challenge both.

Significant world issues arise within the 'ontology of nothing', which tries to establish whether nothing exists. In his book *Being and Nothingness*, Jean-Paul Sartre explores nothing.[25] Nothing was the basis for many creationist ideologies, because the existence of nothing provided a void that needed a god to fill it. For many religious advocates, God was The Creator who made the world out of nothing, but this requires them to prove that nothing existed. Secular philosophers such as Jacques Lacan argue that nothing does not exist, and so a god as 'the creator' does not exist.[26] The deployment of nothing goes beyond creation myths and amusing arguments, and sometimes underpins major disputes.

thinking zone: what happens when nothing exists?

deploying nothing

The concept of nothing is very useful in political discourse, because it creates an impression that there is a gap that needs filling, which legitimates the actions of those who fill it. Consider:

- *Power vacuum* – an absence of political or other leadership.
- *Democratic deficit* – an absence of a Euro-American-style democratic government.
- *Terra nullius* – Roman law, 'Land belonging to no one' – Australian aboriginal history.
- *A land without a people for a people without a land.* – 'No other people, no other power, has ever created an independent state' in the land that is now Israel.*
- *Desert* – Latin *dēsertum* – 'an abandoned place' – The 'Great American Desert'.
- *Plains* – flat empty land. 'American Great plains', and home to the 'Plains Indians'.
- *Empty Quarter* (Rub' al Khali الربع الخالي) – the large oil rich desert in Saudi Arabia.
- *Namakwa* (Kalahari Desert, South Africa) – a 'kind of vast, empty place', with large diamond and mineral mines. Namaland was the home of the indigenous *Nama*.

(Continued)

(Continued)

- *Res nullius* – Roman law, 'Property belonging to no one'.
- *Void* – housing law: accommodation without an occupancy agreement. Hence, the 'Occupy' movement.
- *Failed/collapsed state* – a state that apparently has no, or an ineffective, government.
- *Frigid zones* – the Polar regions.
- *Space* – the place beyond Earth's atmosphere, containing everything except us.

[*See References for further information.[27]].

Because of the large scale of world events, and the increasing use of big data (C6.5; C9.4), understanding how we, or others, know something is especially important within world studies. ***Epistemology*** – the study of theories of knowledge[28] – asks questions such as:

- What is the *origin* of the knowledge?
- How did the *empirical research* (and other experience) and *reasoned arguments* contribute to creating the knowledge?
- How *certain* (valid and error free) is the knowledge?
- Was the knowledge created *critically* (sceptically)?
- How has, or might, the knowledge *change* as other knowledge and understandings change?
- To what degree would the knowledge be seen as *generally true* (as 'a theory')?[29]

An international perspective also raises questions about *cross-cultural* understandings of knowledge. Anthropologists would argue that 'traditional' or 'indigenous' knowledge might come more from practical experience, dreams and the spirit world, elders and other authorities.[30] Whose 'knowns' count most, and why?

thinking zone: how do we know the unknowns?

knowns

Former US Secretary of State, Donald Rumsfeld, concluded:

> 'There are things we know that we know. There are known unknowns. That is to say there are things that we now know we don't know. But there are also unknown unknowns. There are things we don't know we don't know.'

so...

What are the significant 'known knowns', 'known unknowns' and 'unknown unknowns' in:

international relations, development studies, environmental politics, religion, war studies, human capabilities, international organizations?

information systems

Identify examples of *direct primary data* about states, i.e. the data does *not* reach you through indirect 'authorities'.

- From your personal perspective, are there any *certain* 'known knowns' about the examples you identify?
- Are there any *'unknowable* knowns' in the examples – seemingly factual claims which cannot be known because there are no methodologies to discover the truth about them?

archive

If we could set up a database of the misuse of 'unknowns' in international politics, what would be in that archive and who should maintain and fund it?

Because of the distance and scale of events, international knowledge is often based on an 'argument from *authority*',[31] such as a government or commercial expert. The credibility of expert views assumes that:

1. the expert is usually correct about the subject,
2. there is a professional consensus that the expert is usually correct, and therefore
3. any further opinion from the authority on this subject is likely to be correct.

But the views of international experts are susceptible to the *halo effect*.[32] We might judge an authority to be correct because the 'halo' of one particular above-average trait – wealth, tradition, position – can generate a perception that other qualities are above average – honesty, intelligence, diligence. These problems were recognized long ago by Arab historian Ibn Khaldūn. Like al-Bīrūnī, in 1377 he complained about unreliable authorities – 'Reliance upon transmitters' – and he recognized the 'halo' problem of 'authorities' (Figure 1.3).[33]

> People as a rule approach great and high-ranking persons with praise and encomiums [tributes]. They embellish conditions and spread their fame.
>
> Students often happen to accept and transmit absurd information that, in turn, is believed on their authority.
>
> Ibn Khaldūn (1377) *The Muqaddimah*
> (Bk 1: Preliminary Remarks)

Figure 1.3 The 'halo effect' (Ibn Khaldūn)

International knowledge is often created to deceive, in the form of *propaganda*.[34] From the 1950s to 1980s, Eisenhower, Nixon and other American leaders deployed the *domino theory* to justify the Vietnam War – that if Vietnam became communist then other countries in South East Asia would also fall.[35] The claim had no evidence-base. More than 5 million Vietnamese died in a pointless war, which cost America around $165 billion. Misinformation is not just simple retrospective lies to cover up previous mistakes or misdeeds. It also comes in the form of *pre-emptive deceit* – political knowledge-creation that aims to get in first so that subsequent truth is less likely to be believed – as concerning Iraq in 2003.[36] This is explained further on the website.

Ontology and epistemology are often confused. Roy Bhaskar calls this the 'epistemic fallacy'.[37] But although they are not the same, they are linked, and should both be kept in mind throughout a whole study, particularly when data is being reported, to avoid repeating questionable discourse. Where did the idea of an 'axis of evil' and 'good and evil' come from? The source is probably the Persian prophet Mani (ماني) (circa 216–276AD).[38] So when, (then) US president G.W. Bush deployed his 'good and evil' rhetoric about the 'axis' of supposed US enemies, including Iran, he was repeating an Iranian ideology.

1.2 Reflexivity

When the two Wright brothers were developing their ideas for the first aeroplane, if they argued about something, at some point they would deliberately swap sides in the argument.[39] This is an ancient Greek technique called *Dissoi Logoi*. Philosophers analyse how false logic arises, and an awareness of this can help to avoid weaknesses in arguments. Material on the website explains the familiar problems.

There are many relevant approaches to *reflexive* or *reflective* thinking – turning our mental processes back upon themselves. When developing intelligence tests in 1904, Binet assessed 'auto-critique' – the critical understanding of oneself.[40] Bourdieu provides philosophical arguments for reflexivity in sociology,[41] and many writers develop the methodological implications.[42] Organizations or groups use *sense-making* or *mindfulness*.[43] But these ideas are not new. The *Comprehensive Mirror for Aid in Governance* (資治通鑑) by Ssu-ma Kuang (司馬光) (1018–1086), provided a history of China from 403BC to 959, and aimed to help subsequent rulers *reflect* (in the 'mirror' it provided) on the mistakes and success of their predecessors.[44]

Techniques for reflective thinking are not complicated. Using simple words – if, but, or – can expand thinking. Sociologists often talk of viewing events through different *lenses*. Materials to explore these techniques are on the website.

Arguably, complete *objectivity* is impossible,[45] so researchers should aim 'to understand the effects of [their] experiences rather than engaging in futile attempts to eliminate them'.[46] It is helpful to consider the strengths and weaknesses of *positionality*[47] – the *exogenous/etic* perspectives as an *outsider*, or the *endogenous/*

emic perspectives as an *insider.*[48] But assessing personal identity is not always straightforward, particularly for international students and scholars who return to a "home" country to do research.[49] Would a Pakistani student from a middle class family in Islamabad be an insider or outsider if she did research among the Taliban in North Eastern Pakistan?

Most reflexive methodology is not specific to international research but geographers provide useful insights about fieldwork, feminist perspectives[50] and researching elites.[51] Careful consideration of the implications of working across languages[52] and using translators[53] is clearly important for much international work, but is also increasingly relevant within multicultural countries. There is discussion concerning international collaboration in research,[54] and cross-cultural management studies,[55] but international relations has 'lacked a sociology of itself'[56] and is arguably less internationally reflexive in its approach to research than might be expected.[57]

Research diaries or ethnographic notes can provide a basis for reflexive thinking. Notes might be based on self-reflexive contextual impressions, which may later become data or help to explain data (Figure 1.4). Alternatively, they can be structured more formally as: *observational notes* (a purely factual account), *methodological notes* (what happened during data collection), *theoretical notes* (what might be the broader explanations) and *analytic memos* (initial comparisons of data, theory and literature).[58] Notes might also include how researchers and others are feeling – tired, angry, stressed – because later this might warn of unreliable data.

MAY 3 - First impressions: lots of concrete, beautiful mountains in the distance. The welcome is very warm, people are so polite and hospitable; it makes me feel very welcome.

MAY 4 - Outside of the home, things are a bit different. I had to change my shirt before going out as it is a little see through (I had never noticed that before!). So that put me on my guard. But people are very friendly. It is interesting seeing how people dress. Men can get away with more and many dress in 'Western' styles. Girls all wear hijab. Some women do wear clothes that reveal the outline of their body shape, but hair, arms and legs are always covered. There are both cultural and legal aspects to this. The head being covered draws you to their faces, and particularly the eyes. I never noticed so many different subtle shades of brown, green, blue before.

MAY 6. As a foreign man, you must be careful. There is no physical contact with a woman if you are not family. You can shake their hand if it is offered, otherwise you simply say Assalam o Alaikum. I bumped into a woman in a shopping mall, and quickly said 'sorry', reaching out in a reassuring way (something I would do at home). The woman looked shocked, and A. said that if I had touched her it would have been very offensive.

Figure 1.4 A self-reflexive contextual diary

(By a European man in a Muslim country)

More broadly, the UN concept of *international understanding* provides a framework for reflecting on world research.[59] A Deputy Director General of UNESCO, W.H.C. Lewis, provided a nuanced explanation:

> International Understanding is the ability to observe critically and objectively and appraise the conduct of [people] everywhere to each other, irrespective of the nationality of culture to which they may belong. To do this one must be able to detach oneself from one's own particular cultural and national prejudices and to observe [people] of all nationalities, cultures and races as equally important varieties of human being inhabiting this earth.[60]

To transcend nationalistic and other divisive approaches, the concept of thinking and trying to act ***without borders***, which derived from *Médecins Sans Frontières* (MSF), is now applied to over 60 world organizations including musicians, reporters, monks and clowns.[61] The idea reflects the formation of international organizations in the 19th century,[62] and the present-day movement is assisted by books such as *Activists Beyond Borders*,[63] initiatives like the *Reporters Without Borders* and the *Electronic Frontier Foundation*. But, as George Orwell reminds us, progress does not intrinsically lead to international understanding or a borderless world:

> We were once told that the aeroplane had '*abolished frontiers*'; actually it is only since the aeroplane became a serious weapon that frontiers have become definitely impassable. The radio was once expected to promote international understanding and co-operation; it has turned out to be a means of insulating one nation from another.[64]

thinking zone: potatoes without borders

Potatoes are now grown in more than 100 countries around the world, but:

Belarus

- Belarusians eat the most potatoes – 335 kg per year. The world average is 33 kg.
- The average potato production in Belarus each year is 865 kg per person. In the USA – 69 kg per person.
- Belarus is the 10th largest potato producer in the world.
- Belarusians know more than 300 recipes for potatoes.
- There is a Belarusian national dance called *Bul'ba* – 'potatoes'.
- In the Soviet Union, Belarusians were sometimes called *bulbashi*.
- In January 2014, Russia accused Belarus of potato smuggling from the EU.

global potatoes

- Potatoes came originally from Peru and Bolivia, not Belarus. So how, and why, did the potato get to Belarus, and become so popular?
- Potatoes came to Spain from South America. Peter I brought a small sack of potatoes from Spain to Russia in the 18th century.

- Peter I wanted to grow them in Russia but farmers didn't know how. They ate potato tubers and died. The potato became known as the 'Devil's apple' and people refused to grow it.
- Belarus and Ukraine were under Russian domination at that time, and Belarusians grew them instead.

potato politics

- Potatoes are the world's fourth largest food crop, after rice, wheat and corn.
- The UN *International Year of the Potato* (2008) promoted the idea that the potato is crucial to avoid global food shortages.
- In Europe, only a quarter of potatoes are now eaten by humans. Half are fed to livestock. The rest is used to produce alcohol and starch used by food chemical and paper industries.
- *GMO-Compass.org* claims that 'extending the benefits of potato production depends on improvements in...potato varieties that have reduced water needs, greater resistance to pests and diseases, and resilience in the face of climate changes'.
- In 1998, Hungarian researcher Árpád Pusztai claimed on British TV that rats fed with GMO potatoes suffered damage to their intestines and immune systems. The next day he was suspended by his employer, the *Rowett Institute*, his research team was disbanded, and data seized. UK government officials, *Monsanto* and (then) heads of state Blair and Clinton were implicated in the actions.

Where, and what, next for the potato – what is its global future?

[See References for further information.[65]]

Note: Most online information about GM potatoes stems from the GM industries. *Genewatch.org* provides alternative views.
(Research: Belous Daria, Minsk State Linguistic University)

main ideas

The construction of ***international knowledge*** needs to consider:

- how we can prove that relevant things *exist* (ontology).
- how we *know* about things (epistemology).
- *cross-cultural* understandings of existence and knowledge.
- why the *authority* for any source of information is credible.
- how we detect *propaganda* and *pre-emptive deceit*.
- whether *definitions* and *assumptions* are clear and international.

A ***reflexive*** approach should aim to avoid:

- bias caused by ethnocentricity, nationalism, or worldviews.
- bias caused by human psychological traits.
- simplistic conclusions from complex data.

And should aim to achieve:

- an examination of the research design, data and analysis from *different perspectives* – self, others, mirrors, eyes, lenses.
- contributions to *international understanding.*
- researchers and readers who think *without borders.*

key reading

Audi, R. (1997) *Epistemology: A Contemporary Introduction to the Theory of Knowledge.* London: Routledge.

Eagleton, M. (2009) 'Examining the case for reflexivity in international relations: insights from Bourdieu', *Journal of Critical Globalisation Studies*, 1: 111–123.

Effingham, N. (2013) *An Introduction to Ontology.* Cambridge: Polity.

Keck, M.E. and Sikkink, K. (1998) *Activists Beyond Borders: Advocacy Networks in International Politics.* Ithaca, NY: Cornell University Press.

Woolgar, S. (1988) *Knowledge and Reflexivity: New Frontiers in the Sociology of Knowledge.* London and Beverly Hills, CA: Sage.

online resources

To access the resources – search on the name in italics or use the http.

International knowledge

Future of Humanity Institute – do we exist, and will we continue to exist? – existential-risk.org

Ontology.com – ongoing discussions from an American perspective

Epistemology for dummies – a good start – www.epistemologyexpress.com/efordummies.htm

Interdependence Movement. Citizens Without Borders

Electronic Frontier Foundation – protecting the freedom of electronic communication across borders

TWO

Theories and concepts in world research

A story from the Silk Road tells of an argument between *wine*, *tea* and *milk*. *Wine* claimed he was most important because he made people happy, *tea* claimed the same because tea made people calm, and *milk* argued that she was best as babies would not survive without her. But then *water* said, 'You are all wrong. I am the most important, because all drinks depend on me.' *Water* won the argument, with a theory.

This chapter outlines relevant theories (a system of ideas that helps to predict things, such as a proven hypothesis) and concepts (a general idea) under three headings – *peoples*, *places* and *systems* (see Figure 2.1). It does not (and could not!) provide an in-depth critical discussion of all world theories, and the synopses should be followed up through the references. Experts in particular fields should probably ignore the sections they are familiar with, and investigate the relevance of other approaches. Good theories have *predictive* or *explanatory* power. Philosophers argue about whether theories represent truth[1] and the degree to which world theory emerges from, or helps to form, evidence.[2] Present-day world theories have a strong European-American bias, and are often ethnocentric.

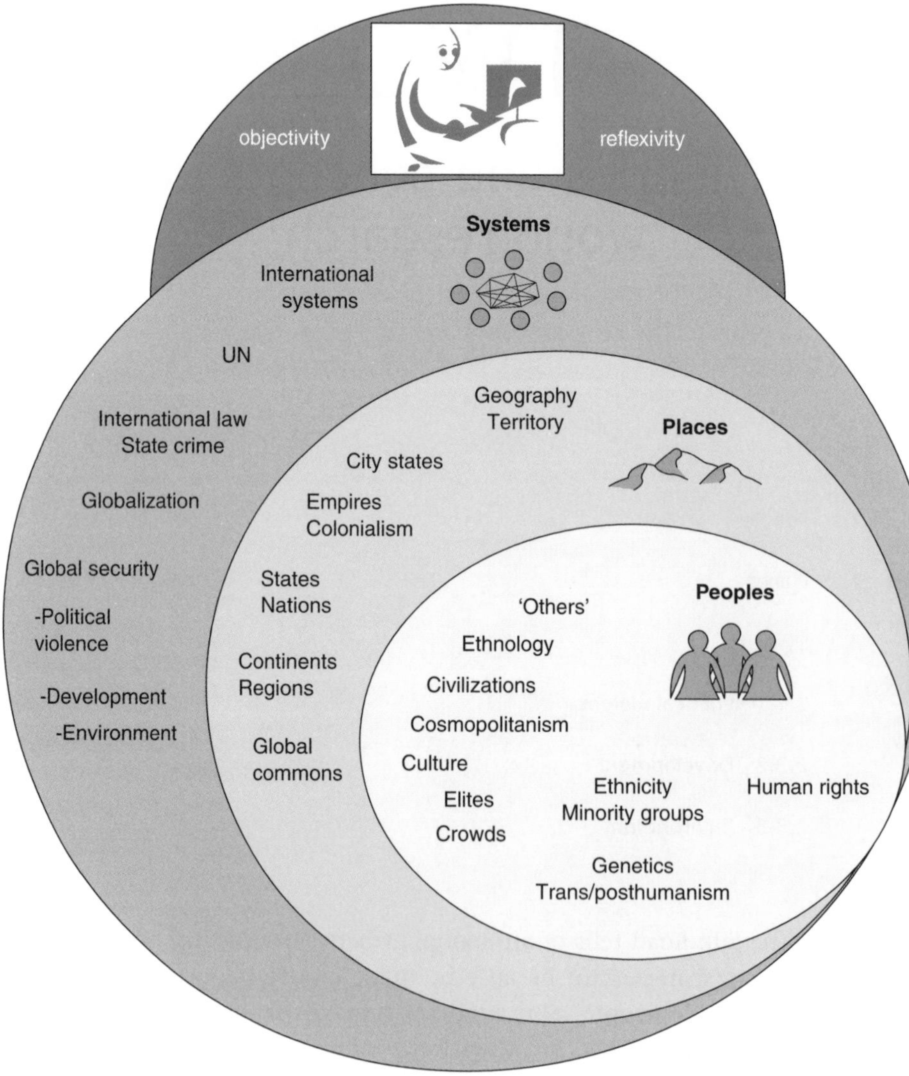

Figure 2.1 World theoretical frameworks

2.1 Peoples

'Peoples' may be the subjects of a ruler, a group to which individuals feel they belong (tribe, clan, racial group), or a group of citizens who legitimize power elites. But this creates the notion of outsiders who do not belong, and world research has often generated worldviews of **others** as representing a threat because of appearance, race, religion, nationality, class, gender, civilization and similar perceived differences.[3] The study of different peoples has been central to:

- ***religious studies***, which wanted to prove the content of religious texts, and that the peoples of some religions were better than other religions.
- ***anthropology*** and ***ethnology***, which often constructed **others**, and rationalized colonial policies to demean and control.
- ***scientific racism, ethnic nationalism*** and ***eugenics***, which tried to prove that peoples were different and some were inferior.
- ***historical studies***, which tried to understand the rise and fall of *civilizations*, but also gave rise to *nationalistic* views.
- ***cosmopolitism,*** and the idea that everyone is a 'citizen of the world'.
- modern ***ethnography***, which tries to understand different cultures, of many forms.
- ***social stratification***, ***elite*** and ***crowd*** studies.
- ***human rights***, which aim to protect all individuals equitably.
- ***human biology***, which now proves the common genetic roots of all peoples, considers the future of the human race, and provides understandings of the 'global brain'.

Although many of the unethical approaches to world research seem to be part of past eras, understanding the failings of the past can help to avoid repeating past mistakes.

The understanding of **others** has a problematic history. Even Hippocrates used racial descriptors such as 'industrious' versus 'sluggish'.[4] The outcomes have been:

ethnocentric – promoting the centrality and paramount importance of one's own people,
xenophobic – creating a fear strangers or foreigners,
supremacist – claiming a right to rule "inferior" groups,
exceptionalist – believing that one's own group is different from, and better than, others.

The biological explanation is that hostility towards other groups seems to be a 'human universal'.[5] But this is made worse by social manipulation because human instincts can be exaggerated to reinforce political interests. For example, young children will tend to eat what their parents eat because that is an evolutionary mechanism to avoid being poisoned. But this can then be turned into a cultural food taboo and a life-long habit, which keeps the young within the group, and alienates others.[6]

Jacques Derrida provides a psychological explanation – if there is a perception of 'self', there must also be a perception of **others** to define that self.[7] But this may not always have been the case.[8] European exploration by ship emphasized difference – to sailors voyaging East from Lisbon, Japanese people would look suddenly different. But travellers on land, for example along the Silk Road, would see diverse similarities across the whole continent, from Tehran to Nara.[9] Silk Road researcher al-Bīrūnī was again progressive, and tried to understand how those he studied viewed others (Figure 2.2).[10]

> ...all [the Hindu] fanaticism is directed against those who do not belong to them – against all foreigners. They call them mleccha, i.e. impure, and forbid having any connection with them, be it by intermarriage or any other kind of relationship, or by sitting, eating, and drinking with them, because thereby, they think, they would be polluted. They consider as impure anything which touches the fire and the water of a foreigner...They are not allowed to receive anybody who does not belong to them, even if he wished it, or was inclined to their religion.
>
> ابوريحان محمد بن احمد بيروني
>
> Abū Rayhān al-Bīrūnī, *India* (circa 1030)

Figure 2.2 Researching 'othering' (al-Bīrūnī)

Religious **ideologies** often underpinned hatred. Arab historian Ibn Khaldūn was vitriolic in 1377 (Figure 2.3).[11] Compte de Gobineau's *Essai sur l'inégalité des races humaines* promoted 'our white species'.[12] The South African *Dutch Reformed Church* (NHK) justified *apartheid* on Biblical grounds – that the non-Israelite Gibeonites were to be 'slaves, and hewers of wood and drawers of water'.[13] The old Jewish texts appear to justify many other evils against peoples. Moses condoned rape as a reward for victorious soldiers.[14] Deuteronomy justified *genocide* – 'Of these peoples...you shall let nothing that breathes remain alive, but you shall utterly destroy them',[15] and stoning on suspicion of adultery – 'the young woman because she was in a town and did not scream for help'.[16] The doctrine of present-day evangelical churches still supports these views. Paradoxically, Iran's penal code still maintains the Jewish ethic of stoning women,[17] as does Afghanistan, Nigeria, Pakistan, Sudan and the United Arab Emirates. Most UN codes now preclude racial discrimination; the UN *Genocide Convention* (1948) now covers acts that intend 'to destroy, in whole or in part, a national, ethnical, racial or religious group...';[18] and sexual violence became a war crime in 2008.[19]

> **مقدّمة ابن خلدون**
>
> To the south of this Nile, there is a Negro people called Lamlam. They are unbelievers...Beyond them to the south, there is no civilization in the proper sense. There are only humans who are closer to dumb animals than to rational beings. They live in thickets and caves and eat herbs and unprepared grain. They frequently eat each other. They cannot be considered human beings
>
> Ibn Khaldūn (1377) *The Muqaddimah*
> (Bk 1: Preliminary Remarks)

Figure 2.3 Theological 'othering' (Ibn Khaldūn)

Ethnology became the study of *races*, and the **comparative method** assumed that other races represented "living fossils" which Europeans could use to study their origins. Theories of **ethnic nationalism** legitimized nations,[20] and **scientific racism** conflated race, mental disability and animals using meticulous comparative methodology (Figure 2.4). **Eugenics** then aimed to improve the genetic make-up of European populations. Although associated with Nazi Germany, the ideology was expressed by many elites including Thomas Jefferson[21] and Winston Churchill.[22]

An "Asylum Mongol"

A Kirghiz man (Racial Mongol)

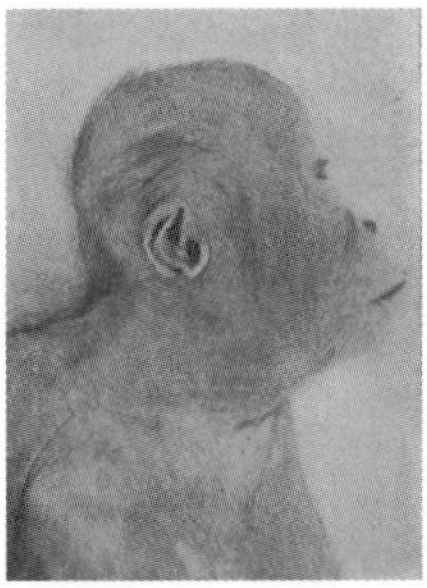

A young Orang-utan

A Japanese priest

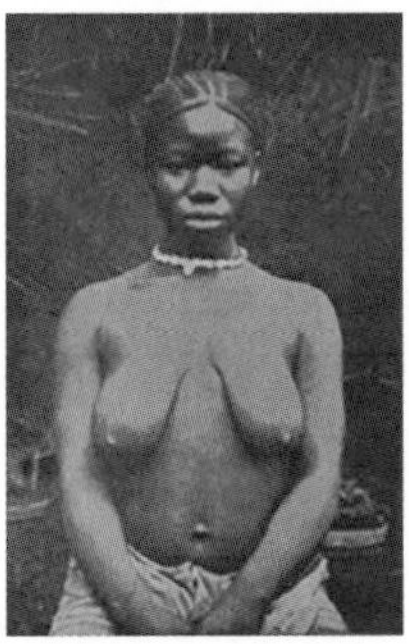

A "black" woman

A "yellow" woman (Chinese)

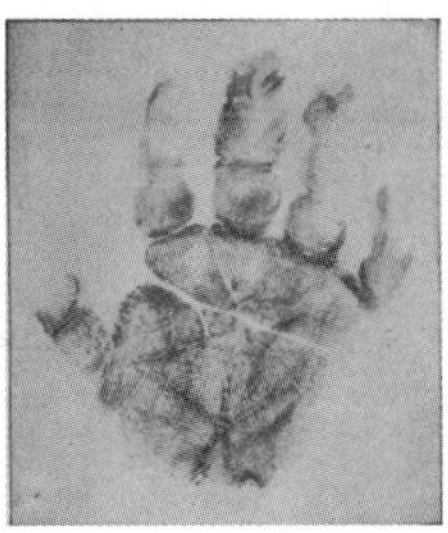

Hand-print of "Mongolian" imbecile

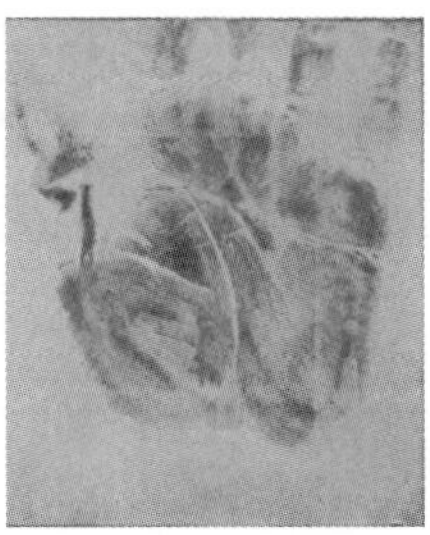

Hand-print of a Tonkinese sailor

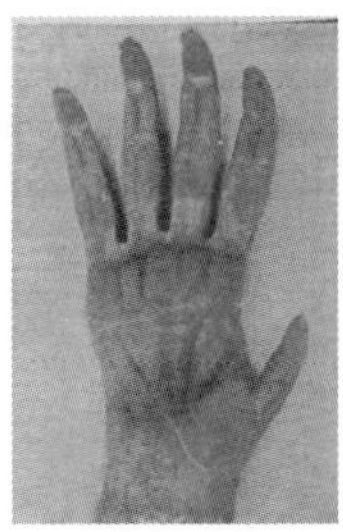

Hand of an Orang-utan

Figure 2.4 Scientific racism

Full version on the website.
Crookshank, F.G. (1924) *The Mongol in Our Midst: A Study of Man and his Three Faces.*
Note: Please use these photographs responsibly. Do not send digital versions.

Ethnicity[23] traditionally meant national *identity*, and Amartya Sen argues that the construction of identity can fuel enmity and violence.[24] Ethnic theories continue in relation to IQ,[25] but the general conclusion among psychologists is that although certain tests may show differences between ethnic groups, this is because of the linguistic or cultural insensitivity of the tests, not racial differences.[26] But now 'ethnicity' usually implies a less specific ancestry or cultural heritage. The term *ethnic background* is often used in relation to **minority** groups ('minority' usually meaning power not size) and terminology is confusing. Chinese people in New York might be described as a *minority ethnic* group, but in the world Chinese people are clearly not an *ethnic minority*. Although racial distinctions have often been harmful, there are arguments that a 'denial of difference' can also be problematic.[27]

Within ***historical studies***, the concept of **civilizations** is used to understand large groups of peoples, but is hard to define.[28] Studying the main legal traditions of the world can help.[29] Success and failure has been a common theme, since Ibn Khaldūn's *Muqaddimah* (1377).[30] In 1911, G.G. Rupert's *The Yellow Peril; or, the Orient vs. the Occident* promoted a fear that the Biblical 'Kings from the East'[31] – China, India, Japan, and Korea and Russia – would attack England and the United States, but Jesus would stop them.[32] The evidence for Rupert's rhetoric was the Bible, and he promoted a German worldview to construct American enmity, which prefaced the destruction of Hiroshima and Nagasaki, the Cold War against 'Russia', the 'axis of evil', and ongoing mistrust of 'Arabia', 'Persia' and 'Afghanistan'. Rupert's ideas and map seem a prototype for Huntington's *clash of civilizations*.[33]

thinking zone: are 'clashes' between or within civilizations?

'clashes'

Huntington warns of 'the clash of civilizations'. How do the following events fit that concept?

- World War I, within Europe.
- The 'troubles' between Catholic and Protestant Christians in Northern Ireland.
- Imperialism and enmity among states that share Confucian values – China, Japan, Korea.
- Disagreements and war within Abrahamic religions – Judaism, Christianity, Islam.
- Conflicts between Shiite and Sunni Muslims, e.g. Iran and Iraq.

Since 1945, when has large-scale political violence occurred *between*:

- Asia and Europe?
- Asia and Africa?
- Africa and Europe?
- America and anywhere else?

Are wars between civilizations, or between powerful people who use ordinary people to fight their wars?

[See References for further information.[34]]

Nationalistic ideologies of "them and us" continue and research continues to study how different groups are represented, for example in films and video games,[35] and the government funding of film and video game research.[36] Games are often contrived to reinforce enmity between peoples. The US *Homefront* game is based on a fictional invasion of America by North Korea, and the theme was mirrored in the story of the film *Olympus is Fallen*, and *The Interview. Operation Flashpoint: Dragon Rising* presents the Chinese People's Liberation Army as hostile, and the Chinese *Glorious Mission*, which was originally created for military training, presents the enemy as American.

Present-day **ethnography** (C6.1) is often described as a study of **culture** – a 'design for living'.[37] *Cultural lag* proposes that social problems arise because culture does not keep pace with technological innovation.[38] *Cultural relativism* argues that there are no clear relationships between culture and race, nor absolute standards for judging different cultures. Many disciplines adopt cross-cultural approaches, including philosophers[39] and psychiatrists.[40] **Cultural imperialism**[41] has been a means to increase colonial and neocolonial power. But *cultural diplomacy*[42] builds on cultural exchanges to improve relationships between nations, and *political arts* is becoming an academic field of study.[43] ***Cultural studies*** (which is distinct from area studies) is an interdisciplinary approach using critical theory and literary criticism, which considers the political aspects of modern culture. It makes distinctions such as 'high cultural production' (film, literature, theatre, art, music, new media), and 'cultural identities' (ethnicity, gender, language, social organization), but not necessarily from the perspective of formal governmental politics.[44] Studies often combine ethnographic and other approaches, for example in relation to cross-national research about the politics of food.[45]

thinking zone: are MOOCs educational imperialism?

MOOCs

The *Massive Open Online Courses* (MOOCs) provide free or cheap access to American and other English language university courses.

why?

MOOCs are good advertisements for universities, and countries. But are they also a form of:

- cultural imperialism?
- cultural diplomacy?
- soft power?

What is the likely future of MOOCs, and how might other countries, and universities teaching in other languages, respond?

[See References for further information.[46]]

All peoples seem to give rise to **elites.**[47] Classical elite theory is rooted in the work of Italian sociologists Pareto (1848–1923) and Mosca (1858–1941), who argued that personal characteristics, such as organizational skill, create an inevitable distinction between select groups of powerful people and others. Traditional theorists often claimed that elites are morally and intellectually superior.[48] International perspectives include *The Comparative Study of Elites* (1952), which aimed to 'reveal the significance of the vast revolution that is reshaping our contemporary world', on the assumption that, 'by determining what is happening to the elites of societies around the globe...we can test the underlying hypothesis...that a world revolution is under way during our epoch'.[49] Future developments may include updates of national elite studies – including South America,[50] Russia,[51] Europe[52] and East Asia[53] – and studies of 'global elites'.[54]

Elites usually perceived **crowds** – the masses – as a threat. From the Greek notion of *ochlocracy* (mob rule), *majoritarianism* carried negative implications, as did the Roman word *demokratia* – rule of the people. J.S. Mill warned of the 'tyranny of the majority' in 1859,[55] and the idea was perpetuated in books such as *Extraordinary Popular Delusions and the Madness of Crowds*[56] and *The Crowd: A Study of the Popular Mind.*[57] Following World War I, the concern about crowds continued, for example a Spanish perspective in *The Revolt of the Masses,*[58] and a German view in *The Menace of the Herd.*[59] Theories evolved to represent polarized perspectives of bad crowds[60] and good crowds.[61] The advent of the internet revealed the potential of the crowd as a resource, and Surowiecki's *The Wisdom of Crowds* argued the value of crowd perspectives.[62] The word 'crowdsourcing' was coined by Jeff Howe, a writer for *Wired* magazine, in 2006, as analogous to outsourcing (2009),[63] and crowdsourcing is now becoming an exciting new research framework (C6.4).[64] But the fear of crowds has not disappeared, and is often manipulated to create a fear of crowds of **others**, based on race or nationality. The lesson from history is that, when it suits the interests of elites to present peoples as crowds that threaten security, they will always find supposed research that supports their views.

Social stratification, whether based on race or other factors, was not a European invention.[65] Jewish tradition delineates judges, kings, priests (*Kohen*) and prophets. Korea had five classes – intellectuals (*yang-bang*), professional and military (*jung-in*), farmers and commercial (*nong-sang-min*), untouchables (*chun-min*) and a slave class (*nobi*). The Indian caste system divided people into hereditary groups – *Brahmins, Kshatriyas, Vaishyas, Shudras,* and the alienated 'untouchables'. Stratification is still intrinsic within honorifics in languages such as Burmese, Korean and Japanese. Within European sociology, class systems evolve as societies change. In Britain, a 'technical middle class' and 'new affluent workers' have been added to traditional categorizations which reflect new forms of *cultural capital.*[66] Classes may now have greater international than intra-national affinities – the well-educated middle classes of India, China, Europe and the Americas may have more in common with one another than with the poor, rural or marginalized people in their own countries.

A **cosmopolitan**[67] perspective promotes an undivided view of humanity and power.[68] The cosmopolitan Greeks apparently considered themselves to be 'citizens of the world'. And the Stoics declared allegiance to universal ideas of justice rather than to the city state – 'we should regard all human beings as our fellow citizens and neighbours'.[69] This concept of *global citizens*[70] and *global ethics*[71] parallels ideas of *global justice* – a fair distribution of 'goods' and 'bads'.[72] Many cities celebrate their *diversity, multicultural*[73] populations, and *cross-border families*.[74] The term *social cohesion*[75] develops previous ideas of *cultural assimilation* and *melting pot*.[76] Many individuals see themselves as having multiple *identities*,[77] and Rumford talks of a 'strangeness' as globalization blurs community boundaries and identities.[78] Appadurai proposes viewing globalizing society in terms of relationships between 'public worlds' comprising *ethnoscapes, technoscapes, financescapes, mediascapes* and *ideascapes*.[79]

When the UN *Charter* used the phrase, the 'peoples of the United Nations', it prefaced an era of codifying the **rights** of everyone, and formalized this in the UN *Declaration of Universal Human Rights* (1948). The website explains more. The first international agreement was probably the *Declaration of Geneva*, which affirmed children's rights and was accepted by the *League of Nations* in 1923. But rights are not a European invention. The *Code of Hamurabi* (circa 1790BC) limited the power of ruling elites, and the Persian *Cyrus Cylinder* (539BC), often called the world's first human rights code, gave religious freedoms and abolished slavery. (It seems that the Iranians abolished slavery 2293 years before the Americans discovered it.) A few Islamic countries objected to the 'universality' of what they saw as a European-American imposition of moral standards, and created the *Cairo Declaration on Human Rights in Islam* in 2000.

The concept of rights usually implies related ***responsibilities***, fulfilled reciprocally by other people, or by states through public services or remedies for wrongdoing. But political leaders often fail to fulfil their responsibilities, and many try to avoid being bound by the same rules as the people.[80] Rights are sometimes restricted on the basis of an apparent inability to fulfil responsibilities. Full rights were often denied to indigenous groups, who were perceived as too "primitive" to understand their responsibilities. The *Declaration on the Rights of Indigenous Peoples* (2007) now guides the UN *Permanent Forum on Indigenous Issues*, and introduces the concepts of collective rights and cultural rights, but the idea of group rights is often questioned.[81] Similar arguments delayed giving people with mental disabilities equal rights. The Christian church talked of the 'grave mistake of treating human-looking shapes as if they were human, although they lack the least vestige of human behavior or intellect'.[82] The Catholic Church only extended its right of Communion to disabled people who could not state their belief in the Eucharist, in 1983. Even the UN *Declaration on the Rights of Mentally Retarded Persons* (1971) talked of 'restriction' or 'denial' of rights 'whenever mentally retarded persons are unable...to exercise all their rights in a meaningful way' (Art. 7). This has practical implications, such as the denial of justice to victims with disabilities.[83] The rights of the unborn child, in relation to toxic environmental impacts, have also been hard to establish, because they are hard to reconcile with a woman's right to have an abortion.[84] Paradoxically, the rights of future generations – *intergenerational rights*[85] – are also impeded by arguments that unborn people cannot fulfil any responsibilities, as are arguments against animal rights.[86] But distinctions are evolving. Philosopher John Gray reminds us that humans are just another form of animal.[87]

In parallel with these social constructs of humanity as a planetary whole, advances in science – **human biology**, psychology, evolutionary theory, archaeology – are increasing the understandings of humanity. Mithen's *Prehistory of the Mind* explores the common roots of art, religion and science.[88] Taylor provides convincing arguments that *Homo sapiens* evolved as *artificial apes*, all humans are intrinsically a technological species, and the use of simple technologies shaped the modern brain.[89] Bloom envisions the *Global Brain* as a 'complex adaptive system' of which all human endeavours, including the internet, are interrelated components.[90] There are now good understandings of why humans tend to be overoptimistic,[91] and why *positive illusions* cause military and political leaders to be overconfident.[92] Kahneman explains why it is useful to understand the difference between the 'fast, intuitive and emotional' and the 'slower, more deliberative and more logical' use of the mind.[93]

Practical insights for international research are also coming from *neuroscience*. Susan Greenfield addresses questions about how the pervasive use of recent technologies, principally IT, may change the way human minds work,[94] including our sense of identity.[95] Brain imaging shows not only that we share common thought processes, but researchers are starting to explain how our brain addresses world problems. Functional magnetic resonance imaging of the brain has been used 'to investigate the central problem of distributive justice: the trade off between equity and efficiency'.[96] The researchers examined brain responses while participants considered an aid scenario about distributing food equitably in a famine stricken region. The dilemma was, should they strive to be equitable and distribute food fairly even if it becomes rotten, or be efficient and distribute the food to those nearest to the distribution networks before it goes bad, but leaving some people to die? In the experiment, a similar scenario was about distributing money and food to children living in an orphanage in Uganda. The study found that two different regions of the brain respond to efficiency and inequity, but a third area 'encodes a unified measure of efficiency and inequity'. This experiment does not provide instant answers to the problems of global justice, but it shows that human beings across the world, from government ministers to school children, have the same mental equipment to try to reconcile dilemmas like these.

Advances in science increase the understandings of humanity, and raise new questions. Will *human enhancement* create **transhuman** generations and then a **posthuman** condition in which humans cease to exist?[97] Would that amount to *neo-eugenics*?[98] Could present-day genetics and neuroscience mutate into another unethical use of science for world research?[99] Might humans suffer *dysgenics* because of changed reproductive or survival behaviour,[100] or *regressive evolution* of the brain because of adaptation to environmental changes?[101] Is Cambridge cosmologist, Stephen Hawking, correct when he predicts that a biological virus, or the development of self-replicating artificial intelligence (AI), could mean the end of the human race? How, as he suggests, might exploration beyond Earth help to solve these problems? The *Institute for Interstellar Studies* considers how human societies would exist in space, and the *Centre for Astrobiology* works to understand 'life in extreme environments on the Earth and beyond', which may also answer the question: Is there life beyond Earth?

But the most pertinent outcome from recent science is to show that the genetic differences between "races" are marginal. Evolutionary theorists now conclude that all modern humans almost certainly have genetic roots in Africa.[102] Even culturally distinct peoples, such as Palestinians and Jews, share a genetic heritage.[103] Their conflicts are wars between imagined histories. Neuroscience shows not only that we share common thought processes, but that our brain addresses world problems in a common way.[104] Science is also underpinning an extension of human inclusiveness to animals?[105] A court ruling from Argentina, in 2014, concluded orangutans are 'non-human persons', and have basic rights to freedom. However although it seems that we share 98% of our genes with chimpanzees, Steve Jones provides a reality check – 'We also share about 50% of our DNA with bananas, and that doesn't make us half bananas.'[106]

2.2 Places

'Humanity is decidedly a territorial species...Territorial expansion and defence by tribes and their modern equivalents the nation states is a cultural universal', concludes biologist E.O. Wilson.[107] Theories of place (a specific space) consider: the creation of **territories**, the **legitimacy** of claims to land, **international organizations**, non-nation **global commons**. In practice, claims to territory reflect three justifications: historical, "It's ours because we've always lived here" – passive, "It's ours because we were given it" – or imperialist, "It's ours because we took it." A sense of territory is politicized by demonizing the peoples of other places.

Geography explores the physical and political characteristics of territories.[108] In Europe, geographical methods emerged in the 3rd century BC, and focused on physical aspects until the 19th century. Islands were probably the first places to develop a sense of *territory* on a large scale. Elsewhere, borders were marked by physical features such as rivers and mountains. Boundaries subsequently became political rather than physical constructs, and diverse 'geographies' have emerged.[109]

In continental regions, castles expanded into walled **city states** – Ur, Uruk, Canaan. Linked city states appeared around 400–500BC. From the 7th century BC, the Great Wall of China evolved apparently to enclose the emergent states of the Chinese Empire. Present-day city states include Monaco, Singapore, the Vatican,[110] and arguably Pyongyang. Walls remain significant in constructing cities and state territory.

City states often merged into **empires**. The Holy Roman Empire (which was not Holy, Roman or a true Empire) comprised a string of self-ruling, but loyal, 'Free Imperial Cities'. Powerful rulers controlled their domains by giving land to loyal subordinates – *fiefdoms* to warriors, *principalities* to family members and *bishoprics* to religious leaders. **Expansionism** entailed moving borders forward into other lands, as did China. The ancient Chinese name for the Roman Empire was *Dàqín* (大秦) – *Dà* suggesting that the Roman Empire was part of the extended 'greater' Qin state.[111]

But as maritime technology improved, strong navies appropriated distant **colonies**, as did Portugal, Spain, Holland and England. These were often populated by exporting surplus citizens. Britain was still exporting its unwanted children to its former colonies in the 1970s. But colonial theory was not an invention of the Renaissance Europeans. Plato's vision of a *Republic* and its *Laws* envisaged a state from which any 'surplus' person could simply be exported to the 'colonies' – albeit, 'with mutual goodwill between the emigrants and their mother-city'.[112]

Postcolonial writers explain how colonizers legitimized colonial rule,[113] including collusion with missionaries and anthropologists,[114] and abused indigenous peoples, particularly through *slavery*.[115] Franz Fanon's *The Wretched of the Earth*[116] and Edward Said's *Orientalism* are seminal postcolonial texts.[117] Conversely, *Occidentalism* considers the view of 'the West'.[118] **Neocolonial** theories describe how former colonies used economic, commercial and political influences to prolong their power.[119] This continues in the form of *soft power,* by superpowers such as America and the EU,[120] and China's international activities provide a further dimension.[121] The concept of soft power was originally Chinese – *li* (soft) versus *fa* (hard).[122]

Early **nations** originally comprised people of the same ethnic group, but were not always confined within territorial borders.[123] But the concept of 'nation' is not precise. Companies, notably the *Dutch East India Company,* tried to claim the rights and power of nations, by making laws and signing treaties. Many national claims are 'invented',[124] or 'imagined',[125] and conflated with religion.[126] Muslims still talk of their 'nation' or *Ummah* (الأمة), as meaning the world community of Islamic peoples who are united by a common history. What is the legitimacy of the *Islamic State* (ISIL, ISIS)?

Large historical populations – Egypt, India, China – claim **sovereignty** on the basis of being **civilizational states.**[127] In Europe, the affirmation of the **sovereign state** is usually attributed to the *Treaties of Westphalia* (1648). These were largely symbolic,[128] but they provided the bases for the *Congress of Vienna* (*Wiener Kongress*) (1814–1815) which tried to affirm borders following the Napoleonic and other wars, the *Concert of Europe*, and then the *League of Nations* (1919). (*Wikipedia* provides a *List of sovereign states*.) States were often constructed in relation to war, and *land rights* gave powerful people certain land.[129] *Land reform* requires the redistribution of land from powerful to less powerful people.[130] But in reality, the concept of *property* is arguably always based more on power than claims of ownership.[131] The *CIA World Factbook* maintains a list of territorial disputes.

State theory[132] argues that states should exist in fact (*de facto*), and in law (*de jure*). The *de jure* view[133] requires a *sovereign state* to have a *legal personality* – it should be accountable in courts such as the ICJ or ECHR. *Declarative* theory maintains that a state must have a defined territory, a permanent population, a government, and be able to have formal relations with other states. *Constitutive* theory argues that a state is a state if it is recognized as such by other states. State governments claim a *national interest* (*raison d'État* – reason of the State), reflecting the security and cultural aims of a state.[134] *Hegemony* explains how nations position themselves in relation to the power of other nations. *Pluralism* describes a mixed-actor model, and a less state-centric view of world systems. In the light of the rise of the BRICS and MINT countries, Kupchan talks of a 'global turn' creating a 'no one's world' in which there are no constant superpowers.[135] And what of the self-declared *micronations*?[136] The legitimacy of states is not as clear as it seems.

thinking zone: how is state status constructed?

Vatican

Vatican City was created by Mussolini and his fascist government though the 1929 *Lateran Treaties*. It claims state privileges about diplomatic relations, banking irregularities and child abuse. Yet it has no permanent, independent population. It is a non-member state of the UN *General Assembly*, which set a precedent for Palestine to gain the same status.

precedent

How might the case of the Vatican create precedents, about the potential statehood, or city statehood, of:

- Kosovo
- Taiwan
- Kabul
- Jerusalem
- The *Gaesong* industrial region in Korea (the 'Hyundailand' territory inside North Korea, but run by South Korean industries)?
- Islamic State (ISIS, ISIN)

[See References for further information.[137]]

The ***United Nations*** (UN) recognizes around 193 'member' states, two 'observer' and 11 'other', but many are disputed. The territories of *discontiguous states* – Angola, Argentina, Palestine, Croatia and the USA – are divided by land claimed by other nations. Some regimes have been dubbed *collapsed states,*[138] *fragile states,*[139] or *failed states* but the last has no meaning in international law, and seems to have come from the *CIA State Failure Task Force*. The UN programme on *Small Island Developing States* (SIDS) is increasingly relevant in the context of sea level rise and other changes.[140] *Protectorates* are small countries that have political and military protection by larger countries, in return for political favours.[141] Attempts to legitimize these lands include spurious explorers and dubious coats of arms (Figure 2.5). *Wikipedia* provides *Lists of countries and territories* and a *List of national institutions and symbols*.

Sir Francis Drake's arms, bestowed by Queen Elizabeth I in1582.

The "Falkland Islands" arms, created by the British government in 1948.

A sea captain of Queen Elizabeth I, John Davis, is said to have "discovered" the *Islas Malvinas* in 1592. But there is little evidence about his existence or voyage. The (British) Falklands' coat of arms reflects that of Francis Drake, but it was only created in 1948.

Calling the Falklands, a 'British Overseas Territory', strengthens the British claim to the nearby 'British Antarctic Territories'. But this is also disputed because the *Antarctic Treaty* (1959), signed by Britain, precludes sovereignty rights. The British government renamed the Antarctic region 'Queen Elizabeth Land' in 2012, after Queen Elizabeth II, and labelled it a 'British Overseas Territory' on government maps. These claims are therefore spurious.

Figure 2.5 Legitimizing overseas territories

The creation of nation states also created **stateless peoples**, who have been recognized by the UN since 1954.[142] Some are considered to be *refugees* under the UN *Convention Relating to the Status of Refugees* (1951). *Environmental refugees* are a new aspect, which is not formalized.[143] Discussions also continue about unrecognized states – *non-nation states, non-self-governing territories* and *stateless nations* – ethnic groups with no territory which claim the status of 'nation'.[144] The *International Romani Union* represents 12 million people, talks of becoming a 'non-territorial nation' with its own government and court.

The **continents** are usually divided into Asia, Africa, North America, South America, Antarctica, Europe and Australia. But Europe and Asia are sometimes called Eurasia. **Region** can mean small local districts and prefectures, or large land masses embracing many countries. The BBC delineates – Africa, Asia, Europe, Latin America, Middle East, the US and Canada. The UN M.49 codes comprise nine regions (including 'world'), and sub-regions, for administrative and statistical purposes (Figure 2.6).[145] UNSTATS also uses regional categorizations based on development – 'developed and developing regions', 'least developed countries', 'landlocked developing countries', 'small island developing states' and 'transition countries'.

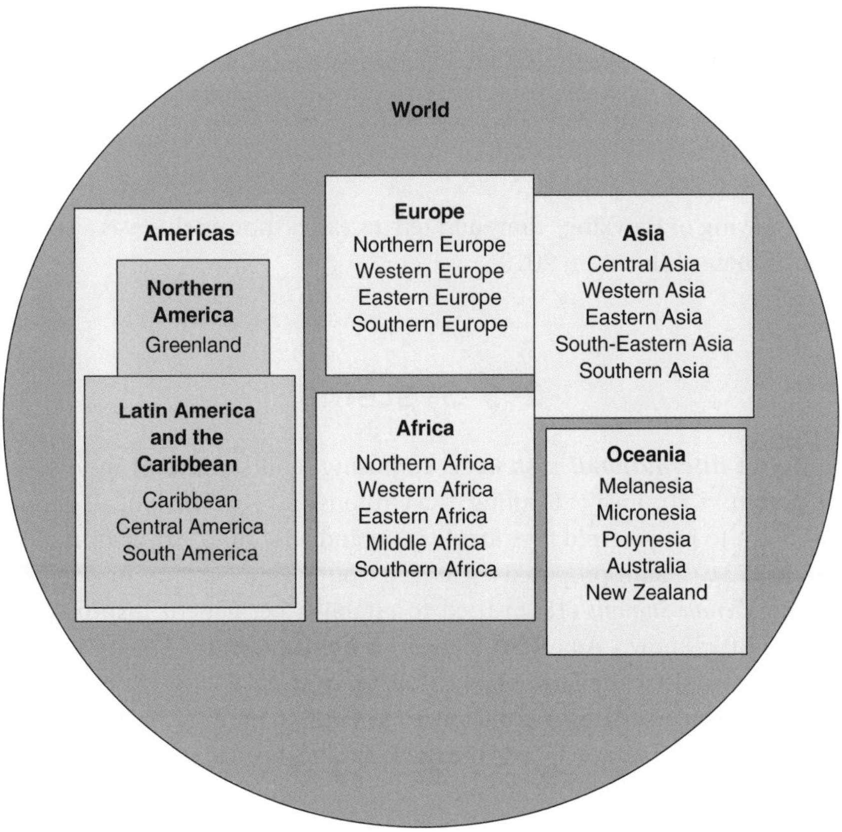

Figure 2.6 The UN regions

Source: UNSTATS

Political regions comprise groups of nations with shared economic and political interests – the *European Union* (EU), *African Union* (AU), *Union of South American Nations* (UNASUR), *Andean Community of Nations* (CAN) and *Association of Southeast Asian Nations* (ASEAN). The *Commonwealth (of Nations)* is united by a common history of British colonial rule. Similarly, the *Commonwealth of Independent States* (CIS) (Содружество Независимых Государств, СНГ) comprises former Soviet Republics. Academics also use groupings based on shared culture – MENA (Middle East North Africa), WANA (West Asia and North Africa), NAWA (North Africa-West Asia). The innovative EC concept of *Euroregions* describes contiguous or non-contiguous areas, based on common interests – environmental problems, fishing stocks, or economic development.[146] *The United Nations University Institute on Comparative Regional Integration Studies* (UNU – CRIS) develops regional analysis.[147]

The concept of **global commons** extends the tradition of common land to areas of the Earth and its biosphere (C10.5), as discussed by the *Coalition for the Global Commons*, and is acquiring meaning in international law.[148] Agreements about the use of cyberspace,[149] and the exploitation of minerals on asteroids[150] and other planets are becoming significant. A prognosis by cosmologist Stephen Hawking indicates how territorial claims may evolve in the future:

> I believe that the long-term future of the human race must be in space...It will be difficult enough to avoid disaster on planet Earth in the next hundred years, let alone the next thousand, or million. The human race shouldn't have all its eggs in one basket, or on one planet.[151]

Without knowing of Hawking, 'draw and tell' research showed this was already in the minds of Chinese children, in 2010.

2.3 Systems

The history of ***international systems*** is confusing, and significant innovations are often forgotten.[152] The idea of forming 'the virtuous and good men of all nations into a regular body, to be govern'd by suitable good and wise rules', came from Benjamin Franklin, in 1731.[153] Kant proposed a 'General Congress of Nations' in *Perpetual Peace* (1795). The *Vienna Summit* (1815) tried to establish permanent institutions across Europe.[154] A little-known American Consul to England, Elihu Burritt (the 'learned blacksmith'), organized the *International Conference of the Friends of Peace* in Brussels in 1848,[155] and spoke at similar conferences in Paris chaired by Victor Hugo (1849), Frankfurt (1850) and London (1851) (Figure 2.7). The website provides a brief history of international organizations.

I present to this assembly a proposition [for]...a Congress and High Court of Nations for the regulation of the intercourse and for the adjustment of the difficulties which may arise between them, according to the principles of justice embodied in a well-defined code of international law...

The measure proposed is not American, either in origin or argument. It had taken shape and form in the public mind before America was discovered as a world or born as a nation...The idea of international law ...has come down to us...through Egyptians and Persians, through Greeks and Romans...[Around 1650] a French author, in a work entitled "Le Nouveau Cygne"...proposed the convocation and establishment of a great International Senate, composed of a representative from every recognised kingdom or Government in this world – a body which would not only serve as a perpetual Court of Equity and Arbitration, but also as a standing convention or congress to project and propose great international works of improvement.

Elihu Burritt, Speech at the *Peace Congress at Frankfurt,* 24 August 1850

Figure 2.7 Elihu Burritt and a Congress of Nations

Bartlett, E.S. (1897) 'Elihu Burritt – The learned Blacksmith', *New England Magazine,* June, XVI(4): 386.

Within the ***United Nations*** (UN),[156] organizations have differing status and abilities to create international agreements (Figure 2.8). The *Security Council* has the greatest power, but its legitimacy is questioned. The *General Assembly* deals more democratically with world issues, but its decisions are less binding. The UN *International Law Commission* is the main authority, the system is explained on the UN *International Law* site, and documents can be found through the UN *Documentation Research Guide.* The *International Bar Association* provides professional insights including press analysis.

International law[157] is not easy to define, and law internationalizes in different ways:

- *international court* charters and decisions at the *International Court of Justice* (ICJ), *International Criminal Court* (ICC) and *European Court of Human Rights* (ECHR).
- *multilateral* UN and sister organization (*jus gentium*) agreements among nations (treaties, conventions, trade rules).
- *bilateral* (*jus inter gentes*) agreements between nations (ODA, border agreements, extradition).
- *regional* human rights and law (EU, AU, CIS).
- *incorporation* of international agreements into national law (torture, corruption, human rights).
- *national law* that extends its jurisdiction to create international reach (international paedophiles, abuse of vulnerable people, pollution abroad, the US 1789 *Alien Tort Claims Act*[158]).

America argues that it creates *international doctrine* through *unilateral* acts such as the invasion of Iraq, the extra-judical killing of Osama bin Laden and use of drones in other countries. Understanding the differing legal traditions helps to understand the arguments about differing cultural perspectives.[159]

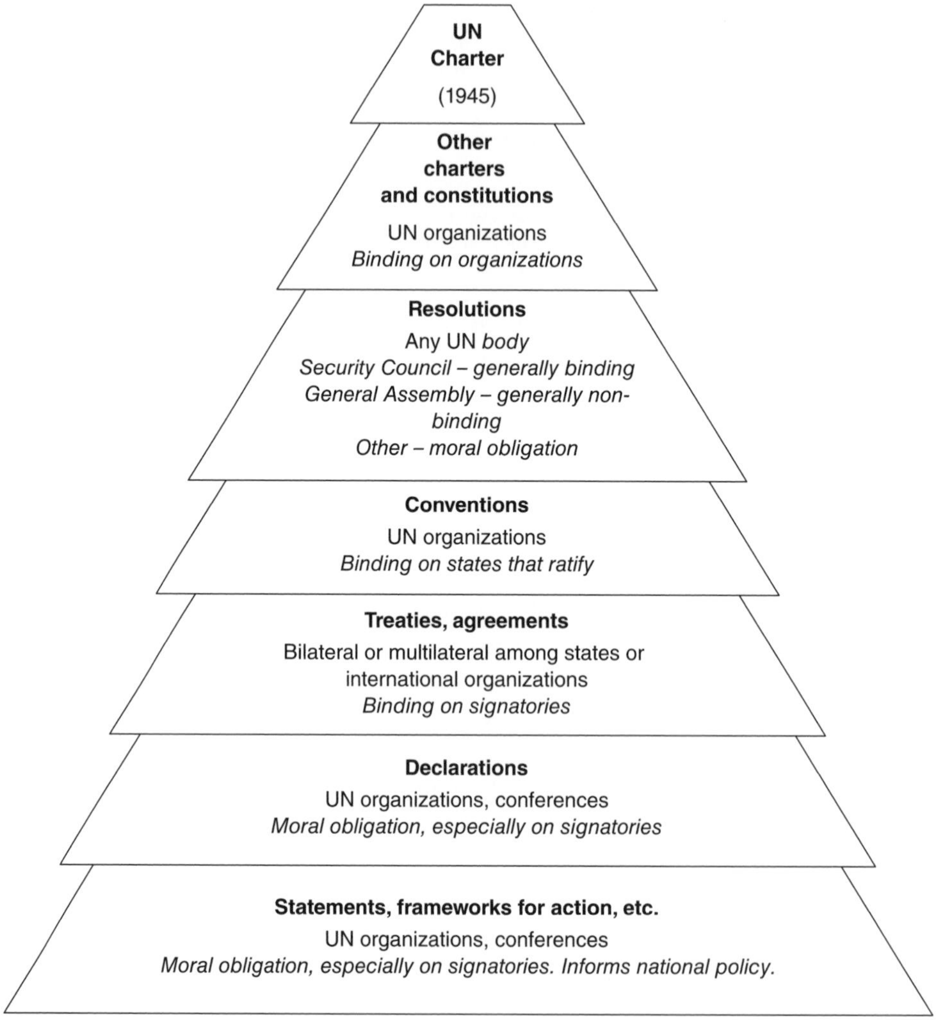

Figure 2.8 The status of UN codes

The UN is only partially democratic, and its future form is not certain.[160] It is neither truly international nor global, and its decisions are limited by the national interests of the member states. It therefore has difficulty addressing many issues, such as **state crime**.[161] There are ongoing arguments for UN reform,[162] and the *Centre for UN Reform* provides information and a non-state view.

Theories of **globalization** describe systems that potentially affect the whole world, and seem to transcend national boundaries – communications, economic, trade, arts, politics.[163] But these systems usually only affect sectors of the world population (often the richest) and are usually legally based in nations. So far, there are no global governments, banks, courts, or companies which completely transcend nations. Gordon Mathews argues that *low end globalization* – the trade in cheap, 'knock off goods', mainly from China – is the real driver of global change because the effect percolates into the masses in less wealthy countries.[164] Emerging ***global governance***[165] arises from agreements about global problems such as climate change[166] and justice.[167] *International civil servants*[168] have a small but significant degree of autonomy. UN organizations demonstrate limited global powers independently of nations.[169] The INGOs,[170] social movements[171] and an 'international'[172] or 'global'[173] civil society[174] all contribute to developing *international ethics*[175] and *global ethics.*[176]

The *global* or *human security* framework provides a basis to study international systems and conceptualize the relationships between them, in terms of:[177]

- *political violence* – the use of *power*, through 'soft' influence or 'hard' military force, by nations.
- *development* – the creation of resources and services to sustain human wellbeing, including *humanitarian assistance* in response to emergencies.
- *environment* – the benefits and limits of natural resources.

Across which theories consider *human dimensions, agency* and *institutions.*[178]

This framework is reflected in international agreements. The *Helsinki Final Act,* among the 57 states of the *Organization for Security Co-operation* (OSCE), covers politico-military, economic and environmental, and human aspects of security, including 'arms control, confidence and security-building measures, human rights, national minorities, democratization, policing strategies, counter-terrorism and economic and environmental activities'. This *new security* framework encourages analysis across relevant areas, for example understanding how water resources are constrained by environmental factors, and that if disputes are not resolved, violence may result.

2.3.1 Political violence

International relations (IR) constructs, describes and studies the *bilateral* and *multilateral* systems and their interactions across national borders, principally about peace and security, trade and cultural activities.[179] Although IR methods have traditionally been based on history, history is, as A.J.P. Taylor points out, just 'a version of events'.[180] At present the prevailing 'version' within IR is European-American, and asserted, as Wilkinson explains:

> The main schools of general theory of international relations (IR) are not proven in any scientific sense: rather they constitute ways of perceiving international relations, metaphors or models which appeal to their adherents because that is the way they prefer to view the world.[181]

And the underlying problem is seen as methodological:

> There are many different scientifically valid ways to produce knowledge. The field of International Relations should pay closer attention to these methodological differences, and to their implications for concrete research on world politics.[182]

Much of the literature is based on an assumption that the purpose of IR theorization is to defend the "west against the rest".

The criticisms are that IR processes are rarely democratic,[183] are not fully based on international ethics,[184] do not recognize increasing cosmopolitanism,[185] do not include global issues such as health[186] and gender,[187] lack a self-critical reflexive perspective, [188] and it has been a *less* international approach than other fields of study.[189] Lewis Fry Richardson provided a rare example of a non-partisan empirical attempt to measure the causes of war and conditions of peace, through differential equations and probability theory.[190] IR theories need to be viewed critically and developed from an evidence-based *among* nations, rather than a defensive *between* nations, perspective. Methods are evolving.[191]

In traditional European-American discourse, there are two main approaches: **realism** (*classical-, neo-, offensive-, defensive-, neoclassical-*) and **idealism** (*rationalist, liberal, neoliberal*). Recent theories blur the distinction and merge ideas from both approaches, for example *liberal realism* (English School). In practice, IR is often based on expediency and 'muddle through' policy.

Realism (power politics) is associated with Machiavelli's *The Prince* (1513) and Hobbes' *Leviathan* (1651). But there are earlier examples from outside Europe. Within Hindu tradition, Chanakya (circa 350–283BC), a professor at Takshashila University and Prime Minister of the Mauri Empire (India), is attributed with compiling the *Arthashastra* ('The science of politics'), which represents a realist manual for autocrats.[192] The German term *realpolitik* originally meant well-focused policies that were likely to succeed, and the meaning was not intrinsically negative. *Structural realism* proposes that the dynamics of the world system, principally the relative power of states, more often determines political acts and policies.[193] *Neorealism* also sees security as paramount, but points to the changes in a globalizing world, and that states are no longer the sole, or most powerful, international actors. *Neoliberalist* writers argue, on the basis of methodologies such as *game theory*, that states should aim for absolute gains – a win-win among nations – not just relative gains to enhance one nation at the expense of others.[194]

The underlying **realist** assumptions are that other states are "guilty until proven innocent" of actions that are potentially hostile to the *national interests* of the "home" state, and that the world would become **anarchical** without forceful national stances.[195] Much of the realist debate depends on an 'ontology of **anarchy**',[196] (Figure 1.2) which reflects the old 'madness of crowds' ideologies (above), scaled up to apply to a global population. Do power elites maintain fear in order to maintain their control? The threats may change their persona – barbarians,[197] religions, nationalism, cults, terrorism, cyber-war, environmental and other liberal concerns[198] – but public fear has often been deployed to make the masses easy to govern. *Military Keynesianism* argues that politicians use wars to pump money into their faltering economies,[199] and into their own pockets. Is *perpetual war*, in some form, necessary to all forms of world order? George Orwell's novel *Nineteen Eighty-Four* provides the most famous exposé,[200] but in earlier writings he questioned the concept of anarchy, and invented the term 'cold war':

> ...looking at the world as a whole, the drift for many decades has been not towards anarchy but towards the reimposition of slavery. We may be heading not for general breakdown but for an epoch as horribly stable as the slave empires of antiquity... [T]hat is, the kind of world-view, the kind of beliefs, and the social structure that would probably prevail in a state which was at once unconquerable and in a permanent state of 'cold war' with its neighbors.[201]

Idealism (utopianism) is based more on moral values and international law, and is reflected in ideas such as *ethical foreign policy*. Realist critiques argue that the idealist approach ignores "what was and is" (the *positivist* view), and emphasizes "what ought to be" (the *normative* view). *Functionalist* perspectives arose mid-20th century, and saw the common interests of states and non-state entities as of increasing importance.[202] *Neofunctionalism* returned towards a realist view, and argued for integration, rather than unification, within international systems.[203] *Neo-Gramscian* analyses examine power relations more historically, in terms of agency and structure, which circumvents the realist versus stalemate.[204] Nation states are significant, but so are many other non-state actors, particularly economic institutions and INGOs, and *regime theory* argues that cooperation between non-state entities influences how states operate.[205] *Neoliberalism* provides a more inclusive approach which builds on, and questions, the traditional realist–idealist dichotomy.[206]

Diplomacy should enable 'states to secure the objectives of their foreign policies without resort to force, propaganda, or law'.[207] The continued use of the term 'foreign policy', and not 'international policy', by nations reflects the ongoing adversarial ethos of diplomacy. Theories of state diplomacy are also being used by others who work internationally and cross-culturally within states – INGOs, financiers, tourist companies, commercial negotiators. Skills include: negotiation, conflict resolution and cross-cultural communication, which are used for pre-negotiations (talks about talks), around the table discussion, maintaining diplomatic momentum, packaging agreements and following up. Techniques such as *constructive ambiguity* avoid contentious specifics until there is broad agreement about aims. *Mediation* among nations is increasingly important, and also between governments and non-state actors.[208] *Strategic moral diplomacy* moves forward from the traditional adversarial style and encourages diplomats to acknowledge the 'moral universe' that underpins the vital interests of others, which is especially relevant when religion and similar ideologies are factors.[209] *Public diplomacy*, through a range of social networking, is of increasing importance, as is *cultural diplomacy* (above). China's *resource diplomacy* provides new dimensions.[210]

Diplomacy often involves trade-offs ("if you do this, we'll do that"), but also tries to find *coincidences of interest.* Water shortages in West Asia and North Africa, which are more important than minor ethnic disagreements, can provide a basis for agreements and systems around which other issues can also be resolved. But alliances can be surprising. In 2013, a declaration proposed by the UN *Commission on the Status of Women,* to end violence against women and girls, was opposed by Vatican City, Iran, Russia and Egypt. A year earlier, when Germany proposed banning circumcision on the grounds of child abuse, Muslims and Jews joined together to object. The old quip that diplomats are "sent to lie abroad for their country" has taken on renewed meaning in the light of *Wikileaks,*[211] and the *Independent Diplomat* site provides interesting insights.

Regional **collective defence** agreements are based on the idea that an attack on one country would be treated as an attack on all. The *North Atlantic Treaty Organization* (NATO) is probably the most active, and the NGO *Nato Watch* provides critical perspectives. The *Inter-American Treaty of Reciprocal Assistance* (*Tratado Interamericano de Asistencia Recíproca* – TIAR) is based on a 'hemispheric defence' doctrine across the Americas. The *Collective Security Treaty Organization* (CSTO) (Организация Договора о Коллективной Безопасности Organizatsiya Dogovora o Kollektivnoy Bezopasnosti) has similar aims for Central Asia, and the *Shanghai Cooperation Organization* (SCO) (上海合作组织) links China and Central Asia, and also fosters economic and cultural interaction. The *Community of the Sahel-Sahara States* (CEN-SAD) demonstrates that collective security now includes environmental threats, such as desertification.

The idea of a **security regime** may be agreed by non-allied countries, such as the US and USSR during the Cold War.[212] The *League of Nations* (above) formalized the idea of international collective defence, and the UN *Charter* provides for *collective military action,* if agreed by the *Security Council.* Difficulties arise when a nation is in more than one organization. When Argentina tried to liberate the Falklands (1982), should the US have assisted its NATO ally, Britain, or its TIAR ally, Argentina? But perhaps the untidy *plurality* of regional defence alliances prevents a major war between power blocs. The significant hypothetical question is, would any form of attack lead to an agreement about collective action from the whole world? What if hostile aliens landed?

Traditional *conflict resolution* methods assume symmetry in the type of violence used in international aggression, but **asymmetrical** relations and conflicts can be much harder to conceptualize and resolve. This was foreseen by George Orwell in 1945:

> A complex weapon makes the strong stronger, while a simple weapon – so long as there is no answer to it – gives claws to the weak...But [recently] every development in military technique has favoured the State as against the individual, and the industrialised country as against the backward one...
>
> The one thing that might reverse it is the discovery of a weapon – or, to put it more broadly, of a method of fighting – not dependent on huge concentrations of industrial plant.[213]

Digital power groups, such as *Luiz Security* and *Syria Electronic Army*, challenge state systems and other digital power elites through hacking and disrupting organizations such as the CIA.[214] *Cyber-war* could include attacks on hospitals, water supplies and other vulnerable entities of the high-tech nations. But it could also be a progressive revultionary force against tyrannical regimes which, from some perspectives, might include the US. Nye explores the changing role of technology in state power.[215] Novel robotic weaponry[216] – *Unmanned Combat Aerial Vehicles* (UCAV) 'Drones' – may cause new dilemmas, particularly *Lethal Autonomous Robots* (LAU). These could 'track and recognize non-cooperative targets (people of interest) in urban or rural environments',[217] through 'Future Attribute Screening Technology' which could detect 'mal-intent' such as terrorist activities.[218]

thinking zone: would killer robots start a war?

killer robots

Smart weapons are now able to take autonomous decisions to kill human beings, without any control by a human being. Some can "eat" bio matter to provide energy to power themselves.

war law

Killer robots could also be programmed to obey the international agreements about war.

so...

- would killer robots ever *start* a war?
- would their autonomous decisions be better or worse than decisions made by humans?
- might they decide to wipe out all humans on the basis of 'pre-emptive action', because we threaten to destroy the planet? If so, would that be ethical?

[Search: Nobel Women's Initiative. Jody Williams. Killer robots.]
[See: film, *WALL-E*, 2008.]

2.3.2 Development

Short-term humanitarian assistance[219] follows wars, disasters and emergencies, which interrupt or impede development. This reflects the work of the *International Committee of the Red Cross* (ICRC) since 1863. The concept of neutrality has been central to the ability of the *Red Cross* to provide assistance quickly and equitably during wars and other disasters.[220] There was an assumption that assistance should cease as soon as possible to avoid disrupting local economies and cultural systems. The UN *Office for the Coordination of Humanitarian Affairs* (OCHA) now coordinates international humanitarian responses to avoid duplication of effort or significant gaps in assistance.

The term *complex emergencies* describes the compounding factors of natural and human-made threats and vulnerabilities,[221] such as the damage to a nuclear power station by a tsunami at Fukushima (Japan) in 2011, and the cross-border nature of disasters.[222] There are no finite definitions of what constitutes an emergency or disaster – should it be above a certain size, speed or complexity? Consequently, the level, or absence, of responses is often political rather than needs-based.[223] Individual and collective resilience is often stressed to redress the impression that people are simply helpless victims of emergencies.[224] Words such as *rehabilitation, reconstruction* and *restoration* are also common. But these stem from the postwar reconstruction in Europe (see below) where the aim was clearly to return nations to their former condition. In present-day emergencies, basing a response on a return to a former condition is often less straightforward.[225] Arguably, many humanitarian organizations now function as businesses.[226] The *Humanitarian Futures Programme* provides wide-ranging discussion of developments.

Longer term economic **development assistance**, to reduce poverty, was initially conceived to reconstruct Europe after World War II. The Marshall Plan was quickly successful, and the concept was then applied to the so-called Third World countries, mainly the former European colonies. Early theories reflected a modernization view of development, which was often inappropriate elsewhere, and did not question the assumption that the development of non-industrialized countries could be achieved in the same way as the reconstruction of industrial European countries. The *ethics* of *Overseas Development Assistance* (ODA) has to balance helping others in other countries, and helping people at home. Peter Singer framed the argument in 1972:

> ...there is a conditional duty "to prevent what is bad, and to promote what is good...[but] only when we can do it without sacrificing anything that is, from the moral point of view, comparably important". This ethic should take "no account of proximity or distance". It is therefore a duty to prevent people starving in another country, but not if our "immediate group" – family and friends – starves as a consequence.[227]

But that does not consider the complicated ethics of the relationship between donor and recipient.

Bilateral aid – ODA from wealthy to less wealthy countries – became a tool of the Cold War powers to gain allies around the world. Aid was usually *conditional* and *tied* through agreements to buy goods and services from the donor countries. *Dependency* theories argued that the less powerful countries were being made reliant on the powerful nations, but a few countries, including Tanzania and North Korea, proposed that *self-reliance* was important. Often funds were wasted or usurped by corrupt politicians.[228] **Multilateral** agencies, such as the *World Bank*, only started to insist on accountability for the money they were spending at the end of the Cold War after 1989.[229] *Structural adjustment* programmes then aimed to create stricter controls and better governance, but often made the daily lives of poor people worse.

The differing **donor** rationales for aid are rooted in national interests. Harry S. Truman set the ethos of European-American ODA in 1949.[230] Less is known about Soviet motivation, for example in Afghanistan.[231] But by 1994, Soviet premier Boris Yeltsin was planning a *Russian Agency for International Cooperation and Development*, and Russian ideas became more tangible in 2007 in the *Ministry of Foreign Affairs* paper 'Russia's participation in international development assistance'.[232] Other BRICS countries are evolving similar plans. China's large-scale assistance is not in the form of traditional ODA, and Euro-American writers often conclude that the Chinese government provides finance in return for promises to support China in UN discussions about Taiwan and other contested claims, the long-term lease of agricultural land, and access to mines and other resources.[233] In 2011, the Chinese government explained its own perspective.[234] Whatever the rhetoric, it is clear that in ODA, "there is no such thing as a free lunch".

Assessments of donor *contributions* are also problematic,[235] and politicized. It is often unclear whether or not military aid is included, and aid is increasingly used to remedy the impacts of military interventions, as in Iraq and Afghanistan, or to achieve NATO security goals, as in Pakistan. Levels of ODA are compiled by the *Development Assistance Committee* (DAC) of the OECD.[236] This index only includes official government donations which promote economic development and welfare, or loans on reduced terms, for DAC members. Private donations are excluded, and in 2009 the top donor countries, in absolute amounts, were: the USA, France, Germany, the UK, Japan and Spain. But if calculated as a percentage of Gross National Income, this becomes: Sweden, Norway, Luxembourg, Denmark, the Netherlands and Spain. And if figures from *Global Humanitarian Assistance* (2010) are used, which includes countries outside the DAC, the top six are: Saudi Arabia, UAE, Kuwait, Russia, India and South Korea.[237]

Many *UN organizations* contribute to development, and there is considerable overlap among them. Development concerns reflect the usual *public services* of any country, and there are many common cross-cutting issues such as gender[238] and disability.[239] The justifications for *Education for All* (EFA) include economic-based *human capital* theories, which see universal education and skills training as the key to poverty reduction. The EFA *Global Monitoring Report* provides assessments. But is the purpose of education only to improve employability, or is it a basic *human right* because employment outcomes depend more on economic contexts than individual achievement, or is it essential to ensure *positive survival* and *human security*?[240] How do schools create and redress *conflict*,[241] including *extremism*?[242] *Perpetration theory* argues that many schools do children physical and mental harm.[243] The *World Health Organization* (WHO) assesses and prioritizes *international health* demands[244] – the spread of infectious diseases, resistance to antibiotics, cheap generic drugs for HIV/AIDS, the environmental health impacts of war – which often requires complicated international agreements. *Global health*[245] and *global public health*[246] consider world pandemics such as lifestyle diseases (obesity, diabetes, alcoholism), genetics[247] and health impacts from environmental change.[248] The UN and *World Intellectual Property*

Organization (WIPO) and the *World Trade Organization* (WTO) work to get agreements about the development implications of intellectual property,[249] including pharmaceuticals,[250] and the patenting of traditional knowledge and resources by powerful organizations.[251] Demographic and lifestyle changes increase the need to consider energy and resource security – including oil,[252] land[253] and food[254] – in relation to demand, concentrated production, new producers, new interdependencies, new consumers, short-term flashpoints, policy choice matters and long-term instabilities. The *UN-Industrial Development Organization* (UNIDO) assesses mined resources and utilities,[255] which are often overlooked within development studies. The *Resources Futures* website provides visual data,[256] and the *BBC Global Resources Stock Check* an overview.

Since, 1990, European and American donors have emphasized improving **democracy** and **governance** through *capacity building* in ministries, including *anti-corruption* and *accountability* systems.[257] But this often means the imposition of western-style voting and other systems, and does not account for the fact that 'democracy' simply means 'government by the people', not necessarily a European-style voting system. This can be achieved in many ways, for example, in Japan, by consensus – *goi* means a 'putting' + 'together' of 'opinions'.[258] What would happen if a 'democratic' country agreed to be undemocratic through democratic processes? Of young people in Pakistan, a 2013 study found that 29% believed in democracy as the best political system, 32% preferred military rule, and 38% Sharia law.[259] Many aspects of imposed governance are not truly democratic, for example the creation of constitutions. In contrast, in 2012, Iceland became the first country to 'crowdsource' its new constitution through *Twitter* and *Facebook* (C6.4).

Small countries often provide interesting models. Iceland claims the oldest parliament in the world, and the Isle of Man's *Tynwald* is the world's oldest continuous parliament, existing since 979AD. The *International Institute for Democracy and Electoral Assistance* has excellent materials about differing democratic systems across the world. China's recent involvement in international development questions the idea of intervention in the governance of countries (above), and this new resource diplomacy does not fit the prevailing European-American models.[260]

Traditional models for ***delivering aid*** reflect polarized top-down versus bottom-up approaches.[261] Prescriptive policies argue for a staged approach based on the history of Euro-American progress, moving through agricultural development, industrial and technological improvement, to modernity.[262] This entails involving governments, and research about *capacity building* in ministries to ensure there is ability to 'absorb' aid efficiently.[263] Conversely, perspectives that advocate channelling aid to local people and NGO projects, and avoiding government interference, are usually based on participatory needs assessment research about the micro-problems of poor people.[264] Strategies such as microfinance – notably the *Grameen Bank* – aim to empower poor people. Encouraging local initiatives is becoming more significant, for example within the context of atrocities,[265] and the *Global Entrepreneurship* *and Development Index* provides ways to assess local business endeavours.[266] Put more simply by a British official from *UKAID* the broad decision is 'whether to give all the money to governments and later wondering where the money has gone, or to fly a helicopter over poor villages throwing dollar notes out of the back, and later wondering where the money has gone'.

Assessing the ***impact*** and ***effectiveness*** of aid depends on whether the criteria are humanitarian aims – alleviating poverty, improving justice, ensuring gender participation – or political aims – gaining allies, improving trade, power over raw materials. Unsurprisingly, some analysts conclude that development theories have been flawed,[267] and ODA is ineffective or harmful.[268] The *OECD Paris Declaration on Aid Effectiveness* (2005) and the *Accra Agenda for Action* (2008) provide a framework for the former, and many related approaches, such as the *Development Progress* project, are intrinsically optimistic. *Counterfactual* methodologies ask, would this outcome have happened had the intervention not been made? Amartya Sen talks of improving *capabilities* – equitably distributed, 'substantive freedoms' such as political participation, and living a full and healthy life. Poverty is measured by the degree to which less wealthy communities can convert natural resources (rubber, minerals, crops) into necessary activities, goods and services (medicines and hospitals, books and schools).[269] The *Human Development Index* provides the relevant indicators, which try to accommodate *social development*, such as gender equity. The UN *Millennium Development Goals* (MDG) aimed to set an international political agenda for poverty reduction,[270] but assessments find that economic growth does not intrinsically reduce poverty.[271] The goals will be reframed as *Sustainable Development Goals* in 2015. The *MDG Indicators Dashboard* provides ongoing MDG data.

Development studies comprise many, often conflicting, theories.[272] The *World Bank, Development Studies Internet Resources* and *British Library for Development Studies* (BLDS) provide access to documentation. The concept of development is still mainly associated with less wealthy nations. But, of course, development happens, in different forms, within all nations. The focus on less wealthy nations means that much research has studied failure rather than success. That approach can be useful, but there is also much to be learnt from wealthy countries which demonstrate successful development outcomes, such South Korea, which was the world's second poorest country in 1946. The development of China[273] should be a major interest, not least because China now deploys the lessons from that experience within its own form of ODA (above).[274] The international concern should be that certain problems of development are currently more urgent in some places than in others, and that this is not only about economic issues. Arguably, the future conceptualization should be global development.[275]

International economics concerns trade, investment and the monetary system,[276] and the study of legal[277] and political[278] aspects such as centrally planned economies and economic collapse. Indicators used to measure and compare national economies reflect the production, distribution and consumption of goods and services. But this is problematic, and technological change provides challenges for traditional economics. The distinction between goods and services is increasingly clouded, for example by investment in software or systems design which does not show up as 'production' in standard assessments. Macroeconomic measures, such as Gross Domestic Product (GDP) and Gross World Product (GWP), do not show whether wealth is spread evenly among that population. These indicators calculate the measurable market value of transactions, and count the same cash many times. Microeconomic theorists argue that these measures ignore significant economic exchanges such as barter transactions, and feminist theorists point out that non-cash labour, such as housework and caring for children and elders, is not valued.[279]

Environmental economists argue similarly that the negative costs of environmental impacts are deemed externalities and ignored (below). The standard indicators measure flows of money but not whether that money adds true value, is wasted, or simply pays to correct avoidable mistakes. In 1850 Bastiat proposed his *broken window fallacy*,[280] which argued that smashing windows could be seen as good for the economy, because of the wealth theoretically 'created' to mend them. Industrial pollution, conflicts and car crashes can all increase GDP as money flows around for medical costs, legal fees and cleaning up environmental toxins (below). Similarly, *military Keynesianism* explains how war can be good for economies (above).

International ***financial systems*** are managed by the UN 'sister' (*Bretton Woods*) organizations. The *World Bank* was originally financing development projects through loans or grants, initially to foster American and European Cold War allies, but soon after 1989 it changed its emphasis towards being a 'knowledge bank' providing expertise, advice and resources to improve development. The *Asia Development Bank* (ADB) and *African Development Bank* are similar. The *International Monetary Fund* (IMF) pools money from wealthier countries, so that countries with financial problems can take short-term loans, but assessing why countries takes loans, and the outcomes of conditionality and austerity programmes, is complicated.[281] The more recent *World Trade Organization* works to liberalize international trade, and replaced the old *General Agreement on Tariffs and Trade* (GATT). It is based on five principles – non-discrimination, reciprocity, binding and enforceable commitments, transparency and 'safety valves' – and has been a focus for activists and protesters, notably at the 'Battle of Seattle' in 1999.[282] World systems currently tend towards a *neoliberalist* perspective which promotes reducing the public sector and increasing the private sector, through privatization and deregulation, and free trade and open markets across the world.[283]

Perceptions of ***global capitalism*** scale up state-based concepts,[284] and discuss differing versions such as *state capitalism* in China,[285] and why capitalism seems to work best in 'western' countries.[286] Economists seem to understand global *markets* convincingly, but not the whole capitalist system. In the wake of the collapse of the Soviet Union, Fukuyama erroneously predicted the 'the end of history' which would culminate in capitalist liberal democracy across the whole world.[287] Mulgan argues that the balance of *predatory* and *creative* mechanisms must be maintained or the former dominates through illusory financial mechanisms that do not create genuine wealth, and also make financial risk assessment very difficult. He cites Estonia, Iceland and Brazil as examples of a return to people-based economic systems which reaffirm human values and genuine productivity, and hold wayward politicians and commercial leaders to account. Sao Paulo has banned public advertising, and 1% of its GDP is ring-fenced for innovation that benefits the public.[288]

The idea of cognitive capitalism[289] considers how highly intelligent physicists[290] and mathematicians are employed within the financial sector to devise algorithms and IT systems that play the financial markets, using large sums of money to make significant profits in seconds. The experts are content because they enjoy playing an intellectual game on a world scale, and the managers are happy because they make a lot of money. The problem is that neither group understands what the other is doing. The result of High Frequency Trading ('algorithmic trading') is inexplicable financial crashes. During the '2010 Flash Crash', the Dow Jones Industrial Average fell around 1000 points (9%), and recovered, within a few minutes, because of erratic computer behaviour. The reasons are still not fully understood.[291]

Global ***financial crises***[292] have inspired innovative critiques of traditional economics and financial systems.[293] *Forecasting* is very unreliable. An IMF study found that there was a 97% failure among economists to predict 60 national recessions in the 1990s, and the other 3% underestimated the severity.[294] Yet philosopher John Gray's *False Dawn* foresaw the problems underlying the crashes of the new millennium, in 1998.[295] Amato and Fantacci predict *The End of Finance*.[296] Acemoglu and Robinson assess *Why Nations Fail* and compare exploitative extractive institutions within which elites appropriate resources from the population, with *inclusive institutions* that are equitable and law abiding.[297] (Other definitions of 'extractive economies' describe countries with a 'substantial non-renewable mineral and energy resource extraction activity', which can be related to national development and poverty.[298]) Keen asks why private debt is ignored by traditional economists.[299] The global chief economist at HSBC warns that 'western' growth is a 'historical anomaly', and that the failure of current financial systems could lead to social upheaval.[300] A fundamental question is posed by the NGO, *Positive Money*, where does money come from? It seems that even the *Bank of England* cannot answer the question. More importantly, where does money go, in the fog of 'inflation'? In the UK, in the years 2010–2013, inflation amounted to a 'stealth tax' on the whole population of 11%.[301] About 97% of the world's cash now exists solely in cyberspace,[302] which seems no more secure than *Local Exchange Trading Systems* (LETS), or *Bitcoin* and other global e-money systems.[303]

Although economic success has been predicted on the idea of infinite economic ***growth***, many authors question the assumptions.[304] In 1972 the *Club of Rome* warned of the *Limits to Growth*,[305] and the argument has been continuously repeated and refined.[306] There has been an assumption that the improved wealth of a nation equates with improved ***wellbeing***. But in *The Spirit Level*, Wilkinson and Pickett provide convincing evidence that human wellbeing is correlated with the income ***inequality***[307] between the richest and poorest people in a nation, not the gross wealth of the nation. Therefore the child wellbeing in countries like America and Britain is lower than in some less wealthy but more equitable nations, such as Portugal.[308] Stiglitz assesses the causes and economic impacts of inequality.[309] The worldwide protests of the *Occupy Movement* operationalized public concerns about wealth inequity.[310]

Economic theories are clearly in need of fresh thinking, and linking with real-world value in relation to environmental resources. In 1981, Nico Colchester provided an example when he argued that *Mars* bars would be a better *unit of account* ('gold standard'), for assessing and comparing economies over long time periods,[311] than currency which changes value because of inflation, or gold. In 2013, gold fell around 22% in value, which put it in the category of 'bear market'. As the *Mars* bar comprises a number of staple commodities – cocoa, vegetable fats, milk solids, sugar – the real-world value was more consistent and genuine than that of currency or gold bars. The theory could be applied to international convertibility, transatlantic arbitrage, and how consumption limits money supply. Colchester showed that, although a young ICI employee would have earned £275 in 1940 and £5700 in 1980, that is not an impressive increase. In *Mars* bars the increase would only have been from MB33,000 to MB38,000. *The Economist Big Mac Index* assesses purchasing power parity, and similar indexes are based on baked beans, popcorn, lipstick and dating agencies. The logic is fun, but also thought provoking.

thinking zone: should water be the "gold standard"?

value

Water is finite and chemically irreplaceable. Without fresh water (2.5%), there would be no life, and we would be dead within a week. Without sea water (96.5%), the Earth's life support systems would collapse. Water is also vital for industrial processes and hygiene.

price

The price of fresh water as a 'commodity' relates to its availability to a particular population, and is affected by factors such as pollution, desalination technology, temperature, infrastructure costs.

the "LFW"

If an Australian earned AUD$100,000 in 2008, and the same in 2013, and the cost of fresh water doubled in that period, at an 'exchange rate' of AUD$0.003 per litre, what is the change in the value of that salary in "Litre of Fresh Water" (LFW) currency?

[Answer: LFW333.333 to 166.66]

Are there any faults with this argument?

[See References for further information.[312]]

2.3.3 Environment

Meteorology provided the bases for understanding what we now call 'the environment'. The foundations were not only scientific, but based on the international systems of weather observation and UN *World Meteorological Organization* (WMO). The relationship between weather and climate became significant following Russian cosmonaut Yuri Gagarin's orbit around the Earth in 1961, and the spaceship to Venus in 1969, as humans started to realize the fragility of their planet. Soviet innovation created the race for Cold War space supremacy, and the resultant US moon landing in 1969, which inspired the international environmental movement.

NGOs took the lead – the *World Wildlife Fund* (1961) in Switzerland, *Club of Rome* (1968) in Italy, *Friends of the Earth* (1969) in America and Britain, and Greenpeace in Canada (1970–1972).[313] Adlai Stevenson used the term 'spaceship earth' at a UN conference in 1965, and Barbara Ward produced a book of the same name a year later.[314] The US *Environmental Protection Agency* (EPA) was founded by President Richard Nixon in 1970, Ward wrote *Only One Earth* with René Dubos following the UN *Conference on the Human Environment* (Stockholm Conference) in 1971,[315] and in the same year the *Canadian Broadcasting Corporation* ran a 'radio symposium on the environmental crisis', *Balance and Biosphere*.[316] In 1972, the *Club of Rome* produced its report, *Limits to Growth,* on 'The Predicament of Mankind'.[317] As a result of the Stockholm Conference, the *UN Environment Programme* (UNEP) was founded in 1972, and the EC (later EU) created its first *Environmental Action Programme* in 1973.

After 10,000 years of warring human civilizations, the peoples of the United Nations had started to agree how to formalize the protection of their collective territory, within the short period of a decade. The concept of international **environmentalism** was born. Early conceptualizations were mainly *Malthusian* – that there were limits on the number of people that the Earth's resources could support. But subsequent theoretical frameworks were innovative, cogent and comprehensive. Rachel Carson's book *Silent Spring* (1962) argued the dangers of DDT, and the unknown risks of environmental pollution.[318] Lifton's *Death in Life: Survivors of Hiroshima* (1967) warned of the hideous outcomes of nuclear war,[319] Schumacher's *Small is Beautiful* (1973)[320] provided the basis for *environmental economics,* and James Lovelock's *Gaia* (1979)[321] inspired a holistic *Earth system science.* In the late 1970s *Green Parties* in Belgium and Germany gained parliamentary seats.

But the originators of ***environmental activism*** were Japanese. Polluted wastewater, including mercury, had been dumped in Minamata Bay by the *Chisso Company* between 1908 and 1968.[322] The response was activist fishermen's alliances and cooperatives, and large-scale protests winning compensation in 1926, 1943, 1958, and the movement is ongoing. This predated American and European environmental activism, and contributed to the democratization of Japan.[323] But little was known of this outside Japan. Language was a barrier, the postwar world did not provide the right context for perceiving Japanese people as 'victims', and postwar geopolitics dictated that everything progressive should be seen an originating in America.

The collaboration between NGOs and the UN in the 1970s had taken national governments by surprise and, as industrialists realized that this movement was likely to reduce their revenues, pressure was put on governments to reassert *national interests* and subvert ***summit*** conferences about environmental threats.[324] In 1987 the UN *World Commission on Environment and Development* (WCED) introduced the pragmatic concept of *sustainable development*, and the need to balance development needs with environmental limitations was affirmed in the *Brundtland Report, Our Common Future*. But this was often interpreted to equate 'development' with unhindered industrial and economic growth. The UN *Earth Summit* (1992) produced the *Rio Declaration on Environment and Development*, the *Forrest Principles*[325] and *Agenda 21* which could be implemented locally, and the *Convention on Biological Diversity* was opened for signature. The South Africa follow-up in 2002 created agreement about fisheries,[326] but the virtual boycott by the US frustrated efforts to move forward. The 2012 follow-up in Qatar seemed to achieve very little, except to formalize the idea that *environmental services* should be incorporated into economic measures. Only seven agreements started, 'We commit', whereas 50 used 'We encourage'.[327]

In parallel, the *UN Framework Convention on Climate Change* (UNFCCC) and subsequent *Kyoto Protocol* (1997–2005) created binding obligations on countries to reduce emissions of greenhouse gases.[328] It was supported by all major countries except the US, which usually signs but rarely ratifies international agreements.[329] In 2011, Canada, Japan and Russia withdrew. Although Canada had shown a lead in environmental awareness in the 1970s, it might, like Russia, gain access to new resources if the climate warmed and ice melted. Although radical change to the agreement was arguably needed,[330] the efforts to amend and renew the agreement in 2012 were fraught. The *Alliance for Climate Protection* and *Wiki Portal Global Warming* provides ongoing data.

The outcomes of these conferences in terms of international ***environmental law*** are complex,[331] but the main international principles include *sustainability, polluter pays, precautionary principle, transparency and freedom of information* and *intergenerational justice*.[332] Mechanisms include *quotas, tradable emissions permits* and *taxes* on pollution. A practical problem, from an international perspective, has been how to extend principles and practice across borders, regionally and globally,[333] for example about *transboundary* pollution. Areas of domestic law are internationalizing by extending common law on homicide and injury, health and safety and damage.[334] But victim nations, which suffer cross-border impacts such as acid rain and radioactive fallout, are reticent to seek redress, because they might set precedents that are later used against them. Nation-based law cannot create internationally equitable environmental law. There is a need for a legal mechanism that can, when necessary, supersede *national interests*, and reflect a 'common', global or *planetary interest*.[335]

In America, the idea of ***environmental justice*** started in the 1980s. Initially it related to activist groups, but later became an academic field of study,[336] assessing issues such as market mechanisms.[337] The US EPA formally recognizes the movement. In parallel, the concept of ***green criminology***,[338] and discussions of ***environmental victims*** analyse the human outcomes of events such as the Union Carbide poisoning in Bhopal, oil pollution in the Niger Delta and the Chisso mercury poisoning at Minamata Bay (C10.9).[339] Distinct problems include establishing causation, the legal status of the unborn child, victim syndrome and environmental blackmail. Justice systems are not well prepared to address these novel types of victimization.[340]

Environmental economics assesses the effects of policy and human behaviour on the environment, which challenges traditional ideas.[341] Since 2000, China has discussed theories of a *circular economy*, based on recycling.[342] *Population* increase demands new economic theories.[343] *Environmental impact assessments* (EIA) predict negative and positive outcomes of projects, on people and place, hopefully before they are implemented.[344] *Valuations* of the environment can be assessed in terms of *natural resources* and *ecosystem services*,[345] and the degree to which these are *global/public goods* which are non-excludable and non-rivalrous. Traditional economics, based on measures such as GDP (above), has often discounted the environment as an *externality*.[346] Arguably measures of wealth creation should include concomitant irreversible 'loss costs',[347] and the idea that less wealthy countries should receive aid for 'loss and damage from climate change' gained legal meaning for the first time at the 2012 *Climate Change Conference* in Qatar.[348] *Ecological economics* builds on *ecological ethics*.[349] It reverses the basis of traditional economics, and puts the ecosystem central and economics as a human *subsystem*,[350] which makes *environmental services, biodiversity* and *species* loss more significant.

The *ecological footprint* is an ambitious measure of human demand on the Earth's ecosystems.[351] Usage is compared with *biocapacity* – the ability of land and sea to produce and dispose of human-made resources. The 'overshoot', by 2007, indicated that humans needed 1.51 planets to sustain their existence. The *National Footprint Accounts* relate to 200 countries, but international trade makes conclusions difficult. If China manufactures American electronics, which then are bought in Europe, which country footprint should be debited with the environmental costs?[352] Ongoing debates are managed through organizations such as the *Association of Environmental and Resource Economists* (AERE), *International Society for Ecological Economics* (ISEE) and *Institute for Green Economics*.

Ulrich Beck's vision of the risk society[353] extends to global environmental aspects,[354] particularly to *uncertain* concerns such as *genetically modified organisms* (GMOs). Many of the risks represent what Prins terms, 'threats without enemies' – new security problems which demand military scale responses, but radically different ideas such as the need to counter 'lock-in' and 'linear thinking'.[355] The concepts of creeping disasters, slow emergencies, or long wave events[356] describe problems that humans do not recognize because they are too slow or too vast, such as loss of biodiversity, air pollution and marine degradation. Our evolutionary mind[357] is attuned to hazards such as fire, but 'brain lag' means we do not readily perceive new threats such as UV radiation.[358]

Philosophers now consider the 'threats to humanity's future' in terms of existential risk and prevention[359] and *Cambridge University* runs a *Project for Existential Risk.* The *Club of Budapest* argues for the creation of a holistic multidisciplinary international approach to survival studies, which links new understandings from brain science, ecology, economics, governance and ethics.[360] Some theories seem counter-intuitive, for example that increasing diversity can increase risk, because there are more things to go wrong.[361] Framing environmental risk in terms of security has the potential to create a problem-led, or solution-oriented, approach which precludes simplistic mono-disciplinary approaches. The problem, as Prins (above) points out, is that 'You can't shoot an ozone hole.'

The goal of preventing environmental harm has shifted to *mitigating* the worst impacts. This has culminated in literature that is *apocalyptic*,[362] again reflected in book titles. The authors are leading scientists, academics, politicians, from a wide range of disciplines, not sensationalist amateurs. Canadian philosopher John Leslie's *The End of the World: The Science and Ethics of Human Extinction* (1996)[363] was followed by biologist E.O. Wilson's warning about species extinction in *The Future of Life* (2002),[364] and *Our Final Century: Will Civilisation Survive the Twenty-First Century?* (2003) from British Astronomer Royal and President of the *Royal Society*, Martin Rees.[365] Australian philosopher Clive Hamilton explains, 'why it is now too late' in *Requiem for a Species: Why We Resist the Truth about Climate Change* (2010).[366] James Lovelock returned with a pessimistic postscript in *The Vanishing Face of Gaia: A Final Warning* (2009).[367] The idea that the planet had entered a new historical period was reflected in Paul Dukes' *Minutes to Midnight: History and the Anthropocene Era from 1763*, which took as its starting point the *Doomsday Clock* created by the Manhattan Project physicists in 1947,[368] a sentiment also reflected in the *Doomsday Handbook.*[369] *Existential risks* include climate change, infectious diseases, nuclear war and vulnerable e-based systems. But might apocalyptic information create a *self-fulfilling prophecy* as people either give up and live selfish short-term lives, or go into denial about environmental problems?[370]

Contrasting perspectives came from 'deniers', who were often organized by the oil industry and other interest groups.[371] Bjørn Lomborg's *The Skeptical Environmentalist* (2001) questioned the whole environmental movement.[372] A belief that there are technological solutions was demonstrated by Mark Lynus in *The God Species: Saving the Planet in the Age of Humans* (2011),[373] which advocated the potential of nuclear power and genetic engineering. *Geoengineering* aims to mitigate global warming through reducing solar radiation, with technology such as space mirrors, and removing carbon dioxide with techniques including ocean iron fertilization.[374] The proponents are often from industries that would benefit from developing the systems. In *Earth Masters: Playing God with the Climate*, Clive Hamilton raises the obvious concern – engineering on this scale cannot be tested before irreversible application, and the amount of technology and energy to remove carbon would need to equal that which produces the carbon, which will itself produce more carbon.[375] Philosopher John Gray argues the need for caution:

> Late modern cultures are haunted by the dream that new technologies will conjure away the immemorial evils of human life...[But there] is no power in the world that can ensure that technology is only used for benign purposes. Partly that is because we cannot agree on what those purposes are. Partly it is because even when enough people are agreed there is no power that can enforce the consensus. The institution which we would have to rely on for such enforcement – the modern state – is not up to the job.[376]

The start of international awareness about environmental problems was optimistic and human-centred, but has ended in pessimism and advocating techno-fixes. In 1962, Thomas Kuhn famously argued that knowledge and research do not proceed in a neutral manner following their own internal logic and laws, but instead reflect *scientific paradigms* – widely accepted sets of ideas 'that for a time provide model problems and solutions to a community of practitioners'.[377] 'Paradigms' are often shaped by socio-economic demands and intellectual fashion. It is interesting to consider how he would have assessed the environmental literature.

Innovative ethics emerged in 2008 when Ecuador's new Constitution declared that 'nature…has the right to exist, persist, maintain and regenerate its vital cycles, structure, functions and its processes in evolution'.[378] The concept of *ecocide*,[379] suggests that the planet Earth has rights, and raises the question, are all humans guilty of this crime? Whatever the disagreements, the recent realization is that the territory of the peoples of Earth is finite and entropic. We now know that sometime, the planet will die. The *real politick* questions for international research are how might we hasten or defer that end, how can we mitigate harmful effects on the species, and how do we respond to that inevitable decline fairly across the entire planetary population without violence? Alternatively, we can take the advice of English philosopher Bertrand Russell: 'The universe is unjust. The secret to happiness is to face the fact that the world is horrible, horrible, *horrible*.'[380]

thinking zone: what is your water footprint?

industry

Industrial water use comprises:

- World: 22% of total water use.
- High-income countries: 59%.
- Low-income countries: 8%.

Annual usage will rise from 752 km³/year in 1995 to around 1,170 km³/year in 2025.
Source: UNESCO *World Water Portal - World Water Assessment Programme (WWAP)*

(Continued)

(Continued)

footprint

'A water footprint, or virtual water, is the amount of water used in the entire production and/or growth of a specific product. For example, 1 kilogram (2.2 lbs) of beef has a water footprint of 16,000 liters (4,226.8 gallons); one sheet of paper has a water footprint of 10 liters (2.6 gallons); one cup of tea has a water footprint of 35 liters (9.2 gallons); and one microchip has a water footprint of 32 liters (8.5 gallons).'
Source: *Circle of Blue* (2013) '10 things you should know about water'.

"throwing money down the drain"

It costs 5 litres of Fresh Water (FW) to make a 1 litre plastic water bottle. So the FW cost of a bottle of water is FW6 litres.

In $FW, that is like paying $6 to buy $1. (And in many countries the same water is virtually free, from the tap.)

How can other arguments like this help us to save water?

main ideas

When using ***international theories and concepts*** consider the European-American *bias*, and unsubstantiated assertions and rhetoric.
Theories about ***peoples*** have often been used to promote:

- the demeaning of *'others'* – *ethnocentric, xenophobic, supremacist, exceptionalist,* racist and eugenicist ideas.
- *cultural imperialism* to impose colonial culture on others.

But other approaches have increased *understanding* through:

- historical assessments of why *civilizations* come and go.
- *ethnographic* methods that create accurate perceptions of different cultures.
- developing concepts of *human rights* and *global justice.*
- explaining *cosmopolitan* views of humanity.
- evidence-based *science* which shows our common genetic roots, and can help to predict future changes.

Theories of ***place*** are based on *geography* and territory, and consider:

- the *legitimacy* of claims to land, including *nations* and *regions.*
- *empires* and *colonialism.*
- the governance of *global commons.*

Theories of international ***systems***:

- reflect the work of the *United Nations,* and international law.
- consider the possibility of *global governance.*

- should, but rarely, consider major *changes.*
- can be based on the *global/human/'new' security* framework – *political violence, development* and *environment.*

key reading

Appiah, K.A. (2006) *Cosmopolitanism: Ethics in a World of Strangers.* New York: W.W. Norton.

Hough, P. (2013) *Understanding Global Security.* London: Routledge.

Laszlo, E. and Seidel, P. (eds) (2006) *Global Survival.* New York: Select Books.

Malesevic, S. (2013) *Nation-States and Nationalisms.* Cambridge: Polity.

Seth, S. (ed.) (2012) *Postcolonial Theory and International Relations: A Critical Introduction.* London: Routledge.

Weiss, T.G. (2012) *What's Wrong with the United Nations and How to Fix It.* Cambridge: Polity.

online resources

To access the resources – search on the name in italics, use the http, or search on the generic term in 'quote marks'.

Methods for assessing civilizations – www.ianmorris.org/docs/social-development.pdf

NASA Landsat. Google Earth. National Geographic – satellite maps

Dymaxion Map – the Buckminster Fuller projection showing the continents as a near-contiguous land mass

Globaia – cartography of the anthropocene – maps of the human impact on the world – http://globaia.org/en/anthropocene/

UN structure and organization – explanations and links to most of the UN system

UN International Law site – www.un.org/en/law/index.shtml

UN Rule of Law – www.unrol.org

International Bar Association – professional legal perspectives

UN Documentation Research Guide – www.un.org/Depts/dhl/resguide/index.html

CIA World Factbook

Wikileaks – open access to confidential and other government documents

Independent Diplomat – a dynamic non-state perspective – www.independentdiplomat.org/

MDG Indicators Dashboard – ongoing *Millennium Development Goals* data – http://esl.jrc.ec.europa.eu/dc/mdg_unsd/index.htm

THREE

Searching and reviewing world literature

How would donkeys review the books of the Bible? They would probably write about all the donkeys – there are lots in the Bible. The problem when reviewing world literature is to maintain reflexive objectivity (C1.2), and not focus on the familiar things that affirm our personal worldviews. Otherwise, the review might as well be written by a donkey.

Around 90% of world information has been produced in the previous two years, and obviously the old idea of basing a literature review on what can be found in a few libraries is no longer sensible. Literature reviews must now be fast, vast and ongoing. For world research, a review has the important function of starting to *focus* a study (C4.2). A good review is particularly important before fieldwork. Mistakes are very expensive, and researchers look very foolish if they visit a country to do research that can easily be done in a home library or online.

This chapter helps with searching and reviewing world literature critically. International literature is notoriously unreliable, not least because it is usually copied many times. But this problem is not new (Figure 3.1).[1] The website elaborates on reliability in relation to international sources.

> The Indian scribes are careless, and do not take pains to produce correct and well-collated copies. In consequence, the highest results of the author's mental development are lost by their negligence, and his book becomes already in the first or second copy so full of faults, that the text appears as something entirely new, which neither a scholar nor one familiar with the subject, whether Hindu or Muslim, could any longer understand.
>
> Abū Rayhān al-Bīrūnī, *India* (circa 1030)

Figure 3.1 The reliability of international sources

3.1 Searching world literature

What is 'literature'? The distinctions in Figure 3.2 help to decide. A literature review does *not* include the new data or findings from the research study it forms part of, but it should provide new understandings about the texts that have been reviewed, and other insights. There are also different reasons for a review,[2] which are explained on the website. A search will probably start as a simple bibliography – a list to see what is available and to find possible gaps. Then this can be developed into a more detailed assessment.

Literature, for a literature review, is usually in the form of single research reports, statistics, texts about specific topics, specialist websites, news media and other front-line accounts of events. These reports may be by academics and other field-researchers, journalists, NGO staff, public officials, sailors, staff from international companies, explorers, travellers and bloggers. 'Literature' can include audio, film and video texts – scripts, commentaries, credits.

Documentary research (C13.2) goes further, and is a data collection *and analysis* method, which treats a text as a source of data. But some of the approaches used to review literature may be similar.

Biographical research also goes further than a literature review, to study specific people. But a review may provide the background for biographical research by, for example, assessing similar biographies, or contextual factors.

Theories and **concepts** (C2) usually derive from assessments of many empirical studies, reasoned arguments and relevant literature sources within a significant time period, and are usually created by academics.

Figure 3.2 What is 'literature'?

Searches are likely to start through using keywords on internet search engines such as *Google, Google Scholar* and *Amazon* books, or bibliographic software such as *RefWorks.*[3] *Google Books Ngram Viewer* helps to locate texts worldwide (Box 3.1). Sites like *YouTube* and *Pathe News* provide video and audio data, and texts in the form of commentaries. *Wikipedia,* and other information-bases, may have information that is biased, flawed, incomplete, or managed by government intelligence services. But entries can help to map (conceptually list) the main concepts of a topic and indicate further reading and people to contact. Comparing entries for the same topic, on *Wikipedias* in different languages, can help to build a balanced view.

Exciting IT can lead to overlooking simple and long-standing ways of finding important literature – reading the *references* and *sources* lists in previous relevant studies, and looking along library shelves for books *next* to the one you thought you wanted. Journalists often phone or email authors to ask for relevant material, whereas academic researchers might spend many hours trying to obtain publications through libraries. Journalists sometimes ask why academics conduct searches as if all their counterparts are dead.

Starting points for an ***area study*** could be the *CIA World Factbook* and BBC *Country Profiles*. Cultural attachés at embassies and consulates, and national cultural organizations such as the *Institute Français* and *Korea Foundation* may have helpful documents. For events, international media sites such as *Reuters* and *Associated Press* can be compared with views on *China Daily, al Jazeera, Press TV* (Iran), *Russia Today, Redditt* news, the BBC and UN Web TV.[4]

Academic databases – such as *ISI Web of Knowledge* and *WorldCat* from the *Online Computer Library Centre* (OCLC) can then be searched. *Retrospective* searches entail searching backwards through the literature, as in a traditional library. *Prospective* searches use software that facilitates setting up an ongoing search on specific keywords, and as new sources appear they are reported to the user. Some databases permit tracking the citing of a particular study from the date of publication, which creates a network of related literature. Many university libraries provide useful advice.[5] The *online resources* list at the end of this chapter suggests the standard sites, and more specific sites are on the website.

Initial searches will probably produce an overload of sources, and many will be irrelevant or unreliable. Even if the sources are overwhelming, the ***meta-data*** on search engines can be used – how many hits do certain terms get in relation to certain countries? A mass of data can also help to identify keywords, significant writers and relevant organizations, or to develop conceptual and theoretical frameworks.[6]

Non-digital searches are equally important. Not everything is stored on a database. Libraries in less developed countries sometimes have excellent press-cuttings collections together with archivists who know their collections well. Families often have fascinating material – colonial records, locally published books, old guidebooks. Sometimes the content of *archives* cannot be found through a simple online search – it is necessary to know which collections are relevant, and to then use their own search engines or paper indexes. Old archives and chained libraries have hidden gems, for example forgotten musical manuscripts which can be transcribed and published for performance.[7]

3.2 Doing a literature review

Most research reports include some form of literature review, which comes from an awareness of a *general* literature (politics, international relations, world music) and then identifies, describes and assesses the related *specific* literature (Icelandic politicians, gender and international relations, Mali jazz). A literature review should be based on, and cite *methodologies* of doing literature reviews, such as in Hart's *Doing a Literature Review*.[8] The review process is likely to entail:

- creating relevant *aims, questions, hypotheses,* and *conceptual frameworks* - deciding good *outcome variables* is crucial (trends, schools of thought, international influence, impact of the literature).
- a 'trawl' - *searching* for all potentially relevant literature (C3.1).
- *screening* - filtering and sorting the search results into a manageable form.
- *quality control* - how sound are the sources?
- in-depth *reading, categorizing* and *coding.*
- *checking facts* with authors, if possible.
- relating *findings* to aims, etc. (above).

Any review must have a good ***introduction*** explaining the methods. This should explain succinctly:

- its ***purposes***. Clear aims, questions, hypotheses and conceptual frameworks focus the content. ("How has the literature changed since the democratic government?" - "How does local literature differ from European-American perspectives?")
- the ***parameters***. What's in and what's out, and why? What period does the review cover? Which fields/disciplines are included? What types of literature are assessed? What countries and languages are considered? How are relevant terms defined?
- the search ***methods***. Which databases were used and why? What keywords were relevant? Are there any unique problems, such as confusing terminology? How were searches for non-text based material (photos, videos, films, *YouTube*) carried out? How was foreign language, non-digital, historical and "grey" literature accessed?
- the ***methodologies*** that were used to create the review - how were sources selected, categorized and coded in relation to *purposes* (above)?
- ***language aspects***. How were keywords in different languages searched and used? Were there translation problems? Was some literature "invisible" for language reasons? How is material in different languages listed and systemized?
- the ***critical*** (quality) approach. How were sources tested and assessed? How were the principles of epistemology (C1.1) applied?
- the ***structure*** of the review. Which headings are used, why, and how do they link with the main research questions?

The introduction can then be used to structure the ***conclusion*** to the review.

There are many ways to ***structure*** a review, and the reasons should be explained. The structure might simply copy the structure of previous similar reports. Alternatively, it might relate to *sources* of literature – UN reports, civil society organizations, internet material. Or it could be *thematic* – perceptions of immigration officers, immigration rules, the training of civil servants. A review might be arranged in terms of *linked issues* – child trafficking in Laos, political corruption in Asia, Asian gang leadership. Sections may be *chronological*, or for small-scale narrowly focused research the whole review might be chronological to show the development of a specific area of literature, such as Russian policy on international corruption. Large reviews may combine a number of these systemizations.

A ***concluding assessment*** of the literature should address the review *aims* and/or *questions*, and summarize and provide new insights into the nature of specific aspects of the literature as a whole. This might identify key writers, schools of thought, trends in knowledge production and influences. The results might be presented as flow charts, spidergrams, tables, or *Ngram* graphs showing historical trends (Box 3.1). See other examples on the website. An academic review will also explain how there is a gap in the literature that will be filled by the new research. It will demonstrate that the new study passes the "so what's new?" test.

Box 3.1 Using *Google Books Ngram Viewer*

'Comfort women' and the Japanese military

Hypothesis: That the term 'comfort women' would have become increasingly known in English since the end of World War II, 1945.

Method: The phrase 'comfort women' may not always relate to Japan, e.g. "Men try to comfort women who cry". Using 'case sensitive' can distinguish the use of Comfort Women and COMFORT WOMEN, which are more likely to be collective nouns and book titles. The boxes show yearly statistics. Clicking the *Google Books* search leads to specific literature.

Initial findings: There also seems a sudden increase since the end of the Cold War.

Further findings: Using maximum smoothing (50) confirms the predicted trend since 1945. Minimum smoothing (0) reveals a sudden increase around 1990. The boxes show no use of the terms in 1987, but used from 1993.

Further analysis: The recent increase started before the UN *Security Council Resolution on Sexual Violence against Civilians in Conflict* (2008), and so was not driven by this UN initiative.

Further research: Has the term been politicized since the 1990s, to encourage regional acrimony and destabilize East Asia?

[See: *Google Books Ngram Viewer* – http://books.google.com/ngrams]

3.3 Checking reliability

World texts are often very unreliable. Most international data is controlled in some way by national governments. From her study of Guatemalan military elites, Jennifer Schirmer concludes of the CIA, 'They get promotion by listing assets, not for getting information right.'[9] It is important to treat all international sources very *critically* when reviewing apparent facts that claim to describe things on a world scale. Epistemology (C1.1) and documentary analysis checklists provide useful starting points (C13.2). An important question is – which methodologies could support this claim, and do robust methods even exist that could support this claim? But the key to being innovative is to ask a smart question. A famous study of the literature on cannibalism did not ask simply, "Did cannibals exist?" It carefully asked, "Are there any *first hand* reports of *socially sanctioned* cannibalism?"[10]

thinking zone: did cannibals exist?

cannibalism

European literature talks of witches, Jews, savages, Orientals and pagans as eating human flesh.

- In 1098, Christian armies in Syria, apparently ate local Muslims.
- Paleontologists report that Neanderthals ate one another in Moula-Guercy (France) and El Sidrón (Spain).
- The first permanent British settlers in James Fort, Virginia, North America seemed to have eaten one another in 1609–1610.
- Swiss biologists found that fruit fly maggots will eat one another, if starved in a laboratory.

but

William Arens tested the literature about cannibalism by asking if there were any *first hand* reports of 'socially sanctioned' cannibalism, i.e. excluding eating for survival, or weird individuals who broke social rules. He could find no 'adequate documentation' and therefore humans should be seen as "innocent until proven guilty" of cannibalism.

so

- Does the evidence from Neanderthals, Syria, Virginia or fruit flies change or support Arens' argument?
- How important is *definition* in Arens' claim?
- How might Arens' approach to reviewing literature relate to other apparent facts about peoples of the world?
- How reliable is present-day literature about cannibalism in North Korea?

[See References for further information.[11]]

Another relevant question is – what is being measured? Politicians, who are opposed to the EU, claim that between 6–84% of national law 'is made by Europe'.[12] Those extremes cannot both be correct, so what was counted – regulations directives, European Parliament legislation then passed by the EU, rules passed by member states, the number of regulations (a regulation may be one line or many pages), the number of paragraphs (many relatively unimportant rules have numerous paragraphs), or the significance? One paragraph concerning immigration control is surely more important than 100 pages regulating duck eggs.

The internet has significantly increased the availability of information but also opportunities for *manipulation*, and these problems might be mentioned in a review. Dubious facts can gain *authority* (C1.1) because they come from a government internet site. Much international information is deliberately misleading, 'pheets' – phony tweets – for example.[13] 'Shills' – people or organizations that pose as independent experts and create fake sites or news stories – are common.[14] But 'fake news'[15] can itself represent literature or data for analysis.

Care should therefore be taken not to *repeat information and terminology* uncritically. Oppositional groups that may be termed 'terrorists', 'rebels', or 'insurgents' by some writers are, from the perspective of others, 'freedom fighters', 'patriots', or 'resistance movements' which may well become the next legitimate government. Questionable statistics are often repeated uncritically. Hazel Smith provides an example:

> Foreign observers have regularly cited the figure of three million dead from famine, or 10 per cent of North Korea's population. Those who use these figures also frequently argue that the government left the people in the northeastern provinces of North Hamgyong, South Hamgyong and Ryanggang to starve to death...The figure of three million was extrapolated from a 1998 survey of North Korean migrants and refugees in China, and was published in the reputable British medical journal *The Lancet*. These North Koreans in the main came from North Hamgyong province, and the scientific work in question specifically stated that their findings could not be extrapolated to the whole country. Firstly, the North Koreans interviewed in China were not a representative sample of their home province; secondly North Hamgyong, which has an urbanised, non-agricultural population, was not representative of the country as a whole. There is no doubt there was a terrible humanitarian disaster in the 1990s...However, the truth is that nobody – including the government – probably knows the real figure.[16]

Two warnings, old and new, should be above the desk of a researcher when dealing with world literature: *Accept nothing on authority* (motto of the *Royal Society*, 1660), *Trust nothing, debate everything* (Jason Calacanis, internet entrepreneur, 2010[17]).

thinking zone: where do international "facts" come from?

a British colony

Minister: "And how do we collect these wonderful population statistics?"

Governor: "Oh. Thank you Sir. My extremely excellent Chief District Officers provide them."

Minister: "And where do the CDOs get the numbers from?"

Governor: "Oh. They send census forms to their very excellent Assistant Chief District Officers."

Minister: "And how do the ACDOs fill in the forms?"

Governor: "Oh. The ACDOs require our quite excellent District Education Officers get their very efficient secretaries to collate them."

Minister: "And so where do the DEOs' secretaries get the numbers from?"

Governor: "Oh. They request the highly diligent Assistant District Education Officers to gather them biannually."

Minister: "And then where do the ADEOs get the figures from?"

Governor: "Oh. Our dedicated missionaries collect the basic returns from the village chiefs?"

Minister: "AND SO where do the chiefs get the numbers from?"

Governor: "Oh THEY just put down what they damn-well like. But it doesn't matter."

Minister: "WHY doesn't it matter?"

Governor: "Because most are illiterate and can't count anyway."

SO

How might this relate to present-day international statistics?

main ideas

There are many ***reasons*** for a literature review, and these need to be clarified.

- What were the aims or questions, and parameters? How were searches done, and what critical methods were used?
- How was it organized – chronologically, thematically, linked issues?
- The reasons, aims and introductory questions need to be addressed in the conclusion to the review.

Internet ***search engines*** provide a mass of information quickly, but:

- may overwhelm with *information overload.*
- can also provide useful *meta-data.*

Wikipedia and similar sources:

- may be *unreliable*, and are used by authors (especially American) to promote their writing.
- can help to understand how a topic is *framed.*
- may list *key texts*, and sometimes *unusual sources.*

Non-digital sources are equally important, and can often lead to original and innovative research. They include:

- *small local libraries* – church records, local government offices, cemeteries.
- *press-cuttings* archives, especially in less wealthy countries.
- *government archives*, for example the release of secret documents.
- *monuments* – gravestones, statues, inscriptions on buildings.
- *family collections* – photos, letters, scrap books.

International evidence is very ***unreliable,*** and must be reviewed ***critically.*** Consider:

- the whole *chain of evidence* – a UN statistic is only as reliable as its local sources.
- how, *methodologically*, the information was created.
- why sources may want to *mislead.*
- whether *repeating* information or terminology is valid.

key reading

Cooper, H. et al. (eds) (2009) *The Handbook of Research Synthesis and Meta-Analysis.* New York: Russell Sage Foundation.

Ford, N. (2011) *The Essential Guide to Using the Web for Research.* London: Sage.

Hart, C. (1998) *Doing a Literature Review: Releasing the Social Science Research Imagination.* London: Sage.

Rocco, T.S. and Plakhotnik, M.S. (2009) 'Literature reviews: conceptual and theoretical frameworks', *Human Resource Development Review*, 8 (1): 120–130.

online resources

To access the resources – search on the name in italics, use the http, or search on the generic term in 'quote marks'.

Google Trends – indicates when and where certain topics and writers become of global interest

Google Books Ngram Viewer – provides trend graphs showing the frequency of key phrases and titles, since 1800, with links to relevant books

Virtual Salt or *Colossus* list numerous search engines by country

DiRT – provides a wide range of research tools

WorldCat – searches numerous academic libraries

Endnote – can help to organize material, but this is more efficient for very specific topics rather than generalist studies

Mendeley – creates a sophisticated networked data collection system

Exaronew – may have interesting information for investigatory research

UN Research Guide and *Columbia University UN Research System* – offer an introduction to UN sources and organizations

Global Research – provides access to world data indexed thematically

Wikileaks – subverts state secrecy by presenting leaked material in searchable formats

MORE ON THE WEBSITE

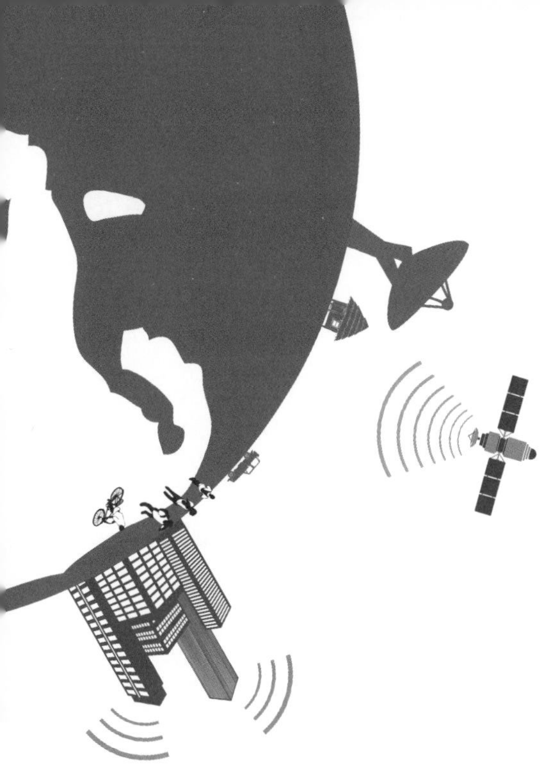

PART II

Planning the research

Chapter 4 – Planning and *research designs* are especially important for world studies because mistakes can be expensive or impossible to correct. Research design must reconcile the intellectual objectives of a study with the practical constraints of fieldwork, relevant technologies and pragmatic research management. The goal is to do micro-research that has macro-significance.

Chapter 5 – The *integrity* of a project depends on sound, workable *ethics* and an unbiased approach. International and local law is a significant consideration, because small mistakes can have big consequences. Consideration for *others* is vital to avoid the unethical practices of former, colonially-minded, researchers. Remote and online research raises new and fast-changing dilemmas.

Chapter 6 – *Frameworks* provide the basis for collecting data. They reflect the level of the study – *peoples, territories, systems* – and include cross-cutting frameworks – *cross-sectional analysis, crowdsourcing research* and *online research.*

FOUR
Research design and logistics

Albert Einstein apparently said that if he had only one hour to solve a difficult problem to save the world, he would spend 55 minutes analysing the problem, and deciding which questions to ask. A research design is a plan to solve a problem – intellectual or practical. If a 'problem' is well analysed, it will nearly solve itself. And good planning is vital for world studies because mistakes may be expensive or impossible to put right.

A *research design* is a plan for discovering something significant that is *not* known already, and it shows that ideas can be transformed into action. Plans often seem linear and inflexible, but in reality they should just provide a provisional conceptual *map* which may change and 'emerge' as methods are thoroughly explored and implemented.[1] As world research usually entails researching **others** in some way, the first consideration is how the purpose of the study reflects the likely concerns of those 'other' people (C5.3). It should be possible to locate a planned study within the chart on the website – the degree to which research is *about others, from others*, or *with others*. Hopefully, world research will increasingly be framed in terms of the last, to address world problems such as climate change and water shortages.

The conundrum for world research is to design a micro-study in a way that has macro-significance – smart ways to make small-scale work have big-scale meaning. This means carefully defining the *focus* – *topic problematization, hypothesis* or *questions*, and *terms*. If a project includes *fieldwork, logistics* such as *risk assessment* and gaining *access* need to be planned.

4.1 Design – mixed methods and iterative approaches

A ***research design***, explains the *how* of research, based on decisions about *what, who, when* and *where*. But the starting point for any plan should be the *why*, the purpose, rationale and outcomes. Why do you want to do this project, why is the project useful – and what type of data, findings, results and evidence are eventually required to fulfil the *why*?[2] A design also shows which *frameworks* (C6) *and data collection methods* (C7–C13) are likely to be feasible, efficient and cost-effective. Charts can help with planning, and examples are on the website. Many methods books explain 'research design',[3] some take design as the central aspect of methodology,[4] there are online resources,[5] and some discuss specific international concerns such as development.[6] The specific problems of planning world research are outlined on the website. A design may also eventually form the basis for a *funding proposal*, or an outline research plan to apply for a Master's or PhD course.

Traditional studies often started with a decision to use a qualitative *or* quantitative approach, but modern world research is likely to combine the two. It is therefore more helpful to consider the 'degree' to which a world study needs to be quantified,[7] and to 'move beyond' the traditional distinctions.[8] Comparative analysis can help (C6.3; C14.1).[9] Unless the intent of the research is to test and develop a specific method, a world study is very likely to entail ***mixed ('multi') methods***.[10] Different types of data are collected in different ways, which may or may not be compared, and may involve a *multidisciplinary* combination of social and other sciences.[11] But whatever approach is used, don't collect any data before thinking about how it will be *analysed* (C14).

In real life (outside methods books), an ***iterative*** process of mixed-methods data collection and analysis is becoming common. This entails repeated incremental "bite-sized" micro mixed-methods data collection and initial analysis to "snowball"[12] more data and build towards *further analysis* and final conclusions. Much social research is now done in this muddle-through way, but this is rarely acknowledged in methods books. Yet 'iterative' product design is well tried and tested, especially in software companies.[13] There are many variations, but Figure 4.1 gives an impression of how it can happen.

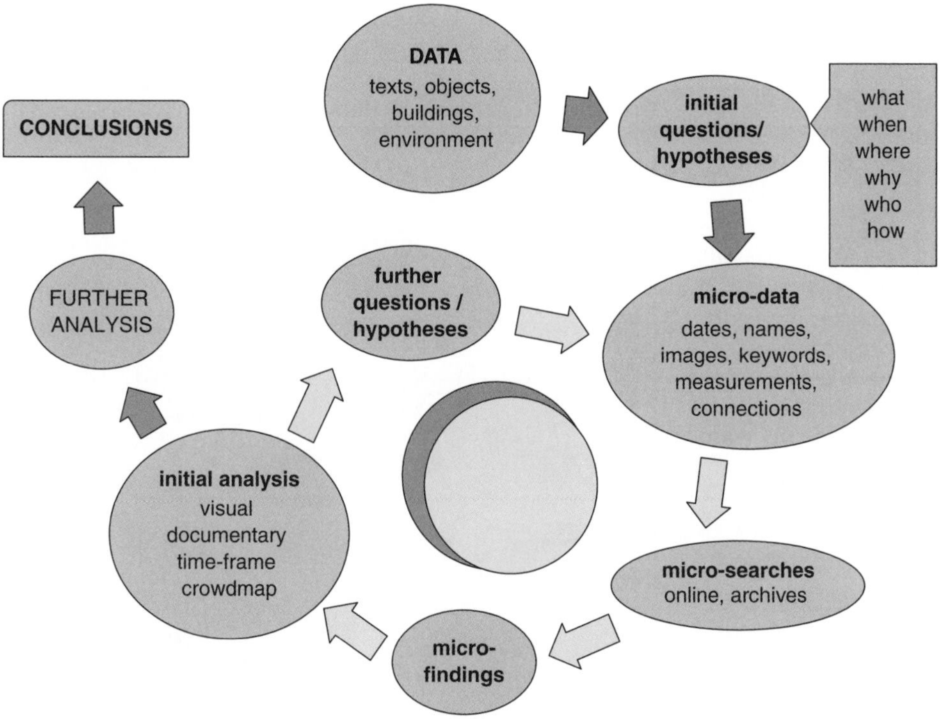

Figure 4.1 Iterative "snowball" data collection analysis

Box 4.1 outlines a case study, and the website provides the details. Starting from an old photo of an unknown statue, an iterative process helped to track the origins and significance of the statue. This included:

- checking *infrastructure* (C10.8) – online transport maps, bus routes.
- *observation* (C8.3) – walking the bus route to find the site of the old photo. (*Google Street View* might help, but it is very clumsy unless the exact location is known.)
- *visual analysis* (C10.6) – how and why the photo was taken. *Photo enlargement* – magnifying glass, digital. (Optical enlargement is often better than digital, for example by putting the original image on a *PowerPoint* slide and projecting it onto a screen.)
- viewing/acquiring additional *textual data* (C10.6) – photos, cigarette cards, stamps, from *eBay*.
- searching *archives* for relevant *documents* (C13) – museums, galleries, government, libraries, press.
- creating *time-frames* from visual data – technology/vehicles, seasons, political events.
- *timeline analysis* comparing events with the "life" of the statue.
- *big data* – using *Google Image* to find other copies of photos and *Google Books Ngram* to find relevant documents.[14]

Box 4.1 Iterative research design – case study

Investigating 'statue diplomacy'	
What is this photo? An unlabelled photo of a horse-drawn bus, and statue of a uniformed man riding a camel. Photo enlargement showed the **destination names** on the bus.	
Where was the statue? Searching **online bus maps**: using **destination names**, found a similar bus route. Architectural style is probably near a city-centre **Street observation:** walking along the bus route, from the centre.	 **Found**: a site with similar buildings, but no camel statue.
Compare: by holding the original photo in line with landmarks at the site. **Found:** site verified. Camel statue would now be in the middle of the road.	

Full case study on the website.

Recent photos: Author's own

The results supported a hypothesis that imperial statues reflect international events and were used as colonial soft power, and that 'statue diplomacy' is worth investigating. And, as always, there were surprise findings. Tracking the history of the minister who dealt with the statue, John Profumo, shows how the postcolonial British government was not only involved in playing games with statues, but also with spies, sex scandals and the courts, leading to miscarriages of justice, the fall of a government, and the death of an innocent man, which became the subject of an Andrew Lloyd Weber musical – *Stephen Ward*.[15]

A ***pilot study*** may be used to test the whole, or an aspect of, a research design before large-scale data collection. Research instruments – questionnaires, interview schedules, observation charts – may have been designed and tested previously by other researchers, or they may be created or adapted for a new study, in which case they will first be piloted to identify ambiguous or misleading aspects, particularly if translation is involved. Instruments sometimes use *proxy* measurements, which measure something that is easy to measure to assess something that is hard to measure (absenteeism to assess 'workplace wellbeing'), or data may be used to create indicators and aggregate indexes (C14.4). All instruments should be tested as part of the research design, to ensure the data can be used to produce the form of findings or analysis that is required. A pilot study for fieldwork could be carried out in a "home" country, using international students or others from the country that is to be visited.

World research is likely to utilize and develop appropriate technologies for ***data management*** (C7), and this needs to be considered when planning a study, not least because of cost implications. The possible technical options for each data collection activity need to be assessed *and tested*. Decisions should be influenced by the best way to obtain the required data, not by technological preferences, unless an aim of the research is to test a research technology. The website provides a checklist for fieldwork technologies. But most importantly, what is the *contingency* plan and *backup system* if things go wrong? Will extra voice recorders and video cameras be available? Are there plenty of notebooks and pencils available, when they all go wrong?

4.2 Focus

Focus defines the boundaries and parameters of a study – "what's in and what's out?" This may entail a 'perspective',[16] 'frame of reference' or 'lens'.[17] World studies are often categorized by their 'purposes', which can be academic[18] or professional (C15.2). The focus will be explained in the ***rationale*** or ***justification*** section of the report, and should include relevant statements from objective authorities. Consider the *levels* of inquiry? If the topic is 'the future of eco-tourism', this could be investigated at the level of individuals in one country, state policy, or international regulation. Alternatively, a *cross-sectional analysis/study* might study a 'slice' across all levels.[19] If the study is for an academic degree, it is useful to check the formal requirements before planning the study and report (Box 15.2). Materials elaborating, and providing templates for these aspects of focus are on the website.

The way that *purpose* and *rationale* are presented can affect ***access*** (below), and careless phrases, for example on a university or funder's website, can bring fieldwork to a sudden halt. People are more likely to cooperate with a research study if they understand and appreciate its purpose, see it as unthreatening, and believe that they might benefit in some way. Sometimes purpose can be presented more appropriately by reframing a large-scale study in terms of one specific area. Data collection for a book about "Brain-Drain in Islamic Countries" might be better presented as "Career aspirations among Muslim MBA students".

The ***title*** of a study is important to communicate the focus to others. Topics expressed in terms such as "Youth tourism" or "World poverty" might provide a good title for a book, but do not describe a practical piece of research. The title is what first impresses potential funders or examiners. And most importantly, it must be relevant to those the research concerns – "Refugee health services in Iran" is better than "Persian clinical traditions of hospitality". It is crucial that the title of a study, and section headings, include the relevant *keywords*, not least for embedding in project websites. A good title is best constructed by identifying the main keywords, and then assembling them into a title. This can then be tested on search engines for its originality and effectiveness.

Definitions and ***concepts*** clarify the focus, and help to identify *keywords* for data searches (C3.1). These come from noting keywords in similar studies, and by authors thinking about how they would search for their own study. *Wordle* provides an interesting visual way to test if the frequency of words in a text reflects the keywords.[20] *Dictionaries* are a useful starting point. *General dictionaries* remind researchers that some words have many meanings – 'development' might refer to nations or babies. *Specialist dictionaries* – politics, sociology, philosophy, social psychology – help to ensure that the terminology in a study reflects current usage in relevant disciplines. A *thesaurus* helps to find relevant keywords and related concepts. *Etymological dictionaries* not only explain the roots and linguistic derivations of words, but show linkages that can inspire interesting lines of thought. When working in more than one language, a meticulous approach helps with basic understandings of different cultures, which can be useful when writing questionnaires and analyses (Box 4.2).

Box 4.2 Conceptualizing a study of leadership in Korean and Arabic

The Korean word for leader – *ji-do-ja* – means 'instructing person', but another – *dae-tong-ryong* – means 'big controller of territory' and is used only to refer to the head of state. In Arabic, *zaa-a-ma* means 'to command people', but another word – *qya-da* – literally means, 'to walk in front of the animal in order to give it direction'. A separate term – *al-rais* – only describes the head of state, as in Korea.

Concerning 'elite', the Korean *sag-ryu-in-sa* means a 'higher type/system/tendency of people', and this is distinct from *bu-ja*, which is reserved for wealthy people.

> In Arabic, the general term for elites is *aaliyatul-qaum*, meaning 'high profile people', but *al-kheirou fi al-qaoum* is also used, meaning 'the best of men'. Like Korean, there is a separate term for wealthy elites, *aghniya*.
>
> [Source: Lee, Y.-j. (2011) 'Leadership and development in South Korea and Egypt: the significance of "cultural shifts". Unpublished PhD thesis, SOAS, University of London.]

The website outlines how focus might be explained. The important point is that all elements of focus are logically connected to one another and to other relevant parts of the report. Whatever the style, the outcome should be that the researchers could explain what the research is about, and why it is 'international' or 'global' (Introduction), in a few words. And to be able to do this to anyone at a party in one minute, without ending up as the bore who no one else wants to talk to.

4.2.1 Problematization

Problematization formally focuses a study, and entails turning a *topic* into something that can be researched. A topic such as "Mobile phone use" does not intrinsically describe a research problem – "What is the per capita ownership of mobile phones in North Korea?" does. Problematizating a topic is also a way for the researcher to reflect (C1.2), gain more objectivity, and not jump to hasty conclusions about a topic.[21] World research is often *problem-solving*[22] or *solution-oriented*[23] in relation to practical and/or intellectual problems. Research for campaigning organizations is often action-oriented. If data is to be used for specific purposes – court cases, documentary films, political advocacy – the design must produce appropriate data and findings in relevant action-oriented forms. A research ***problem*** is an unknown that invites a *solution* or *resolution*. The *Club of Rome* report *The First Global Revolution* was structured in terms of a world '*problematique*' and '*resolutique*'.[24] Holmes talks of a 'problem (solving) approach'.[25] But not every issue is amenable to a solution, as Gwyn Prins argues in relation to climate change:

> ...there was a fundamental framing error, and climate change was represented as a conventional environmental 'problem' that is capable of being 'solved'. It is neither of these...climate change is better understood as a persistent condition that must be coped with and can only be partially managed more – or less – well.[26]

'Tame' problems may be complex but have 'defined achievable end states'; 'wicked problems' are 'issues that are often formulated as if they are susceptible to solutions when in fact they are not'. It may be possible to solve the research problems about "migration rate", but it is probably not possible to solve the "problem of migration".

Having problematized a study, this can be expressed as initial ***hypotheses*** and/or *research questions* which have emerged from the literature review (C3). A hypothesis is an informed guess which can be tested to create a generalizable conclusion. Usually, hypotheses test causal relationships (C14.2) – that W did Z – or they might test a predictive theory – that if A happens, B will follow. The likely relationships within hypotheses are often framed in terms of *variables* (C9.3.2). Formal hypotheses need to be proved or disproved on the basis of statistical probabilities, which is very difficult outside experimental research.[27] A guiding or *soft hypothesis* can also be used, which is *addressed* but not proved or disproved in the conclusions of the study.

Research questions similarly guide a study. Questions are also usually *addressed* rather than *answered*, unless the study is investigative or evaluative and demands finite answers. Questions need to be framed in relation to the data collection and analysis methods (Parts Three and Four).[28] *Initial* research questions/hypotheses may be elaborated as a result of an ongoing literature/theoretical review, or other data collection, to create sets of *specific* hypotheses/questions, which can be investigated through interviews and surveys, observation or interrogation schedules.

To operationalize the hypotheses/questions, a study can be further focused by determining a hierarchy of ***aims*** – aim, sub-aims, sub-sub-aims – but terms relating to this are very muddled. For example, one study might be framed in terms of – PURPOSE > AIMS > OBJECTIVES – but another study might use the terms – GOAL > OBJECTIVES > AIMS – to imply the same hierarchy. The website suggests how a table or spidergram can show how the aspects of focus might relate to one another, and also possible overlap in terms of practicalities such as fieldwork planning. In any study, it should be possible to trace the chain of systematic inquiry from any conclusion – back through analysis, findings, methods – to aims, questions, rationale and purpose. The evidence of a systematic process is what makes research different from a casual conversation in an airport lounge.

It is necessary to distinguish clearly between what a study aims to discover, and the ***assumptions*** of a study. Assumptions form the taken-for-granted bases for the hypotheses or questions, and are accepted as correct and are therefore not questioned further – "women are disadvantaged", "children are vulnerable". But assumptions must be referenced to theory, strong evidence, or ontological and epistemological arguments, which support their general acceptance (C1; C2).

4.3 Fieldwork and project management

Some world studies will entail ***fieldwork***, and large-scale projects will require formal ***project management.*** These two areas are discussed further, with resources, on the website. But think first about the ethics of going abroad to study another country, including how those being studied might view the research design (C5).

thinking zone: how would humans respond to alien researchers?

aliens

Alien researchers have landed. They say they are from an organization called *Save the Humans*, and are carrying out a project called *Omnicide of the Earthlings.*

research design

- **Aims** To discover why humans are destroying their habitat, and to modify their intelligence appropriately.
- **Questions**
    - Why is the human brain the only thing in the universe that threatens its own wellbeing and survival?
    - What type of mental disability do humans have, which causes this self-destructive behaviour?
    - Why do women continue to have babies that have this mental disability?
    - How is it possible to save the human species through genetically enhancing the human brain to prevent it being self-destructive?
- **Literature review** Indigenous texts on eugenics, human enhancement and transhumanism.
- **Methods**
    - Genetic analysis of humans who appear most, and least likely to destroy their habitat.
    - Action research to enhance the brains of babies with the most favourable genetic profile.
- **Outcome** Participatory grassroots health and education programmes to ensure the appropriate intellectual enhancement of the human race.

response

How might humans respond from the perspectives of: disability rights, feminism, ecology, philosophy, science, religion, transhumanism and being a planetary minority group?

[See references for further information.[29]]

Whatever the scale, world research entails some form of ***risk assessment***. Even if working from home and asking a few friends to do some interviews in another country, their safety must be considered. The main consideration is risk to local people and participants, such as the safe disposal of unwanted equipment – cars, electronics, confidential material. A simple starting point is to sit with others and list everything that could go wrong, and what could be done if these things happened. Even humorous brainstorming can be valuable. Ask international students about their home countries. But keep in mind that local people are not experts in everything. Try to build up a portfolio-picture of a country from many different sources.

How can risks be minimized? Is protective clothing required? In hazardous or polluted settings, masks may be necessary. Can communications technology help – tracking devices, alarms, satellite phones? Is kidnapping a possibility? But however good the planning, the unexpected often happens, and risk assessment must include ***contingency plans***. Relatively small incidents such as a hotel fire or small bomb can interrupt all communications and transport, including airports. A significant risk factor when suddenly being caught in an emergency is lack of local information. The first indication that a war has started may be a sudden silence punctuated by rumblings and bangs. It could just be heavy construction vehicles backfiring – or it could be tanks and shooting. Check the TV, ask cafe staff, watch how local people are reacting – are you in the middle of a war? But while seeking information about an apparent conflict, the important thing for foreigners is not to reveal information about who they are or where they are. Sending emails or tweets that indicate a hotel and room number – which can be deduced from a room phone number – may not be wise.

Many governments have online country assessments such as the UK *FCO Travelling and Living Overseas* site, and the *US State Department – travel.state.gov*. Many books provide advice,[30] and big organizations will provide online or other training packages, checklists and forms. The BBC *myRisks* site is very helpful. But most importantly, chatting to local people, and careful observation at fieldwork sites, can indicate the significant dangers already known to local people. Press articles, radio and TV news and street posters can all provide information about local hazards.

main ideas

World research often uses ***mixed-methods***, ***interdisciplinary*** approaches, and ongoing ***iterative*** data collection analysis using new technologies.
A research design should:

- create a "map" to convert *ideas into actions.*
- provide the basis for *communicating* the research project clearly to others.
- include creating *research instruments, pilot studies* and a *technology plan.*

The ***focus*** of a study should clarify:

- the *purpose,* conceptually and practically.
- the *rationale* for doing the study.
- *definitions* of concepts and terms.
- the *levels* that are being researched.

Problematization entails:

- differentiating between *wicked problems* that cannot be solved, and *tame problems* that can.
- formulating *hypotheses* or *research questions.*
- clarifying the *assumptions* that are being made – what is taken-for-granted?
- stating the specific *aims* and *objectives.*

Fieldwork means thinking about:

- *why* it is necessary to travel to a research site.
- using *checklists* and the experience of others.
- negotiating *access* to research sites and key people.
- deciding the organizational and individual *personas* of the researchers.

Small- and large-scale research requires ***project management*** which means:

- *responsibility* for other people.
- doing *risk assessments* and making *contingency plans.*

key reading

Cresswell, J.W. (2009) *Research Design: Qualitative, Quantitative, and Mixed Methods Approaches*. London: Sage.

Horwood, J. and Moon, G. (2003) 'Accessing the research setting: the politics of research and the limits to inquiry', *Area*, 35: 106–109.

Lee-Treweek, G. and Linkogle, S. (eds) (2000) *Danger in the Field: Risk and Ethics in Social Research*. New York: Routledge.

Sriram, C. et al. (eds) (2009) *Surviving Research: Doing Fieldwork in Violent and Difficult Situations.* New York: Routledge.

Thomas, D.R. and Hodges, I.D. (2010) *Designing and Managing Your Research Project: Core Skills for Social and Health Research*. London: Sage.

Winser, S. (ed.) (2004) *Expedition Handbook.* London: Profile Books.

online resources

To access the resources – search on the name in italics, use the http, or search on the generic term in 'quote marks'.

Fieldwork

Royal Geographical Society Expedition Handbook **–** a comprehensive and updated site

Insurancewide – comparisons of 'long stay travel insurance' products – www.insurancewide.com

Risk assessment

FCO Travelling and Living Overseas. US State Department travel.state.gov site – country risk assessments

BBC *myRisks* – checklists and forms – www.bbc.co.uk/safety/resources/forms-and-documents.html

Funding sources

European Research Council – http://erc.europa.eu/
Kickstarter – crowdfunding
World Bank. Evoke. Global Giving Challenge. Crowdfunding – www.globalgiving.org/evoke

FIVE
Research ethics and integrity

Too often, the design for world research is – "get in, get what you want, and get out" – and this also applies to online research. Researching another country can create a feeling of intellectual impunity, because repercussions are minimal for researchers once they finish. Yet the consequences of bad practice can harm local research participants, hosts and assistants, local and other visiting researchers, and the reputations of universities and organizations.

The overall integrity (moral soundness) of a research project entails thinking about research ethics (rules of conduct), together with methodological aspects such as objectivity, impartiality and bias.[1] Unethical research practice often leads to biased data collection and analysis, and *vice versa*.[2] Ethics can seem an irritation, but developing ethical standards for international work can be an 'outcome' of any study, which could be more significant than the basic work. This chapter outlines the cross-border and cross-cultural considerations of *world research ethics*, relevant *law*, the abuse and inclusion of **others**, the new conundrums of *online research* and the ethics of *ethics committees*. But, for world research the big question is, whose ethical standards take priority – those of the researchers' "home" country and funder, or those of the countries where the research is carried out?

5.1 World research ethics

Many books explain the basics of social research ethics,[3] and usually the focus is ***human participants***. These principles may need to be developed for international work, particularly in less developed countries.[4] In many contexts, a standard ethical practice may be very dangerous. Getting informed consent in the form of a signed document may be accepted by university ethics committees in wealthy countries. But if the research were being carried out among illiterate village elders in a war zone, other considerations may be more important. Those concerned may not have the background knowledge to be, or to become, 'informed'. And signing anything may be a meaningless or very risky act, which breaches confidentiality.

There are numerous ethical codes available from research bodies, universities,[5] public services, government departments,[6] civil service and professional organizations such as journalists.[7] These should balance good practice with *academic freedom*, but ideas about this differ across the world.[8] There are many national codes about international research, but few internationally agreed standards, such as the EU *RESPECT Code* and the *Singapore Statement on Research Integrity*. The 'ethics' section of any study should mention ethical standards used previously in similar studies, and relevant codes. It should then identify and discuss aspects that are not fully covered, seem unique to a particular study, or require adapting for different settings. This is explained further on the website.

Confidentiality is a significant concern for cross-border research, because local people in other countries can be put at significant risk by careless use of data and personal information. This is not just because of state action – families and other interpersonal relationships can easily be destroyed. When research is by an INGO such as *Amnesty International*, carelessness could endanger the same people that the organization is trying to help. And there is a self-interest aspect. Media coverage of harmful outcomes from research by a few individuals could put the credibility and future of the whole organization at risk. Proper data management, including safe transfer, is increasingly important, and better technology does not always increase security (C7.7).

Ethics discussions often confuse ***harm*** and ***deceit***. The aim should be to avoid or minimize harm, but it is virtually impossible to do research without deceit in some form. If research subjects were fully aware of the nature of the research, this would inevitably bias the way they responded or behaved. Deceit may be acceptable to facilitate observation and evidence gathering, especially about deceitful people, but it is less acceptable to use deceit to entrap people into doing wrong – 'setups' and 'stings'. Is *covert research* reasonable? How far is 'blagging' acceptable – getting data by posing as someone else? Is it ethical to adopt a false persona, or gain access by joining an organization or providing a service?[9] Dress can create a conundrum – should it reflect the persona of the interviewee or the interviewer? If a non-Muslim woman wears a *hijab* to interview a Muslim leader, is that respectful or deceitful (Figure 5.1)? NGOs doing research in poor communities in Colombia consider it ethical to wear conspicuous T-shirts with the logo of the NGO, to show people who they are.

Figure 5.1 The cultural persona of the researcher

A Korean researcher, Yun-joo Lee, wearing Muslim dress to interview an Islamic leader, Professor Muhammad S. Tantawy, Grand Sheik of *Al-Azhar*

Any information that is already in the ***public domain*** can usually be used freely without further permission, even if it is incorrect, but some countries still take action against those who repeat unfavourable information. Although *Wikileaks* is seen by many people as unethical and even unlawful, when leaks become public they can be widely used, even for court cases.[10] A broad ***public interest*** is often argued by journalists and by whistle-blowing organizations, but there are significant differences in national laws.[11]

If research participants cannot understand and/or ***consent*** to the research, there are ways to argue that a *non-consensual approach* is ethical. If public officials are in a public place, it seems reasonable to assume that, whatever they say or do, they know that they are acting in an *official capacity* and can therefore be quoted or recorded freely. The concept of *best interests* is often applied when research subjects cannot give informed consent, for example studies concerning children's rights.[12] Is reporting the findings of research likely to be better for all those concerned, than any potential harm? Medical, military and police ethics address the same concern in terms of *proportionality* – is the risk of harm less than the benefit arising from taking that risk?

Similarly, *substituted judgement* may be applied in non-consenting circumstances – people with mental disabilities and children.[13] This asks a counterfactual question: if those concerned could fully understand the research, and its risks and benefits, what might they decide? This can be applied to right previous wrongs. In the 1990s, international journalists in China presented the care of orphaned children negatively. But from shadowing the journalists it was possible to record how they manipulated images and reports, and Chinese care workers explained how photographers used tricks such as photographing children through the safety bars of their cots, to create prison-like images. This badly affected the morale of staff who were doing their best in difficult circumstances. Permission to take accurate photos was granted by the manager – had the children and all staff understood the purpose of documenting the truth, they would probably have agreed.

Photos of children, or people in vulnerable situations, can be considered unethical, but there are no clear rules. If children are photographed in a school or other private space, permission should usually be sought from the children and/or responsible adults. But when children are in the street, this is public space where photographing anyone is normally acceptable, unless they are in distress. If showing the identity of people may cause harm, faces can be *fuzzed* very simply. But try to maintain the aesthetic of the picture – colour, tone, shape – because people can be upset by fuzzing that makes them look silly, and distortions can distract from the purpose of using the photo. Some people are upset if their face *is* hidden. From the children's perspective, often the main ethical concern is that they want payment or an immediate print of the photo. The only rule is, if possible, ask and note what individuals prefer.

Increasingly, it is seen as ethical to ensure ***open access*** to research findings that may help disadvantaged people. Organizations such as *Research4life* make vital research available within disadvantaged communities, about UN priorities including health, development, environment and agriculture. This raises arguments about intellectual property. Ethics discussions about the production of cheap generic drugs to address world pandemics like HIV/AIDS, in less wealthy countries, are an increasing concern. Medical charities such as *Welcome* demonstrate progressive approaches.

5.2 The law

Legal issues are closely related to research ethics.[14] It is not possible to give comprehensive advice for all countries, but the website discusses the relevant issues including visas, local rules, restrictions in public places, copyright and defamation. The *Index on Censorship* provides updated information about changing laws and actions against journalists and other researchers, internationally. The UK *FCO* site details 'local laws and customs'. Relevant laws are often very unclear, even to local people, for example what is a 'public place' where photos can probably be taken, and private property where they cannot (C10). Major problems can arise from minor infringements which can give police an easy excuse to inconvenience unwanted researchers because, for example, they take nasal sprays into Japan, cover their face in France, or feed pigeons in Venice.

The law may sometimes conflict with research ethics, for example about confidentiality versus freedom of speech, the research participants' desire to publicize or conceal their views, state officials who want to know everything, and researchers' views on academic freedom. Some researchers may have a professional *duty of care* which overrides other considerations. If, in an interview, a doctor admits abusing a patient, a researcher who is a health worker would have a duty to report this.[15] In some countries, France for example, there is a legal requirement to report suspected crime.

Laws can seem an irrelevant irritation to researchers. But before simply ignoring them, it is worth considering the penalties for being found doing research illegally in another country. The police are likely to take any reports very seriously, and charges may amount to terrorism or spying.[16] Being caught without the right papers in a foreign country can suddenly cause a surprisingly short, or shockingly long, stay.

5.3 'Others' and 'othering'

The ***othering*** of people within world research has been common (C2.1), and it was often done with meticulous methodology. It is easy to look back and criticize practices a century ago. But it is less easy to identify unethical representations of others in the present-day. Professional bodies such as the *American Anthropological Association* publish useful online ethical codes. Yet there are ongoing arguments, for example about the use of ethnic group names – such as Khoisan, Bantu and Bushman – in the biogenetics literature.[17]

How will future academics judge present-day medical researchers who sell photos taken in clinical settings to sites such as *Documenting Reality*, which shows 'Human Deformities and Medical Problems' or 'Africa Diseased and Deformed' to make money from the accompanying advertisements? How should we judge modern missionaries who use similar photos of children with major facial disfigurements, such as cleft lip and *noma*, on their websites, for fundraising? Health researchers can unwittingly become implicated in similar practices.[18]

The unthinking repetition of ***politicized terminology*** is common in international studies. International reports often use a lazy style that conflates the political leaders of a nation and ordinary people – many North Koreans, Somalis, Congolese, Israelis or Americans are the victims, not the perpetrators, of state abuses of power. Terms such as 'illegal immigrant' often describe asylum seekers and others who are more accurately 'undocumented immigrants' because they have not been found guilty of any illegal action. Naming disasters after places rather than perpetrators punishes the victims and hides the villains – the 'Bhopal disaster' is more correctly 'Union Carbide negligence', and 'Minamata disease' should be the 'Chisso Company poisoning' (C10.10).[19]

Present-day human rights organizations such as *Survival International* argue that ***stereotypical portrayals***, even if well meaning, can fuel harmful politics against indigenous peoples, and anthropologists continue to be criticized. Jared Diamond's book, *The World Until Yesterday*, was questioned for claiming that, 'tribal societies offer an extraordinary window into how our ancestors lived for millions of years'.[20] This assumes that tribal peoples, past and present, can be treated as a distinct homogeneous group, and that modern humans are also one distinct homogeneous group. Would a study of present-day nomadic Bedouin in Palestine help us to understand how the nomadic tribes of Moses lived? And would that help us to better understand modern Israelis?

The ***intellectual property rights*** of people in less wealthy countries are often ignored. The *Society for Ethnomusicology* advises, 'Sensitivity to proprietary concerns regarding recorded materials, photographs, and other documentation.'

> Ethnomusicologists recognize the need to be informed regarding copyright and other laws pertaining to the ownership of intellectual and cultural property and to be aware of the potential protections and liabilities of contractual arrangements dealing with depositing, licensing, and distributing musical sound and audiovisual recordings.[21]

Similar concerns should apply to indigenous art and design (often copied to create "ethnic" factory-made fabrics), poetry, aural histories, and other intellectual and creative assets that the originators may not recognize as their property. UN-WIPO researches international disputes, for example when a US company wanted to patent Basmati rice, and a Japanese company, curry. NGOs like *Light Years IP* research intellectual property issues for indigenous groups, for example the use of the brand name 'Masai' by *Louis Vuitton*.

In the past and present, the dynamics are the same. Unethical othering, in the guise of research, enhances the power of the powerful through disregard for those less powerful, and usually has a racist or nationalistic aspect. And online research raises new questions (below 5.4).

thinking zone: should avatars be treated ethically?

avatar ethics

Online, an avatar represents a user in some way. When researching and analysing avatars:

- Should avatar participants be asked for their consent?
- Should any material, including avatar names, be kept confidential?
- Is it OK to misrepresent how avatars behave?
- Would it be acceptable to try to 'unmask' and identify the humans behind the avatars?
- If an avatar behaves unethically – racist hatred, being violent to women, sexually abusing children – should this be reported?
- If a researcher created a game or online environment to research human behaviour through avatars, what would be the ethical considerations, for example about closing the site when the research ends?
- The word 'avatar' comes from Hindu, meaning a godlike being that manifests itself on Earth in another form. Might Hindus view the ethics of avatar research differently?

What would be the answers to these questions if the researchers were from another planet, and we were just avatars in their game?

5.3.1 Inclusion and participation

The focus on world issues can lead to ignoring problems that are familiar everywhere, but become hidden in some countries. There are often forms of ***double discrimination*** which ethics discussions should consider – disabled people from minority groups,[22] disadvantaged children in repressive countries,[23] people in psychiatric institutions in war zones.[24] And powerful people deserve the same basic ethical standards as anyone else, unless there are clear reasons why they should be treated differently.[25] In relation to minority groups, it is well established that a research design should aim for the best possible ***integration*** ('inclusion') of the people that the research concerns, for example disabled people, within the whole process. Many books explain how,[26] and sites such as *inclusiveresearch.net* exemplify good practice.

Full integration means involvement in:

- *deciding what to research* – What are the important issues, and the hidden details that a project needs to investigate?
- *writing research proposals* – Which funders might respond best to participatory grassroots research, which will be more impressed by expert involvement, and how can proposals secure funding by optimizing all levels of involvement?
- *planning* – What are the strengths and weaknesses of those who should be involved?
- *creating ethical protocols* – How can the ethics be decided by, and presented appropriately for, those who the study concerns?
- *carrying out research tasks* – How can tasks be adapted for those with special needs and abilities (languages, disabilities, qualitative-quantitative skills, analysis, reflexive practice, writing and presentation skills)?

- *presenting findings* – What are the most appropriate, accessible and ethical ways to present at conferences and in the media, in printed or online formats, through video, theatre, poetry and other arts.[27]
- *profiting from the study* – Who can gain financially, emotionally, reputationally, or by having fun, from doing a study?

NGOs, health researchers, anthropologists and development studies researchers implement these ideas within *participatory research* frameworks.[28] Disability sites about access technologies, like *Ability.net*, not only show how to include people with disabilities as participants and researchers. They test and explain devices that can be helpful to any researcher.

But the reason for an integrated (inclusive) approach is not just ethical. It improves the design, implementation and outcomes of the whole project. And that means working with everyone who is involved in the research, in every aspect, including the ethics decisions. Visual methods explaining ethics can apply to anyone who cannot fully understand formal research ethics. And this probably includes everyone, including the trained researchers.

5.4 Online and remote research

Online research is increasingly important for international work (C6.5). There are distinct ethical questions,[29] but few agreements about standards.[30] The best starting point is simply to follow the *terms and conditions* of individual sites, such as the *Facebook Community Standards*. The broad ethical discussions revolve around the

Intrusiveness – Discuss to what degree the research conducted is intrusive ("passive" analysis of internet postings versus active involvement in the community by participating in communications).

Perceived privacy – Discuss (preferably in consultation with members of the community) the level of perceived privacy of the community. (Is it a closed group requiring registration? What is the membership size? What are the group norms?)

Vulnerability – Discuss how vulnerable the community is: for example, a mailing list for victims of sexual abuse or AIDS patients will be a highly vulnerable community.

Potential harm – As a result of the above considerations, discuss whether the intrusion of the researcher or publication of results has the potential to harm individuals or the community as a whole.

Informed consent – Discuss whether informed consent is required or can be waived. (If it is required how will it be obtained?)

Confidentiality – How can the anonymity of participants be protected? (If verbatim quotes are given originators can be identified easily using search engines, thus informed consent is always required.)

Intellectual property rights – In some cases, participants may not seek anonymity, but publicity, so that use of postings without attribution may not be appropriate.

Figure 5.2 Ethical considerations for online qualitative research

Source: Eysenback, G. and Till, J. E. (2001) 'Ethical issues in qualitative research on internet communities', *British Medical Journal*, 323: 1103–1105.

questions, are websites *private* or *public* spaces, and what is the distinction between *human-centred*[31] and *non-human centred* research? Health researchers have identified the basic considerations, but there are still few finite conclusions. The *Journal of Mass Media Ethics* provides an ongoing discussion and the website lists the main issues. The considerations are often qualitative, not just technical (Figure 5.2).

Questions when doing online research should consider human aspects and content, and include the following.

- ***Human participants:***
  - How do we *define* 'human participants', online?
  - When is *consent* needed to use communications between people (blogs, *Twitter*, chat rooms, *Facebook*)?
  - Should *different* people be treated in different ways – children, older people, religions, nationalists, ethnic groups, gender – and if so, how does the researcher know who people are?
  - Is *anonymity* required when information is already part of the global commons of the internet? Does *public interest* sometimes override privacy?[32]
  - Do the originators of online material need (or want) to be anonymous or do they want recognition? Should material be disguised at different levels ranging from – 'none, light, moderate, to heavy'.[33]
  - How can *rapport* between researcher and participants be developed across cultures, online?
  - How can researchers *protect participants* from harm, or *evaluate* local threats, from a distance?
  - How do researchers *protect themselves* and assistants, for example from cyber-attacks?
  - Should researchers use *false IDs*, and can they use different IDs for different parts of a study or different studies, and if so how do they remain *accountable* for their conduct?
  - Can *participants freely use materials* that show researchers – recordings of *Skype* interviews, video conferences, emails? (Perhaps the 'participants' are actually covert researchers, and if so should they have admitted to this when they were recruited online?)
  - What is the *power relationship* between researchers and participants, and how can this be assessed internationally?
  - What special *training* should online researchers have?

- ***Online content:***
  - When is *consent* needed to use general 'global commons' material – what are the *copyright* issues?
  - Who is being *excluded*, and what is being ignored, for example when online big data is being used, and how does that bias results?
  - Should *user-generated* content (tweets, responses to BBC news items) be treated differently from content created by *site owners* (*Twitter* terms and conditions, BBC news items)?
  - To what degree can internet material be *sampled* properly, and does it matter?
  - If *crowdsourced material* (contributed resources, crowdmaps, analytical discussion) is being used (C6.4), what is the responsibility towards the 'crowds', especially if they are in repressive countries?[34]
  - If online project content is *taken over* by others (hijacked, or goes viral) after it formally ends, who is then responsible for how it is used?

Whatever the final agreements about online ethics among academics, it is very likely that commercial and government researchers will be operating to different standards. That raises the question, can academics therefore adopt the standards of the commercial or government researchers, when researching commercial or government entities online?

Remote research from a "home" country is increasingly attractive to reduce cost and increase speed, and goes beyond standard online research, for example by using satellites or drones (UAVs – Unmanned Aerial Vehicles). Analysing what an interviewee says during a TV interview in another country might appear reasonable, as the interviewee has seemingly already consented to that interview. But would they consent if they knew that it was not their words that were being studied, but their dress and body language in terms of sexuality? How are we sure that ordinary interviewees have consented in any way, and are not just following orders from powerful people? Similar considerations apply to analysing online material from the ICC and other international courts, particularly if the defendant is eventually acquitted. A court camera can pick up details about stressed people, which are far more intrusive than what could be observed by researchers who are present in a courtroom.

Robots can now fulfil basic research roles, for example to collect information from hospital patients in waiting rooms, and in the form of remote doctors controlled by physicians many miles away. Increasingly, robots are able to take autonomous decisions. Weapons are being developed which can take decisions about how to behave, which can include killing people. Research robots could evolve similarly, for example by using natural language processing to invent questions. Should the ethics of robot research be different from online and other research ethics, and if so, how?

thinking zone: what are the ethics for robot researchers?

rules for robots

In *Runaround*, Isaac Asimov determined 'Three laws of robotics' (1942)[35]:

1. A robot may not injure a human being or, through inaction, allow a human being to come to harm.
2. A robot must obey the orders given to it by human beings, except where such orders would conflict with the First Law.
3. A robot must protect its own existence as long as such protection does not conflict with the First or Second Laws.

How should these 'laws' relate to robot researchers?

Should robots be free to:

- select who to interview?
- suggest that there may be consequences from not answering questions?

(Continued)

(Continued)

- report interviewees who say they have done something illegal?
- discard extreme or unintelligible data?
- create their own questions?
- choose what to research?

[See References for further information.[36]]

5.5 Ethics committees

Ethics committees are an increasing concern among international academics.[37] Committee members sometimes have little experience or knowledge of work outside their own country, and sometimes seem more concerned to protect themselves than to protect others. Researchers who have worked in dangerous countries sometimes explain that they only described the safe part of their work to their research ethics committees, to avoid complications.

Hammersley and Atkinson provide a useful reminder of reality and balance:[38]

> Some discussions of the ethics of social research seem to be premised on the idea that social researchers can and should act in an ethically superior manner to ordinary people, that they have, or should have, a heightened ethical sensibility and responsibility. There is also a tendency to dramatize matters excessively, implying a level of likely harm or moral transgression that is far in excess of what is typically involved...Yet the ethical problems surrounding ethnographic research are, in fact, very similar to those surrounding other human activities...Above all, in everyday life ethical issues are subject to the same uncertainties and disagreements, the same play of vested interest and dogmatic opinions, and the same range of reasonable but conflicting arguments. All that can be required of [researchers] is that they take due note of the ethical aspects of their work and make the best judgments they can in the circumstances. Like anyone else, they will have to live with the consequences of their actions; and, inevitably, so too will others. But then this is true of all of us in all aspects of our lives.

Ethics discussions can be the most significant part of a project, or they can become self-fulfilling iterations of personal righteousness by people who themselves have done little world-scale research. The academic response to unreasonable objections by ethical committees might be, "Do you have any significant evidence that this has ever caused serious harm?"

Ethics committees should be an informed source of expertise that can help researchers to recognize and address new and difficult world ethics problems. This has become more evident for medical research,[39] but less so for other international work. New technologies, such as satellites and robots, raise new questions – what are the ethics of NGOs and academics remotely monitoring sovereign states without consent from their governments?[40] Ethics committees should create regularly updated online codes because issues change rapidly, but this rarely happens. Domestic ethical standards usually need further consideration when applied internationally (Box 5.1).

Box 5.1 Adapting research ethics for world research

Principle	**General considerations**	**World research considerations**
Voluntary participation	Research participants should be acting freely and not pressured or coerced into taking part in a study.	In some cultures certain people – women, children, subordinates – may want to seek permission before participation in an interview. If they are told or asked to take part by a superior, is that still 'voluntary'?
Informed consent	Research participants should understand the research and its implications, and agree to take part. Informed consent should be recorded. But this usually does not apply to observation in a public space.	Illiterate people from remote areas might not be able to understand the idea of research. Recording consent could be meaningless, or even dangerous to participants. Media and online research raises new questions. Satellites and drones (UAVs) are increasingly used for remote observation, by both government and commercial and civil society researchers, but there is little discussion of the ethics of this when private places are observed.
Privacy, confidentiality, secrecy, anonymity and *disclosure*	Data and participants should be protected and disguised.	For international organizations this has distinct implications, and international human rights law protects *privacy*. Is anonymity always possible, or wanted, in relation to public figures holding specific posts that will inevitably identify them? If they want privacy, to what extent is it acceptable to investigate the private lives of public figures, particularly if wrongdoing is suspected? If someone mentions a criminal or abusive act, should that be reported further?

Further examples on the website.

The significant world consideration is that, while other forms of research might harm local communities, or even occasionally cause the death of individuals, the scale is limited. Domestic research does not usually have the potential to contribute to genocide as in Nazi Germany, decades of hatred of people labelled 'communist', racial tensions as in Africa and America, animosity among East Asian countries through book titles such as *The Rape of Nanjing*, or wars resulting from the misleading presentation of intelligence research as in Iraq.[41] The best, but not perfect, guiding principle is the 'Golden Rule' of *reciprocity* – behave to others as you would like them to behave to you. At least this has multicultural roots, and could potentially make ethical committees more ethical.

thinking zone: what would my brain want if it were theirs?

reciprocity

The 'Golden Rule' occurs in many philosophies and religions:

- That which you hate to be done to you, do not do to another – Egypt, Late Period papyrus 664–323BC (trans. R. Jasnow, 1992).
- Do not do to others, what you would not want for yourself. 己所不欲，勿施於人。– China, Confucius, 552–479BC, Analects XV.24.
- Do not do to others what would anger you if done to you by others – Greece, Isocrates, 436–338BC, Nicocles, 6.
- Treat others as you treat yourself – India, Mahābhārata Shānti-Parva (9th–8th centuries BC, 167:9.
- Hurt not others in ways that you yourself would find hurtful – India, Buddha, 563–circa 483BC, Udanavarga 5:18.
- Therefore all things whatsoever ye would that men should do to you, do ye even so to them: for this is the law and the prophets – Roman Syria, Jesus, Matthew 7:12 (circa 100AD).

are ethics free?

Matthew cites his source as Jesus, and Jesus attributes the idea to 'the law and the prophets', but not to any of the earlier international thinkers. Is it ethical to plagiarize ideas about ethics?

but

'Do not do unto others as you would that they should do unto you. Their tastes may not be the same', advised George Bernard Shaw in *Maxims for Revolutionists* (1903).

So, if a masochist said to a sadist, "Hit me", what is the ethically correct answer for the sadist?

"Yes" or "NOOOOO"!?

neuro-ethics

The 'Golden Rule' is seen as a 'neuro-ethical principle' – an ethic honed by evolution, which is fundamental to the survival of the whole human species. How might this idea be applied to:

- the study of comparative ethics?
- the formation of international law?
- international research ethics?

[See References for further information.[42]]

main ideas

When using ***ethical guidelines*** for international work consider:

- whose ethics take *priority* – those of the researchers' "home" country, or the countries where the research is happening, or both?
- the difference between causing *harm*, and *deceit*.
- how decisions are made when *consent* is not possible – 'best interests', 'substituted judgement', 'public interests'.
- the tendency to fuss about *small* moral details, which makes us feel good, and *big* issues that are easy to ignore but can fuel wars, commercial exploitation, and life-long problems for local people.
- *reciprocity* – how would I want "them" to behave to "us"?

When thinking about the ***law***, consider:

- the need for research visas.
- local rules – taxes, currency exchange, import/export laws.
- restrictions on recording in public places – photos, videos, audio.
- copyright and defamation.

When working with ***'others'***, consider how research:

- has often *demeaned* people, and caused *hatred* and *conflict*.
- can be fully *integrated* (*inclusive*), at all stages, including decisions about ethics.

When using ***online*** and ***remote*** methods, consider:

- if, and why, people online, and/or in other countries, should be treated *differently*.
- the distinction between *human-participant* and *non-human participant* research.
- whether internet sites are *private* or *public* spaces.

key reading

Dawson, J. and Peart, N.S. (2003) *The Law of Research: A Guide*. Dunedin: University of Otego Press.

Halai, A. and William, D. (2012) *Research Methodologies in the 'South'*. Karachi: Oxford University Press Pakistan.

Hammersley, M. and Traianou, A. (2011) *Ethics in Qualitative Research*. London: Sage.

Robinson-Pant, A. and Singal, N. (eds) (2013) Special issue. 'Researching ethically across cultures', *Compare*, 43(4).

Swan, N. et al. (2011) *Ethics Protocols and Research Ethics Committees.* Sonning Common: Academic Publishing International.

Ward, S.J.A. (2010) *Global Journalism Ethics*. Quebec: McGill-Queen's University Press.

online resources

To access the resources – search on the name in italics, use the http, or search on the generic term in 'quote marks'.

Social Research Association – ethics guidelines

Singapore Statement on Research Integrity – an attempt to identify global principles

EU *RESPECT* project

Yale University – conducting research abroad – http://world-toolkit.yale.edu/research_overview

UNESCO – European cross-national research – www.unesco.org/most/ethissj.htm

International research ethics subject guide – medical research – http://bioethics.iu.edu/reference-center/ireguide

World Association of Professional Investigators – www.wapi.com

Inclusive Research Network – research by and with people with learning disabilities – www.inclusiveresearch.net

Internet research ethics – www.nyu.edu/projects/nissenbaum/ethics_elgesem.html

MORE ON THE WEBSITE

SIX

Choosing research frameworks

Buildings have different frameworks – steel, concrete, wood – which provide the main structure. And within these frameworks different, or similar, materials are used – carpets, paint, heating. Similarly, *research frameworks*[1] (also called 'strategies',[2] 'approaches',[3] or 'designs'[4]) provide a structure within which different, or similar, data collection methods are used (C7–C13). A research design may be based on more than one framework, frameworks may overlap, and a framework can involve a combination of different data collection methods and analysis.

In the past, research design often started with a decision to use either a ***quantitative***[5] (*positivist* – numbers, measurement, statistics) or ***qualitative***[6] (*interpretive*[7]– words, images, meanings) framework.[8] World research can use the standard frameworks, and many methodology books explain these,[9] so they are only outlined here (Figure 6.1). But the qualitative–quantitative distinction is not now so clear-cut. New technologies are producing data that does not fit neatly into the old paradigms. Satellite images are visual data, but the images can be measured quantitatively (the number of tanks in a war zone), or observed qualitatively (the type of tanks and their movements). More importantly, frameworks should be chosen to address the research problems in the most appropriate way, not because the researcher favours one way of doing research. There has been a belief that qualitative analysis is not viable on a world scale, except within ethnographic fieldwork,[10] but approaches have been developed,[11] and are applied to topics within international politics/relations such as gender, race, religion and secularism.[12] The internet has made online qualitative work viable and innovative.

Framework	Characteristics	Difficulties	Advantages
Action research	Cycles of interventions and evaluations to understand and change a situation.	People may not welcome interventions. A study may collapse before the cycles of planned interventions are complete.	Provides a clear focus. Applicable to training and change management.
Case studies	A study of something because it is either typical (common) or atypical (unique).	If selection of the case is opportunistic or convenience, the academic rationale may be poor.	Clear boundaries. Typical cases can be generalized.
Cross-sectional	A study of the same thing at different levels of a population or organization.	Difficult to ensure that the same things are being studied.	Multiple perspectives which increase validity.
Experimental	An intervention is tested, perhaps on one group, and comparisons are made with another similar 'control' group that did not experience the intervention.	Role play and simulation do not reflect real-world circumstances. Powerful people are unlikely to cooperate.	Useful for informing and evaluating training and pilot projects.
Longitudinal	Repeated observations of the same things over a long time period, compared with 'baseline data'. 'Cohort studies' track the same people; 'panel studies' survey a sample of a population at each stage.	High attrition rate of cohort subjects. Baseline data cannot be amended. Context changes can confound results.	Indicates effects of major policy changes. Can track development of cohorts experiencing a particular intervention.
Psychological	Assessments of the minds of individuals – personality, cognitive style, mental health.	Difficult to get data directly from actual leaders/elites, 'distance psychology' is problematic, and simulations are hard to generalize.	Insights can inform international intelligence analysis, decision-making, negotiation and conflict resolution.
Surveys (see C9)	Large-scale interviews, or postal/e-questionnaires across a population or sample.	Busy or powerful people rarely respond to postal/e-surveys or get staff to provide standard responses.	Respondents are often keen to give anonymous views about sensitive topics.

Figure 6.1 Standard research frameworks

This chapter concentrates on other frameworks which can be relevant for world research. Specialists may find the explanations very basic, but the intent is to make researchers aware of the potential of diverse ways to structure data collection, which is often lacking in international studies.[13] These data collection frameworks are explained in relation to the *conceptual framework* for this book – *peoples, places, systems*. Some studies may be *cross-sectional* looking at a topic across all three levels. *Crowdsourcing* (C6.4) and *online research* (C6.5) are also relevant across all areas. Figure 6.2 shows the frameworks that can be relevant for world research, and the website has related diagrams and templates.

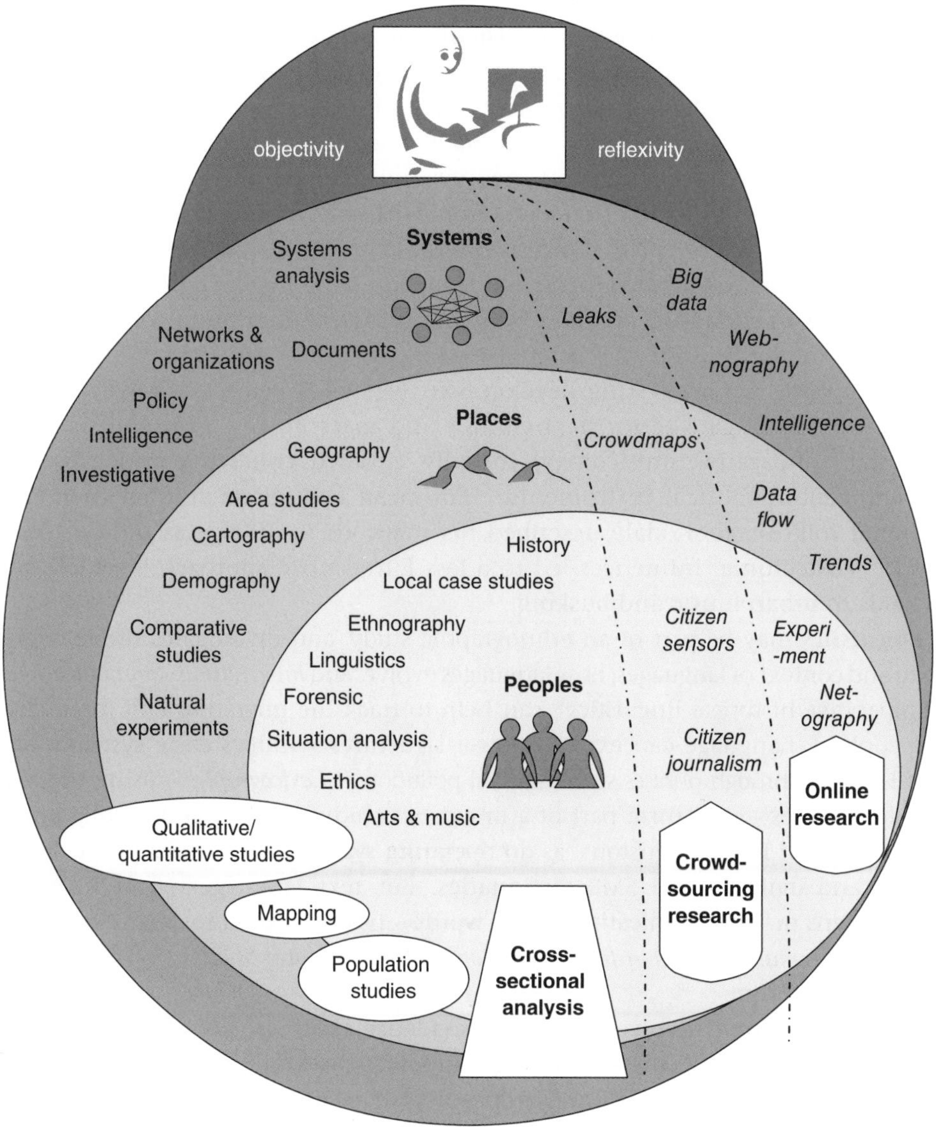

Figure 6.2 World research frameworks

http://openclipart.org/collections

6.1 Studying peoples

Local case studies are usually small-scale and focus on particular aspects of particular people's lives in a specific place.[14] They rarely concern a whole population or system, as *area studies* do (C6.2). General case study methods are relevant,[15] and the choice of the 'case' is usually because it is either *typical* (common) or *atypical* (uncommon). A case study should be structured to make it comparable with similar studies across the world, and it may be *cross-sectional* looking at the same issue at different levels in the same country.[16] The crucial factor for any case study is to define the boundaries – "What's in and what's out, and why?"

Ethnography ('culturology'[17]) is usually associated with *anthropology*, and aims to provide a holistic account of peoples or other groups, including their languages, history, place, environment, buildings, kinship, elites and objects.[18] *Fieldwork* and *participant observation* have been central,[19] and ethnographic methods can be related to critical theory[20] and reflexive thinking.[21] *Endogenous* perspectives consider things that come from within a cultural group (food taboos, house decoration); *exogenous*, concern external views (nutritional standards, symbolism). Similarly, *emic* accounts come from someone inside a group ("our gods say..."), and an *etic* account comes from an outsider ("their moral values are..."). 'Distance methods' were discussed by Margaret Mead in 1953,[22] and online ethnography is an interesting development (see C6.5 below). Forensic anthropologists[23] investigate terrorist bombings and mass graves. ***Ethnomusicology***[24] (cultural/comparative musicology) initially entailed collecting and categorizing indigenous musical instruments.[25] European composers studied their own national folk music. Kodály described his methods in 1906,[26] as did Bartók in 1931.[27] Postcolonial influences led to a less Eurocentric approach,[28] which now extends to urban music and busking.

Linguistics may be part of an ethnographic study, and investigates the meaning, form and context of languages, how languages evolve, and *intercultural communication*.[29] Comparative/historical linguistics[30] can help to track the migration and interaction of peoples.[31] Language can explain power structures – India's caste system is built into language through phrases such as 'ritual pollution'.[32] ***Lexicography*** – using or creating dictionaries – may form part of a linguistics study. Internet and mobile phone translators add new dimensions, as do operating systems (OS) that support diverse scripts and dialects, and SMS dictionaries. But text language is not new. The *rebus* – signs or letters indicating whole words – has been used for many centuries. The *International Association for Translation and Intercultural Studies* (IATIS) provides an academic forum.

Forensic research involves collecting evidence that can be used in courts as bases for 'toxic torts',[33] cross-border litigation, ICC cases and holding governments to account.[34] Anthropologists and archaeologists examine mass graves, in places such as the former Yugoslavia, and historical photos can help. They might use private photos, and regime records, and physical evidence such as 'saw and tool marks on bone', 'surgical effects on bones (including amputations)' and 'stigmata of torture'.[35] Satellite images have been used at the ICJ, ECJ and *Inter-American Court of Human Rights* (IACHR).[36] Specific methodologies are used to organize and analyse data in a way that is appropriate for courtroom arguments,[37] and specific software is available.[38] Presenting digital evidence effectively is increasingly important.[39] Forensic evidence collection needs to be done very carefully.[40] Court records of cases can provide very reliable data for other researchers. Most importantly, researchers doing fieldwork for other reasons may suddenly find they are in a position to collect valuable evidence of abuses of power, such as children's drawings in a war zone.[41]

Situation analysis (SA) happens in many different forms.[42] It may be an independent piece of work, incorporated into planning tools such as Log Frames, or be based on *crowdsourcing* (C6.4). SA is likely to consider how people are affected by obvious factors – geographic, economic, political, cultural/social, environmental. Often *SWOT analysis*[43] (Figure 12.2), *risk analysis* (C14.3.1), and *predictive analysis* are used (C14.3). SA is often used to plan *international development* projects, or during and after *emergencies* and organizations have developed comprehensive checklists, available on the website. Project ***evaluations***[44] usually compare project *outcomes* in relation to *aims*, conceptual or legal criteria, and specific *impacts*.[45] *Rapid Rural Appraisal* (RRA) is an alternative to survey-based evaluation methods.[46] *Participatory Rural Appraisal* (PRA)[47] makes greater use of tools and techniques such as *participatory mapping, ranking* and *prioritizing, community memories* and *life histories, timelines* and *calendars*.[48]

Ethics (moral philosophy) research compares the behaviour of people against ethical norms – international law,[49] human rights agreements, traditions, codes, professional standards.[50]

- *Theoretical* studies assess and provide the bases for ethical claims.[51]
- *Normative* studies consider the 'normal' pragmatic bases of moral behaviour.
- *Applied* studies identify how ethical standards should be used in particular circumstances.
- *Descriptive* research discovers how moral standards are actually applied.
- *Psychological* studies assess moral capacity and agency.

Global ethics considers macro-issues such as *distributive justice, environmental ethics* and the conduct of international organizations.[52] Some discussions of *global justice* assume that this can only happen within a nation state system;[53] others that the concept is older reflecting the world distribution of 'goods and bads'.[54] When analysing historical issues, distinguish between *retrospective* and *retroactive ethics* (C13.2).

Arts and music ('culture', 'media') research has been the domain of itinerant poets, musicians, storytellers and artists. Practitioners search for new materials and techniques, check the factual bases of their work, or seek inspiration. They may be *participants* through living in slums, or working rubbish dumps. The international community is interested in *cultural diplomacy*,[55] and *culture and development*, for which UNESCO has created a set of indicators.[56] Examples of *cultural imperialism* substantiate claims about colonial and neocolonial influence.[57] How governments use the arts to promote national identity can be studied by analysing policies.[58] Work within *arts management* investigates international trends and fashions, and administrative aspects including intellectual property. Journals such as *Art & Research*, and organizations like the *European Artistic Research Network* (EARN) provide ongoing discussions. A 'framework' may just be an inspirational collection of words and images, but within this a way to collect data can be devised.

6.2 Studying places

Area studies have a long tradition,[59] and usually concern major aspects of a whole country – public service systems,[60] politics,[61] religion.[62] Initially used for training international security experts,[63] the scope has now broadened.[64] Some studies are based on city data,[65] and the *Council of Europe* programme on *Intercultural Cities* provides ongoing debates. Area studies need to be structured in a way that makes comparisons with similar things in other countries feasible. The style and methodologies of area studies can be seen on sites like OECD and the *CIA World Factbook*. A series of area studies does *not* intrinsically create an international or global study (Introduction), unless they are designed to provide a world perspective. Large-scale economic and other forms of migration can make defining an 'area' population very difficult. And think about whether 'nation' is always the best unit of analysis – does it really make sense to compare China and Russia with The Maldives and St Lucia, in an index (Figure 0.2)?

Cartography – mapping and using maps – is often a basis of an area study, and many interesting methods do not require a high level of technical expertise (C11). Old maps, such as the *Atlas of the World's Commerce* (1907), can help to design a present-day study. But the most important aspect of using maps is to remember that they can deceive.[66] ***Demography*** relates populations to territory (C9) – the statistical changes in human (and other) populations. The *UN Population Division* (UNDESA-PD) now collects data and maintains international databases. Studies include trends such as shrinking cities,[67] *transnational migration*,[68] *mobility*[69] and *hypermobility*.[70] Ideas such as *global nomads*[71] and *Third Culture Kids* (3KC, TCK) describe the globalized identities of many young people.[72]

Comparative studies[73] are based on local and area case studies.[74] A research design is usually similar across all cases, and can be focused through a set of common questions or theory. If this is not possible, data is usually *contrasted* rather than formally compared. The design can be:

- *synchronous* – similar things happening at the same time in different places – "Immigration to EU countries in 2012".
- *asynchronous* – similar things happening at different points in history in different places – "Street children in 19th century Europe and the 20th century 'Third World' ".[75]
- *longitudinal* – *cohorts* of people are assessed at different points in time – "Health outcomes of children from rich and poor families in England, from 1950–2000".
- *multivariate* – statistics about numerous places can be complied into *indexes* and *indicators* (C14.4).

Numerous methods books discuss comparative methods[76] including specific advice on: politics,[77] political economy,[78] environmental politics,[79] education,[80] social policy,[81] law,[82] social justice,[83] health policy,[84] media,[85] history[86] and working with children.[87] *Descriptive* comparisons are usually based on two area studies, but rarely more than five – analysis becomes very messy across a large number of cases (C14.1).

Natural experiments entail *opportunistic observation* and *comparison* of circumstances created by 'nature' not experimenters, and can be based on *present* or *past* events, within particular places (C14.1). The *present* collapse of a government could provide an opportunity to research how civil servants cope in a crisis. Press letters, online comments to media sites such as the BBC[88] and tweets can provide a wealth of data for analysing public perceptions and the understanding of *present* events. Family histories, local official records and archaeological findings can provide evidence for *past* ('historical') studies. Historical cases can be analysed comparatively.[89] Understanding the 'collapse' of *past* societies can provide insights into the vulnerabilities of present societies.[90]

6.3 Studying world systems

Systems analysis (C12) was developed during the Vietnam War.[91] It tries to provide a holistic understanding of interconnections and interrelatedness, within a 'closed' system, such as a nation, or 'open' systems such as religions. *World systems analysis/theory*[92] was developed by historians, including Immanuel Wallerstein,[93] in the 1970s, as it became evident that using nations and regions as the main units of analysis of world economies was inadequate. The world could be divided into *core*, *semi-periphery* and *periphery* countries.[94] *Earth systems science* investigates the interactions among the atmospheric, water, geological and biological systems. This provides the context for social science studies such as those related to the IPCC.

Network analysis[95] identifies 'nodes' of individuals or organizations who are 'tied' by interdependency arising from characteristics such as kinship, interests, beliefs, status, profession and ethnicity. Physicists are contributing to the analysis of *complex networks* in global finance.[96] Journalists use simple versions to suggest political influence,[97] and *big data* permits social media analysis (C6.5). *Supply chain analysis* may seek to make global logistics more efficient, reduce environmental impacts, or understand international crime networks (Figure 12.3). ***Organizational analysis*** considers the systems within organizations, by analysing factors such as context, and situations.[98] The purpose is often to gain a competitive advantage over rival organizations.[99] *Organizational network analysis* specifically studies communication,[100] and can be linked with *policy analysis* and *network analysis*.

Policy analysis[101] considers how to *make* policy, and how to *assess* policy-making, concerning public services, international politics[102] and foreign policy.[103] *Game theory* is a mathematical approach to understanding how strategic decisions might be made, when the outcome for one person/entity depends on the decisions of other people/entities in the same context.[104] Game theory does not account well for real-world dynamics such as irrational behaviour and unexpected contextual factors. Game theorists did not manage to predict the end of the Cold War.

Intelligence analysis[105] of military, political and commercial systems is used in settings such as embassies and transnational companies.[106] For outsiders, the blogs of the 'independent diplomat', Carne Ross, provide fascinating insights.[107] *Security intelligence* techniques are sometimes outlined on defence ministry websites.[108] *Centre of Gravity Analysis* determines the strengths and weaknesses of 'principal protagonists' ('the elite of the group') – friendly and hostile – in relation to critical 'capabilities', 'vulnerabilities' and 'requirements in order to act'. Human geospatial analysis can be used to assess power and populations in relation to space.[109] Software can assist. The *GeoTime* programme can map people's movements from data such as cash transactions and mobile calls.[110] ***Protocol analysis*** is based on the unwritten rules about the courtesies of interpersonal international relations.[111] Specialist consultancy companies provide advice,[112] and protocol manuals provide the chance to check what should have happened with what actually happened at a particular public event.[113]

Investigative research[114] is relevant to many forms of world research.[115] It usually aims to prove specific facts about state or commercial systems, and can be an element of a broader academic study. Investigative research *by* states[116] uses case-specific methods – about murder,[117] drugs dealing,[118] fraud[119] – and traditionally involves looking for *means, opportunity* and *motive*. The starting point might be a suspicion from computer-assisted profiling of a particular population.[120] Methods include electronic surveillance, informants[121] and *undercover research*.[122,123] A distinctive feature is that *groundwork* (intelligence monitoring, psychological profiling, nurturing informants) tries to achieve well-focused investigations of the 'right people in the right place at the right time'. Investigations *of* state wrongdoing have traditionally been done by *investigative journalists*.[124] State and corporate[125] crime are significant aspects. UNESCO provides a hypothesis-based inquiry approach for journalists, which entails: starting with a few clues or facts, hypothesizing the facts that are not yet known, trying to confirm the hypothesis from open sources, questioning people who can fill in the gaps in the information found in open sources. It advises, 'Don't search for secrets. Work out what they might be from open sources.'[126] Hypotheses may come from noting what may be missing in government reports.[127]

6.4 Crowdsourcing research

Crowdsourcing (CS) can relate to all frameworks, and is probably the most exciting development in world research, because it is a way to get verifiable primary data about states, which is not controlled by states. It entails: 'an organising entity that outsources research tasks, which that entity could not achieve alone, to large groups of self-selected people (lay and expert)'.[128] This might mean managing and triangulating diverse electronic sources, such as on-the-ground mobile phone video or sensor data, satellite photos and media reports. Crowds can make handwritten records accessible by transcription and tagging. But some crowd data is hard to verify – reports of air pollution may or may not come from a particular event. Therefore the use of monitors that relay data directly to internet platforms, perhaps via smart phones, can 'take the human element out of the crowd' to transmit scientific data directly to central databases.[129]

Crowdsourced research may be organized by civil society organizations, companies or governments. Experts may contribute by systemizing and presenting complex data in easily searchable formats and analysing particularly interesting findings. Volunteers and others can be organized to contribute to data collection, data management, evidence testing (triangulation), analysis, the development of relevant technologies and dissemination. To optimize the process, research planners need to ask, what can:

- *people do that technology cannot?* (decipher unconventional handwriting)
- *people do better than technology?* (scan-reading)
- *crowds do better than individuals/experts?* (repetitive tasks)
- *individuals/experts do better than crowds?* (research design)
- *technology do better than people?* (mass data storage)
- *technology do that people cannot?* (aerial surveillance)
- *several technologies do better than one?* (robotic sample collection and spectrometry analysis)

The 'crowd' is often a social or professional network, which often parallels state structures – doctors/health, teachers/education, lawyers/justice – and so evidence about how systems operate becomes easier to track and analyse. Professionals are also likely to be seen as embodying more integrity and neutrality than activists. But crowdsourced research need not depend on the internet, and identifying non-digital methods can help to optimize the relationship between humans and e-devices. The website provides a basic CS research framework.

thinking zone: how can we crowdsource research without internet?

historical

- 1563. *Foxe's Book of Martyrs* documented 'persecutions and horrible troubles' perpetrated by the 'Roman Prelates'. This included testimony evidence from 'both men and wemen, whiche can and do beare wytnes', including prisoners. The 1583 edition was three times bigger than the first, and four times bigger than the Bible. *Amnesty International* now uses similar methods.
- 1858. *Oxford English Dictionary* was created by 800 volunteers who scan-read particular texts, and copied relevant quotations onto slips. Their endeavours created two tons of paper. *Wiki* texting dictionaries are now compiled similarly.
- 1890. *The Golden Bough.* Scottish anthropologist James Frazer investigated and compared instances of human sacrifice, scapegoats, the burning of humans, the sacrifice of sacred kings, and countless other violent ritual practices from around the world. He sent questionnaires to missionaries and colonial officials in many countries, including Japan, China, Africa and the Americas. In modern terms, he used social networks for a snowball survey.

recent

- 1979. *The Iranian Revolution.* When the Americans evacuated their embassy, they shredded all sensitive documents. But hundreds of students placed the shreds on the floor and numbered and indexed them manually. Local carpet weavers reassembled the pieces. The documents were published as a book – *Documents from the US Espionage Den*, which revealed the contents of telegrams, correspondence and reports from the *American State Department* and the *CIA*.
- 1985. *Bikini Atoll.* The *Hata High School Seminar* engaged in community research about the effects of *US nuclear testing.* They interviewed fishermen who had been exposed to the radiation, and mapped their stories together with family testimonies, secret government documents and evidence of how the US tried to obstruct news about what had happened.
- 2000s. *El Nadeem Centre.* Egyptian doctors working with torture victims put red dots on a map, marking police stations where torture had reportedly happened, recording the type of injuries. The same methods and 'appliances' were being used, which showed 'systematic practice' and a 'policy' dictated by senior state officials.

human–machine cooperation

Analyse examples of internet-based crowdsourcing, and consider how they might be enhanced by more use of human-based methods.

[See References for further information.[130]]

The Kenya-based *Ushahidi Project*[131] provides online CS tools which permit mass research, including election monitoring via mobile phones.[132] The *American Red Cross Digital Operations Centre, iRevolution* and the *Digital Humanitarian Network* organize ongoing discussion about humanitarian assistance initiatives[133] and emergencies,[134] and the *Harvard Humanitarian Initiative* is providing analysis.[135] *Tomnod Crowdrank* software helps to assess, triangulate and validate CS data that has been tagged by thousands of people. The development of $250 personal *KickSat Sprite* satellites, carrying sensors controlled from smart phones, will provide new dimensions.

6.5 Online research

Online research can also relate to all frameworks, and includes using the internet,

- as a *research tool* (email, *Skype*, search engines, internet surveys, remote viewing of real-time videos), which can increase the inclusiveness of world research (C5.3.1; Box 6.2).
- as a *source of data* (websites, blogs, social media), which is outlined here.
- for *methodological research* – online research about online research – transmission speed, nodes, specific patterns, data blocks, data management and storage.

Relevant data collection methods are discussed further in the chapters about *people* (C8) and *populations* (C9). Methods for using online data fall into two categories – researching *knowns* and *unknowns* – but there are overlaps. The website provides tools to clarify this.

Box 6.1 Big data research – terms and processes

big data – Data sets that are too big, too fast or slow, too diverse (sources and types) and/or too complex to be managed and analysed by traditional systems (climate, environmental, population movement, tweets).

distributed data – Data stored in more than one place, which needs to be combined (hazardous factories near borders + weather patterns + transport links + nearest **emergency services** + airlift capability = modelling cross-border emergency responses).

unstructured data – Data that is not clearly labelled (tagged), or systematically organized into typologies or categories (video, audio, social media postings, photos).

meta-data – data about data, often collected and stored "invisibly" (ID, time place, from smart phone use).

algorithms – a computer decision-making programme that can sort data).

text – written word or images (texts/texting – SMS messages on mobile devices).

GPS – Global Positioning System, shows 'geo-location'.

(Continued)

(Continued)

tags – labelling of digital data (topic, what/who is on a photo).

profiles – demographic (age, gender, nationality, etc.).

user ID – a unique digital identifier.

frequency – the number of times specific things happen (keywords, phone use, internet searches).

A longer list is on the website.

When searching for ***knowns***, researchers know broadly what they are looking for. They know the likely data *sources*, or how to find those sources,[136] and use data that is collected specially for a particular study. They are usually trying to understand *why* specific things happen, through *in-depth* analyses of online *content*,[137] and often include researching specific *people*, or groups such as children.[138]

Searching for ***unknowns*** entails *big data* research – 'big' in terms of volume, velocity and variety. Researchers often do *not* know exactly where to look, or even what or who they are looking for,[139] and their studies usually concern *populations* (C9.4). The data is often *by-product* or *exhaust data*, which was collected initially for a non-research purpose (location of mobile phones, IP addresses). Programmers set up these data searches by designing algorithms – a flow chart of logical repeated actions. It is helpful for non-experts to understand the basics of these, so that research can be designed appropriately.

Big data research may occasionally provide answers to research questions, but more often identifies where to look for those answers. State *intelligence* services capture masses of digital data – emails, phone calls, texts – and then try to find something useful in relation to actual or likely events – riots, organized crime, terrorism, political dissent.[140] Researchers are often searching for *patterns* (clusters, outliers, associations),[141] *networks* (who 'shares' with who) and *trends* (frequencies, data flows), perhaps based on keywords in mass *content*. They look for indications of *what* is happening (interest in products, concern about events), and *how* large groups of people organize themselves (social networks, the leaders of e-chat), but not *why*. Understanding the basic terms and processes helps to demystify the jargon, and provides an idea of what big data research can achieve (Box 6.1).

The attraction of online methods is that they seem to link the researcher to the large and distant world easily, quickly and in a way that has never before been possible. But online methods are sometimes not well understood and over-hyped, which can lead to bad decisions.[142] The *ethical* considerations are unclear and fast-changing (C5.4), and many methodologies seem to assume that everyone in the world writes English and that the 'overwhelming majority' has access to a mobile phone.[143] Twenty percent of the people in our world still do *not* have access to electricity.

Box 6.2 Online inclusive interviewing

It is important to choose a comfortable setting to conduct an interview, so for people with visual impairment online interviews are excellent. The interviewer and interviewees are enjoying the comfort of their own homes, and sitting using their own computers which are adapted to their specific needs. And so it feels just like chatting with a friend.

هبة خليف Heba Kholeif
(International Student Advisor)

main ideas

Research frameworks provide *structures* to *collect* data.

The ***basic frameworks*** are: documentary analysis, case studies, surveys and experiments.

World research will also use ***other frameworks*** to collect data in relation to *peoples, places and systems, and across these:*

- *cross-sectional studies* which consider a topic at all three levels.
- *crowdsourcing research* – getting micro research tasks done by large numbers of people, often avoiding state control.
- *online research* – using the internet to search for 'knowns' to explain '*why?*', and for 'unknowns' to explain '*what?*'.

key reading

Buchana, D. and Bryman, A. (2009) *The Sage Handbook of Organizational Research Methods*. London: Sage.

De Smith, M.J. et al. (2006) *Geospatial Analysis: A Comprehensive Guide to Principles, Techniques and Software Tools.* London: Matador.

Ford, N. (2011) *The Essential Guide to Using the Web for Research*. London: Sage.

Hammersley, M. and Atkinson, P. (2007) *Ethnography: Principles in Practice*. London: Routledge.

Hantrais, L. (2008) *International Comparative Research: Theory, Methods and Practice.* Basingstoke: Palgrave Macmillan.

Williams, C. (2013) 'Crowdsourcing research: a methodology for investigating state crime', *State Crime*, 2 (1): 30–51.

online resources

To access the resources – search on the name in italics, use the http, or search on the generic term in 'quote marks'.

Library of Congress – 'public domain use', country studies – http://lcweb2.loc.gov/frd/cs/

BBC Country Profiles. CIA World Factbook. OECD Country Reports. The Economist World-in-figures app – country case studies

Google Trends – shows trends in the use of keyword searches, and the level of interest for basic demographics, including country

Maps of World – www.mapsofworld.com

UNStats – international statistics

OECD Data Lab – indexes and ranking of public service systems in developed nations

Ushahidi Project – online crowdsourcing tools

American Red Cross Digital Operations Centre Digital Methods Initiative – creates and provides links to web search tools

Collaborative Online Social Media Observatory (COSMOS) – open access, integrated set of social media research tools (data harvesting, together with detection and representation of topics, sentiment, tension, frequency, information flow, geospatial location and social network analysis), with the capability to link with official curated and administrative data sources – www.cs.cf.ac.uk/cosmos

GDELT – Global Data on Events, Location and Tone – open access, 200-million geolocated global news events, 1979 to the present – http://gdeltproject.org

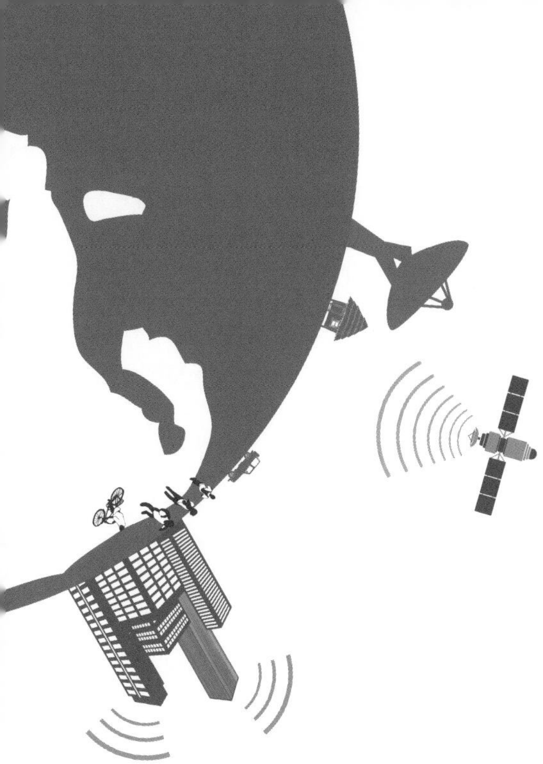

PART III

Doing the research

Chapter 7 – The obvious problem about world data is that the world is a big place, and so innovative technologies are central to efficient *data management*. Plans for finding, selecting, collecting, testing and transferring relevant data need to be considered before starting to collect data.

Chapters 8–13 then explain the techniques for collecting data in relation to the conceptual framework of the book:

- *peoples* – identifiable individuals and groups (interviews, observation), and *population studies* (surveys, big data).
- *places* – streets, urban, rural and coastal regions (texts, objects, buildings, environment), and *mapping*.
- *systems* – administrative and organizational research, and formal documents.

Understanding how technology has developed in the past can inspire innovations, but also help with understanding and reinterpreting previous world studies.

SEVEN

Data management

Before you plan data collection, make a cup of tea. But remember that (unless you are in China) this is only possible because of an innovative data transfer technology, and theft. The invention of the *Wardian Case* – a mini greenhouse – permitted a Scot, Robert Fortune, to smuggle Chinese tea plants from Shanghai to Assam, in 1824. The result of this botanical espionage, by the *East India Company*, was the wealthy tea business in Europe.[1]

Most studies will need a plan for data management, and that starts by researching relevant and innovative methods in methods books, specialist sites and technology magazines such as *Wired*. This chapter specifically considers the *finding, selecting, collecting, testing* and *transfer* of data. But innovative IT means that these aspects are often now carried out simultaneously. Robo-journalism systems can analyse online texts and write articles without human intervention, within three minutes of events such as earthquakes.[2]

The following chapters about data collection (C8–C13) assume a *mixed-methods* and *iterative* approach (C4.1). Not least, field trips are expensive, and when at the research site it is sensible to collect a range of relevant, or opportunistic, data in all possible ways. These chapters include doing *initial analysis* to create *findings* – the presentation of the data in a usable way with comment about possible biases and weaknesses. Chapter 14 then explains *further analysis*. But the broad aim of Part Three is to implement Marcel Proust's advice – 'to see the universe through the eyes of...others'.[3] And this does not come just from smart technologies. It needs smart researchers.

7.1 Research technologies

World research has always been influenced by new technologies to overcome problems of distance, access, scale, dispersed data, recording, and understanding others. So it is helpful to remember how technology has influenced similar research in the past, and how ideas can be reinvented and adapted to new needs. Many present-day innovations have a long history. In 2013, Google's *Project Loon* returned to using balloons to provide internet in remote regions. This uses stratospheric wind currents, much as the navigators of early sailing ships used sea currents and trade winds, and also the techniques of balloon research first used in the Boer War in 1900, which created the first *Google Earth* style maps.

A technology checklist should consider how devices might help with *access* (satellites, robots), *data capture* (life-loggers, sensors), *new interpretation* (dating, x-rays), *safety* (walkie-talkies, GPS tracking), and full *participation* of other language speakers, minority groups and people with disabilities (C5.3.1). The practicalities of using technologies abroad includes: checking the power supplies, taking spares, using robust common-brand equipment that can be repaired easily, and proactive thinking about who might repair devices in remote areas.

In sensitive settings, be aware that people might also be using devices to watch you, especially near embassies.[4] A handheld *Snoopy* device can monitor all mobile phone content, at gatherings like conferences or protests. Hotel rooms may be bugged. 'Bug detectors' are available, and there are basic strategies such as looking for small lights and listening for clicks and other noises.[5] Surveillance technologies are now cheap and available to all researchers. To be aware of what you, and others, could use, search 'spy equipment', monitor the *Surveillance Industry Index*, and check the local spyware shops.

thinking zone: how might "they" research you?

In many countries, outsider researchers may be seen as spies, sources of valuable information, or a way to make money through scams. The problem may be worse in so-called advanced counties such as America and Britain. Even friendly local colleagues may innocently report information back to line managers who are less friendly.

documents

Personal details can be used by others to send spam mail, or to create false personas, so take care with business cards, digital profiles, etc. Avoid personal identifiers that you might use on internet banking sites.

Internet

Anything you say, do or write can be compared with things about you online – university/organization CVs, *Wikipedia* sites, publishers' sites, papers in repositories, *Twitter*, *Facebook*, blogs. Research proposals are often open access, and must not contradict other explanations about research study visits.

listening

In some countries, hotel rooms are bugged with devices in electric sockets, light fittings, and phones. Phones may be tapped, including mobile phones. At venues like conferences, all mobile phone content can be captured on small handheld devices. Metal phone boxes, or wrapping the phone in tin foil, can deter this.

talking

Anyone who you talk to may be reporting, or recording, what you say and do – even people who you know well. Be suspicious of unknown people who are very helpful or friendly.

watching

In any public place CCTV, or people, may be following you.

IT

- Any form of software or hardware may also be spyware. Be suspicious of free USB sticks, CDs, downloads, etc.
- Any document that you send/give digitally can be used or plagiarized by others. Simple defences include not putting full references on conference papers, and only putting keywords or images on *PowerPoint* slides.

online

When doing online ethnography, how do you know that those you are researching are not also researching you?

so

Brainstorm improbable, funny scenarios around these issues, in relation to your trip. How would you know if the hotel toilet were listening to you, cats were filming you, and people you are researching online were also researching you?

7.2 Data management systems

A simple data ***management*** system may just entail setting up files that reflect the stages of the project and headings of a final report. Many books explain how to create good systems.[6] All forms of data need accurate *labelling*, and standard templates need to be used by all members of a research team. International standards for digital data are provided by the *Inter-University Consortium for Political and Social Research* (ICPSR). Tools such as *bulkrenameutility* can rename large data sets, if necessary. For digital data, the *formats* for the final data and reporting need to be considered early, because transferring formats can be problematic, and some formats are better than others for long-term storage – PDF not *Word*, TIFF or JPEG2000 not GIF or JPG, ASCII text not *Excel*. Sites like *MullermediaConversions* can reformat data. Photo management software – *Picasa, iPhoto, DigiBookShelf* – can sort and improve masses of digital photos. If a system is set up well, writing up a study simply entails working through the files and reporting what is relevant to the narrative of the report. If the filing system is good, the report will "write itself".

Secure storage is important, because data loss can wreck a project and waste money, and ethical considerations (C5) often dictate that data must be kept safe and destroyed at certain points. Many research funders and university departments require a *data management plan* before projects start.[7] *Loss or damage* might happen due to:

- *theft or malicious damage* – How will stores and systems be locked, who will have access, and how will access be recorded?
- *impacts* from floods, rain, fire, temperature extremes – Are proofed or sealed storage and transport systems needed?
- *power surges/losses* – Are electrical problems likely, and which devices can protect equipment?
- *systems problems* – Is professional help needed to set up and manage the system?
- *human error* – Is training, and ongoing reminders, needed to minimize mistakes?
- *hacking, virus attacks, blackmail or interception* – Might someone want to steal or destroy data, and if so, how?

Responsible funders will usually be willing to pay for setting up effective data management systems. If data is politically sensitive, or could endanger anyone, keep in mind that software now exists that can overcome any encryption, and restore all 'deletes', to some extent. The most secure practice is to isolate computers (no internet or wireless), and hard drives and other storage devices when in use, and afterwards to physically destroy them by grinding or burning. Alternatively, use handwriting and manual typewriters as top secret military departments do. The *Centre for the Protection of National Infrastructure* (CPNI) provides good advice and reports about security research.

For large projects, a designated person may be responsible for data ***risk analysis*** (C4.3) and ***curation***. This includes software updates, ensuring that data is anonymized (removing identifiers – file names and meta-data that indicates locations and time, etc.) and removal of redundant data. Backup systems are essential, and these must be tested for compatibility, ease of use, accurate restoring, correct meta-data and network access. Remote cloud storage may be useful, through companies such as *Elephant Drive* or *Jungle Disk*, or simply by sending documents to an email file. It is usually best to separate data *storage* from data *processing* – devices can go wrong and are more likely to be stolen. Use separate hard drives, and use many small storage cards (especially in digital cameras) rather than one large card. The *Get Safe Online* project has good up-to-date advice. Security also includes thinking about paper-based data – What if a notebook is lost or stolen immediately after, or during, an interview? Can data be coded as it is being written? How will paper data be disposed of safely? Simply leaving it to soak in soapy water makes it easy to mash and often removes or smudges ink. The dried mush can then be burned.

7.3 Finding data

Locating the sources of relevant world data – "knowing where to look" – often comes from personal experience, colleagues, or literature searches (C3). For archival work the *finding aids* systemized by the *International Council on Archives* are useful. It is helpful to develop systematic ways to search for world data, because these systems may reveal data sources in surprising places. Understanding the historical context of data can provide clues, for example, that artworks may be hidden during wars.

Basic questions can structure a search for data sources, often by using big data searches (C6.5; C8.4; C9.4):

- *Who* might provide information? Most organizations have 'staff' lists, and country desk officers in international organizations such as the UN often have a responsibility to help their compatriots. Sites such as *Facebook*, *LinkedIn* and *Twitter* may provide basic information on named people, which can be followed up through electoral lists, registers of births, marriages and deaths, property and company registers. *Google Images* may locate people through photos.
- *When* did relevant things happen? A keyword search on *Google Trends* or *Google Books Ngram* (Box 3.1) might indicate periods of relevant events or media interest in people or organizations. Archives and specialist librarians may help with historical events.
- *Where* did relevant things happen? Searches through media sites such as *al Jazeera* or *Russia Today* may reveal regional events. Big data sites, based on media feeds, such as *GDELT* may help to locate global events.

But sources near the researcher's home may provide better information than can be found by field visits – colonial archives, museums, or immigrant and refugee community centres.

Once at a ***research site***, simple *observation* – in shops, cafes, newspapers – can help locate, and understand minority and hidden groups (Figure 7.1). Local journalists and intelligence agencies address the problem of knowing where to look by ongoing *intelligence gathering* from informants, NGOs, other journalists and media, which is stored in organizational databases and archives. Companies and security services may also use *profiling* to develop sets of characteristics of those they may be interested in, which entails:[8]

- *defining problem-solution aims* – "to identify children at risk of trafficking".
- *identifying data sources* – "places attracting wealthy tourists (demand), and places with poor large families (supply)".
- *selecting out irrelevant data* – "places where children are locally available for sexual exploitation".
- *data mining* – "search for likely supply-and-demand networks".
- *verification* – "do results match on-the-ground reports (local press, NGO reports, TV documentaries)?"
- *refining profile* – "clarifying the characteristics of supply-and-demand networks".
- *decision to act* – "improve border checks at key places".

But profiling raises ethical considerations about collecting predictive data.[9] If it were possible to identify likely child-traffickers reliably, should people who fit the profile be forcibly detained or tagged, to protect children?

'Kangnam Cafe', with newspapers for the Koreans in Kazakhstan.

Figure 7.1 Finding minority groups

Photo: Author's own

7.4 Selecting data

Having found likely data sources, specific ***units*** of analysis then need to be selected. These will reflect the topic and focus of the study (C4.2) and also the level of the study. Studies of populations may entail researching the whole population of somewhere, but more usually a *sample* from that population (C9.3.3). This will either statistically represent a whole population (refugees, chefs) or qualitatively represent a small unique group (child refugees, immigrant chefs). But in real life, selection is often *opportunistic* – you just happen to be somewhere when something interesting occurs, and you use that opportunity to gather data (Box 7.1).

Box 7.1 Opportunistic data collection

Travel for my work as an army officer presented occasions for opportunistic data collection for my PhD. While in Iraq, Bosnia-Herzegovina and Cambodia, I was able to use personal notes, and reports and statistics from international organizations working in those countries. These provided an understanding of the context in each place. However, opportunistic data collection was potentially problematic.

- There was a risk that data sets were incomplete.
- Data that was easily available was likely to be partial and biased, particularly as it was only in English and freely shared with someone who was clearly a representative of the international community.
- Ethically, I had two distinct roles and identities – as a PhD student and an army officer – which needed to be acknowledged and kept separate depending on what I was doing.

In international research, understanding the context is particularly important. While there will be issues around any data obtained, opportunistic data collection should not be overlooked as a part of a wider approach to gathering evidence.

[Source: Johnstone, C. (2014) 'Adult education as a stabilizing response to conflict'. Unpublished PhD thesis, IoE/University of London.]

A further selection process is involved in qualitative studies, after data collection. This entails a method for extracting and organizing relevant data from notes, transcripts or observation records. The data is usually ***coded***,[10] perhaps in relation to research questions, and how this is done should be explained. Software such as *QDA Miner* can help. Coding is likely to entail a *coding frame*,[11] which can be developed when the questionnaires or schedules are being devised. At a basic level, coding may just mean reading a transcript and putting the research question number next to the relevant data. At a more sophisticated level, each question might link to a research hypothesis, and even to specific "mini-hypotheses" – detailed predictions about the expected response to each question, based on literature or theory. Alternatively, inductive or open coding permits the categories to emerge from the data, as in *grounded theory*.[12]

After expected types of data have been selected and coded, *saturated coding* can be used to assess the unexpected data that does not seem to fit anywhere. This data will either be the most important data in the study, because the researcher did not envisage it. Or it will be garbage.

7.5 Collecting data

There are three ways to ***access*** world data, explained further in C8–C13:

- Data that has already *arrived* at the researcher's "home" and is available in places like museums or archives, or through international travellers.
- Data that can be *acquired* – collected, sent, or purchased. (But consider the ethics if 'acquiring' represents stealing.)
- Data that can be *recorded* – through field notes or digital recording.

The degree of control the researcher has over data collection, on an international scale, needs thought. Obtaining first-hand *primary data* entails data collection that is controlled by the researcher, and collection often involves *fieldwork*. *Secondary data* has already been collected by someone else, collection methods cannot be controlled, but this data can be analysed in new ways, for example by museum researchers.[13] *Meta-data* is data about data, over which there is no control, such as records about computer or mobile phone use and other big data (C6.5).

Whatever the system, the aim is to create ways to find the right data, in the right form, about the right things, at the right time. Hybrid innovations that combine old and new are important. Thinking broadly about how world data has been found and collected throughout the long history of world research can inspire new ideas and the adaptation of old ideas (Figure 7.2).

Mode	Historical examples	Current examples	e-access
Arrived data just "turned up" via other people.	*Alexandria Library.* Private collections. Seals. Letters. War captives. Pilgrims. 'Human zoos'. World fairs.	Museums, archives, galleries. Documents at embassies or companies. Immigrants, international visitors, international newspapers.	TV/radio, film, music. *YouTube*. Photo galleries. Websites, blogs.
Acquired data was bought, given, taken or stolen.	Archaeological and anthropological objects. Botanical samples. Human exhibits.	Artefacts, books, merchandise. Samples from polluted sites or mass graves. Presents from friends & family.	Online auction sites. Downloaded files, photo galleries, digital archives.

Mode	Historical examples	Current examples	e-access
Recorded data was copied, noted, or curated.	Maps. Ships' logs. Travellers' notebooks. Military reports. Scientific drawings.	Fieldwork notes, diaries, photos, testimony. Video/ audio recordings. UAVs (drones).	Online research. Crowdsourced data. Satellites and sensors. Screenshots.

Figure 7.2 Ways to access world data

7.6 Testing data

Data is just a measure or account of something, and does not necessarily represent 'fact' or 'truth', and so it needs to be tested. The starting point is to revisit the relevant aspects of ontology and epistemology (C1.1). Testing may happen as data is being collected, soon after, or during analysis.

Interview and ***documentary data*** might be tested by asking: who is speaking, who are they speaking to, for what purpose are they speaking, and under what circumstances?[14] Other factors include style, manner, experience and social position.[15] Certain forms of evidence may be more trustworthy than others. Data from interviewees with little public accountability, such as spies, may need greater corroboration.[16] Defector and asylum seeker *testimony* is particularly problematic, as people in these situations often need to present a specific view of why they have fled from their persecutors, or are 'countering' a prevailing view of recent history.[17] And after testimony data has been collected and analysed, respondents are rarely asked to check its accuracy.[18] Corroboration against other factual evidence is therefore vital.

Triangulation tests a piece of data by comparing it with two or more other relevant pieces of data, as a police officer might test a witness statement against other statements and mobile phone records. The aim may be to validate a significant report, but it can also be to analyse the reasons for differences. Triangulation might entail comparing evidence through different 'lenses':[19]

- *methods* – observation ('demonstrated behaviour') can be used to check documentary accounts ('stated behaviour'), interviews can check survey data.
- *respondents* –the perspectives of politicians, social workers and refugees could be compared.
- *investigators* – data collected by English and other language speakers, insider and outsider researchers.
- *theories* – post-conflict education understood through human capital, peace stabilization and human rights theories.

More usually, different types of *data* about the same things are compared – press reports, drawings, photos and political songs.

Validity describes the degree to which data and findings represent what they claim to represent. Validity is often assessed through mixed methods[20] and *triangulation*. Validity tests are often applied to interviews.[21] The *aggregation* of statistical data ('composite data') can increase validity because the likelihood of a misleading score from a single source is greater than from taking the average score of a range of sources (C14.4). This can be tested further by a *split-half* check which randomly divides the indicators into two groups, and checks if the aggregate figure is similar for both.[22] If data is not valid, no form of testing or IT tricks can correct the problem.

Significance tests assess statistically how likely a result is due to chance (but not the degree of the causal relationship). Testing starts with a null hypothesis – that there is no difference between two variables – which the tests confirm or not. In statistical terms 'significance' implies that there is little likelihood that a result occurred by chance – usually less than 5%. But these 'significance levels' have arisen from tradition not objective statistical fact.[23] Statistical tests also do not assess the quality of data – if it was collected carelessly, that will probably not be detected or corrected by tests.

Reliability is the degree to which, if the study were repeated in exactly the same way, it would provide the same findings. If three researchers independently drew flow charts of the networks of the same transnational corporations (TNCs), would the findings be the same? Assessing reliability is often hypothetical in world research because the likelihood of repeating a study is low. But the reliability of previous studies can be assessed by, for example, identifying unclear questions or concepts, particularly with translations – does "people who voted" include people who voted but deliberately spoiled their papers as a protest? Simple *test-retest* checks can also assess reliability. In an interview a key question might be repeated throughout the interview, in different ways.

Understanding the checks used by large reputable media organizations, such as the BBC, can provide practical insights into the rapid testing of world data (Figure 7.3).[24] Professional verification is usually a mix of assessing validity and reliability, and triangulation, and a lot of common sense.

Verifying world evidence **BBC**

Check:

- stated locations on maps. Is it plausible that someone in that place could report that event?
- images with existing images from those locations. (Is that the correct 'parliament building'?)
- images with weather data. (Was it really snowing at that time in that place?)
- audio data to see if accents and language are correct for the location. (An Egyptian would greet by saying '*Iziak*', a Jordanian with '*Kifhalik*'.)
- the original source of the upload/sequences as an indicator of date.
- weaponry, vehicles and licence plates against those known for the given country.
- previously verified material.

Figure 7.3 BBC processes for verifying social media content

7.7 Transferring data

In the 1930s, explorer Thor Heyerdahl was caught when returning to Norway from the Marquesas Islands with a gun butt carved by the artist Gauguin. Unfortunately it was still attached to the gun, which did not amuse immigration officials. But one official had the wit to ask him to detach the butt from the gun. The official kept the gun, and Heyerdahl took his precious data home. Most researchers are not so lucky.

Transferring ***physical*** data entails checking what can legally be exported and imported, and how this must be done safely. Many countries regulate the export of any object deemed an antique, which could be a string of beads from a market. And import restrictions can include items such as nasal sprays into Japan. Posting items may be prohibited if they are hazardous, or be very expensive and attract import duty. Some postal services, such as Britain's *Royal Mail,* will levy very exploitative charges for collecting small amounts of import duty. To minimize the seriousness of loss, post many smaller packages, each with mixed copies of data, not one large parcel. If carrying sensitive data, put it in innocent but unobtrusive places in luggage, but do not hide it in secret compartments because customs officials look for these, and obvious deceit can lead to criminal charges. A micro-SD card is probably safe in a toiletries bag, if you can find it afterwards.

Documentary data, including digital, can often be seized on the dubious grounds of national security, impropriety, or politicized regulations. This could include photos of women not wearing *hijabs* in an Islamic country. US border officials operate like Wild West bandits, and can seize anything they like, without any reason. Carrying data in seemingly innocent formats can help to avoid attention. Art may be a less conspicuous means to transfer interesting political data. A street child's drawing of police violence in Soweto during the apartheid era was unlikely to attract the attention that photographic data would, although a child's drawing of the police could also be illegal.

Postal services will provide lists of what cannot be posted without using formal ***hazard*** procedures, which may include batteries, human and animal remains, knives and poisons.[25] The WHO provides detailed advice about transferring hazardous materials and infectious substances,[26] and the *International Air Transport Association* (IATA) (which provides a *Dangerous Goods Manual*[27]) can help with training about classification, documentation, labelling, packing and supervision. But, of course, sometimes the most important data *is* transferred illegally. In 2013, blood and urine samples smuggled out of Syria to the British military Porton Down centre provided evidence of chemical weapons use.

Transferring data ***digitally*** not only applies to documents and statistical data. As devices such as 360° cameras, mini video recorders and 3D scanners and printers become more available, visual and audio data is increasingly transferrable online.

Platforms such as *Dropbox* and *Skydrive* facilitate transferring large amounts of data, and the trend towards 'open access' encourages researchers to put raw data from research sites immediately online. Toolsets such as UNICEF's *Rapid SMS* permit data collection, streamlining complex workflows and group coordination, using basic mobile phones, and the system can then present information on the internet immediately. This can assist with things like remote health diagnostics, nutrition monitoring and supply-chain tracking.

Transferring ***politically sensitive*** data is obviously problematic because online systems are not secure. Although seeing the 'https' lock indicates an encrypted transfer, the US, UK and other intelligence agencies can intercept and decode this. There are ways to avoid IP-address tracking.[28] The free *TOR* software encrypts data and masks the original IP address. Simpler strategies include photographing or scanning written material, and sending as JPG files, because writing on image files is harder to detect than emails or *Word* attachments. End-to-end encryption claims to be totally secure, but ultimately we never know who has set up, controls or infiltrates seemingly secure systems, and sometimes the use of secure systems attracts attention. Even governments are unable to transmit data securely, as *Wikileaks* demonstrates. Meshnet systems such as *Firechat* may be better.

New technologies are bringing significant changes to how we can transfer data around the world. Organizations such as the *Public Initiative for Information Security* support the development of more secure systems, such as *Hiding Duck*. Tracking with *Radio Frequency Identification* (RFI) means that physical data is much less likely to get lost in transit. Robots – such as the *Dolphin-cam* which can swim at 20 mph – can now stream video instantly.[29] With hydrogen fuel cell engines, UAVs, carrying cameras, will be able to stay in the air, streaming video data, for up to 30 hours. Improved 3D scanners and printers will permit the reproduction of objects quickly, from anywhere to anywhere. Conservation groups such as *Factum Arte* can digitally recreate damaged historical objects, and even small buildings, such as Tutankhamun's tomb.[30] Eventually nano-fabricators will extend this to recreating the actual materials. And if researchers still want to write and draw their field notes by hand, robot arms will be able to replicate what they do, in real time, anywhere.[31]

Data management technologies have always been significant within world research. And they have helped us to move from state-controlled companies stealing data as with the *Wardian Case*, to states and companies being deterred from stealing data with the *Hiding Duck*. Micro-cameras now come in many disguises. But always keep in mind that the people you are studying with a spying device may also be studying you with a spying device. Those blank windows at the top of US embassies and other government buildings might be hiding powerful listening and interception equipment.[32]

main ideas

Data management systems entail thinking about:

- *secure storage*, which protects from theft or malicious damage, and other impacts.
- *asking funders* to pay for setting up systems.
- who is responsible for *risk analysis* and *curation* of data.

Finding data entails asking:

- *who* can provide information?
- *when* did relevant events happen?
- *where* did things happen?
- is *intelligence gathering* useful?
- are *profiling* systems relevant?

Selecting data entails identifying *units of analysis*, and *samples from* relevant *populations.*

- *Probability* samples will statistically *represent* the whole population.
- *Opportunistic* and other samples are useful to study small interesting groups.
- Qualitative data will be *coded* to ensure unbiased use.

Collecting data is likely to entail thinking about data that

- has already *arrived.*
- can be *acquired.*
- can be *recorded.*

Testing data includes:

- *triangulation* by comparing different types of data, or differing views about the same data.
- *validity* tests to assess whether findings represent what they claim to represent.
- *significance* tests to assess if a result is just chance.
- *reliability* assessments to judge if similar results would be found if the study were repeated.

Transferring data is a distinct problem on a world scale:

- *Physical data* may be lost because of theft or carelessness, export or import regulations, or be expensive to post. If materials are *hazardous* they require special packing and sending in line with international regulations.
- *Digital data* is very easy to manage and send, but also very vulnerable.
- New technologies permit real-time video streaming of data, the 3D replication of objects anywhere in the world, and smart systems to deter interception.

key reading

Hesse-Biber, S.N. (ed.) (2013) *The Handbook of Emergent Technologies in Social Research*. Oxford: Oxford University Press.

van den Eynden, V. et al (2011) *Managing and Sharing Data*. Colchester: UK Data Archive.

online resources

To access the resources – search on the name in italics, use the http, or search on the generic term in 'quote marks'.

Surveillance Industry Index – tracks state and commercial surveillance systems – www.privacyinternational.org/sii/

ICPSR – international standards for labelling digital data

Trade Quotes – converting old data to current formats – www.tradequotesinc.com

Renaming files – http://renamer4mac.com

Get Safe Online – www.getsafeonline.org

Remote storage – *Elephant Drive* – www.elephantdrive.com. *Jungle Disk* – www.jungledisk.com/mote

ICPSR – international standards for file formats. Social science data – www.icpsr.umich.edu/ICPSR/access/dataprep.pdf

QDA Miner – qualitative analysis tool, including coding – http://provalisresearch.com/products/qualitative-data-analysis-soft (*QDA Miner Lite* is a free smaller version)

Public Initiative for Information Security – www.publisec.org

WHO – transporting hazardous materials and infectious substances – www.who.int/ihr/infectious_substances/en/

EIGHT

Researching people

When travelling, annoying people – corrupt police, arrogant officials and inept hotel staff – are not a nuisance, they are a wonderful source of data. The starting point for most research by outsiders should be chatting to, and watching, people in airports and train stations, buses and taxis. Human data is everywhere. If you are studying child labour, your data will probably meet you from the airport bus, carry your bag to your hotel, and turn up next morning to clean your shoes.

As in Europe 300 years ago, present-day coffee shops, bars and cafes are productive research venues. Pubs might have old music boxes, or clocks, which play music recorded by pins in wooden drums, tongued metal disks, or holes.[1] Comparing performances on these early "CDs" with written scores shows that music was not always performed as it was written. For example, 300 years ago, notes *written* equally might be *played* unequally (*inégale*), like 'swing' in jazz.[2] A study of local arts could be informed by visiting bars next to theatres, and political research could start with a cake in an underground cafe. It is useful to find out how local researchers research local people. They may have locally-appropriate methods, and realize things that an outsider would not. How else do you find out that the face iced on your cake is a South Korean political prisoner, or that the photos of the beautiful Japanese actresses are all men?

This chapter concerns research with *people* who belong to a particular place – identifiable individuals or small specific groups – ***human subjects***. Data collection about large groups of people – *populations* – is explained in C9, and the study of transient, anonymous groups of people in *public places* in C10. *Reading, asking, watching, listening* and *online research* will provide a mix of primary and secondary data. *Cross-cultural* approaches to analysis are likely to be necessary,[3] but this must be done with an awareness of the dubious history of researching *others* (C2.1; C5.3). The basic methods come from *history*[4] and *ethnography*,[5] *cultural studies*, or '*culturology*'.[6] But early data about **other** peoples needs to be interpreted carefully.

thinking zone: what if...?

othering

Theories of 'othering' peoples on the basis of race and other perceived differences were created and promoted by respected elites – doctors, anthropologists, religious leaders, politicians.

counterfactuals

'Counterfactual' – contrary to the facts – analysis asks "what if..." certain things had or had not happened, to understand causal factors better.

- What if... ordinary people had *not* learned racist ideologies from elites? Would racism still exist among the masses? Would nationalistic wars have happened?
- What if... Nazi Germany had *not* put eugenics theories into practice in the death camps, leading to a worldwide condemnation of scientific racism? How might the theories of scientific racism and eugenics have developed?
- What if... Meiji Japan had not learned of the European eugenics theories? How might the ethnocentric ideologies of the Meiji rulers have developed?

futures

- What are the present, and possible future, equivalents of scientific racism?
- How can we identify 'othering', ethnocentricism and exceptionalism in our own research?
- How can the ethics of research funding try to prevent harmful research about 'others'?

Outsider researchers are inevitably shielded from certain types of local people, and so a study design should aim to *triangulate* (C7.5) a range of views from:

- *elites* – select people, often decision-makers, who can provide an *overview* of something – leaders, managers, administrators. But they may present a politicized or self-promotional perspective.
- *experts* – people who can explain *objective knowledge* gained through professional endeavours or specific skills – scientists and artists, doctors and agronomists. But their view might reflect a specific school of thinking or disciplinary outlook.
- *representatives* – people who identify themselves with a certain group and may explain *group-related experiences* – tribal or nomadic groups, young/old, male/female, professionals or manual workers. But they may only represent a partial, perhaps self-interested, viewpoint.
- *locals* – people (including visitors) who know about a particular *location* – town, village, coast – or *setting* – factories, hospitals, prisons. But they may not be able to explain their circumstances in a broader context.
- *transitionary people* – people experiencing a movement from one circumstance to another – geographical, political, personal, cultural – who have knowledge about that *change*. But during the period of change they may not fully understand what is happening.

Elites and *experts* are likely to provide *exogenous* or *etic* data; *representatives, locals* and *transitionary* people will probably provide *endogenous* or *emic* accounts (C6.1). In the 1980s, a 12-year-old South African street child might provide an insider view of prison, but would probably not be able to explain the political context of the apartheid system. Of course, the same individuals may have different personas or roles in different circumstances. Relating to these can sometimes help to win trust and gain access to people in sensitive jobs. For a gender study, going to a local football match with an army colonel may be more productive than interviewing her in her HQ.

8.1 Reading about people – documents, biographies, texts

Numerous types of ***document*** provide information about people, which helps to discover and compare life histories and viewpoints – press, blogs, prints and photos, letters, company or government reports. These may be *about* or *by* relevant individuals. Many countries have useful national *archives*, the homes of historical figures may have libraries, and there are countless family collections of material. Old documents can also be analysed as *objects* (C10.7). *Documentary analysis* and *content analysis* are explained further in C13.2.

Biographies provide an in-depth account of the lives of individuals, but they are often based on secondary data, and so may be unreliable.[7] *Oral histories*[8] and psychological approaches[9] can provide better empirical evidence. *Autobiography* may come from many years of methodical diary-keeping, and *diaries* themselves can be a valuable source of data.[10] *Memoirs* tend to be more personal, focusing on feelings and emotions about significant events. Autobiographies and memoirs usually disclose little that is new or interesting about the author, but may reveal a lot about their colleagues, friends and family. A selection of autobiographies might need to be studied systematically. To study Ms Z:

1. The autobiography of Ms Z is analysed in relation to a *relevant and specific time period.*
2. Friends, colleagues and others are identified, within this time period.
3. Autobiographies and biographies of those people (2) are analysed during the same time period.
4. Further data for that time period is sought through online research.
5. Analysis compares all sources, relevant to Ms Z.

Biographical analysis might compare numerous biographies, which are categorized under relevant headings (violent, non-violent), looking for factors (negative self-image, victimization, corruption), and rating the degree of these factors on a scale, to identify predictors of a characteristic (violent leadership).[11]

Images within documents need to be understood critically, especially historical ones.[12] Early 'data capture' was often set up in a studio, and the purpose was sometimes to emphasize the "primitive" nature of indigenous people, and the superiority of the elites. Looking at context can help to validate depictions. Photos showing people in the context of foreground, background and consistent natural shadows are more likely to be genuine than those showing no context, just a backdrop, or remarkably good lighting. Common sense is a good fake-detector, and with digital images, increasing the 'contrast' can help to detect changes. Unfortunately, *Photoshop* can now fix things like shadows. But *Error Level Analysis* (ELA) – on free sites such as *Imageforensics* and *fotoforensics* – can indicate digital changes and additions, and reveal meta-data that can verify the integrity of photos.[13]

The alteration of images by, or about, powerful people can sometimes be more revealing than the original image. The airbrushing of people who had gone out of favour, from formal photos, was common in Communist China and the Soviet Union. In the former Yugoslavia, Milosevic's photographers added extra people to make crowds look bigger at his political rallies – the same group appeared many times across one picture.

8.2 Asking and listening – interviews, participant observation, focus groups

Data collection through asking and listening might involve formal *interviews, participant observation* and *focus groups,* or by informally asking questions at public presentations, radio phone-ins, or during opportunistic chats. Researching people does not only mean investigating lives, but also understanding death (Box 8.1). This has many applications – in health care, counselling, forensic investigations. And as communities become more cosmopolitan, cross-cultural understanding and empathy are becoming more important.

Box 8.1 Researching death in an African context

Death must be studied within the contexts of the cultures and religions that shape people's lives.

Among healthy people, a discussion or interview about death and dying would usually be uncomfortable as it may suggest impending doom. The Igbo tribe in Nigeria prides itself as a culture that celebrates life and despises death. Likewise, in the religious context, discussing death could be seen as a curse.

However, to those who are dying, there is a more open acceptance of death. Riding on religion, the time of death and its circumstances are believed to be beyond human control, and so easily accepted, even with gladness.

Sensitivity to cultural and religious traditions is therefore important, for example asking a female to interview women.

[See: Murray, S.A. et al. (2003) 'Dying from cancer in developed and developing countries', *British Medical Journal*, 326 (368): 1–5.]

Olúgbénga Awòlaràn
(International Student Advisor)

The main problem was recognized by al-Bīrūnī a thousand years ago – 'lies' (Figure 8.1). Methods books often give a lot of credence to interview data, though this may be less true in world contexts, not least because of language and cultural differences. Even if people do not 'lie', interview responses are only what someone says, about what they think about something, at a particular moment. They may have never thought about that question before, and they may have a different view tomorrow. And the presence of the interviewer can influence the responses – people may try to give "clever" or "correct" answers, and poor people may give responses that they think may benefit them in some way.

Follow-ups are therefore valuable to see if answers are consistent or if views have changed and, if so, why? This is difficult if time is limited, but it is possible to build in a follow-up mechanism, by using email, or giving stamped-addressed envelopes and cards with *Questions for next week*. A responsible local person – teacher, village head, health worker – might be asked to do follow-up interviews and forward the responses. Following up initial explanations about places and objects can also provide valuable in-depth insights about a country, which would not be evident from initial explanations.

We must distinguish different classes of reporters.

One of them tells a lie, as intending to further an interest of his own, either *by lauding* his family or nation, because he is one of them, or *by attacking* the family or nation on the opposite side, thinking that thereby he can gain his ends.

Another one tells a lie regarding a class of people whom he likes, as being under obligations to them, or whom he hates because something disagreeable has happened between them.

Another tells a lie because he is of such a base nature as to aim thereby at some profit, or because he is such a coward as to be afraid of telling the truth.

Another tells a lie because it is his nature to lie, and he cannot do otherwise, which proceeds from the essential meanness of his character and the depravity of his innermost being.

Lastly, a man may tell a lie from ignorance, blindly following what others told him.

Abū Rayhān al-Bīrūnī, *India* (circa 1030)

Figure 8.1 Lies

Informal chats might include off-the-record meetings in a bar or cafe to understand the background to something. The difference between a casual chat in a bar and 'data collection' is that researchers will talk in a way that is *intentional, planned* and *systematic* – they chat with a purpose. They will have a specific *interest, research questions*, or *hypotheses*. Opportunistic chats in a shop or marketplace might not use notebooks or voice recorders, but could entail casually using the key questions of a study, for example about tourist behaviour, supply chains, or corporate corruption. But keep in mind that your interviewee may also be researching *you*. Traders may watch your face to judge your level of interest, or ask where you are staying to have your room searched or burgled while you are out.

Formal interview techniques are discussed in-depth in standard methods books,[14] including *group interviews*, and may include observing body language. Advice about interviewing in different contexts covers: international organizations,[15] political settings,[16] national contexts,[17] national leaders,[18] cross-cultural discussions,[19] spies[20] and intelligence officers.[21] Different disciplines discuss specific approaches, such as those of international relations[22] and development studies.[23] Less is written about interviews with people who have mental health problems, learning disabilities,[24] or visual or other impairments (See: International Student Advisors, Heba Kholeif. Boxes 6.2, 8.2)

Structured interviews follow a detailed interview *schedule* or *questionnaire*. This might be graduated from semi-structured to highly structured, or move from 'non-threatening' to 'threatening' questions.[25] The structure may be staged, in terms of 'the opening, the grand tour, and the follow-up', reflecting different styles – 'journalistic', 'therapeutic' (building trust and rapport), or 'investigative'.[26] In general, contentious but important topics are usually left until the end of an interview, in order to avoid the possibility that an interviewee may walk out before answering most of the questions. The format is often complicated if it entails *routing* – "If no, then go to..." Tablet or laptop-based interview schedules can make this easier, and when answers are in-putted initial analysis may be immediate.

Semi-structured interviews permit flexibility yet maintain focus, but it is hard to maintain consistency if they are done by more than one interviewer. These might explore *life histories*, or memories of a significant event, in-depth. Alternatively, mixed approaches might be used by 'tandem' interviewers who switch roles strategically – one notes body language while the other asks questions.[27] How will interviews be *recorded* – notes, audio recorders, videos? There may be no second chances, and so backup recorders may be vital. If the setting has a lot of background noise, or the interviewee does not speak the interview language clearly, lapel microphones can help.

Investigative interviews often use psychological methods, and in forensic settings interviewers need a good knowledge of process and relevant jargon.[28] *Cognitive interviews*[29] use techniques to enhance memory and increase recall by people who appear unconfident when replying to questions. Techniques include reconstructing context, insisting on complete unedited descriptions, recalling events in forward and backward timescales, changing the perspective of the recall – seeing from a different angle or as another person. A central principle is that each interview needs to be planned in a way that is compatible with each interviewee, especially traumatized people such as defectors.[30]

Experienced interviewers may use techniques for ***extending interviews***. Having asked a few key questions they might:

- *comment on an object in the interviewee's room* – a picture, vase, carpet – which may lead to a discussion about where it came from, which provides data about social and family networks.
- *build on what the interviewee has just been doing* – if they have just come from a meeting or field visit, ask about it.
- *ask for advice* – "If I (my son/daughter/friend/students) wanted to get a job like yours, what would you suggest?" – "What would you put in a curriculum for management training?"
- *use flattery* – "Your staff all seem so cheerful. Why is that?" – "I don't think there is anyone else who could explain this properly." – "I think you understand this better than anyone else."
- *mention mutual, or impressive, friends or colleagues* – "I also studied English at that college, did you know...?"

Interviews may be optimized if the interviewee believes she or he will be compared with others. Other interviews can be mentioned to prompt or provoke more discussion – "I believe that the *Imam* does not completely agree with you..." It is always worth asking, "Who else would you suggest I talk to?" because this reveals networks and provides the basis for negotiating access. Providing feedback of initial analysis may be an effective means to gain more data and improve accuracy, because at that point interviewees have invested time in the work and have an interest in ensuring its accuracy.

Focus groups[31] provide a compromise between interviewing and a full survey (C9.3). They can be done online,[32] utilize a range of technologies,[33] and be used internationally for topics such as health[34] and media studies.[35] A facilitator will ask basic questions, and perhaps use prompts to elicit further views.[36] Group dynamics can be noted – how members influence one another, and how discussions evolve. For some groups, a more visual *non-verbal* method might be more appropriate. Reliable recording is essential, as it is not possible to repeat anything. A simple focus group might be recorded with two voice recorders. A lone researcher might use a *smart pen* which links an audio recording to written notes. A captioner (court recorder) could use a stenotype machine linked to a laptop. If clear and comprehensive records are needed, individual radio microphones can be linked to different channels on the recorder. Different video cameras might film specific aspects such as group-shots, leadership, body language, males and females. Another researcher might note non-verbal body language, and things of especial interest in a notebook (Figure 8.2).

Figure 8.2 A focus group

Photo: Angela Latorre (with permission from participants)

Translation and interpretation are often main considerations. Phone-based translation services and smart phones are useful for the basics, and this includes *Video Remote Interpreting* (VRI) using sign language for people who have hearing, speech or other language impairments.[37] Bilingual research assistants are likely to do a better job if they have a good understanding of the aims of the whole project. For distance interviews, sending interview questionnaires to interviewees who speak other languages might help them to prepare clear responses. Or it could lead to sanitized answers prepared by lawyers. A compromise is to outline the areas of questioning – "What you learned from your sitar teacher in Bangladesh?" – but not the exact questions. Online and smart phone translation software creates new opportunities.

Transcription of recorded data is expensive. For a linguistics study, full transcription may be essential to understand the detail. But when general interview data contains a lot of irrelevant material, a researcher might just note the counter numbers on the recorder when something relevant is said, and then only transcribe those parts. If translators or interpreters are used, how will they be briefed, and will their transcripts be double checked by back-translation? This was understood 1000 years ago (Figure 8.3).[38] *Voice recognition software* (*Word* – 'accessibility', *Dragon Naturally Speaking*) can create transcripts, but it needs to be trained to recognize specific voices.

> ...we have sometimes written down a word from the mouth of Hindus, taking the greatest pains to fix its pronunciation, and then afterwards when we repeated it to them, they had great difficulty in recognising it.
>
> Abū Rayhān al-Bīrūnī, *India* (circa 1030)

Figure 8.3 Back-translation

Interviews with ***elites*** and ***experts*** usually entail a brief one-off chance to meet a busy person at an inconvenient moment, and present distinct difficulties.[39] Not least, people who have power on a global scale may try to control an interview.[40] The strategies for gaining *access*, *"surgical" questioning* and *prolonging interviews* are explained in *Researching Power, Elites and Leadership*.[41] Interviews with politicians may amount to extracting specific 'memoirs' rather than information.[42] Promising feedback of initial analysis to managers may be an effective means to gain more data and improve accuracy, because at that point they have invested time in the work and have an interest in ensuring its accuracy. Preparation is vital. Asking busy people obvious questions that are answered on their website is not a good way to start an interview.

Talking and listening with ***representatives, locals*** and ***transitionary*** people may not be so pressured, but the techniques may need to be more sophisticated to ensure inclusion of vulnerable or minority groups, children[43] or women. Indirect methods may work best with vulnerable people, who may have had bad experiences from answering formal questions. Thematic drawing (draw and tell) is an effective methodology, and people "tell a story about the drawing" rather than answering direct questions.[44] Asking children to do thematic role play with glove puppets – made quickly from plastic bags, tape and paper cups – can also overcome inhibitions (Figure 8.4).[45]

Figure 8.4 Using puppets

Source: Williams, C. (1990) 'Street children and education' – http://etheses.bham.ac.uk/698

Certain people, cultural groups, contexts and places may require greater ***sensitivity*** (Box 8.2), and this is not only because people are vulnerable. In his research among Taliban leaders, Matt Waldman used a 'divide and rule' strategy – 'all interviewees were contacted and interviewed separately...none is based in the same district as another, and none disclosed to comrades that they were being interviewed'.[46]

Box 8.2 Sensitive interviewing

In Egypt, talking about anything related to sexual experiences is considered a taboo. This is even more difficult when the interviewees are visually impaired, as society has very low expectations for these girls as wives-to-be. Educating them about sex is very rare, and families, especially mothers, do not discuss this.

So I avoided asking the interviewee directly about herself. I used the third person, or I tried to ask as if I were asking their general point of view about sex education, or if it is different for a female with visual impairment, or how society views her as a wife. I asked a mother as if I were talking about her view of *other* parents of girls with visual impairment.

And things changed after the 25th of January Revolution, because before that Egyptians lived in an authoritarian regime, and discussing politics was not allowed. Now, everyone is discussing politics. But because there is a strong attack on the Muslim Brotherhood from the media, people who are pro the Brotherhood are afraid to declare this as they are scared of the criticism they will face from the general public.

هبة خليف Heba Kholeif
(International Student Advisor)

Voice Over Internet (VOI) and ***phone interviews*** require careful preparation,[47] because misunderstandings are hard to remedy at a distance. Not least, check time zones. Like any interview, the opening 'warm-up', to establish rapport, needs to be planned. If *Skype* or other video systems are used, the question of what to wear may be important, because the image will probably be small and poor quality. Similarly, check what is behind you – a glamour poster may not create the right impression. If possible, use a separate camera and microphone, because the quality is better. Microsoft has developed fully interactive translation software that can be used on VOI systems. Photos and *PowerPoint* slides can be used with VOI, as a basis for questions. An online interview can have gaps – for minutes, hours, or weeks – while interviewees find helpful materials or check facts. Similarly, it is possible to do experiments online, and to ask interviewees to talk to colleagues, family or others.[48] Short ***email questionnaires*** can work well. But, unless it is certain that the respondent will provide a long reply, put the questions in the email, visible in one email screen. Attachments or a seemingly endless list will probably not get a reply. Online surveys are outlined in C9.3.

Life-logging – automated diary-keeping – provides an alternative to interviews. Devices such as *Autographer* can capture visual and audio data at intervals throughout a day, automatically about people with interesting lives – traders, refuse collectors, farmers. Alternatively, they might become research assistants – 'human sensors' – and record specific data occurring during their daily life – tourists, fishing, police conduct. *GPS tracking* devices can be used, but this requires full explanation and consent from those who wear them. *Walkie-talkies* can permit assistants to send commentaries directly to researchers, and to keep in touch for safety. 'Electric tattoos', in the form of tiny microphones stuck to the throat, may soon be able to transmit speech wirelessly, and eliminate background noise. This creates the possibility of very unobtrusive real-time data transmission. These techniques obviously require specific training, ethical discussion and risk analysis (C5.4).

Advances in ***robotics*** and ***natural language processing*** are presenting new possibilities.[49] Robots are able to have interactive discussions – to teach languages, provide therapy,[50] chat with astronauts,[51] monitor elderly people. Robot-mediated interviews have been tested with children, using a familiar 'schedule': establishing a rapport, asking for free narrative recall, asking questions, closure and thanks.[52] Independent robot interviewers present many potential advantages. Robots will keep to their script consistently across countless interviews, and work in many languages. They could route yes/no answers quickly, use Likert and other rating scales, record video and audio, and use voice recognition to transcribe and translate answers. The data could be sent wirelessly to a cloud platform, in real time. Robot interviewers can smile, wink, nod encouragingly and sing songs. They have infinite patience and stay polite, appear confidential, and require no training after being programmed. Robots are much cheaper than humans and, if they disagree with you, then you can just switch them off (Figure 8.5).

Figure 8.5 A robot Interviewer (Japan, 2013)
Photo: Author's own

8.3 Watching and listening – observation, group discussions, experiments

Observation[53] – *watching* how people behave and *listening* to what they say and to the music and sounds they make[54] – provides the chance to analyse language[55] and body language.[56] Observation can also happen during interviews (C8.2), group discussions and experiments,[57] and might include reflection on how the experience affected the researcher. As with interviews, *translation* and *recording data* need to be considered. *Observation schedules* provide a framework for logging data, and use time-frames and shorthand symbols. They might note the frequency of certain behaviour in one-minute blocks, for example how often police take bribes from motorists at checkpoints. 'Rapid' methods are evolving.[58] Observations are usually recorded as *field notes,* which are often in digital form.[59] But in sensitive contexts, some form of *encryption* of notes and sketches may be necessary, in case they are seen by participants. This can use very simple signs such as circles, lines, crosses for different types of people or activities.

Within ***ethnomusicology*** (C6.1) listening and observing are complemented by *listener research.* Recording devices not only capture data, but can present audio material to elicit responses. A study might play respondents folk or pop music from other countries, to discover how they perceive it. Researchers from countries that were formerly the "object" of study are now researching how their own cultures have international influence, for example the influence of Kazakh music in Europe. Mobile phone and other audio recorders make basic ethnomusicology feasible as part of any fieldwork.

Participant observation[60] has been central to ethnography,[61] and is based on intensive, usually long-term, involvement, which may range from partial to total. This raises ethical and risk concerns (C5), which entail trade-offs between deceit, personal safety and over-influencing the behaviour of those being observed. A range of standard methods are used, and data collection may be overt, covert, or 'unobtrusive'.[62] *Visual research* may consider accessories such as clothes, hair-styles and electronics.[63] For an outsider, blending in with a group is not always easy, and there are sometimes no simple solutions, except to be aware of how others will see you.

New technologies are creating many opportunities for ***remote observation***, and the principles of traditional forms of observation can still be applied. Parliaments, war crimes tribunals, shareholders meetings and many similar events are webcast in real time, and have archives, podcasts and transcripts of proceedings. These provide the chance to observe people in challenging situations in great detail. Observation can include question–response styles, the use of prepared versus spontaneous responses, media skills and obfuscation. *Emotions analytics* software can use 10–15 seconds of speech, irrespective of language, to analyse *how* things are said, rather than *what* is said, to assess mood, attitude and emotional personality.[64]

8.4 Researching people online

Online research (C6.5) can use the internet as a research *tool* (examples are in the relevant sections above), or as an *object* of research (discussed here and C9.4).[65] Online studies about people are usually small-scale, feasible for single researchers, and are explained under headings like 'digital anthropology',[66] 'virtual ethnography',[67] 'online ethnography,[68] 'netography',[69] 'multi-sited ethnography'[70] and 'social media research'.[71] Studies might focus on behaviour that is uniquely online, such as online grooming.[72] Data collection may simply entail capturing relevant material for later analysis using screen shots, or researchers may make notes like traditional fieldwork notes. The internet also creates the opportunity for large-scale cross-national/cultural web-based ***experiments***, which are mainly in the field of psychology.[73] Simple online tools are available, and the *Web Experiment List* helps with recruitment and lists experiments. Open source software is increasingly available, in specific fields such as *international development.*[74] Examples of online questionnaires are on the website.

Relevant ***online texts*** may be found under headings such as 'staff profiles', 'management structure', or 'chair's report'. *Wikileaks* proposes a simple methodology for accessing and *crowdsourcing* analysis (C6.4) of its online data:[75]

- search for events you remember that happened, for example in your country.
- browse by date or search for an origin near you.
- pick out interesting events and tell others about them.
- use *Twitter, Reddit,* mail – whatever suits your audience best.

Online texts are not always what they seem and the sources need to be verified through checking the web address and contact details against other information. Comparative research can be based on keywords and likely names (Figure 8.6).[76]

As I got older, that gut instinct – that America is the greatest country on earth – would survive my growing awareness of our nation's imperfections (Missouri, June 2008).

I believe in American exceptionalism, just as I suspect that the Brits believe in British exceptionalism and the Greeks believe in Greek exceptionalism (NATO, Strasbourg, April 2009).

I believe we should act. That's what makes America different. That's what makes us exceptional...let us never lose sight of that essential truth. (Speech to the Nation, 10 September 2013).

Some may disagree, but I believe America is exceptional, in part because we have shown a willingness, to the sacrifice of blood and treasure to stand up, not only for our own interests, but for the interests of all. (Speech to UN General Assembly, 4 September 2013).

Barak Obama, President of the USA

It is extremely dangerous to encourage people to see themselves as exceptional, whatever the motivation...We are all different, but when we ask for the Lord's blessings, we must not forget that God created us equal. (*New York Times*, 20 September 2013)

Vladimir Putin, President of Russia

Figure 8.6 Comparative exceptionalism

Simple searches of ***big data*** can sometimes provide clues for further in-depth research, and can be very easy to do. A name search on *Google Trends* or *Ngram* (Box 3.1) may indicate periods of online activity or media interest. Looking at the metadata for simple searches should show the number of internet hits for a particular name and phrase. Sometimes, studying the ***human networks*** around online networks may be more significant for addressing particular research questions, but these may be hard to access and understand. Some user groups, such as hate-groups, may use chat rooms as a perverse game, and the content may reveal little about what they actually think or do. How could the disability comments around the Korean ILBE site be interpreted and researched? ILBE purports to be a conservative political group, and users call themselves 'retards'.[77]

8.5 Data capture

The technology for ***data capture*** about people is increasingly simple, but the ethical, legal and safety considerations are increasingly problematic (C5.4). Photographic and other electronic data permits retrospective *categorization* and *typologies*, which may not be evident just from observation, but each piece of data raises unique ethical considerations (Box 8.3).

Box 8.3 Photographing street-working children

		Photographs of children working provide data about dress, health (note legs), hygiene (note clothes), occupation, behaviour, relationships and networks, abuse, and micro-economics. But should working children be paid for their time? Is it different if they also provide a "service" such as entertainment? (Bombay/Mumbai, street circus. Istanbul, Roma musicians)
		Working boys are conspicuous; girls are not, especially sex-workers. The boy said he was working on construction sites with his family. The girl said she wore a "party dress" during the day, and changed into jeans to go home in the evening. If the boy were paid for an interview, because it was done during his "working time", should the girl be paid for the same reason? (Bombay/Mumbai)

Typological analysis: Photos help to place children within analytical typologies, such as:

- totally abandoned, *of* the streets, *on* the streets, in families.

Note: potentially violent adults may be watching and using street-working children, and can pose a safety hazard for researchers and children.

Procuring appropriate devices is not simple, and comparisons can be made using checklist headings like: *device, capabilities, examples, advantages, problems*. Relevant equipment is listed and explained under these headings on the website. But keep in mind that the use of any devices could be used by police as evidence of spying or terrorist activities. Although small hidden devices are less likely to attract attention, if found, they will appear more like spy devices. Check country law about the use of all devices. Remember, the people you are watching may also be watching you.

main ideas

When researching identifiable ***people***, consider methods from *sociology, anthropology/ethnography, elite studies, biography* and *investigative* journalism. A triangulated sample of people might reflect:

- *elites* – select people, decision-makers, who can provide an *overview.*
- *experts* – relevant professionals and skilled people who can provide *objective knowledge.*
- *representatives* – people with group identities who can provide *insider* perspectives and explain things about their group.
- *locals* – those who can provide *first-hand information* about a familiar location or type of place.
- *transitionary people* – people moving from one state to another, who can *describe that change.*

Data collection methods include:

- *reading* – biographies, websites, blogs, CVs, 'staff profiles'.
- *asking and listening* – using informal chats, formal structured or semi-structured interviews, with individuals or groups, which may require interpreting from other languages, including signing.
- *watching and listening* – observation of speech and behaviour, and the music and sounds people make, to study language, body language and culture.
- *online research* – ethnographic examination of people, experiments, big data searches, using the internet.

key reading

Barbour, R. (2007) *Doing Focus Groups.* Thousand Oaks, CA: Sage.

Gillham, B. (2008) *Observation Techniques: Structured and Unstructured Approaches.* London: Continuum.

Jorgensen, D.L. (1989) *Participant Observation: A Methodology for Human Studies.* London: Sage.

Makagon, D. and Neumean, M. (2009) *Recording Culture: Audio Documentary and the Ethnographic Experience.* Thousand Oaks, CA: Sage.

Weiss, R.S. (1995) *Learning from Strangers: The Art and Method of Qualitative Interview Studies.* New York: The Free Press.

online resources

To access the resources – search on the name in italics, use the http, or search on the generic term in 'quote marks'.

Emotions analytics – assessing mood and personality from speech intonation – www.beyondverbal.com

Dragon Naturally Speaking – voice transcription software – www.nuance.co.uk/dragon/index.htm

Digital photo analysis – Imageforensic.com – fotoforensics.com – www.imageforensic.org/

Qualitative Researcher – recording techniques – www.qualitative-researcher.com

Evaer – recording VOI (*Skype*) data – www.evaer.com

Recording radio – http://radio.about.com/od/recordstreamingaudio/

MORE ON THE WEBSITE

NINE
Researching populations

If we met five men from Mars, and they said they had come to earth for medical treatment because the Martian health service is very bad, we would tend to believe them – they are "real Martians", we haven't met any other Martians, and therefore they seem to represent all Martians. But what would women from Mars say, Martian health professionals, Martians with disabilities, or the whole Martian population? The point of population research is to find out if individual opinions and anecdotes, and small-group characteristics, are evident across large groups of similar people. It relates large numbers of people (C8) to places (C10).[1]

The large-scale national and international studies require large-scale resources, and their methods are explained on websites and critically discussed in academic publications.[2] Governments have specialist departments for national population research, such as the British *Office for National Statistics*, which provide methodological advice and survey data.[3] Organizations like the OECD and EU research populations regionally. The UN compiles many of these statistics, and the *Population Division* of the *UN Department of Economic and Social Affairs* and the *UN Population Fund* (UNFPA) look specifically at reproductive health, gender equality and population and development strategies.

Most non-specialist researchers will need to use, rather than to do, population studies on a world scale. This chapter therefore concentrates on *understanding* population research, and only outlines how to do *surveys*, and the use of *big data*. Many surveys are designed to be *predictive*, and analysis methods should be considered early (C14.3). But first, it is useful to think about historical population studies, and how *non-digital studies* might still be relevant.

9.1 Non-digital studies

The pervasive use of computers can lead to overlooking non-statistical and non-digital ways to understand populations, which remain relevant. For centuries, historians have studied how certain groups of people inhabit particular places. When linguists studied a particular language with a few people, the findings could apply to the whole population of people who spoke that language. Colonial administrative reports in the 19th–20th century combined basic statistics and descriptive analyses to inform political decision-making, and press reports influenced public opinion.[4] Historical studies can provide valuable data and background information for present-day research, but might also suggest how low-tech methods may still be useful in some circumstances.

An early ***international survey*** was devised by the Scottish anthropologist James Frazer, for his copious collection of magical and mythical beliefs in *The Golden Bough* (1890). He investigated and compared instances of human sacrifice, scapegoats, the burning of humans, the sacrifice of sacred kings, and countless other violent ritual practices from around the world. Yet he had only travelled to Italy and Greece. His method was simple but effective. He sent questionnaires to missionaries and colonial officials in other countries – Japan, China, Africa and the Americas – and got them to contact others and do his research . In modern terms, he *crowdsourced* (C6.4) his *social networks* to do *remote research* and a *snowball survey* of world populations.

Present-day ***opinion polls*** trace their history back to a straw poll carried out by *The Harrisburg Pennsylvanian* in 1824, concerning a presidential election. Then in 1916, the *Literary Digest* carried out a national survey, which predicted Woodrow Wilson's victory. The editors simply sent out millions of postcards and counted those that were returned. In 1936, a similar endeavour failed because there was no accounting for bias in those who received and returned the cards. In the same year, George Gallup carried out a smaller but more methodologically sound survey, which correctly predicted the success of Franklin D. Roosevelt. Gallup had demonstrated the value of proper sampling, and provided the basis for present-day polls and household surveys.

Another innovative method occurred in Britain from 1937 – ***mass observation*** – the study 'of the masses by the masses for the masses'.[5] Researchers believed that the press was presenting a biased view of public opinion, and organized 500 untrained volunteer observers to keep diaries or reply to open questionnaires. Amateur *crowd-sourced* (C6.4) investigators recorded people's discussions and behaviour on the street, in pubs,[6] in factories,[7] during war[8] and at events. Similarly, in 2006, the online *One Day in History* project invited diary entries, and 46,000 blogs were uploaded.[9] The film *Life in a Day* crowdsourced 80,000 clips on *YouTube* (4500 hours), which were edited into a record of micro- and macro-events, in 192 countries, on 24 July 2010. In 2013, the *British Library* (BL) announced that it would capture data from social media sites such as *Facebook* and *Twitter*, including data from pay-sites. *The Listening Project*, by the BL and BBC, is building an archive of short conversations between ordinary, but interesting people.

A population in a particular locality can be studied through *secondary data* about anything relating to that population – goods and services, media, cultural events, church records (C8). Transport networks reveal much about demography. In any location there are also many informal population experts – politicians, police, youth workers, health professionals – who have a lot of information. Interviewing elites and leaders can provide general insights into the populations they head. Many things are already based on population data, and so the population can be studied by studying these things. Adverts are useful because the advertisers will already have done a lot of market research about a local population. Researching the price of a cup of tea in different locations can indicate the wealth gap in a population – in London that would range from tea inside the *Ritz Hotel*, to free tea for homeless people just outside.

9.2 Understanding population studies

Many population studies are local or national, but this chapter only considers types of study that are relevant for world research, and these are generally at three levels:

- *Case studies* are about an aspect of a place or country, and are designed to make comparisons with similar studies elsewhere. ("Women's rights within a northern Nigerian village", to compare with similar studies elsewhere in Islamic Africa.)
- *International studies*, which concern two or more countries, and might be based on comparable case studies or national (often government) data about whole countries. ("School achievement in Europe", to compare European countries.) *Wikipedia* provides useful international lists.[10]
- *Global studies* are a *cross-sectional* investigation of a particular global sector that is not nation-based. ("Lifestyle diseases", to compare the causes globally.)

Population studies start from a broad *purpose* (C4.2) ("To improve health"), but there are many ways to design different studies that have the same purpose.

Demographic studies assess the numbers, types and characteristics of the inhabitants of a particular place. Demographers relate population to factors such as distribution (rural, urban, coastal), structure (age, gender, nationality), groups (religious, ethnic, migrants), status (education level, health, employment), or systems such as economy, education and health (epidemiology). *Dot maps* are a simple method to relate populations to places (C11.1). 'Stocktaking' studies, such as the UNDP *Human Development Index*, assess resources and public services – the availability of water, food, health care, education – and are often created from regular monitoring data ('returns'). National *census* data (based on everyone in a country or place) forms the basis of most national and international demography, but this is often very unreliable, especially in less wealthy countries where groups such as homeless people, immigrants, hill tribes children, and older people are often missing from data. Even in countries such as Britain and the US, census data becomes out of date very quickly, and other methods are being considered.[11] *Population modelling* uses data on births, deaths, migration and life expectancy to predict population size and characteristics.[12] (The 'model' is *built* from algorithms and equations based on relevant variables – life expectancy, technological impacts, desertification, water shortage. The 'simulation' *runs* that model to predict the effects of changes in those variables.) Better computers have greatly improved the modelling of world economic systems.[13] But, even if the models and maths are correct, small data errors, or technological changes, can lead to very inaccurate predictions: the GIGO problem, "Garbage In – Garbage Out". Predictive modelling (C14.3), such as the 'carrying capacity' of the Earth,[14] is very problematic.

Perceptions studies, including *opinion polls* (above), are based on people's stated views not objective facts. They often use *Likert scales* – respondents score questions from 1 (don't agree), to 5 or 7 (strongly agree).[15] There should always be a 'don't know'/'no opinion' option, which is different from the middle score, otherwise respondents are forced to express a numerical opinion that may have no basis. Cultural factors are important. Muslim women may tend to use middle scores, and men the extremes. A scale without a midpoint, of 1–4 or 1–6, may help to overcome this. The *Corruption Perceptions Index* (CPI) from *Transparency International* (TI) explains its methods clearly, and warns that although the 'score' is calculated consistently across years, the 'rank' may change in a way that does *not* imply that countries have "gone up" or "gone down" – the change may simply be because new countries have been added, or previous ones omitted.[16] The objectives and methodologies of studies like this are constantly debated.[17] In a slightly different form, perceptions studies may be used to detect hidden things, such as the level and type of crime that is not reported to the police, which is then compared with similar 'reported crime' data.[18] 'Global' studies need to be viewed with caution. The *Pew Research Center's Global Attitudes Project*[19] ignores most of Africa, Central Asia, Scandinavia and Central and Eastern Europe. Most of its findings show the US favourably.

Market research,[20] which assesses markets, and ***marketing research***,[21] which is about selling things (goods and services), deploy a wide range of population methods. *Market segmentation* analysis uses the demographics – age, sex, income, interests, personality – of a population in relation to the things they are likely to buy. *Market information* concerns supply and demand, competitors, new products, processes and materials, and international laws, regulations and cultural factors. *Market trends* are a specific aspect, measuring the rise and fall of prices, potential customers and interest. Methods such as SWOT analysis (Figure 12.2) assess the potential of companies to respond to the market, and risk analysis (C14.3.1) assesses the degree to which a company can safely invest in something. Advertising companies will use data from market and marketing studies to plan their campaigns. Psychologists study how people make *choices,* using techniques such as *choice modelling. Evaluation methods* (C6.2) are used to measure the success of strategies and the effectiveness of market/marketing research. Social media are increasingly studied. *Netography*[22] uses online methods to discover the interests of specific groups of potential customers, though studying blogs, chat rooms and specialist interest websites. *Big data* methods use the mass of data on social network sites (C9.4),[23] and other media such as newspapers, resulting in data such as that on *Google Trends. Social marketing* adapts commercial methods to address social issues such as HIV/AIDS and environmental responsibility.[24]

But is simply counting the numbers in a population always going to provide the information we really need? We may use the standard demographics – number of people, age, sex, nationality – but are other characteristics about the people in a population more important, like fat?

thinking zone: how would a butcher research the world population?

carrying capacity

Studies of the Earth's 'carrying capacity' reflect the Malthusian assumption that the problem is population increase. So, most population studies are based on counting people. But is that unit of analysis always best?

human meat

The average global body weight is 62 kg, in North America 80.7 kg, but in Asia 57.7 kg.

'If every country in the world had the same level of fatness that we see in the USA, in weight terms that would be like an extra billion people of global average body mass.' Average *Body Mass Index* (BMI) in the USA is 28.7; in Japan, 22. So living in a wealthy country doesn't need to make you fat.

methods

Country data on BMI and height distribution was used to calculate 'average adult body mass'. 'Average body mass', and population size, was used to calculate 'total [human] biomass'.

car gases

One of the most important determinates of average body mass index is motor vehicle gas consumption per capita. In Arab countries, people eat a lot and they move very little because they drive everywhere." And car use also contributes to greenhouse gases.

cow gases

Methane from ruminants and manure also creates greenhouse gases. More meat means more methane.

therefore

"When people think about environmental sustainability, they immediately focus on population. Actually – it's not how many mouths there are to feed, it's how much flesh there is on the planet." ...and how that relates to car use, and livestock farts.

so

What alternatives to the familiar units of analysis might provide new perspectives on world problems?

[See References for further information.[25]]

9.3 Doing small-scale surveys

Surveys use *questionnaires,* or observation or other *schedules,* to collect data that describes a specific *population* – the inhabitants of a particular place, or a specific group of 'items' (magazines, official documents, websites). For human populations, *demographics* ("age", "sex") and/or *characteristics* ("car use") may be noted, perhaps to test hypotheses ("that women are safer drivers than men"). But there is no point to do a survey if: usable data is already available somewhere else, it is not likely that the results will be accurate, or if the people that the study needs to get data about are very rare within a population – "transgender heads of state".

Surveys are usually statistical, and use software such as *Excel* or *SPSS.* But surveys can also be small-scale, simple, use paper and pencil methods, and be done by calling at households in villages or informal settlements.[26] A population can be human or non-human – "Homeless women in Moscow" – "Gay websites in Russian". Surveys of non-human things will use a schedule in much the same way as a questionnaire, to 'interrogate' the things being researched. But defining a population is not easy. Research based on a population of 'prisoners' may not represent all 'criminals' – only the stupid ones who get caught.[27]

A simple survey design entails deciding:

- whether the research should create *descriptive statistics*, suggest a *causal link* and/or *generalize* from a small sample to a large population?
- the *questions* – will they be 'closed' (yes-no answers), or 'open' (narrative answers), and how will the answers be analysed?

- the *variables* – what are the relevant things that might vary (age, gender, opinion, income), which variables are *independent* (age, gender) and which are *dependent* (opinion, income), and how are these included in the questions?
- the *instrument* – how will the questionnaire or schedule be designed, in relevant languages, and how will it be *piloted* (C4.1)?
- the *population* and *sample* – who or what will be studied, when, where and why? And can they be accessed, and will they respond?
- who will *carry out* the survey – do they need training?
- how will data be *analysed* and *presented* – what are the technology and IT requirements – how will this affect the whole design?

Online surveys can be done through short email questionnaires,[28] or by using online survey tools listed on *Capterra*. Free online basic tools like *Survey Monkey*, software such as the *iSurvey* app for iPads, or reduced cost systems for NGOs such as *EasyGoingSurvey*, all explain the relevant technical methods. *Crowdsourced* (C6.4) *networks* can be used, but likely bias must be considered. Not all those surveyed will respond, and a low or biased *response rate* can make a study invalid.

The general advantages and weaknesses of surveys, and specific considerations for world studies, are explained on the website. For individual researchers or small organizations it is often better to employ professional survey companies. But it is still useful to understand survey methodologies, because companies will usually only take responsibility for the technical aspects of a survey, not for factors like the overall study design, clarity of questions, or the hypotheses or theory underpinning the questions.

From a broad ***purpose*** ("To improve health"), specific *aims* help to focus the study ("To assess the availability of doctors"). The aims are then expressed as *research questions* which the study can answer clearly, by measuring things – "What is the ratio of doctors to population?" But *definitions* are important. What is a 'doctor' – does it include volunteers working for international agencies, and traditional healers? Does the 'population' only include citizens, or also migrant workers, cross-border nomads and aid workers? There may be further significant considerations. Finding out the basic doctor–population ratio will reveal nothing about the distribution of doctors – are they evenly spread across urban and rural areas? *Categories* must be mutually exclusive and unambiguously defined, so that it is clear what counts in which category – in health research 'overweight' and 'obesity' are separate categories, defined by weight, although in general conversation 'obesity' could be included within 'overweight'. Relevant *units of analysis* will be identified, which also needs careful thought. For example children are normally counted like family possessions – like TVs, cars, radios. Using 'household', 'family' or 'child' as the unit will produce different results. The 'number of families' with 5+ children might be 1.5%, but the 'number of children' living in 5+ families might be 5%. 'Child-centred statistics' are just one example of the need for careful consideration of minorities in study design.[29]

It is usually not possible to research a whole population, and so some form of ***sample*** will be used. A *sample* could comprise a few individuals who will be interviewed in-depth, or thousands who will need to be accessed by an online survey. A similar approach could be applied to other forms of non-human 'population' – a few texts for in-depth documentary analysis, or a *sample* of texts from numerous websites for keyword-sentiment analysis. A *sampling frame* lists all the units in a population from which a sample will be selected – all "African bishops", all "religious websites in China".

Non-probability samples cannot usually be generalized, and the findings are only indicative of what may happen within a population. But statistical methods may still be used, even with a single in-depth interview, for example as an aspect of content analysis (C13.2). Counting words or phrases could be used to identify likely patterns within that interview, such as gendered language, and then to detect differences from a predicted pattern. As the scale and cost of world research is usually very large, the non-probability approaches to selecting samples are often very pragmatic:

- *Opportunistic* selection arises from chance or luck, and is sometimes not considered to create a true sample. But any questioning, however informal and brief, can still be systematic and reflect the purpose and main questions of the research. Opportunities may arise at public meetings, on public transport, or by chatting with people in international settings such as airports.
- *Purposive* samples use units that are chosen for a reason, and the reason should be explained. Respondents may have relevant responsibilities or qualities – politicians, performers, prize winners – or comprise small homogeneous groups – indigenous minorities, refugees, senior managers. A relevant and accessible research site may be used – trade fairs, conferences, sports meetings.
- *Chain-referral, network* or *snowball* sampling is arguably more appropriate than probability sampling when studying hidden populations, or exploring social networks or processes. This method is central to investigative research. Investigators "follow up leads", but the aim is to establish specific facts not to provide generalizable findings.
- *Convenience* samples are common in experimental studies. University students might be rewarded for participation in role play by extra credits or small fees. But to what degree can student role play provide indications of how actual people behave in real-life situations?
- *Crowdsourced* samples (C6.4) provide a new dynamic. Although the 'crowd' is self-selecting, it often comprises 'the right people in the right place at the right time'.

These samples are not statistically representative of a population, and cannot usually be generalized to large populations. Representative *probability samples* are necessary for statistical generalization (below C9.3.3).

Specific ***questionnaire questions*** derive from the *research questions* ("Is access to doctors adequate?"), to investigate relevant details ("What prevents you from getting to the doctor?"). With thought, smart questions can be devised which are immediately adaptable to different populations and criteria, and automatically provide statistical findings:

> "Do you think you are above or below average {intelligence / physical attractiveness / leadership / sexiness}, within your {college, workplace, country, the world}?"

Logically, a population should be a 50–50 split, above and below 'average'. Usually, more people think they are above average, and so the data from the smart question *automatically* evidences the theories of human over-optimism.[30] From most population studies, *statistics* – numbers resulting from counting or measuring things – can be produced and analysed in many different ways. Numerous books explain survey methodologies in-depth,[31] and this section only outlines basic *descriptive, inferential and causal* statistics (Figure 9.1). Follow up the references for further explanations in the book *Statistics for Research.*[32]

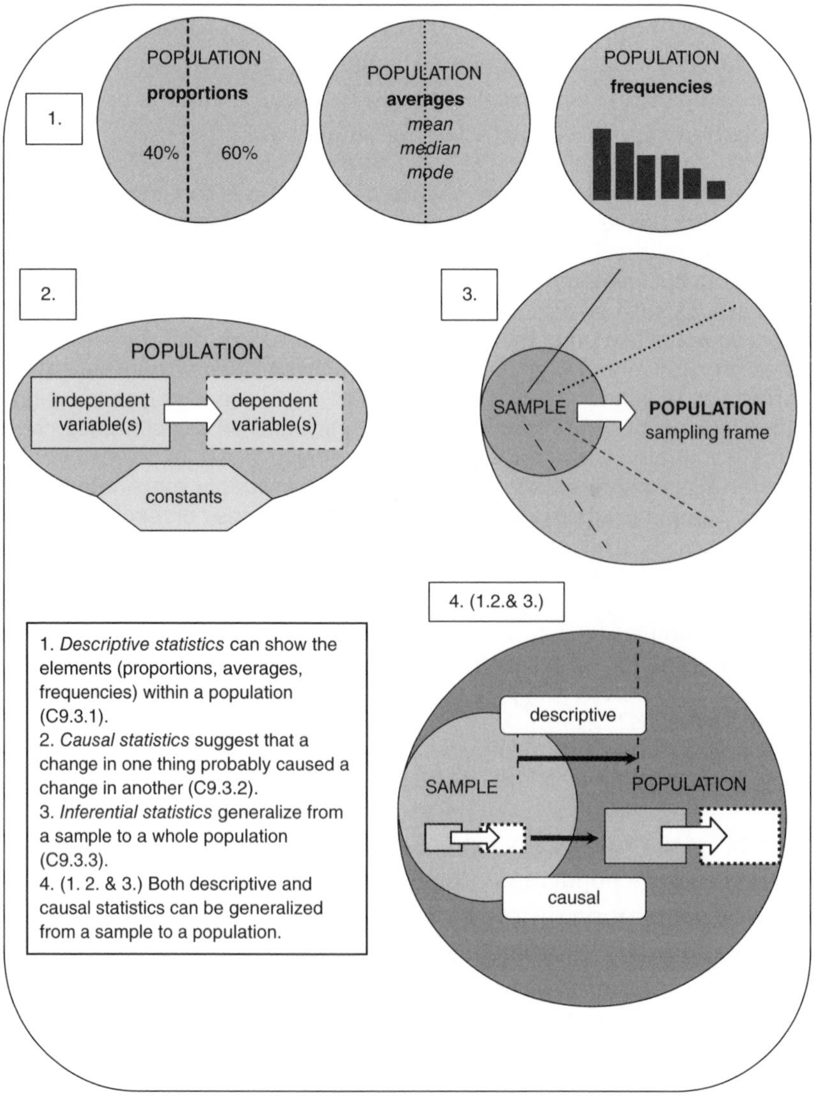

Figure 9.1 Descriptive, inferential and causal statistics

9.3.1 Descriptive statistics

From a quantitative survey, the basic numbers – ***raw data*** – are usually presented as ***descriptive statistics*** – easily understandable tables, or simple visualizations such as graphs and pie-charts. Data might be *disaggregated* to show numbers in relation to particular sub-groups within populations (male/female, rural/urban), or *aggregated* to combine different (perhaps uncertain) data sources, in the hope that, if some data is weak, it will not bias the overall findings because sources are so numerous – *newspaper circulation + libraries + computer owners + books published + self-definition = literacy levels*. Indexes (C14.4) are often aggregated. But aggregation embodies a lot of (usually unacknowledged) qualitative judgement – how does '1 newspaper' equate with '1 library'?

Every form of statistical presentation and analysis hopefully increases the understanding of something, but this also loses information. Percentages lose information about actual numbers, and even basic numbers lose information about who said what. So the choice of how to present and analyse numbers should closely reflect the *purpose* of a study (C4.2). A significant misunderstanding, even when experts explain research, concerns the difference between a population statistic and a personal statistic. If "1 in 5 people die within five years" of contracting a particular disease, that does not imply that every individual person with that disease has a 1 in 5 likelihood of dying. The likelihood of dying for each person is 100% or zero.

Raw data might be presented as simple numbers (26 women, 43 men), or then ***standardized*** to make comparisons easier when the numbers of those surveyed differ. It might show (Figure 9.1):

- the *elements* of population in the form of *proportions* (percentages – 60%).
- *averages* – the *mean* (the total from all scores divided by the number of scores), the *median* (the central point when scores are ordered high to low), or *mode* (the most frequent score). But it is important to consider whether these forms of presentation make sense. A *mean* of 'type of government' does not seem sensible; the *mean* of 'numbers of MPs' might be interesting.
- *frequencies* (1 doctor per 100 patients, 10 times each year).

Frequency tables[33] (Figure 9.2) show how often the same things occur. Data is first *listed* (or entered) for each case (Table A). This can then be converted into a frequency table, *ranked* in the order of highest to lowest frequency, and the frequencies could also be converted into percentages or proportions, which would create a *relative frequency table* (Table B). The data could be *disaggregated* into 'large countries' and 'small countries', and the *cross-tabulations* shown in a *bivariate table*, i.e. it is quickly possible to see that only two 'small countries' are 'theocracies', or that most 'large countries' are 'parliamentary republics' (Table C). But, unless the 'type' is unambiguous ('age', 'nationality') this is not always straightforward and, again, definition is important. The delineation between 'small' and 'large' countries will be arbitrary, and Britain could be classified as a 'theocracy'.

Type of government
(Table A – *list*)

Case (countries)	**Type of government**
1	Single-party state
2	Absolute monarchy
3	Parliamentary republic
4	Parliamentary republic
5	Theocracy
6	Parliamentary republic
7	Single-party state
8	Absolute monarchy
9	Single-party state
10	Parliamentary republic
etc.…to 50	

Type of government
(Table B – *frequency*)

Type of government	**Frequency**	**%**
Parliamentary republic	20	40
Single-party state	15	30
Absolute monarchy	10	20
Theocracy	5	10
Total	50	100

Type of government
(Table C – *bivariate frequency*)

Type of government	**Small countries**	**Large countries**	**Total**
Parliamentary republic	8	12	20
Single-party state	10	5	15
Absolute monarchy	8	2	10
Theocracy	2	3	5
Total	28	22	50

Figure 9.2 Frequency tables

9.3.2 Causal statistics

Population studies often try to suggest ***cause and effect***, that if one thing changes ("a new poverty reduction policy"), something related has changed ("poverty reduced") (C14.2).

Qualitative analysis will argue causation in terms of the existence or absence of variables and the probable nature of cause and effect – "*How* does a scientific education influence the problem-solving skills of politicians?" Statistical analysis assesses *if* a specific causal relationship is evident – "*Does* a scientific education influence the problem-solving skills of politicians?" Statistical analysis assesses the degree of a causal relationship in various ways:

- How the *value* of variables may be relevant – do more educational qualifications equate with greater income?
- The comparative *strength* of the causal relationship – how much qualifications affect income?
- The *completeness* of the causal relationship – what is the gap between the average science graduate's income, and the lowest and highest science graduate's income – big (less complete) or small (more complete)?

But to investigate whether a causal link exists requires a plausible theory/hypothesis that variables are related. It seems plausible that 'education qualifications' and 'income' are related in many countries, but it is not plausible that the number of robots in Japan is related to the number of *Imams* in Iran, yet.

Things that could *not* normally change, are termed ***constants***. If the things could change (vary), they are called ***variables***. Both can be human or non-human. The analysis of variables reflects three main forms:[34]

- *Univariate* (using one variable) – 'religion'.
- *Bivariate* (using two variables)[35] – 'religion' *and* 'attendance at religious meetings'.
- *Multivariate* (using many variables) – 'religion' and 'attendance at religious meetings' and 'place of birth' and 'age' and 'coercion'.

Univariate statistics only show a simple relationship between basic numbers – higher/lower – but these can still be *ranked* into *indexes* or *indicators* (C14.4).

Bivariate and *multivariate* statistics can be ranked, but might then provide the basis for an ***association/correlation***. Some *variables* may also seem ***causally*** related to others – if an *independent variable* changes, the *dependent variable* will change. But influence can be in one direction, or more. It might seem obvious that 'education level' would be *independent*, coming before the resultant *dependent* 'income', but direction also needs theorizing. If the type of 'education level' being studied were 'PhD', that 'education level' might depend on *previous* 'income', because doing a PhD is usually expensive and often happens after or during a period of employment. But when there appears to be a relationship between variables, there may not be *causation*. The number of young smokers may decrease following an anti-smoking TV campaign, but that decrease may have been caused by another factor – a *confounder* – such as a famous rock-star dying of lung cancer. *Probability* theory provides ways to express the strength of a belief that a causal link exists, or could exist – the risk that "the death of the president will affect the economy". But there is never 100% certainty.

Significance tests contribute to validity (C7.6) by assessing how likely a result is due to chance (but not the degree of the causal relationship). Tests set up null hypotheses – that there is no difference between two variables, which the tests confirm or not. In statistical terms 'significant' implies that there is little likelihood that a result occurred by chance – usually less than 5%. But these 'significance levels' have arisen from tradition not objective statistical fact.[36] The word significance can have political, social or statistical meaning, denoting importance. To learn that a prime minister believes that genetically modified (GM) foods are harmful is a politically significant finding; for supermarket CEOs to decide to stop selling GM foods is socially significant; to show that 66% of a population does not want GM foods may be statistically significant. Statistical tests also do not assess the validity of data. If the data was collected carelessly, that will probably not be detected or corrected by tests.

In all quantitative analysis there will be unexplained factors, including data collection errors and the effects of other unknown or omitted independent variables. It is incorrect to assume that these unexplained factors are all known and can therefore be named, because they have not been measured and tested. In an attitude survey about "war", retrospectively naming all the unknown factors, "fear" would not be correct unless fear had been measured.

9.3.3 Inferential statistics

Studies may involve the whole *population* of a particular place – a *census* of all *units of analysis* in a *population.* But often a smaller manageable ***sample*** of *units* will *represent* the *population* that is being studied (C7.4). It is then possible to *infer* ('*extrapolate*', '*generalize*') from the sample data, to describe the whole population.

To create inferential statistics, ***probability*** ('representative', 'random') ***samples*** will be used to create data that can be generalized to the whole population.[37]

- *Simple random* samples comprise *units of analysis* that each have an equal likelihood of being chosen – numbers-out-of-a-hat". (But the selection of one unit must not influence the selection of any others.)
- *Systematic samples* may select every *n*th unit from a list – every 10th item on *eBay*. (But the list must not be organized in a way that may bias the study.)
- *Stratified samples* divide the population into groups ('strata'), which have clear differences, such as geographical districts with different language groups, and then take random or systematic samples from each group. (But the groups must not have different characteristics that may bias the relevant data.)
- *Quota sampling* is often used for commercial surveys, especially opinion polls. The quotas reflect the main demographics of the whole population (age, sex, etc.), but

the actual respondents are chosen opportunistically not randomly, e.g. by an interviewer in a railway station. (But there is no control over who interviewers actually select.)

- *Cluster sampling* – uses relevant geographical areas, and selects a random sample from these – "cities with an airport". (But the choice of clusters should reflect the aims of the research, e.g. airport noise.)

These *representative* samples can usually be generalized statistically to larger populations, but there must be a theoretical basis for the generalization, for example explaining why the whole *population* is culturally similar to the *sample*.

Whatever the scale, type or complexity of a survey, a central problem for world population studies is the difficulty of accommodating ***cross-cultural differences***,[38] and this problem is most evident in opinion/perceptions research. Initially, methodologists tried to create, refine and pilot types of question that were 'culture-proof', but this is difficult, not least because cultures constantly change. There were also attempts 'to measure directly response category incomparability and to correct for it'[39] – tests for cultural difference were put into questionnaires, and the results were then used to weight the responses to the main questions. But this approach can make the questionnaire long, irritating and irrational to the interviewee. The problem becomes more complex in globalized, cosmopolitan communities – 'nation' is no longer a simple determinate of 'culture'. Big data researchers take this discussion a stage further and argue that, with massive data sets, cultural differences become irrelevant.

9.4 Big data

Online, big data methods provide many new opportunities to study populations (C6.5). *Social media analysis* looks specifically for patterns in people's online interaction – web use, mobility and transport, public service demand. *Crowdsourced* data (C6.4) may help to predict and analyse disasters (typhoons, earthquakes, industrial disasters), or events such as epidemics or pollution. Many methods have been adapted for *market research*[40] and other commercial endeavours,[41] under the headings 'webnography',[42] big data,[43] or 'predictive analytics'.[44] The approach is increasingly an aspect of government planning, even in less developed countries.[45] Sites like the *COSMOS* and *GDELT* platforms are making commercially captured data more widely available for academic and civil society researchers, together with tools for analysing and visualizing data, such as IBM's *Many Eyes*.

Big data research uses algorithms to process large amounts of data very quickly, to assess:

- *events* – infectious disease outbreaks, disasters, emergencies, environmental change, political violence. These can be predicted by comparing new patterns with norms, or spikes in keywords in tweets ("wind" "crowd" "earthquake")

- *behaviours* – how people *respond* to events. This uses 'sentiment' – like/dislike – and 'moods', such as 'tension' which may predict events like riots.
- *style* – a *totality* of *behaviours* – "Do international visitors differ from local people?"
- *trends* – significant patterns and changes in *direction* within populations – "Which types of clothes are being bought, in which countries?"[46]
- *networks* – the significant *links* and *influences*, and how are they used – "How are infectious diseases spreading around the world?"
- *interactions* – modelling *influences* and *effects* from some form of online communication or contact – "Which countries have internet dating links?"
- *the future* – forecasting, modelling, predicting events, economic scenarios, social trends (C14.3) – "Might climate change increase violence and conflict?"

It is possible to link big data with standard data, for example the geotags on tweets with standard government data about socially deprived areas. Natural data might also provide a type of 'control group' which can be compared with similar social media data – interview data with tweets, census demographics with website user profiles. Big data also creates the possibility for creating ongoing real-time statistical data – commuter flow, pollution, births-and-deaths.

Many questions are raised about the soundness of big data research, and these are discussed further on the website. In general, big data seems likely to augment rather than replace standard social science methods.

main ideas

When researching ***populations*** consider: whether the data already exists in some form, digital *and* non-digital methods, unambiguous definitions and cross-cultural aspects.

Research ***design*** is likely to be at the level of:

- *case studies* to compare with similar things in other countries.
- *international studies* to compare more than one country or region.
- *global studies* which concern aspects of world society that are not nation-based.

Examples of ***relevant studies*** will include:

- *demographic studies* – how people relate to places.
- *perception* (opinion) *studies* – which assess what people think about things, not objective facts.
- *market research* which assesses markets or investigates how to sell things.

Small-scale surveys may utilize:

- *univariate, bivariate, or multivariate* data.
- *descriptive statistics* – numbers which may *standardize* data, and show *proportions*, *'averages'* and *frequencies*.
- *causal statistics* which hypothesize/theorize causation, and then try to evidence the cause and effect.
- *inferential statistics* which generalize from sample data to a whole population.

Big data studies may use data from:

- social media networks.
- crowdsourced evidence.
- "exhaust data" from other forms of mass data collection.

key reading

Argyrous, G. (2011) *Statistics for Research.* London: Sage.

Blair, J. et al. (2014) *Designing Surveys.* London: Sage

Davidov, E. et al. (2011) *Cross-Cultural Analysis: Methods and Applications.* London: Sage.

Holdsworth, C. et al. (2013) *Population and Society*. London: Sage.

Journal – *Big Data.* Sage.

WEF (2012) *Big Data, Big Impact: New Possibilities for International Development.* Geneva: World Economic Forum.

online resources

To access the resources – search on the name in italics, use the http, or search on the generic term in 'quote marks'.

Survey Monkey – free basic survey tools

Capterra – lists online survey sites

Snap Surveys – attractive presentation of online surveys – www.snapsurveys.com

EasyGoingSurvey – low cost services and tools for NGOs

International Survey – international social, political and economic surveys – www.international-survey.org

iSurvey – app for iPads

Office for National Statistics – methods guidance – www.ons.gov.uk/ons/guide-method/index.html

ESRC *National Centre for Research Methods* (NCRM) – current information on statistical and online methods – www.ncrm.ac.uk

COSMOS – free big data from commercial sites, and tools

GDELT – big data harvested from international media

IBM *Many Eyes* – open source visualization software

MORE ON THE WEBSITE

TEN
Researching places

In any *place*, things that other visitors may find annoying – poor transport, shortages in shops, decaying buildings – often present opportunities for interesting research. The adverts on the road from the airport, or other entry points, are a fascinating source of data. Data collection just entails being prepared, and a small camera with a quick shutter action.

Distinctive locations include *street, urban, rural* and *coastal* settings, and the *'global commons'*. Within these 'human-influenced' environments (Figure 1, p. xxxi) *texts, objects* and *buildings* (including *infrastructure*) provide primary data. There is, of course, overlap – texts might be on objects, objects might be built. The important point is not to miss something significant because it does not fit a preconceived idea about what is relevant.

The approaches of *human geography,*[1] *archaeology*[2] and *ethnography*[3] ('culturology'[4]) (C6.1) provide useful insights into researching 'place'.[5] Data collection may entail *watching* and *listening* to people (C8.3), and probably *mapping*, which is discussed in C11. Data may be *captured* by electronic devices, not least digital cameras, but binoculars and a magnifying glass are also useful. Audio data about places is also valuable.[6] But the first way to understand any place is to read about it (C3) in guidebooks, commercial country-guides, *Wikipedia* and embassy websites. In 1030, al-Bīrūnī provided a neat discussion of the merits of 'hearsay' (speech and documents) versus 'eye-witness' (observation) (Figure 10.1).[7]

> No one will deny that in questions of historic authenticity *hearsay* does not equal *eye-witness*, for in the latter the eye of the observer apprehends the substance of that which is observed, both in the time when and in the place where it exists, whilst hearsay has its peculiar drawbacks.
>
> But for these, it would even be preferable to eye-witness; for the object of eye-witness can only be *actual* momentary existence, whilst hearsay comprehends alike the present, the past, and the future, so as to apply in a certain sense both to that which *is* and to that which is *not* (i.e. which either has ceased to exist or has not yet come into existence).
>
> Abū Rayhān al-Bīrūnī, *India* (circa 1030)

Figure 10.1 Hearsay versus eye-witness

Research about peoples (C8) and places is related, and *following up* observations is often important. To discover national values – the "national psyche" – go beyond current politics. Ask what people learned about their own country at school. Even if they dismiss it as nationalistic propaganda, school learning – good or bad – is a shared experience which unites people in relation to their country. In Belarus, a bison billboard was explained by local students, then by experts, and then through a print from the *British Museum*. It symbolizes the resilience of the Belarusian people.

10.1 The street

A quick walk around a new town or village is a good start for ***urban ethnography.*** Chatting in bars and cafes can provide a wealth of *contextual* information about an unfamiliar place, and clues about how to access hidden groups (Figure 7.1). But street research is not new, and books such as Mayhew's *London Labour and the London Poor* (1850) provide insights into potential methodologies, and international data for historical comparisons.[8]

Researching *people* is considered fully in Chapter 8, but ***street ethnography***[9] provides ways to understand non-specific street populations – 'crowds',[10] transient groups,[11] gangs[12] and street children.[13] A particular problem for a street ethnographer is that *participatory observation* and *interviews* may be difficult,[14] yet *non-participatory observation* can lead to superficial findings. 'Lurking' is one alternative – the researcher 'hangs out at the periphery of a social setting'.[15] Similarly, *phenomenological* approaches might use a 'go-along' method.[16]

But first, it is sensible to find out about local ***law*** and ***customs*** (C5.2). Although photography in a 'public place' is usually lawful, taking photos of sensitive sites and following people may be unlawful. And what is, or is not, a 'public place' may not always be clear. Many street people – beggars, prostitutes, traders – have "minders", who watch them and can become violent. And these "minders" may be local police officers. Noting political posters is useful research, but can also indicate that making jokes about certain political leaders may be unlawful. International buskers have useful research networks about street law, such as *Buskers Advocates*.

From simple ***street observation***, homeless people may evidence discrimination, and graffiti might indicate gang culture and street style. *Transient peoples* – nomads, farmers, traders – may congregate in commercial hotels, markets, or *caravanserai* (camel hotels). *Political data* comes from posters and murals. Simply taping a cheap video "spy camera" to a bike helmet, or car roof-rack, can record large amounts of street data unobtrusively. Put a camera on someone who uses a wheelchair, and you will find out how wheelchair users view a place, and how the public views them.

Streets are also the site of, or gateway to, informal and formal ***events*** – political gatherings, social activism,[17] riots,[18] and places where people have traditionally met to express opinions like Hyde Park Corner (London), or Hong Lim Park (Singapore). The assessment of formal events and festivals has become a useful aspect of *audience research*[19] – why people attend, how they behave, commercial implications. Research about international *event management* is similar.[20] Balloons and kites are useful for aerial observation and audio recording at outdoor events, as they are quiet and safer than motorized UAVs (C11.2). Satellite data can help to assess the size of a crowd,[21] new software is likely to detect faces in crowds,[22] and predicting when crowd movement indicates danger is increasingly significant.[23] *Streamweaver* coordinates mobile phone data, captured by different people at the same event, which can later be analysed simultaneously on a split screen.

10.2 Urban areas

Street research is an aspect of ***urban research***. This takes a broader view, to include less visible data about *organizations* and *systems* – transport, justice, public services – and *permanent communities* – housing, town planning, labour. Urban study has a long academic history,[24] including *ethnographic*[25] and *anthropological* approaches.[26] Many university departments specialize in research about their local environs, and are a good place for outsiders to start their studies. Local public administrations have their own innovative methods.[27] *Cities* are increasingly used as a unit of analysis to explain national and international phenomena.[28] New topics include *megacities*,[29] *conflict* in cities[30] and communities with *declining pollutions*[31] explored by the *Shrinking Cities International Research Network*. The *Urban Affairs Annual Reviews* series provides a good record of significant issues.

Urban spaces also provide access to hidden ***underground*** data,[32] which is often ignored. Tourists in London's beautiful Embankment Gardens are not aware they are walking on a large sewer built to stop the 'Big Stink' of 1858. Different places have different underground characteristics – shopping malls (Montreal), metro architecture (Moscow), lost cities (Derikuyu), abandoned mines (Philadelphia),[33] Cold War defences (Europe, US, Beijing),[34] wartime shelters (London),[35] robotic cycle parks (Tokyo), and sewers (Paris). Understanding underground networks is becoming important in the context of probable flooding from sea level rise, as in Paris.

Primary data might relate to gender issues,[36] migrant labour or social exclusion, and work for independent tourist guides such as *Lonely Planet*. There is a wealth of ***secondary data*** for outsider-researchers, in local media archives, official records and local libraries. ***Mixed-methods*** approaches can provide new perspectives on topics not covered fully by formal public administrative studies, such as social capital.[37] A study might combine formal and non-formal data, for example drug adverts to assess local health service problems, and products available for men and women to compare local gender aspects.

10.3 Rural areas

Rural research considers different ***terrains*** – deserts, steppes, wetlands, coastal, mountains, forests. Many rural places host ***transient populations*** – nomads, traders, hunters – who are often united by common world narratives and cosmologies. Rural research studies remote communities such as hill tribes,[38] but this is sometimes politically motivated.[39] Other rural topics include agricultural techniques,[40] land use,[41] land reform[42] and gender aspects.[43] Demographers have developed specific methods for rural areas,[44] and health[45] and food security.[46] Crowdsourced approaches to rural research (C6.4) address aspects such as *land cover*.[47] Semi-rural, ***peri-urban*** areas – "slums", "shanty towns", "informal settlements" – fall between urban and rural delineations, and present new topics such as urban agriculture and forestry,[48] water and waste disposal.[49] The traditional methods of *anthropology* and *ethnography* have generated a wealth of historical data about rural peoples, and there are recent perspectives.[50]

Historically, ***botanical artists***, who accompanied international explorers and mariners, meticulously recorded plants that might be useful, or saleable, in Europe. They depicted roots, blossom, flowers, seeds, pollinators and different stages of growth in a single *scientific drawing*, while maintaining the aesthetic value. *Kew Gardens* (London) maintains the tradition, a library, archives and a seed bank, which includes samples collected by Darwin. Artists now record pertinent concerns such as 'plants in peril' from environmental change. Landscape artists, including photographers, also created useful records of rural terrains, especially in the European colonies. But much of this work was idealized propaganda, showing how nature has been tamed, to encourage immigration and investment.

Practical methodologies come from ***development studies***,[51] and are often specific to particular communities.[52] *Participatory* approaches adapt standard methods, including using stones as counters and assessing responses to drama presentations about topics such as HIV/AIDS,[53] and try to involve all sectors of the local population including children.[54] *Rapid Rural Appraisal* (RRA)[55] uses informal interviews with villagers, and discussions with key people such as village chiefs and local officials. *Transect walks* with small groups use a 'sample' of land and crops – perhaps from the top of a mountain down to a river valley – which is discussed on site. The key research questions are simple but comprehensive and inclusive:

- What has changed over recent years, and what may change in the future?
- What are the problems?
- How do people think these problems can be avoided or solved?

The *World Bank* provides useful research tools, and case studies.[56] But development studies methods must be carefully piloted to ensure people all understand the processes including the images (Figure 15.3).

10.4 Coastal regions

Coastal peoples live on natural borders, yet perceive their territory as borderless, and 'the sea as our bank'.[57] They inhabit both nation state territory, and the global commons (C10.5). This raises questions about identity, worldviews, belief systems, environmental impacts and cultural systems. Not least of the unique problems is how to measure a coastline. A coast is never straight, and so as the ruler (unit of measurement) gets smaller, the measurement gets longer, because it measures into smaller bays, inlets, rock formations, erosion and eventually microscopic fractals.[58] Disasters – tsunamis, typhoons, pollution, radiation – are prompting innovative research. *Oxfam* researchers found that the 2005 Asian tsunami had killed four times more women than men, because misinterpreted Muslim traditions had prevented girls learning to swim.[59]

The coast is the intersection of diverse areas of ***multidisciplinary*** study – oceanography, wetlands, agriculture, meteorology, archaeology, tourism, engineering, geology, marine biology, ecotoxicology, navigation, customs and excise, security. But studies have often focused on fishing[60] rather than whole coastal populations. Work on *coastal management* assesses government policies and commercial development,[61] and the likely impacts of climate change.[62] Ecosystems are unique,[63] which demands innovative approaches. Much relevant data is 'invisible' because it is 'time-hidden' (too slow to be perceived), 'scale hidden' (too big or small), 'distant' (influenced by large ecosystems or ocean dynamics), 'dynamic' (constantly moving), or 'submerged' (underwater or underground).[64] Underwater robots and imaging devices are providing access to this 'invisible data' (Figure 10.2).[65] *Ramsar* provides ongoing discussion about wetland regions.

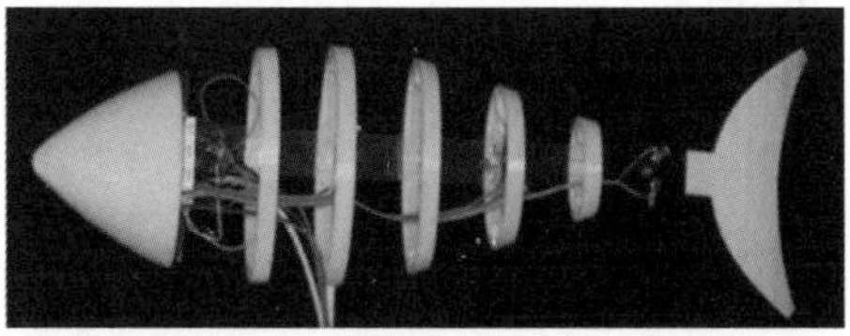	The *iTUNA* swims like a fish to record fish behaviour. The spine is a smart electro-responsive material. The case is 3D printed. (CSIC, Madrid)
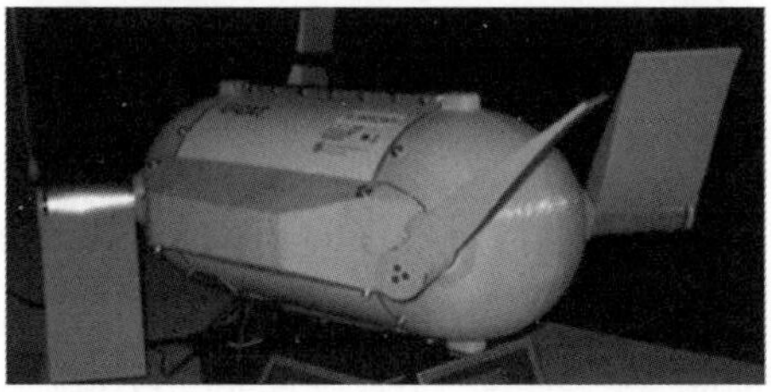	This "turtle submarine" swims in deep water with cameras, sensors and tools to recover archaeological and other samples. (ARROWS, TUT/CfB Tallin, Estonia)

Figure 10.2 Underwater robots

Photos: Author's own

A significant example of coastal research concerns the *Chisso Company* mercury poisoning at Minamata Bay (Japan). Victims and fishing families became the first environmental activists in the world, and the *Soshisha Minamata Disease Museum* has remarkable data about their research. From 1925, Minamata research was complex and innovative. Local nurses observed strange health problems, and local people noticed there were too many rats, and worked out that this was because there were too few cats. Doctors tried to study the mysterious environmental health problems, before ecotoxicology existed.[66] They mapped affected humans, cats and fish. Poisoned fish could be caught easily by the cats and children, because they floated or swam slowly, and so cats died and children became ill. This, and infrastructure such as railways that took fish to distant markets were mapped. Workers in the factory drew diagrams of the processes, from memory, showing that an initial filtering system had been removed as production increased. Lawyers could therefore argue that the company knew the discharge was hazardous, and brought negligence cases to court without environmental legislation. Noting the electric pylons is the key to understanding why the *Chisso* factory started, and continues to exist (C12.2). The region has cheap hydro-electric power. In 2013, the agreement of the UN *Minamata Convention on Mercury* marked the significance of the disaster, and research continues about caring for disabled, and often alienated, survivors.

10.5 Global commons

From the 1960s, arguments about 'the tragedy of the commons'[67] inspired research about the world's shared resources, which informed research about international security, law and regulation.[68] The UNEP/DELC works to consolidate the subsequent disparate treaties. Places of interest include:

- Outer space (UN *Committee on the Peaceful Uses of Outer Space*; *Outer Space Treaty*; *Moon Treaty*) – communications satellites,[69] space commerce,[70] security.[71]
- Atmosphere (*Vienna Convention for the Protection of the Ozone Layer*; *Convention on Long-Range Transboundary Air Pollution*; UN *Framework Convention on Climate Change*, IPCC) – agriculture and fisheries,[72] health,[73] livelihoods,[74] the dynamics of 'environmental refugees',[75] human impacts on the biosphere.[76]
- Sea (*Convention on the Law of the Sea*; *Global Ocean Commission*) – livelihoods and safety of sailors and fishing communities,[77] marine pollution affecting coastal populations,[78] marine resources and potential for related conflict,[79] transport of passengers and goods – ship safety,[80] economic impacts on port workers and communities,[81] modern piracy,[82] environmental change – rising sea levels,[83] loss of island territories, freshwater cycles.[84]
- Polar regions (*Antarctic Treaty Systems*) – exploration,[85] melting ice,[86] human impacts.[87]

There are convincing arguments that *cyberspace* also represents part of the global commons, and research now concerns freedom of expression, access to the digital commons, censorship, privacy and surveillance.[88] The ICRC is investigating how exploiting internet-based vulnerabilities – hospitals, navigation, disaster warning systems – through 'cyber warfare', might amount to a war crime.[89]

The ***human dimensions***[90] reflect how science relates to social research,[91] and that global resources represent *global public goods*.[92] A fundamental area of research is the perceptions and rights of indigenous peoples about the commons.[93] New technologies are making relevant low-tech data collection methods more feasible. These are often a basis for crowdsourced research – mapping polluters,[94] measuring greenhouse gases with mobile sensors[95] and tracking oil spills.[96]

10.6 Texts

Textual analysis can be an aspect of documentary analysis (C13.2). But in public places, texts are usually short sets of symbols – words and images[97] – which communicate messages through media such as inscriptions, posters and memorial plaques. ***Visual research*** methods cover a wide range of topics,[98] and are discussed in the journal *Visual Studies*. *Graphic design* is a significant aspect.[99] Whether visual data is *quantitative* (can be measured) or *qualitative* (can be interpreted) depends on how data is collected and recorded, and that relates to how it will be analysed.[100]

Data about how a country promotes its national identity is readily available on official images on *coins, banknotes and stamps*. Collecting this data does not always entail seeing the actual objects, they can be viewed on collectors' sites and *eBay*. In public places, state posters and murals provide a way to "read" and interpret political messages.[101] Of course, texts and images are often altered – manipulated, airbrushed, selectively framed, defaced – for political or journalistic reasons. Researching alterations is sometimes more interesting than the original text, and often reflects geopolitics.

Data needs to permit an analytical "reading" of texts, beyond the obvious meaning, to address questions such as:

- What is the image?
- Where and when was it created?
- Who created it, and how?
- Who is the image for, and why was it created?
- What obvious 'message' does it send?
- What are the hidden messages?
- What has changed over time, and why?
- What are the power implications - gender, wealth, age, status, nationalistic?
- What languages are used, and why?

Heraldry (Figure 2.5), *logos* and *insignias* indicate the values and identity of states and organizations. The emblem of Kazakhstan is based around the *shangyrak*, the central skyward roof window of the yurt. This not only supports the whole yurt frame, but also acts as a sundial, and is a form of Zenith Telescope to observe the movement of stars.

10.7 Objects

Objects (artefacts)[102] are central to research by archaeologists, anthropologists and museum curators, who have their own specialist methods, including photography.[103] In the past, objects from other countries were usually *acquired*, which often amounted to stealing. New technologies are creating more ethical ways to find, record and research objects, and to transfer data (C7). This includes 3D scanning and photographic replication, or 3D printing. Many interesting objects can now be found by searching on museum, gallery or auction sites such as *eBay*.

Archaeologists and ***curators*** usually deal with objects related to people who are long dead.[104] In the past, this has often entailed guesswork about their meaning and function, which often needs to be reassessed. Objects that were not easily categorized were sometimes termed 'votive', 'ritual', 'symbolic', 'religious' or 'sacred' without much evidence. Their use may have been more prosaic, as maps, calendars, or memory aids. We now realize that some "sacred" objects were probably children's toys,[105] but this did not fit the male-dominated world of archaeology. In contrast, ***anthropologists*** may be studying objects that have contemporary significance for living people. Investigating these may mean talking directly to people for whom the objects have great meaning, which should be done in a sensitive way. Researchers study how and why buildings are created and used, but also the influences between the construction of buildings and objects.

Forensic anthropology and ***archaeology*** links traditional ethnographic methods with police investigation techniques, to study things like objects in mass graves, and this also requires a combination of science and sensitivity.[106] Systematic collection and annotation is crucial, preferably by neutral parties. Reputable police forces have robust systems for ensuring the integrity of forensic evidence.[107] Spent munitions in a war zone can evidence the use of illegal weapons such as cluster bombs and chemical weapons, and many munitions carry precise details about technical specifications, country of origin, dates of manufacture and batch numbers, which can evidence systematic abuse of power. Robert Fisk provides an example:

> Pieces of the US manufacturer's [Lockheed] Hellfire air-to-ground missile lie in the local civil defence headquarters in Bethlehem...The missile engine, fuel pipe and shreds of the wiring system have been sorted into plastic bags by ambulance drivers and paramedics, alongside shrapnel from dozens of US-made fuses for shells fired by Israeli tanks into the Christian village of Beit Jalla.[108]

Investigators need to keep, and photograph or document, contextual evidence to verify location and, if possible, timing. A bullet still embedded in something – a brick or human tissue – is better evidence than a clean bullet. Photographing an object together with a newspaper, clearly showing a date, provides evidence that the photo was taken after the paper was published. A public clock, or the sun and shadows, might verify time. Plants and trees can indicate the season.

New methods also provide new ways to ***reinterpret*** old objects. Improved dating can revolutionize world history.[109] The first sound recording was on a 'phonautograph' in 1857, but the machine could only record graphically and not play back. In 2008, computer-graphic software was able to convert those visual patterns back into sound.[110]

10.8 Built environment

Research about ***buildings***, uninhabited ***built objects*** and ***infrastructure*** systems ranges from historic stone buildings[111] and memorials, to electric pylons. *Google Street View* is useful for remote close-up viewing, when there are precise details about the location. Research is often associated with urban history,[112] or restoration and conservation.[113] Damage and alterations are worth investigating. The damage above the entrance to a government building in Sarajevo has not been repaired, as an ongoing reminder of the 1992–1996 siege (Figure 10.3). Similarly, World War II bomb damage to the *Tate Britain* gallery and *V&A* museum, London, has been left as a memorial.

Entrance to a government building
(Сарајево ¬ Sarajevo, 2007)

Figure 10.3 The symbolism of war damage

Photo: Author's own

Public buildings, such as courts, public baths, churches and museums, are often open to researchers. From observation and interviews, museum researchers might analyse *visitor behaviour*.[114] Older buildings have often changed their use dramatically, this is not always obvious, but can indicate local political values. A former KGB building in Budapest is now a museum, one in Almaty is now a bland-fronted college, and the vast KGB building in Minsk includes a colonnade and panopticon and is still closed for business.

Built objects are usually uninhabited structures – statues, monuments, memorials, gravestones – and data often needs to be collected in a way that permits *textual analysis* (above). Gender researchers might observe war memorials to compare involvement of women in conflict. A British memorial emphasizes the anonymity of British women soldiers by showing empty uniforms of non-combat ranks such as nursing. But in Kazakhstan, women war heroes are presented as named fighters. Kazakh nomadic tradition considers women as strong and equal to men. Other sources can validate visual analysis. The 2012 WEF *Global Gender Gap Index* ranked Kazakhstan highly at 32; France was down at 45.

After *regime change*, new rulers are faced with the conundrum of what to do with the symbolic monuments of their predecessors. To keep them suggests that previous ideas are still valid, but to destroy them equates with political vandalism. Protestant iconoclasts in Reformation England destroyed and defaced – but also punished, tried, tortured and even hanged – Catholic monuments. In 2003, the US military stage-managed images of Iraqi people seeming to pull down a statue of Saddam Hussein.[115] Ideological monuments may have artistic merit, and preserving a history of the former regime can be important to legitimize the new regime. Budapest solved this conundrum by creating a *Memento Park*, which preserves communist era statues (Figure 10.4).

A truncated Lenin

Memento Park, Budapest

Figure 10.4 Communist monument

Photo: Author's own

Infrastructure connects places and spaces – it provides the physical networks and vectors, which transfer people, things, knowledge and ideas along prescribed areas. Methodologies are undeveloped, but *systems* and *network analysis* can provide a basis (C12). Infrastructure *hubs* can provide access to otherwise unobtainable data about a place – sewage treatment plants contain data about the degree of drug use in a locality.[116] Where do things that are stored in 'the cloud' actually exist, and what are the environmental implications?[117] The absence of data can also be significant – the empty highways of Pyongyang reveal a lot about life in North Korea.

Historically, important ***vectors*** were based on natural phenomena – currents and prevailing winds, pathways and passes, routes between oases and wells. And these might be useful when studying things like cross-border pollution, or trafficking networks. On land, early navigation may have entailed using 'ley lines' – 'straight tracks' between landmarks such as hills and trees, and later between buildings such as burial mounds and spires.[118] Cathedral spires (or tall cedar trees by desert monasteries) helped religious travellers to navigate. But this navigation was based on knowledge, and knowledge was based on power. To know that the main entrance to a Christian church faced west turned cathedrals into compasses.

Local buildings and infrastructure may also be used for local research and ***surveillance***.[119] Multi-purpose buildings often contained additional sophisticated research technologies. Towers seem an architectural human universal across nations and throughout history, yet few do anything uniquely useful, except to provide a way for the powerful to observe the people. With negotiation, researchers may be able to utilize some of these facilities for their own research, especially for mapping (C11).

10.9 Environment

'Places' exist in the context of a physical ***environment***. And *texts*, *objects* and *buildings* may all exist, change, or have disappeared because of environmental factors. Although environmental research is normally the domain of natural scientists, social science increasingly explores the *human dimensions* through activist groups, citizen science,[120] crowdsourced research (C6.4) and environmental victims.[121]

Satellite data evidences long-term global change, such as the shrinking of the Aral Sea, and environmental impacts on the global commons. Cheap UAVs are providing ways for aerial environmental monitoring by non-specialists, which may be better than satellite images. Quadcopters, kites and balloons[122] can collect data cheaply and quickly, as for the BP oil spill in Mexico Bay[123] (C11.1). Numerous mobile and handheld sensors make data collection by non-specialists increasingly easy. With many devices, samples can be analysed instantly on-site, and data sent through the internet, which avoids the problem of posting or carrying hazardous substances (C7.7).

Small ***robots*** with cameras or sensors can reach inaccessible terrains. *Rosphere*[124] is a robot ball that will roll along the ground collecting data about the land and plants. Low level *flying robots* such as *GimBall* can hold a course yet negotiate hazards, as in forests. *Unattended ground sensors* can be camouflaged as rocks and use solar power. It seems probable that soon *transient electronic devices* will self-destruct or biodegrade. Thousands of these could be dropped in the sea to monitor pollution, and then dissolve.

An interest in electronic devices should not rule out innovative unobtrusive *low-tech data collection,* including 'human sensors'. Identical white T-shirts and shoes, worn in polluted and clean cities, can collect comparative data about human exposure for analysis in a laboratory back home. Shoes can pick up sample soil, especially if the soles are smeared with grease or *Vaseline*. Keeping samples of water from washing hair is similar – hair is an excellent pollution-collection device. The data might evidence toxic releases from factories or military sites. Data must be dated and tagged, and sealed in separate plastic bags to avoid cross-contamination. Independent photos or videos of the collection can help to verify that data is genuine. Officials – police or emigration – are unlikely to suspect a grubby T-shirt, or smelly trainers, as evidence of subversive evidence gathering. And, if challenged, the objects could be explained as the basis for an art work, or even used to create one.

10.10 Data capture

Former data capture techniques can be relevant to present-day research, and inform the use of modern digital devices. An English engraver, E.W. Lane (1801–1876), provided ethnographic descriptions and meticulous ***scientific drawings*** of daily life in Egypt. His depiction of a street in Cairo shows different trades, goods, inscriptions, ages, sexes, classes, transport, animals, architectural design, female modesty, construction techniques, clothing, and even the sunny weather. But he omits irrelevant information. With electronic devices, the first consideration must be, as for scientific drawing, how to "select the signal from the noise".

The website explains and lists numerous devices that can help with data capture. Cheap small devices are available to collect data unobtrusively, especially in sensitive places – "spy cameras", video and audio recorders, and sensors. They need testing before use, to use the controls quickly and efficiently, and to aim and stabilize shots. But, note the warning at the end of C7 and C8. While you are observing and recording other people, other people may be using similar devices, and buildings, to observe and record *you*.

Sometimes researchers visit a particular place because recently something has happened, an *event* or *incident* – revolution, disaster, environmental change. The purpose is to assess something that is different from the norm, and so a wide range of non-standard data capture may be relevant. Researchers working with political prisoners might ask them about smells and sounds, to identify or verify the place of imprisonment. Good audio recordings in war zones can help experts to identify types of munitions and aerial weapons. Smell could provide initial evidence of unusual chemicals, or disposal on a large scale by burning. In his study of Hiroshima after the US use of an A-bomb, Lifton provides a rare example of 'olfactory imagery', describing 'a terrible smell, like broiling sardines'.[125] Cheap sensors can now capture environmental data easily, and odour recorders – "electronic noses" – are capturing usable data about smell[126] to understand 'smellscapes'.[127] Increasingly, places can be "seen without looking", and non-visual data can provide a wealth of insights, if we remember to note it.

thinking zone: how would a blind person "see" the data?

What did wars, crucifixions and Chinese "death by a thousand cuts" sound like? How did the Catholic burnings of Protestants smell? There are seemingly no documentary accounts, yet this data could easily have been noted.

"seeing"

- If sighted, observe a research site with eyes closed. Are some forms of non-visual data interesting and relevant?
- Ask blind researchers to observe a research site, or listen to recordings. What do they notice that others do not?

recording

Use an audio recorder during general observation in public places, and note the counter number when visual or audio data seems interesting. Check these audio data 'hotspots' later.

validating

Check the audio tracks on secondary video data, e.g. from mobile phones in war zones, or YouTube clips. Does the sound match the video data, and claims about where and when it was taken - clock bells, *muezzin* calls, seasonal birds? If a video appears to be taken from a vehicle (helicopter, bike) or specific place (cafe, coast), does the background sound match? Is a contextual sound missing - engine noise, sea, weather?

future history

- What sounds may soon be lost - dialects, glaciers, technologies, backgammon in cafes, local radio?
- How would odour data improve historical evidence?

[See References for further information.[128]]

main ideas

When researching ***places*** consider methods from *human geography, archaeology, anthropology* and *ethnography* - *reading, watching, talking, recording.* Places can be categorized in terms of:

- **street –** "invisible" people, graffiti, posters, adverts, street markets and shops, informal and formal events.
- **urban –** organizations, public services, permanent populations.
- **rural –** different terrains and transient populations.
- **coastal –** coastal management and communities, "invisible" factors hidden by time/scale/distance or because they are dynamic or submerged.
- **global commons –** shared resources, human dimensions, satellite data.
- **environment –** human dimensions, aerial observation, sensors.

Data about places is likely to come from visual research on:

- **texts** - banknotes, stamps, logos, insignia, political posters, murals.
- **objects –** archaeological and anthropological evidence and museums, reinterpreting old objects with new technologies.
- **buildings –** dwellings, public buildings, industrial and commercial centres - and uninhabited **built objects** - monuments, 'observatories', infrastructure.

key reading

Andranovich, G.D. and Riposa, G. (eds) (1993) *Doing Urban Research.* New York: Sage.

Flowerdew, R. and David, M. (2005) *Methods in Human Geography: A Guide for Students Doing a Research Project.* Harlow: Prentice-Hall.

Kusenbach, M. (2003) 'Street phenomenology: the go-along as ethnographic research tool', *Ethnography*, 4 (3): 455–485.

Sinton, D. and Lund, J. (eds) (2007) *Understanding Place.* Redlands, CA: ESRI Press.

Twumasi, P.A. (2001) *Social Research in Rural Communities.* Accra: Ghana University Press.

online resources

To access the resources - search on the name in italics, use the http, or search on the generic term in 'quote marks'.

Street ethnography - http://blogs.ubc.ca/qualresearch/2012/11/12/street-ethnography/

Buskers Advocates - information for street users - www.buskersadvocates.org

Digital Humanitarian Network (DHN) - interface between formal humanitarian organizations and global networks of tech-savvy digital volunteers

Wiki Sensor – environmental monitoring software platform – http://wikisensor.com

CITI-SENSE – facilitates citizens' observatories – www.citi-sense.eu

PublicLab – development of cheap citizen science devices – http://publiclab.org/blog

Tactical Technology Collective – info activists

Crytek CryENGINE – converts maps and scientific drawings into 3D visualizations

MORE ON THE WEBSITE

ELEVEN

Mapping places

Anyone arriving in a research location by plane should try to look out of the window, and perhaps take a few photos, because this can provide a starting point for local mapping. If that fails, going up tall buildings or hills might be useful. Alternatively, find local people who work high in the air – crane operators can take wonderful aerial photos, especially if the topic of the research is construction and development.

Cartography is a specialist skill, and the purpose of this chapter is first to understand the *terms* and *techniques* of professional *general* maps.[1] But for most researchers, it is more important to create simple *thematic maps*[2] which can complement other research methods, and the methods of *citizen* and *grassroots mapmaking* are innovative and straightforward. Historical and indigenous map-making are useful sources of ideas.[3] Former methods can be a source of data, and were often created by inspired amateurs, with basic materials, and these can often easily be adapted to new circumstances.

11.1 Terms and techniques

Geometrics is the science of collecting, analysing and presenting geographic and spatially referenced information about the Earth. *Geostatistics* combines spatial and temporal data. These endeavours are the foundations of modern *Geographical Information Systems* (GIS), which use IT to manage maps and related information.[4] *Global Positioning Systems* (GPS) provide details of location, based on Russian and American satellite systems, and create the maps for smart phones, SatNav and other devices. But using proper GPS equipment is not simple, and requires training. Researchers often study power and mapping – how and why certain things are omitted or distorted, threats to privacy and security, the digital divide and spatial information, why companies like *Google* are so keen to amass and control so much data, and how maps 'lie'?[5]

The big technical problem for all world mapmakers is ***projection*** – how to depict a spherical world on a flat piece of paper – and this has often been politicized. In 1569, a Flemish cartographer, Gerardus Mercator, produced a projection that became the European standard for many centuries, but it showed the European, northern regions as proportionately much bigger than the southern continents. In 1855, a clergyman, James Gall, corrected this, and in 1967, a filmmaker, Arno Peters, produced the so-called *Peters' Projection* which become the favoured map for INGOs. An innovative projection came from the American polymath Buckminster Fuller in 1954. His 'one island' *Dymaxion Map* projection shows the continents of the world as a near contiguous landmass from Australia, across Eurasia, to the Antarctic.[6] But one of the most interesting projections comes from the sphere of 'borderless' outsider art – a map of the internet.

thinking zone: how do you map the internet?

"outsider"

Kokubo Norimitsu (小久保 憲満) is termed by some as 'autistic', and his work was a centrepiece of the *Souzou Outsider Art from Japan* exhibition at the *Wellcome Gallery*, London, in 2013.

world map

Kokubu's *World Map* depicts 'past, present and future' details of places he has come to know through the internet and other media. This *social projection* of the world reflects the GPS, interactive, real-time and topological maps which increasingly provide information rather than visual locations, about things like traffic flows, disasters, internet traffic, Earth systems and transport.

How might other so-called 'outsiders' map their world, differently – blind people, life prisoners, isolated villagers, robots, aliens from another planet?

[See References for further information.[7]]

Panoramic drawings of European cities were produced from the mid-16th century, often based on a river. Some were compiled by using numerous smaller local drawings;

others appear to be drawn from a single vantage point. From around 1860, panoramic cameras were widely used. Panoramic cameras either controlled the exposure of a long role of film, or took separate shots that were then 'stitched together'. This technique is now easy with digital cameras and software such as *Panomonkey* (*360cities*). *Google Street View* has developed the techniques of panoramic photography, and uses six video cameras, mounted on a car or bike, and the photos are stitched together digitally later. *Google Tracker* is a backpack version of the 360° camera systems which create *Street View*, but can be used in places that are not accessible for vehicles. Other systems use a similar camera, but can stream the results directly to the internet, which cannot be intercepted easily. Good quality panoramic cameras are expensive. But cheap clip-on lens mirrors for smart phones permit fish eye or 360° surround video. Alternatively, single shots can be stitched together using *MapKnitter*. But simply videoing river banks from a boat, or streets from a bus, can also provide a rich 'panorama' of data.

The first ***aerial photos*** were from balloons in 1858, and kites in 1889. Pigeons carried cameras in 1908; the shots were timed but very imprecise. In 1900, British military photographers took the first aerial photos for mapmaking, from manned balloons. The first aerial film was made when the Wright brothers spontaneously fixed a movie camera to the wing of their prototype plane, which became a film *Wilbur Wright und seine Flugmaschine* (1909). From 1916 planes took over from balloons, and satellites provided new opportunities (below).

In 1854, a London doctor, John Snow, marked the houses where people had died of cholera, on a simple street map. He noticed that the frequency increased close to a particular water pump, and correctly identified it as the source of the disease. He had also created a *thematic bivariate* ***dot map***, invented *epidemiology*, and provided the bases for present-day online resources such as *Google Flu Map*, *HealthMap* and the crowdsourced *Flusurvey*. The method has countless applications, such as evidencing that commuting motorists kill children in black areas of American cities,[8] and poisonings from environmental pollution.

In 1869, a retired French engineer, M. Minard, used secondary data to produce a remarkable *multivariate* ***flow map*** of Napoleon's failed attempt to invade Moscow in 1812–1813. The map shows the route the army took, the number of soldiers at each place (in graph form based on the width of line – 1 mm = 10,000 men), combined with a temperature scale below (low temperature at the top). The map showed how "General Winter" had defeated Napoleon. Online research methods can now produce similar multivariate maps in real time. By monitoring tweets, the UN-OCHA in Geneva was able to monitor the trajectory of *Typhoon Pablo* in 2012, and produce the first crisis map from social media data.

Topological maps are distorted representations which show travellers "how to get there", not exactly "where you are". These maps are now common – the London Underground map is the obvious example, but there are earlier instances. Aboriginal 'ground paintings' also emphasize relative position not exact location. Micronesian 'stick maps' help fishermen to navigate between islands.[9] The technique can be applied to many systems from oil pipelines to micro-electronic circuit boards. In simple form, topology can provide quick spatial research records, and simplify complex geopolitics. A topological Venn diagram map can clarify political structures, while still indicating relative geographical position.

Satellite maps can provide quick evidence for situation analysis (C6.2) of emergencies,[10] which can be politically very effective. George Cloony's *Satellite Sentinel Project* started monitoring Southern Sudan in 2010, to warn of potential mass atrocities. The *Peace Research Institute Oslo* (PRIO) provides mapping tools for assessing the potential for conflict, such as shared rivers and long international boundaries. Earthquakes are tracked by the *US Geological Survey*,[11] and mobile technology is becoming easy to use.[12] *Universe Today* provides a useful basic introduction to satellite methods. *Google Earth* and *National Geographic Maps* make satellite maps widely available. NASA *Landsat* images are free on *Earth Observatory*. Archived satellite images, and commissioned work, can be purchased from organizations such as *GeoEye, Digital Globe, Land Info, Spot Image* and *Earth Explorer.* Archived images can cost as little as US$10–50, commissions from organizations such as the *European Space Agency* are more expensive (around $1500) and the timing of shots depends on satellite availability and cloud cover. Mini satellites, as being developed by *Planet Labs,* produce HD low altitude images, and increasingly give power to individual citizen mapmakers. ***Real-time*** maps include *FightRadar24,* which shows all commercial air traffic in-flight. These *live maps* are especially useful for emergency and disaster mapping. Real-time maps can also track slower changes such as land cover,[13] and human activities such as illegal logging.

Remote sensing[14] was initially done from balloons, ships and buoys, but more recently by collecting data through light planes, satellites, UAVs and mobile devices, which can be analysed digitally.[15] Sensing entails gathering non-photographic information about the Earth from a distance – either *passively* though film or sensors, or *actively* by emitting energy and measuring its reflection like radar. Local remote sensing data can be added to maps, and expensive high-tech systems are not always needed. Data about pollution levels can be collected automatically from smart phone sensors (C10.9), or even from pigeons linked to the *Pigeonblog* website.[16] Arguably, humans can themselves be 'citizen sensors', sending *Volunteered Geographic Information* (VGI)[17] back to a website map, either from observations or via mobile devices which operate automatically.[18]

3D digital mapping is a culmination of old and new methods, which makes valuable "invisible" data visible.[19] Following the *Carte géométrique de la France* (1789), mapmakers have added contours to create *topographical* maps of the visible vertical features of territories (mountains, valleys). Soon after, William Smith created the first *geological map* of England (1815), and this *stratigraphic* mapping adds the invisible vertical features (under the ground and sea), which helps geologists to locate minerals and oil fields, and archaeologists to date the things they find. Superimposing sea-depth information on maps of coastal seas can help fishing communities and activists to understand the likely consequences of government coastal developments (C10.4).[20] 3D sensing can reveal 'lost cities' and other archaeological factors such as ancient roadways or quarries, in places such as Easter Island.[21] Software such as the *Crytek CryENGINE* can convert historical maps and scientific drawings into 3D visualizations. *Airborne Light Detection and Ranging* (LiDAR) measures distance by illuminating a target with a laser and analysing the reflected light. It can, in effect, "x-ray" land cover and produce 3D maps which help to find unknown archaeological, or other, sites by showing regular features such as straight lines and circles. Interactive 3D maps permit users to manipulate and add data through hand gestures.[22]

Innovative *thematic maps*[23] include the *Globetrotter* interactive world map, which incorporates DNA mapping to identify human migrations throughout history, evidencing events like the Arab slave trade and Mongolian Empire.[24] But specialist knowledge and high-tech systems are not needed to map features such as police stations that use torture,[25] fishermen exposed to radiation from nuclear testing,[26] or the use of urban spaces by young people.[27]

11.2 Citizen mapmaking

Searching under the keywords *citizen mapping* and *grassroots mapping*, finds free software, advice and numerous mobile mapping devices.[28] Many resources focus on the vulnerability of communities to disasters,[29] and crisis mapping.[30] The *Public Laboratory for Open Technology and Science* (PLOTS) develops and makes available a wide range of low cost innovations and high-tech devices. The *publiclab.org* store provides balloon and kite mapping kits, and a 'grassroots mapping forum'.

Light lithium batteries have made it possible to mount cameras on diverse low cost ***Unmanned Aerial Vehicles*** (***UAVs*** – drones). Although currently the flying time is usually around 15 minutes, new hydrogen fuel cell engines are likely to extend this to around 30 hours. Planes take useful video, but because of the speed, still photos are often poor quality. *Quadcopters* can hover, and take better quality photos of exact locations. These are now sold cheaply as toys, can be pilotted by and send data to a mobile phone, and can be controlled on a retractable dog lead. Using more expensive systems, videos from UAVs can be streamed back to a PC. *DIY Drones* provides ongoing discussion and updates, for example about 'terrain mapping'.[31] Small UAVs fly low, can avoid cloud cover, and can take high resolution shots and infra-red images. Technologies can be up-and-running quickly, are completely controlled by the researchers, and are adaptable as ideas change. Check local laws before using UAVs, and consider safety if flying over people. Indoors use prop-guards. Drones sometimes fall out of the air for no reason.

There are also groups of *Kite Aerial Photography* (KAP) enthusiasts using suppliers such as *KAPShop*. Unmanned *Balloon Aerial Photography* (BAP) is similar. Photos are taken by timed auto-exposure, continuous shooting ('continuous drive'), or are radio controlled. Creating a 'rig' to maintain a stable camera angle is difficult, but a high shutter speed can overcome general wobble. The software *MapKnitter* helps to stitch photos together. Kites and balloons are silent and can therefore record discreetly, including sound, in quiet locations such as wetlands. If balloons have three tethers, they can be steered and held in specific locations for long periods of time, to monitor logging for example. Small flying devices, used by amateurs, may sometimes lawfully circumvent governmental controls on flying. At the start of the BP/Mexico Bay (*Deepwater Horizon*) oil spill, balloons were used to get around the 4000 ft restricted flight zone, which prevented evidence gathering by plane during the first few weeks.

Crowdsourced (C6.4) mapping contributes local details to improve online maps – concerning emergencies and disasters,[32] or land cover (vegetation, forests).[33] Local volunteers, perhaps using handheld GPS devices, may be asked to check out specific places of concern, and add photos or comments. These can then be verified and coordinated by other volunteers, anywhere in the world. Information can also come from big data analysis, which finds keywords in social media chat, about events such as typhoons, and can map their progress before other systems. *Syria Tracker* used *crowdmaps* to match satellite images and local photo/video and testimony to document political violence in Syria (Figure 11.1). The *iWitness Pollution Map* recorded oil pollution from the BP *Deepwater Horizon* oil spill. Citizen cartographers use sites such as *Wikimapia, OpenStreetMap, Google Mapmaker, Ushahidi* and *Crisis Mappers. Map Action* and the *Digital Humanitarian Network* provide GIS assistance to humanitarian NGOs, and the *Crisis Response Journal* has ongoing updates. But amateur mapmakers can sometimes create security problems by revealing safe locations, and perhaps unwittingly provide information that helps repressive regimes or other criminals.

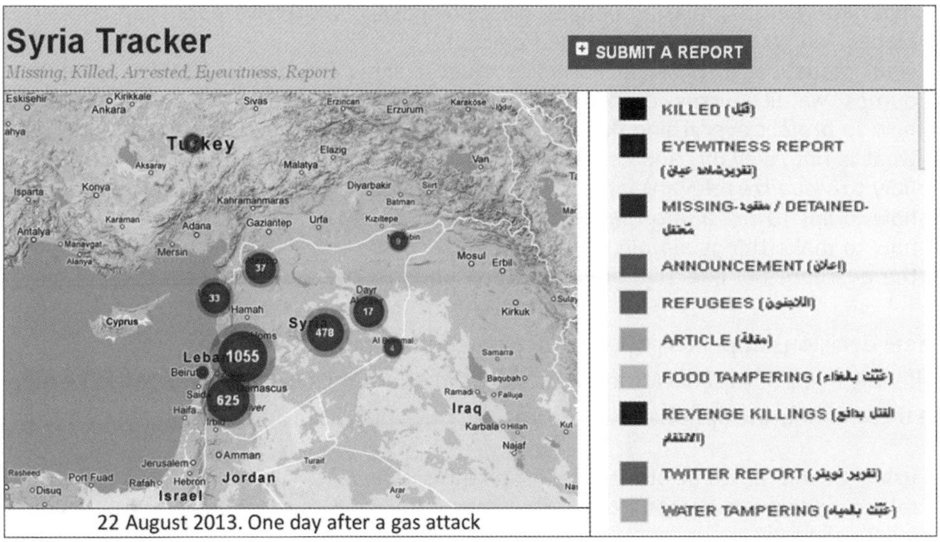

22 August 2013. One day after a gas attack

Figure 11.1 Syria Tracker crowdmap

The *World Bank* provides tools for micro-level ***community mapping***, including discussions of: social factors, mobility, risk and community resources.[34] Development agencies provide useful guides for participatory mapping.[35] Civil society initiatives are contributing local details to online maps,[36] using platforms such as *Wikimapia*. Using *Google Earth*, American students produced *North Korea Uncovered*,[37] which documented 'buildings, monuments, missile-storage facilities, mass graves, and secret labour camps'.[38] The potential for cheap low-tech innovation seems endless. "Spy cameras" can simply be taped to toy AUVs. A camera protected in bubble-wrap can be strung from hydrogen-filled party balloons, tied to a long piece of string, and retrieved when the balloon blows away or bursts.

11.3 Creating simple thematic maps

Mapping does not need to be complicated: it needs to be adequate for the purpose of the research. If assessing the time taken to get to safe drinking water from remote villages, drawing and measuring simple as-the-crow-flies lines on a map, and roughly adjusting the calculation for terrain (mountains, rivers, roads), might provide adequate relative data about different villages, which would not be much better if done using GPS tracking devices.

For researchers or their research participants, making basic maps entails simple decisions:

- the *purpose* of the map.
- how things will be *located* – compass, GPS, grid systems.
- *what* it needs to show – *physical reference points* (roads, rivers, buildings), *objective data* (deaths, missing people, waste disposal), *subjective data* (dangerous/safe places, 'no go' areas, overcrowded places).
- what statistical or physical *variables* must it show (reports of deaths, toxic waste dumps, water courses, drinking wells).
- how to *project* everything flat, on paper or screen.
- what is *not relevant*, and can be omitted.
- how to *visualize* relevant information (dots, colours, key).
- how to *link* to *extra information*.
- how to make things *simple*.
- the *aesthetics* of effective presentation – images, colours, size, title.

These decisions apply to paper, device-based and online mapping.

If basic maps of the area are available, in print or online, relevant features can be drawn on these. If not, the options for recording the basic physical features of an area include:

- using *Google Earth* or other satellite pictures (above).
- taking *panoramic* photos from high places (church or mosque towers, tall buildings, hills) (above).

- using basic geographical *survey methods* to measure ground features, starting with regular shapes (straight roads, square buildings) and landmarks (trees, towers), and then adding irregular features (rivers, crops).
- using *mapping software*, often free.
- *crowdsourcing* data (C6.4) ("Every family will measure and draw the area in front of their dwelling, to the middle of the path").
- using *aerial* photos from UAVs – kites, balloons, planes, helicopters (above).

If the purpose of the map requires a high degree of accuracy, scaling or GPS can be used. If not, maps may be topological (above), just showing significant features, such as safe routes to the market.

But not everyone understands the concept of a map or of a bird's-eye view. People in remote rural areas may never have seen a diagram, and not understand that symbols can represent real things. People with learning disabilities may not understand how physical things can be depicted on paper. (And students that have always depended on GPS devices, are often clueless about real maps.) Using large 3D 'model maps', on the ground or a table, can help to make mapping fully inclusive, for example to show routes and dangerous places. Smaller *tactile maps* can help blind and partially sighted people.[39]

People who are inexpert in mapping may be experts about other things, for example police violence, or state neglect. A South African street child who had been arrested by police for playing dice (using archaic colonial gaming laws) was asked where this happened. Without prompting, he drew a map, which provided convincing and precise evidence of the site of this abuse by police. (Figure 11.2).

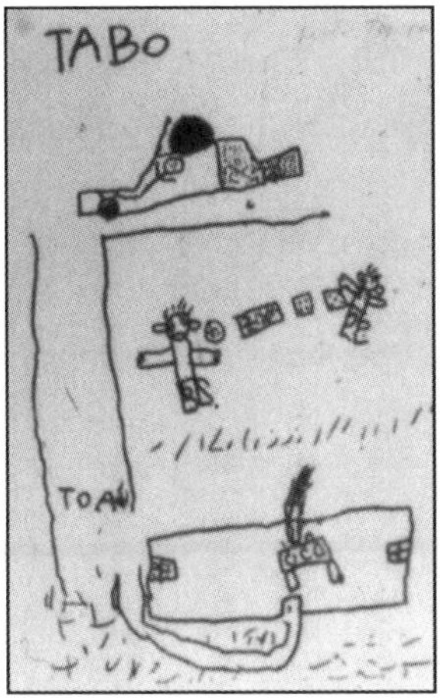

Tabo mapped where police arrested him for playing dice

Figure 11.2 Maps by street children

Source: Williams, C. (1990) 'Street children and education' – http://etheses.bham.ac.uk/698/

main ideas

Understanding ***historical mapping*** methods can help to:

- analyse and compare *historical research*.
- inspire *new non-digital* and *digital mapping* methods.

Cartography includes using and creating:

- *general maps*, which usually requires specialist skills.
- *thematic maps* – dot maps, flow maps, topological maps, satellite images, remote sensing, 3D mapping.

Basic mapping can:

- add relevant details to *existing maps*, paper or online.
- use *aerial photos* from high buildings, kites, balloons, UAVs, light planes.
- *'stitch together'* panoramic or aerial photos.
- use, purchase or commission *satellite photos*.
- use free *crowdmap* sites to link maps to the internet.
- *crowdsource* to get numerous small mapping tasks done by many people.
- use simple *inclusive* methods to make sure that relevant people can participate in research.

key reading

Bankoff, G. et al. (2004) *Mapping Vulnerability: Disasters, Development, and People.* London: Earthscan.

Chuvieco, E. and Chuvieco, E. (eds) (2009) *The Fundamentals of Satellite Remote Sensing.* Boca Raton, FL: CRC Press.

Meier, P. (2013) 'Crowdsourcing to map conflict, crises and humanitarian response', in D. Backer et al. (eds), *Peace and Conflict.* Bethesda: University of Maryland Press.

Slocum, T. (2003) *Thematic Cartography and Geographic Visualization.* Upper Saddle River, NJ: Prentice-Hall.

online resources

To access the resources – search on the name in italics, use the http, or search on the generic term in 'quote marks'.

How to choose and use GPS devices – www.ordnancesurvey.co.uk/blog/2013/12/choosing-a-handheld-gps-device

Reviews of international devices – http://gps.toptenreviews.com/navigation/international-travel-which-gps-device-is-best-.html; www.reviewgist.com/best-gps-device-international-travel

Geocomm – lists free viewers and basic mapping tools – http://software.geocomm.com/viewers/

Free mapping software – www.esri.com/software/free-mapping-software

Crowdmap – mapping software that allows online additions to immersive internet maps

Crisis Mappers – support for mapping disasters and emergencies

360cities – advice and demos about panoramic mapping – www.360cities.net

Panomonkey – software to 'stitch' shots together – www.panomonkey.com

GeoEye. DigitalGlobe. Spot Image – purchasing and commissioning satellite maps

Crytek CryENGINE – creates 3D (computer game) visualizations from maps and drawings – www.crytek.com/cryengine

OpenSourceGIS. FreeGIS – lists of free GIS software

Kite Aerial Phography (KAP) – www.arch.ced.berkeley.edu/kap/

ConservationDrones.org – UAVs for sustainable development research

ResearchDrones.com – UAVs for general research

Tactile maps for blind and partially sighted people – www.tactileview.com/mapmaker

TWELVE

Analysing world systems

If bored on a plane journey, look at the route maps in the airline brochures. They provide wonderful data about world *systems* – economic hubs and networks, political affiliations, human mobility, commercial interests. Which airlines fly to Pyongyang, and why? A historical study of air routes would probably represent a history of the development of the main systems of the modern technologically-based world. The site *Airline Route Maps* provides country-specific detail.[1]

But systems existed across the world well before airlines. Early traders, mariners, scholars and religions had large effective networks (Introduction), and they left information about their networks on buildings and in libraries. Therefore much fascinating data is non-digital, including colonial collections in museums like the *Oost-Indisch Huis (East India Company House)* in Amsterdam, or religious archives like the library of *St Catherine's Monastery*, Sinai. Many sources require field visits, for example to buildings and monuments across the old Silk Roads.

Methods books usually consider organizational, network and systems analysis separately. But for world research the interest is how these relate. Methods of data collection overlap, and so the relevant methodologies are discussed together. *World systems* research starts from some form of *intelligence gathering* – data about 'other' systems. This is then *mapped* using diagrams (but not necessarily in the form of the spatial maps discussed in Chapter 11). These show how the parts of a system fit together.

12.1 Social and administrative systems

Systems can be categorized as 'human-dominated', 'human-influenced' and 'natural' (Figure 1, p. xxxi).[2] Social science is mainly interested in the first two, but understanding how we relate to the natural world is essential for human survival. Human history is shaped by Earth systems such as tides, the weather and climate change.[3]

The *International Society for the Systems Sciences* hosts ongoing discussions about methods, and provides a way to adapt methods across the natural sciences, IT and social sciences. Many guidebooks explain the *international systems*.[4] Contemporary international research is likely to be based around the UN. Many academic sites[5] provide resources about the systems, and research,[6] including the UN 'sister' organizations, the WTO/GATT,[7] *World Bank*[8] and IMF.[9] The *Model UN* research resource site is clear and helpful.[10] The *United Nations System* home page is oriented towards UN staff and experts[11] and provides a useful *Directory of United Nations System Organizations*.[12] Similarly, the *Protocol and Liaison Service* lists permanent missions, representatives and senior UN officials.[13] The *United Nations University* (UNU) produces publications and methodologies about current issues. UN Web TV provides a way to maintain a daily awareness of UN work.[14] By comparison, there is very little methodology about researching global civil society and INGOs.[15]

World systems can be viewed in four ways – *governance* (UN HQ, EU), *political violence* (NATO, *Amnesty*), *development and economics* (WTO, *Oxfam*), and *environment* (UNEP, *Greenpeace*) – and there are many relevant research *frameworks* (C6.3). International systems can be assessed using different units of analysis – elites, power, power blocs, sovereignty, national interests, interdependence, dependency, non-state actors, TNCs. A study might put data on a theoretical framework, such as Wallerstein's[16] world systems theory (Figure 12.1).[17] Data might include:

- *overview* – history, aims and strategies, values, resources, finances.
- *human factors* – power structures and leadership,[18] staff and expertise, networks,[19] communication,[20] 'narratives'.[21]
- *technical* – machinery, vehicles, IT, unique expertise.
- *contextual* – external influencing factors.

But current world theories often reflect colonial values and systems.

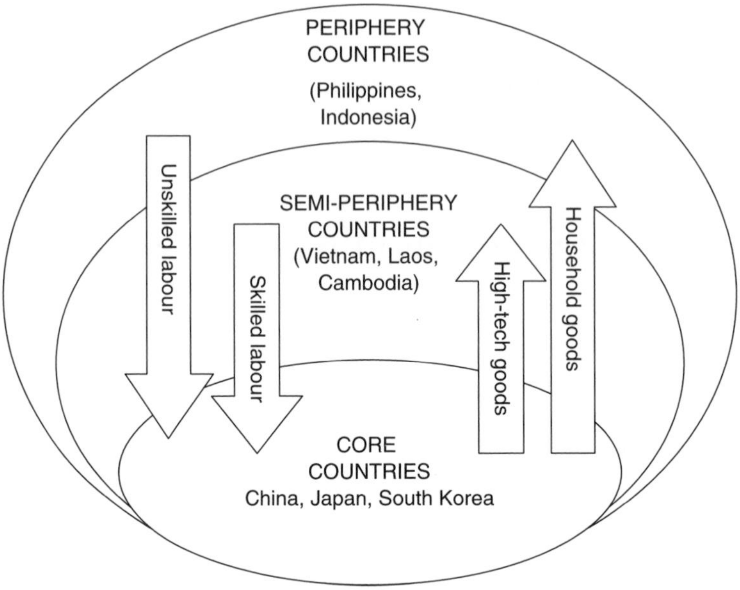

Figure 12.1 World systems theory

Based on: Wallerstein, I. (1974)*The Modern World-System: Capitalist Agriculture and the Origins of the European World-Economy in the Sixteenth Century*. New York: Academic Press.

Systems analysis uses data about interconnections and interrelations – concerning people, processes, methods and procedures – within organizations, or on a world scale. The methods developed for assessing commercial systems can be adapted to public services.[22] *Corporate Watch* provides a useful guide – *How to Research Companies*[23] – which can be applied to other forms of organization. 'Hard systems' are amenable to simple functional analysis much in the way that an engineer would analyse a mechanical system; 'soft systems'[24] are complex, fluid, and definitions and structure are unclear because of human dynamics.[25] *Organizational analysis*[26] focuses on power relations, and *organizational network analysis* on communication.[27] *Network analysis*[28] identifies 'interlocks',[29] 'nodes' and 'ties'. The aims of studies are usually to improve systems, perhaps by comparison with similar more effective systems. ***Evaluative research*** often entails some form of SWOT assessment of the efficiency of a system in achieving its own goals, but also in relation to other world dynamics such as climate change (Figure 12.2).[30]

SWOT ANALYSIS MATRIX		
	positives	negatives
internal	**S**trengths	**W**eaknesses
external	**O**pportunities	**T**hreats

Figure 12.2 SWOT analysis

12.1.1 Intelligence gathering

Intelligence analysis[31] is the basis for understanding commercial, criminal, military[32] and other systems across the world. It usually starts top-down from researching the elites who run the systems.[33] A manual, published in 1954, *Discovering National Elites*, provided a comprehensive methods book for diplomats and intelligence officers, which is still relevant.[34] Research might be based on official announcements, leaks and protocols. The UN *Protocol and Liaison Service* maintains a *Manual of Protocol*, which provides a basis for understanding how international relations *should* operate.[35] In closed countries such as North Korea, workers in organizations providing humanitarian assistance may be the best sources of regional information.[36] Political posters indicate the personas of ruling elites, how they want to present their systems, and who their allies are.

International police organizations such as *Europol* and *Interpol*[37] create systems for international cooperation.[38] Comparing methodological frameworks – for example about military and criminal threats – can assist cooperation and generate new methods.[39] *Data mining* of social media sites, using programmes such as the US *Prism* programme, is said to identify suspicious communications – *traffic analysis* affiliations, which can be mined to analyse beliefs, thoughts, friendships, interests and purchasing.[40] But the number of false positives is likely to be very high.

12.2 Mapping world systems

Most systems research *maps* (using diagrams) the data about elements, networks and processes of a system,[41] perhaps to create comparable *case studies* (C6.2). In the 19th century, models of education systems permitted national governments to compare (C13.2), and copy, the more progressive countries, and the charts used for analysis are still interesting. They use the *similarities* (*independent variables*) such as 'age' to compare the *differences* (*dependent variables*) – like 'type of school'.

Basic ***mapping templates*** can be created using software such as *Word* (Insert – Smart Art; Shapes):

- *Venn diagrams* – show overlaps and common areas, and *nested Venn diagrams* show core and contextual elements.
- *matrices* – list the presence or level of factors, *Excel* spreadsheets.
- *organizational/line management charts* – despict power structures, and systems of control and responsibility.
- *flow (decision) charts* – explain how different processes do, or should, operate in response to "yes/no" decisions about events. These can help to plan or understand algorithms.
- *process charts* – depict *linear* and *cyclical* processes and procedures, and can help to analyse planning or policy-making.
- *spidergrams* and *network charts* – show the linkages that create networks. These are often computer generated.[42] Useful analytical software includes *UCINet*, *ORA*, *Pajek* and *GIU for Linux*,[43] which can handle small and large-scale studies.

- *timelines* – show the order in which things happen (chronology), which can be the basis for analysing how certain events (independent variables) affect other events (dependent variables).

From these basic charts, further analysis may combine different sources or forms of data, to provide a bigger picture. *Critical Process Analysis* (CPA) provides a framework for investigating abuses of power (C12.2). Large systems, including 'soft' complex situations,[44] may be *modelled*, usually on computers, to understand past and future trajectories.

Data for mapping systems (using diagrams) can be collected through:

- *Interviews* (C8.2) within organizations – staff, customers and service-users may explain their local networks (experts, subordinates), who they communicate with (IT security, country offices), and who gives them permission to take certain actions (line manger, finance officers). Similarly, in public space, public officials or company reps may describe their own contacts and communications; victims or operatives of crime syndicates and similar networks, may be able to identify immediate contacts. But interviewing powerful people has distinct problems and methods.[45] Like a jigsaw puzzle, fitting these 'local' pieces together can create the big picture.
- *Observation* (C8.3) can help to identify interviewees, or verify interview data. This can include following people (which may be illegal if seen as 'stalking'), using CCTV, watching from vantage points such as high buildings, or participant observation (C8.3).
- *Tracking* people and objects is increasingly easy by using electronic devices, including cash machine and mobile phone[46] data. Short-distance devices, such as *Radio Frequency Identification* (RFI), are creating an 'internet of things', and researchers will increasingly be able to track how countless contemporary objects move and are being used, in real time. Long-distance *GPS tracking devices* can track any object, almost anywhere – cars, fish,[47] containers.[48] Logbooks and inventories help to track objects. Diaries, passports and travel tickets provide similar information about people.
- *Documents* (C13) may provide sufficient information to map (diagrammatically) an organization, even if not presented in a helpful format. Government or commercial records may list data about *organizational affiliations,* and online CVs may provide *cultural affiliations.*
- *Online ethnography* (C8.4) can include discovering the 'links' on websites and social media to analyse organizational and personal connections.

Data then needs to be presented as concise findings that can be envisioned on diagrammatic *mapping* templates (above).

Spatial mapping methodologies (C11) can also be adapted, particularly topological visualizations, to explain systems such as *supply chains.*[49] This can help to improve efficiency, monitor specifics such as environmental impacts, or track abuses such as human trafficking and illegal logging (Figure 12.3).[50] ***Forensic mapping*** can utilize supply chain methods to demonstrate that events such as state crimes,[51] commercial corruption, food contamination, industrial pollution are *systematic,* and not just isolated incidents. This is often crucial for international courts and similar forums.[52] This may entail evidence showing that: *distinctive events* happen *repeatedly* across a system (a type of torture), there was a *logic* and *reason* – *mens rea* (torture will scare protesters) – the events are *linked* by *communications* and '*command and control*' systems (a line management structure), there is *technical* evidence (the supply of torture implements), there are *causal links* – would Y had happened if X had not? (the torture could not be carried out without the implements) – and that some events amount to 'guilty acts' – *actus reus* (use of torture implements is illegal).

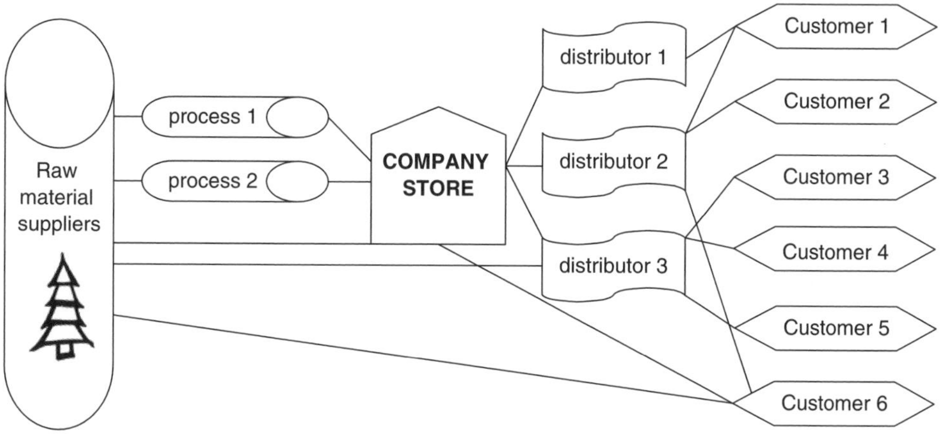

Figure 12.3 Supply chain analysis

Data in the form of ***infrastructure*** (C10.8) represents 'the physical components of interrelated systems providing commodities and services essential to enable, sustain, or enhance societal living conditions'.[53] Data collection may start from infrastructure maps[54] which explain the strategic implications for business and security,[55] and aerial maps (C11), which can indicate likely research sites for field visits. Analysis may compare government or commercial descriptions of infrastructure, with what is actually on (or under) the ground. Networks may include:

- *trade and commercial* – distribution networks,[56] markets.[57]
- *transport* – roads, railways, waterways, air routes.[58]
- *communications*[59] – postal services, telecommunications, internet traffic,[60] submarine cables.[61]
- *energy and water* – electric power lines, gas and liquids pipelines,[62] dams and reservoirs for hydroelectric generation.[63]
- *waste removal* – rivers, drains, solid waste, sewage, pneumatic.[64]

Fieldwork is important. The existence of pylons in Minamata Bay (Japan) explains the *Chisso* mercury poisoning (C10.4). The Bay has abundant cheap hydroelectric power. This makes fertilizer and chemical production very cheap, which is important to the national economy. And this is why the government protected the company.

Triangulating data (C7.6) can help to validate *mapping*, including:

- *historical* – what was the formative context of the system, what did it aim to achieve?
- *conceptual* – what theories, plans and strategies (security, information flow, economic) informed decisions?
- *political* – how do international, national or regional governance and agreements affect the system?
- *administrative* –what are the key institutions and organizations?
- *infrastructure* – how are natural (rivers, trade winds) or built (roads, communications) systems relevant to the research?

The *East Asian Highway Agreement* (the 'New Silk Road') aims to stabilize the region through linking commercial interests, like Europe's postwar E-road network. It will link Tokyo to Tehran across Asia.[65] The existence of AH road signs in South Korea – indicating a road that goes to Japan, China, India and Turkey – evidences the implementation of the *Highway* concept in a tangible form.

Systems are based on ***processes***. *Critical Process Analysis* (CPA) provides a framework for data collection and analysis, which addresses the possibility that a process may not do what it claims to do. CPA combines academic and investigatory approaches to research, and can utilize any research framework (C6) and many forms of data. It is often easier to identify incorrect processes than incorrect outcomes, because processes and related methods have an intrinsic logic – consistency, sequences, scale, audit trails and information channels. Standard *process analysis* usually concerns efficiency in commercial settings,[66] and asks questions about the links between the steps within a process.[67] Within this, *process tracing* uses any data[68] to trace causal links and mechanisms.[69] The term 'critical process analysis' is sometimes used to describe the analysis of processes that are particularly 'critical' – vital – to a system.[70] But CPA is used to critically understand the use of power within a process, not just to make a process more efficient, which reflects the tradition of *critical theory*. Standard process analysis might ask, "How can UN Security Council meetings be arranged more quickly?" But CPA is likely to ask, "The UN could and should have arranged the meeting more quickly, so why did it not do this?"

Although CPA is distinct, the standard process model – input > process > output – provides a basis for first *mapping* an *original process*. This is based on the claims about how the original process was implemented, made by those involved with the process, for example in minutes of meetings or monitoring reports (Figure 12.4). This process *map* comprises:

- the *stated purpose* – policies, aims, intended outcomes.
- the *apparent inputs* and *methods* to make the process work – resources, personnel, information, meetings, research, communication systems, implementation procedures.
- but both the first and second items above operate within *parameters* and *underlying structures* which shape and control the process – norms, regulations,

resource constraints, time-frames, ideologies, religious values, power structures, coercion.

- *outcomes* ('outputs') – decisions, information, policies, actions.

This explanation of an original process is then critically questioned *backwards* through the process and *maps*:

1. *Doubts* raised about the *outcomes* provide the starting point – media comment, profiling, informants, intuition, gossip. Doubts can create *hypotheses* about the causal links creating these doubts – "That pressure from the CEO caused omissions in the minutes of the meeting". These hypotheses provide the bases for then developing:
2. *Meta-methods* (methods to investigate methods) in relation to the 'doubts', to address three guiding questions:

    2.1 How *was* the outcome produced, according to the records? What was the *agency* – who or what made things happen? What was the underlying *function* of a specific aspect, in relation to aspects of the whole process which may be hidden?

    2.2 How else *should* that outcome have been produced – counterfactual scenarios based on standard practice, logic, efficiency, common sense, feasibility?

    2.3 How else *could* that outcome have been produced – counterfactual scenarios of other non-standard alternatives?

    2.4 *Other information* is introduced to investigate questions 2.2 and 2.3 – details about the methods usually used by others to produce similar outcomes, professional standards, procedural norms, legislation.

    2.5 *Comparative meta-analysis*[71] compares the answers to these questions to understand significant differences, and to discover and explain lack of *consistency* (above).

3. Any differences are then analysed in relation to the original stated purpose ('*map*'), to illuminate true motives.
4. Conclusions are then made about the validity and integrity of the original process – was this sound, complete, honest – "the truth, the whole truth, and nothing but the truth"?

CPA therefore entails questioning an original process by reconstructing that process in counterfactual ways that it *should* and *could* have been done, to compare and explain significant differences with the *claims* about what was done. It uses the question "What if …", to interrogate what was claimed.

Most secular world institutions and governance systems reflect the ethos of the UN, and of a supposed 'international community'. But these are relatively new, and not universally accepted. In addition, modern world systems are technologically-based, and therefore vulnerable. The relevant lesson from history, which is often forgotten, is that world systems appear, change and disappear. And any form of systems analysis needs to be aware of that, and recognize the drivers that may create major changes, and plan for the implications.

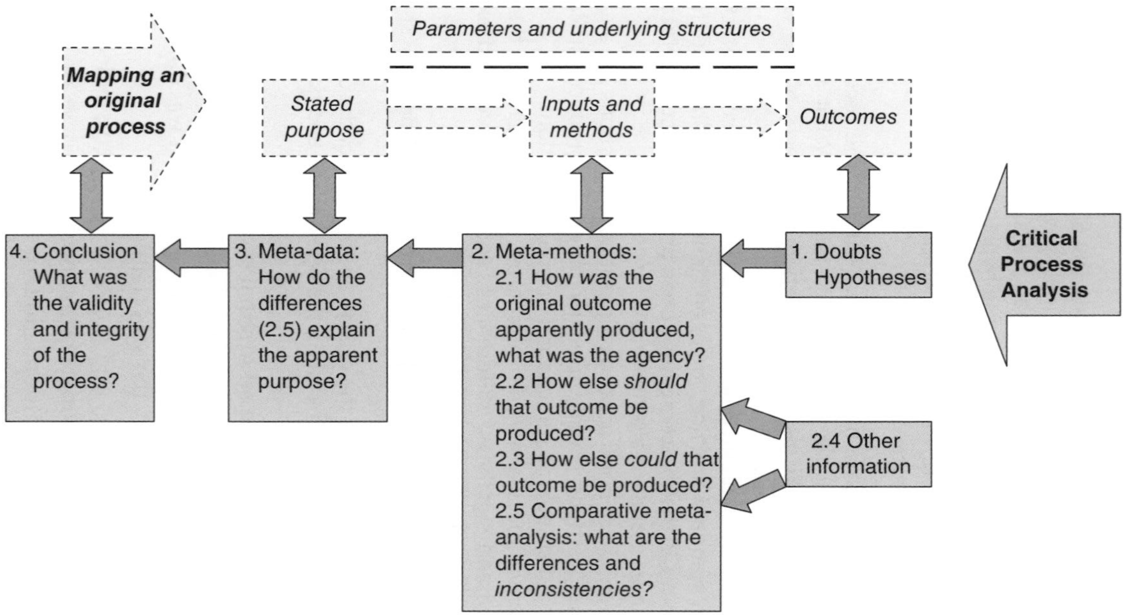

Figure 12.4 Critical Process Analysis (CPA)

thinking zone: how might systems change?

drivers

How might these *drivers* (C14.3) change national and international systems:

- a large earthquake in Tokyo or Tehran?
- a large flood in Paris or New York?
- the unification of North and South Korea?
- Mongolia's mineral wealth promoting it to OECD membership?
- an African country gaining nuclear weapons?
- Iran returning to a secular constitution?
- Israel's land becoming salinated because of sea level rise?
- the Nile drying up?
- the escape of an Ebola-type virus in North America?
- massive wildfires across the Americas?
- a large-scale eruption of the Mount Paektu (aka Changbaishan) volcano on the North Korean–China border, or of Eyjafjallajökull in Iceland?
- a world public that becomes immune to adverts on social media and other internet sites?
- an internet that becomes unusable because of viruses, hackers and overload?
- accelerated climate disruption?
- the unfreezing of the North-West passage and other sea routes?
- the unfreezing of polar regions, making mineral and other resources more accessible?
- massive movements of 'environmental refugees'?
- total toxic pollution in some regions?
- an electro-magnetic storm that destroys the internet and satellite-based communications?
- a large-scale asteroid impact?
- a virus that outpaces all antibiotics?
- Russia, China, EU or South America set up an alternative internet system?
- things costing the same to manufacture, everywhere in the world, even in China?

How could the UN, TNCs and other international organizations prepare for, and respond to, these events?

main ideas

When researching ***world systems*** consider:

- *the historical* context, and how theories reflect this.
- how to use *intelligence* methods to collect information.
- how to *map* systems.
- *templates* for diagrammatic *mapping*: Venn diagrams, organizational/line management charts, flow charts, process charts, spidergrams, networks charts, timelines, and adapting spatial *mapping* methods.
- how *data* can be collected through interviews, observation, tracking, documents, online ethnography.
- how *infrastructure* relates to other systems.
- *triangulation* to assess validity.
- *CPA* provides a framework for assessing failings in systems.

key reading

Babones, S. and Chase-Dunn, C. (2012) *Handbook of World Systems Analysis*. London: Routledge.

Brandes, U. and Erlebah, T. (eds) (2005) *Network Analysis: Methodological Foundations*. Berlin: Springer-Verlag.

Punnett, B.J. and Shenkar, O. (2004) *Handbook for International Management Research*. London: Wiley.

Reinalda, B. (ed.) (2013) *Routledge Handbook of International Organization*. London: Routledge.

online resources

To access the resources – search on the name in italics, use the http, or search on the generic term in 'quote marks'.

International Society for the Systems Sciences – ongoing methodological discussions – isss.org/projects/overview

Airline Route Maps – www.airlineroutemaps.com

ITO – infrastructure maps – www.itoworld.com

Directory of United Nations System Organizations Index – www.un.org/en/index.shtml

Model UN Research – http://bestdelegate.com/research/

United Nations System – www.unsceb.org

WTO/GATT – http://nyulaw.libguides.com/content.php?pid=55653&sid=424226

World Bank – http://econ.worldbank.org/external/default/main?menuPK=577939&pagePK=64165265&piPK=64165423&theSitePK=469382

IMF – www.lib.berkeley.edu/doemoff/govinfo/intl/gov_imf.html

THIRTEEN

Analysing official documents

Take a look at your passport: it is an official international document. Do you understand it all? If you are British and standing in an immigration queue at Heathrow airport for several hours, it might be worth understanding what 'allow the bearer to pass freely without let or hindrance' means. If you have a 2012 Chinese passport, what are those dashes, on the map, around the disputed southern islands?[1] Countless official documents are available for analysis, not least online.

But not all official documents are immediately accessible. Europe has superb *chained libraries* of texts that are not digitalized, which contain manuscripts and maps of world systems by former world travellers. International records are sometimes in the form of texts on buildings (C10.6), handwritten letters, or religious tomes. This chapter discusses how *official documents* can be *found* and *used* to understand how international systems function (C12), and to inform other aspects of world studies.

13.1 Finding documents

Documents are increasingly easy to access online.[2] The UN *Dag Hammarskjöld Library* provides an access point for ***international documents***, and two distinctions are helpful when starting to understand formal UN documents:

> A *document* is a text submitted to a principal organ or a subsidiary organ of the United Nations for consideration by it, usually in connection with item(s) on its agenda.
>
> The term 'United Nations *publication*' refers to any written material which is issued by the United Nations to the general public.[3]

The *UN History Project*[4] maintains archives of non-current material, including photos, radio broadcasts and videos.[5]

National documents also contain international material. Most national *constitutions* can now be accessed online, which provides insights into the values underpinning international relations.[6] The *UN Treaty Collection* provides access to all international agreements between nations.[7] The charters and constitutions of the UN, INGOs and other international organizations, and companies, provide a starting point for a documentary understanding of international institutions.

Other ***organization texts*** can be found online by searching under the organization name, and adding headings such as 'company profile', 'staff profiles', 'management structure', 'financial report', 'chair's report'. Materials that organizations inadvertently leave online might be found by using keywords and adding 'pdf' or 'ppt'. Headers and footers might show that a document's title had been changed at the last minute, leading researchers to seek out earlier versions, as with the UK government's *Iraq Dossier*.[8] Not all online texts are what they seem and the sources need to be verified through checking the web address and contact details against other information, or on sites like *checkdomain* or *whois*.

Using ***archives*** is more complicated than using university libraries,[9] because the material may not all be indexed digitally, and *Google* may not find documents that are on private intranet systems. Keep in mind that many national collections hold material about other countries, but finding the material is not straightforward. In Britain, government documents about wartime "Japan" may be filed under "America", if they are intelligence intercepts. The 'finding aids' for archival research are systemized by the *International Council on Archives*. But usually talking to local archivists is an effective way to find exactly what is needed. Problems with government archives include: incomplete records which give a misleading impression, a focus on administrative process rather than cause and effect, reports that are deliberately misleading, and a 'self-justificatory element'.[10] *Secret material*, collected by organizations such as the CIA,[11] may at some point become available.[12] When the Chinese *Public Security Bureau* archives were opened in 2006, they revealed meticulous records of the brutality of Mao Zedong's regime.[13] Specialist libraries can make declassified documents easier to search.[14] Check what devices can be used in archives. Handheld *wand scanners* are useful for copying paper documents quickly and accurately. If not, try "spy cameras".

During Japanese occupation, and 'Korean War', many Korean documents were destroyed. The South Korean government is working to locate Korean-related materials around the world, and record them. The ICRC (Red Cross) in Geneva is one source.
Documents are archived under:

- *Paper* (Can be photographed but not scanned)
- *Images* (Thumbnails are available on a CD, high definition can be requested on a one-by-one basis)
- *Film and sound* (Often in original format)

The Korean government offers to create high quality digital copies for the archives, and for Korean museums.

Yun-Joo LEE

www.icrc.org/eng/resources/icrc-archives/

Figure 13.1 Using international archives

Photo: Author's collection

Documentary evidence can also be captured from ***non-written sources***, such as radio, TV and film. Philosopher Andrew Chrucky provided interesting data about US military policy in relation to Japan, from the film *The Fog of War*. He explains, 'there is a very fast sequence of frames in which the bombed Japanese cities are named...To get all this information, I had to advance the DVD frame-by-frame – otherwise the whole thing shoots by you in a blur.' And from this he could present the data as a chart, including an effective comparison with US cities.

Of course, world data is often ***censored***, hidden or manipulated by states. *Reporters Without Borders* provides updates and an annual *World Press Freedom Index* (Figure 13.2).[15] *Freedom of information* (FOI) systems[16] provide a 'right to know' in relation to information held by a government. Many countries have helpful legislation – but the efficacy varies. The Canadian government provides a useful international comparative review,[17] and *Open Government: A Journal on Freedom of Information*[18] presents ongoing discussions. Details of how to access FOI systems are country specific, and usually available on websites or from any governmental organization.[19] Officers working in FOI departments can sometimes be obstructive, and may be attached to national intelligence services. Initial inquiries should appear low-key and harmless. If a first attempt fails, try again using a different persona and approach. Asking for a large number of seemingly related documents can provide cover for getting the one that is crucial. Information from central government can often be accessed through local government departments and organizations – sensitive central government information is sometimes repeated in secondary documents such as local policy and planning reports. A CPA chart can help to *map* obvious and less obvious sources (C12.2).

REPORTERS WITHOUT BORDERS
FOR FREEDOM OF INFORMATION
مراسلون بلا حدود
لحرية الإعلام
无国界记者
维护信息自由

FREEDOM OF THE PRESS WORLDWIDE IN 2013

Rank	Country	Rank	Country
1	Finland	176	Syria
2	Netherlands	177	Turkmenistan
3	Norway	178	North Korea
4	Luxembourg	179	Eritrea

LA LIBERTE DÉ LA PRESSE DANS LE MONDE EN 2013

Figure 13.2 World Press Freedom Index

Source: Reporters Without Borders

Crowdsourcing (C6.4) has dramatically improved access to, and use of, old documents. Non-digital texts can be photographed and 'sliced and diced', to give small tasks to large numbers of people. This can include simply typing titles and other biographical information into a database, and *tagging* photos – writing descriptors using keywords such as '2 boys, 3 girls, mosque, car'. If texts are handwritten, the crowd can help to transcribe and digitalize them.

13.2 Using documents

Documents can be used in three ways:[20]

- as the basis for a *literature review* (C3).
- as a source of *specific evidence* ('Lee found that...').[21]
- for *documentary analysis* – the text is treated like an interviewee and *interrogated* in depth, probably by using an analytical schedule/framework. This can help to check the obvious things – who wrote it, why, when, how (C1.1) – and more specific things – who funded the study, what are the obvious omissions – much like an interview questionnaire.

Texts might also be analysed more broadly in terms of *mass communications*.[22] Software such as *NVivo* help with managing and analysing documents, through linking, shaping, searching and modelling.[23] *QDA Miner* helps with mixed-methods qualitative analysis, and includes statistical functions such as coding frequencies, visualization tools including heat maps and proximity plot, and geo-tagging.[24]

Documentary analysis[25] starts by identifying appropriate physical or digital documents (books, reports, magazines, letters), and then useful texts are selected from those documents using relevant criteria – time periods, events, meetings, keywords. A search can start by using big data document sites like *Amazon*, or with keywords on *GDELT*, *Google Trends* and *Ngram* (Box 3.1). In general, most documents are scarce and texts will be selected *purposively* or *opportunistically* (C7.4). But if there is a large *population* of documents – international magazines, political autobiographies, minutes of meetings – they could be selected by random sampling (C9.3). *Wikileaks* proposes a simple methodology for accessing and 'crowdsourcing' analysis (C6.4) of its online documents.[26]

- Search for events you remember that happened for example in your country.
- Browse by date or search for an origin near you.
- Pick out interesting events and tell others about them.
- Use *Twitter, Reddit, email*, whatever suits your audience best.

When certain phrases are extracted from individual documents, some form of *coding* is necessary, which is likely to use a *coding frame* (C7.4).[27] A specific difficulty, when analysing international texts, is to ascertain exactly who wrote them. Were they drafted by speech writers or assistants, and the named authors simply approved and put their names to the script, as with most company or government reports?

Content analysis provides deeper insights into any type of communication,[28] and is often applied to transcripts.[29] Analysis can be based on simple questions to discover the unwritten aspects of a document as in historical research,[30] or can take a more theoretical approach such as analysing rhetoric.[31] When working across a number of different languages, the methods need to be simplified. A study might examine the origins, usage and linguistic source (indigenous, translated, assimilated) of keywords such as 'comfort women', in Japanese, Korean, Chinese and American English. *Google Books Ngram* can provide basic big data content searches (Box 3.1).

Discourse analysis treats any text as primary data.[32] Analysis can be at a detailed level, using methods and theories of linguistics to assess aspects such as the frequency of certain phrases. For 'aphorisms' (summaries to make an impact), analytical frameworks and plotting charts can help to compare and rate (less to more) data effectively (Figure 13.3). Software is available to help.[33] ***Critical discourse analysis*** (CDA) considers how language is used to increase domination and power,[34] and assumes that texts mediate power.[35] Fairclough's CDA framework combines:[36]

- *micro-analysis* of syntax, metaphoric structure and metrical devises – Does this speech reflect a particular linguistic style?
- *meso-analysis* of the production and consumption of the text, and related power relations – How many copies were circulated free, to whom, and why?
- *macro-analysis* of the general societal trends affecting the text – How has Chinese soft power influenced African political speeches?

An ***epistemic*** approach to CDA links discourse and sources of knowledge.[37] It is often relevant to notice what is missing or hidden in a text, but that needs objective criteria indicating what should be included and conspicuous.

A formal document should be assessed in terms of ***consistency*** with itself (internal), or with other standards (external).[38] Consistency is a requirement in the formulation of law,[39] or when drafting of public documents.[40] Ireland's 2009 *Blasphemy Act* outlaws publishing or uttering 'matter that is grossly abusive or insulting in relation to matters held sacred by any religion' (36.a.). Critics point out that therefore religious texts are blasphemous.[41] Jesus reportedly said of the Jews, 'Ye are of your father the devil, and the lusts of your father ye will do. He was a murderer from the beginning, and abode not in the truth, because there is no truth in him.'[42] Muhammad is quoted as saying, 'May Allah curse the Jews and Christians for they built the places of worship at the graves of their prophets.'[43]

Maps (C11), the way they are created, changed and manipulated can reveal a lot about geopolitics. The primary purpose is often to demonstrate power. Maps commonly exaggerate property, colonial lands and the centrality of power elites.[44] A significant use of politicized maps has been in school classrooms, and that continues. Jewish sources complain that Palestinian school textbooks omit details of modern Israel.[45] The Kuwaiti *Not to Forget Museum* displays Iraqi school textbooks from Saddam Hussein's era, in which maps show an Iraqi empire spanning North Africa, and Kuwait as part of Iraq.

Documents can also be analysed as ***objects*** (C10.7), which may happen as part of police or museum work. Analyses might entail discovering how and when the paper was made, what printing process was used, watermarks, changes, damage and incidental marks such as food stains. Infra-red photography can identify different types of ink or reveal what was written underneath obliterations.[46] Diaries, purportedly by Mussolini and Hitler, were found to be fakes because the straw fibres and optical brighteners found in the paper were introduced after the stated dates of writing.[47] Software is now available to reconstruct shredded documents, and has been used to piece together Stasi files that were thrown into 16,000 garbage bags in 1989.[48]

Policy analysis, in relation to national, international[49] or regional policy, is likely to be based on documents, but may also include observation and interviews.[50] Analysis concerns either *making* or *assessing* policy. The model that a policy-making process should have been based on can be *mapped* diagramatically, and what actually happened is then compared with this.[51] The *International Institute for Democracy and Electoral Assistance* (IDEA) provides tools and data for international policy work.[52] Influence between international and national policies is often interesting, but not easy to show. Comparative policy-making, for example relating climate systems to international and national systems, can be *mapped* as a timeline, in two languages.

Many international policy documents relate to ***international law***, which is a contested concept as there are differing cultural views about world ethics (C5). Analysis quickly becomes politicized, and often applies present-day standards to past events, such as 'comfort women' and slavery. It is useful to distinguish between *retrospective* ethics – a counterfactual conclusion that, "If that happened today it would be unethical/illegal", and *retroactive* ethics – "I want compensation for something that happened to my parents". Sadly, the conclusions often reflect 'victors' justice'.

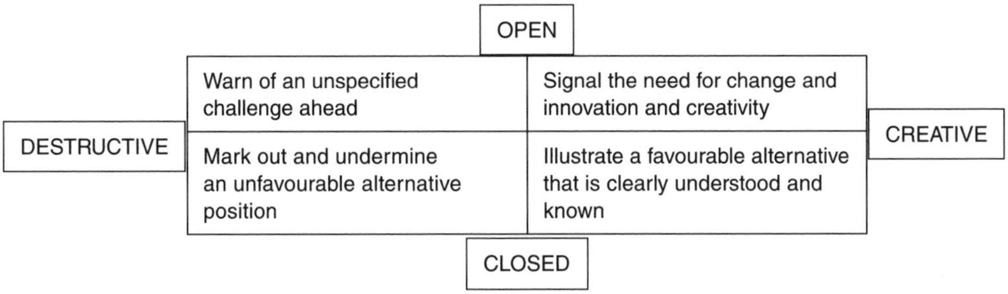

Figure 13.3 Analysing aphorisms

Source: Morrell, K. (2006) 'Aphorisms and leaders' rhetoric: a new analytical approach', *Leadership*, 2 (3): 367–382.

thinking zone: when is a crime a crime?

ICC

The *Rome Statute of the International Criminal Court* addresses crimes against humanity (Art. 7):

> 1. ...acts when committed as part of a widespread or systematic attack directed against any civilian population, with knowledge of the attack:
>
> (a) Murder;
>
> (b) Extermination; ...
>
> (k) Other inhumane acts of a similar character intentionally causing great suffering, or serious injury to body or to mental or physical health.
>
> 2.(a) "Attack directed against any civilian population" means a course of conduct involving the multiple commission of acts referred to in paragraph 1 against any civilian population, pursuant to or in furtherance of a State or organizational policy to commit such attack;

Japan

During World War II, the US air force used napalm to firebomb 67 Japanese cities in 1945. The victims were mainly civilians – women, children and older people. The US knew that the fire service was run by young boys. US strategists calculated wind direction and other factors to optimize destruction of the wood and paper homes. Official estimates range from 1 million dead and 1.3 million injured, upwards. The atomic bomb exploded over Nagasaki was not dropped on the original military target, but through a gap in the clouds, destroying, among other things, the biggest Christian cathedral in Asia.

victors' justice

In the book and film *The Fog of War*, Robert McNamara quoted General Curtis LeMay as saying, "If we'd lost the war, we'd all have been prosecuted as war criminals."

(Continued)

(Continued)

McNamara continued, "And I think he's right...He, and I'd say I, were behaving as war criminals...LeMay recognized that what he was doing would be thought immoral if his side has lost. But what makes it immoral if you lose and not immoral if you win?"

crimes?

Would these events have been crimes:

- Under legal norms at the time of World War II?
- Under the *ICC Rome Statute*?
- Had American allies not won the war?

Might the concept of 'war crime' hide the conceptualization of war as a crime?

[See References for further information.[53]]

main ideas

When researching ***formal documents*** consider how they will be used – for a *literature review*, as a *source of evidence*, for *documentary analysis*, or to analyse *mass communications.*

To ***find*** and ***select*** documents:

- check if they are in archives and "invisible" to online searches, and plan how to find them.
- ascertain if UN documents are *categorized* as a *document* or *publication.*
- decide the *sampling method*, if there is a large 'population' of similar documents.
- design a *coding frame* for extracting particular texts.
- remember *secret documents* may become available after certain time periods, but are often *censored, hidden,* or *manipulated.*
- use *Freedom of Information* laws to gain access to sensitive material.

When ***using*** documents, consider:

- *documentary analysis*, which *interrogates* a document, using questions or an analytical framework.
- *content analysis*, which may be useful for transcripts.
- *discourse analysis*, which may consider the use of language in-depth.
- *critical discourse analysis*, which will assess how the text relates to power including *epistemic* aspects.
- *policy analysis*, which will assist with *making* or *assessing* policy, and investigate how *policy-making frameworks* are/were followed.
- internal and external *consistency*.

key reading

Fairclough, N. (2001) *Language and Power*. London: Longman.

Gee, J.P. (2005) *An Introduction to Discourse Analysis: Theory and Method*. London: Routledge.

Hansen, A. (2009) *Mass Communication Research Methods*. London: Sage.

Hill, M.R. (1993) *Archival Strategies and Techniques*. Thousand Oaks, CA: Sage.

Krippendorff, K. (2004) *Content Analysis: An Introduction to its Methodology*. Thousand Oaks, CA: Sage.

Scott, J.P. (2006) *Documentary Research*. London: Sage.

online resources

To access the resources – search on the name in italics, use the http, or search on the generic term in 'quote marks'.

Constitute Project – national constitutions – www.constituteproject.org/#

UN Treaty Collection – https://treaties.un.org

UN History Project – http://unhistoryproject.org/research/research_guides.html

Wikileaks – databases of leaked government and other documents

Checking internet sources – www.Whois.net – www.checkdomain.com/cgi-bin/checkdomain.pl?domain=who

NVivo – documentary and textual analysis

QDA Miner – mixed-methods qualitative analysis

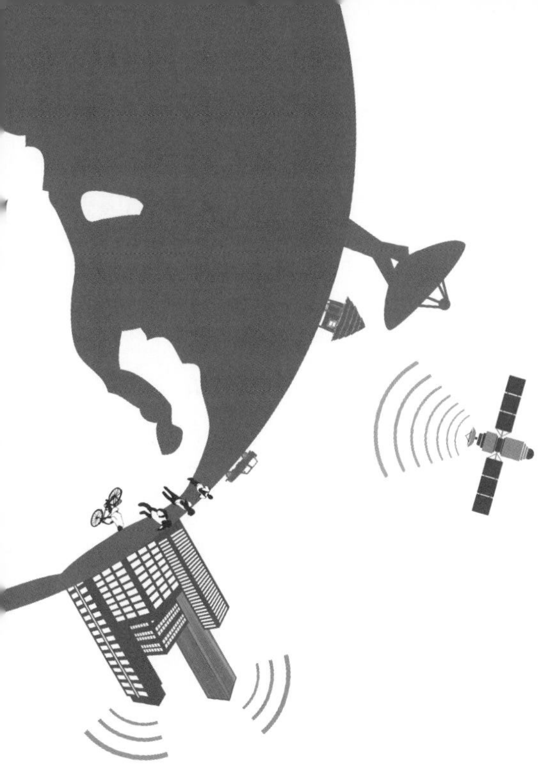

PART IV

Using the findings

Research *findings*, resulting from *data collection* and *initial analysis* (C7–C13), provide the bases for *further analysis* and *reporting* the research.

Chapter 14 explains how, during *further analysis*, a researcher should 'see what others see but think what others have *not* thought' through *comparisons*, establishing *causation, predictive* evidence, creating *indexes*, and *generalization and theorization*.

Chapter 15 then outlines how to *report* the research effectively, using international style, for academic, professional and public audiences, to influence and perhaps change things in the world.

FOURTEEN

Further analysis

Two men saw little baby geese following big mother goose – as we all do. But they thought – could we get baby geese to follow a human? The result was the theory of 'imprinting', and Nobel prizes for Conrad Lorenz and Nikolaas Tinbergen. They saw what other people see, but thought what other people had *not* thought.[1] That is the purpose of *further analysis*.

Further analysis builds on *initial analysis* and *findings* to create broader meanings. Within a 'critical theory' approach, analysis will go beyond discovering "what is" to assess "what could be".[2] This involves *comparisons*, establishing *causation*, explaining *predictive* value, creating *indexes*, and *generalization* and *theorization* to fit research within world frameworks. *Analytical frameworks* help to structure analysis, and examples are provided throughout this chapter and on the website. All *methods of analysis* should be described in the *methods* section of a research report. But Stephen Jay Gould provides a useful warning: 'The more important the subject and the closer it cuts to the bone of our hopes and needs, the more we are likely to err in establishing a framework for analyses.'[3]

14.1 Comparison – the basis of analysis

Analysis *is* comparison – noting similarities and differences between two or more things. Some studies may be designed specifically within a comparative framework (C6.2), but all studies will compare findings with other studies, literature and theories. Comparison is the basis of knowledge creation. John Locke pointed out in 1690: 'Knowledge is the perception of the agreement or disagreement of two ideas.'[4] Knowledge is more than raw data and simple facts.

Formal comparative analysis needs a set of clear ***questions*** that are common across the units being compared. Comparisons may be *overt* – "Iran, Syria, Afghanistan and North Korea have ratified the UN Convention on the Rights of the Child, but America has not". But they may also be *implied* – "powerless" would imply a comparison with a group that has more power, "talented" with others less talented. Comparative analysis accommodates multi-methods research, to 'move beyond' the old qualitative–quantitative divide.[5]

Analysis considers the reasons for ***similarity*** and ***difference*** (*dependent variables*) in relation to *common factors* (*constants* and *independent* variables). This entails comparative presentation, which requires *standardization* to ensure that comparisons are of like-with-like (C9.3.1). For statistical data this might mean creating percentages or averages, and often *aggregation* (below). For qualitative data, standardization may be based on determining categories which can create typologies (Figure 14.1). Software permits quick analysis of many forms of data. Similar texts, such as versions of political speeches, can be compared with online resources such as *TextCompare*, and *Excel* can compare spreadsheets.

The Korean class system

Choson era ***Sinbun* class system**	**Hierarchical status**
Yang-ban	Intellectuals
Jung-in	Professional and military
Nong-sang-min	Farmers and commercial
Chun-min	Untouchable

Nobi (slaves) were not ranked.

Figure 14.1 A typology of the Korean class system

Standard *templates* can help to ***present*** analysis. *Area charts* help to compile country data. Qualitative concepts can be combined with quantitative ratings on *star plots* for comparative multivariate, mixed-methods, analysis – the variables can be compared, but also the volume of the star may compare the overall effect (bigger is better) (Figure 14.2).[6] Checking how comparison sites envision their data can propose how to present similar forms of data. *Index Mundi*[7] presents country profiles very effectively, *Country Reports*[8] has a 'compare and contrast' function, and *If It Were My Home* enables diverse ways to compare countries with 'your home' (or anywhere else), including disasters.[9]

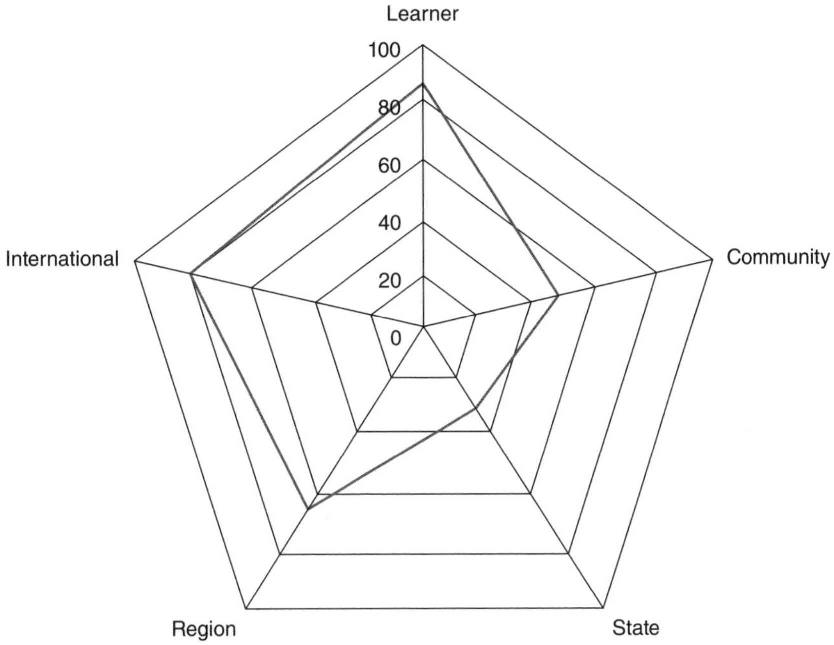

Stabilizing effects of 'English language programmes' in Cambodia. (See website for other examples)

Figure 14.2 Star plot

Source: Johnstone, C. (2014) 'Adult education as a stabilizing response to conflict'. Unpublished PhD Thesis, Institute of Education, University of London.

Jarad Diamond's comparative approach to *historical natural experiments*[10] examines *similarities* or *differences* in:

- *initial conditions* – relevant starting points.
- *perturbations – endogenous* (internal) or *exogenous* (external) influences.
- *outcomes* – factors that can be shown to have a *causal* link to *initial conditions.*

Comparisons may be of cases with similarities and differences in *initial conditions* or *perturbations*. *Confounders* are alternative explanations that may interfere with identifying a causal link. In the example on the website, cases 3–8 had the *initial condition* of access to TV; 1 and 2 did not. Cases 5–8 all had the *perturbation* of access to English Language (EL) TV programmes; cases 3 and 4 did not. Cases 5 and 6 only had *endogenous* influence from Soviet EL programmes, but cases 7 and 8 also had *exogenous* influence from access to European EL programmes. So, cases 1 and 2 with no *initial condition* (TV), and 3 and 4 with TV but no *perturbations* (EL TV) had less political awareness. Cases 5 and 8 had similar *initial conditions* (access to EL TV), but the *perturbations* were different (endogenous Soviet/exogenous European). Yet the *outcomes* were similar – more political awareness. For both there were no *confounders* (poor TV transmission, prohibitions on using English), and a *causal* link seems likely. This creates grounds for a *conclusion* that EL TV may have influenced political awareness, whether or not it was *endogenous*/national or *exogenous*/international, i.e. simply having access to EL TV had an effect irrespective of the content. This could inform present-day policies about cultural diplomacy, for example about providing English language classes in North Korea.

Philosopher David Deutsch argues that knowledge is information that is a basis for action – it has 'reach'.[11] A significant strength of international comparisons, particularly in the form of indexes (C14.4), is that they provide very persuasive evidence for political change, on the basis that, "Other countries are better than us."

14.2 Causation

If a woman pushes a man who has a weak heart, and he dies, is the 'cause' of death her push or his heart? Conundrums like this are central to legal and social arguments about cause and effect. Causation is very significant in world studies because of the need to argue if things were caused systematically – by governments, TNCs, or online networks (C12).

A ***hypothesis*** is often a guess that one thing causes another, and is based on causal theories. Therefore research that is focused by causal hypotheses *must* provide analysis and conclusions about causation.[12] Some research questions have similar causal implications – "Do TV images influence the choices of tourists?" Causal analysis needs to show how *independent variables* and *constants* influenced *dependent variables* (C9.3.2). The theoretical assumptions that explain causal links can be tested through *hypothetical comparison*[13] – "that low police pay causes low morale, low morale causes inefficient policing, and inefficient policing causes corruption".

The fundamental considerations of causation are ***philosophical*** and ***culturally formed***, which must be considered in world research.[14] Indian traditions might argue that an 'effect' is inherent within a 'cause' – that an effect is simply a modification of a cause, and the process is less relevant.[15] Buddhists might add that everything is both an 'effect' and a 'cause', and that every 'effect' results from infinite chains of 'causes'. Confucian writers could say that causation does not arise from human action, but from things that happen independently of humans and are dependent on one another.[16] Diverse traditions underlie how people argue and accept causal links across cultures. Before the 2014 South African elections, (then) President Zuma argued that if people leave the ANC, 'they will attract the wrath of the ancestors, who will also bring that person bad luck'.[17]

Causation must be ***theorized***. If environmental health researchers found an increase in lung disease near a new polluting factory, it is not enough just to say "the factory caused it".[18] They would need to explain the *mechanism* – can the presence of those pollutants cause the particular lung disease, were the ill people exposed, were they healthy before the factory opened, does similar pollution seem to cause a similar impact elsewhere? This might entail laboratory research to show how the poison causes damage in the lung, and what dose levels are harmful. For forensic use, the causation would also need to be theorized in terms of environmental science and law (Figure 14.3). But theorization is not always complicated. We do it every day. If a deodorant caused our armpits to stop smelling, we might try it on our feet, but we would not spray it in our mouth to stop bad breath.

Environmental theory of causation	**Legal theory of causation**	
	Act	*Omission*
***Presence* of environmental agents**	e.g. The *presence* of methyl isocyanate. (*Union Carbide* gas poisoning, Bhopal, India)	e.g. The *presence* of excess lead in water supplies. (Regulatory failure, US)
***Absence* of environmental agents**	e.g. The *absence* of micro-nutrient – iron. (Caused by heavy metal pollution on farmland, Poland)	e.g The *absence* of iodine in salt. (Regulatory failure, Bangladesh)

Combining a theoretical model of the environmental (scientific) causes of brain injury (*presence–absence*), and a legal theory of causation (*act* or *omission*).

Figure 14.3 Theorizing causation

Source: Williams, C. (1997) *Terminus Brain: The Environmental Threats to Human Intelligence*. London: Cassell, p. 230.

Legal processes help to understand the concept of causation in the social world. Some legal philosophers prefer to use the form, 'Z was a *consequence* of Y', rather than 'Y caused Z'.[19] In a court, causal *proof* 'beyond reasonable doubt' is required in criminal cases, and reflects a notional 95% certainty. In civil cases, 'balance of probabilities' reflects 51% certainty – it is more likely than not. But a court never claims a decision is 100% certain. Law also considers both the actions (*actus reus*) and the mental rationale (*mens rea*). For social causation, distinctions can be made between the:[20]

- *responsibility* of relevant individuals or leaders, for their actions, and/or the actions of agents and others over whom they have effective authority and control.
- *blame* for wrongdoing, which may attract punishment or other sanction.

- *liability* of individuals, organizations or states to provide remedy.
- *accountability*, which implies that a senior person has a duty to answer initial questions about events that she or he oversees.[21]

In law, cause and effect must be *adjacent* – 'proximate', 'immediate', 'continuing and operating' – but that becomes difficult when arguing on a world scale, for example about environmentally-mediated impacts.[22]

In the ***natural sciences***, Popper's well-known argument about scientific method is that research can only create a better 'corroborated' hypothesis, not 'truth'. He argues that an initial hypothesis can be disproved ('falsified'), but it can never be confirmed as completely correct, because however many times the research is repeated and gives the same result, the next time may provide a different outcome. He therefore argued for the use of 'null hypotheses', a default position, written in a negative form to be disproved – "That A does not cause B". This reflects the court assumption that a person is 'innocent until proven guilty'.

European ***philosophers*** provide useful distinctions. Aristotle defined elements of causal chains:

- *material* – the *physical* things that are involved (toxic waste).
- *formal* – the *plan* that determines the form of the 'effect' (illegal waste dumping).
- *efficient* – the *agency* creating the result (Italian *Mafia*).
- *final* – the *reason* (blackmail to extort money).

But this does not eliminate *confounders*. Arguing that A caused B implies that B was not caused by C, D, E, etc., and eliminating the other likely causes is very difficult in social research. It is therefore relevant to consider the *ontological* and *epistemological*[23] bases (C1.1) – do the causal factors and links really exist, and how do we come to know about them?

Scottish philosopher David Hume argued the need to identify ***'necessary connections'***, the 'causal nexus',[24] and relational ontology has developed this.[25] Do the ties, causal chains and links exist and are they effective? If mass executions by a despot "caused" people to stop meeting in public, what were the 'connections' that informed them about those executions – TV footage, press photos, posters, gossip – and did people experience these and say that they were consequently afraid? It is also helpful also to consider *'agency'* – the degree to which people could have acted freely and independently – in relation to 'structure' – the systems that limit the choices and opportunities available.[26]

Recent philosophers have made distinctions about the relative influence of the causal factors, but terminology is not used consistently. Calling a causal factor *'necessary'* usually implies that if it were not there, the effect could not have happened. A *'sufficient'* set of factors (which includes the *necessary* factors) means that together they were adequate to cause the effect without any additional factors, and this helps to identify *missing* factors. *Contributory* factors may have influenced the details of the cause and effect, but were not vital for it to happen.

The influences can be tested through '***counterfactual***' analysis[27] – "what if" particular factors had been absent, present or different. Actual and hypothetical data can be compared when assessing or evaluating[28] the impact of an intervention, such as a new policy – "If the new well had *not* been built, would health have improved?" A counterfactual argument might also be used when causation is investigated through an *experiment* – actual or 'natural' (above) – in which one group was exposed to an intervention, compared with another similar group that was not.[29]

Like systems analysis (C12), *mapping* causal systems can help to make explanations clear, each stage of the causal chain can be tested, and contextual factors that may not seem immediately relevant can be included. (The diagrams on the website are just outlines – real-life events are much more complex.)

- *Fishbone diagrams*[30] *map* problems in commercial systems. The main causal factors (weather, maintenance) must be easy to identify and well understood. But the method might omit the more fundamental causes (flawed contracts, corrupt CEOs).
- *Why-Because Analysis* (WBA) was originally designed to assess the causes of accidents.[31] Potential causal factors are identified, the causal links are then tested to see if they were '*necessary*', '*sufficient*' or '*contributory*', and if anything is *missing*.
- *Causal loop diagrams* integrate forward and reverse factors, and show how causal trajectories can be impeded or expedited.[32] This is useful because most causal diagrams are one-directional.

Diagrams can clarify explanations, but can also encourage mechanistic and deterministic thinking. In the social world, nothing is, or was, inevitable, and context can permit or inhibit most human endeavours. Cause and effect in human systems is never automatic.

14.3 Prediction

An English vicar, Thomas Malthus famously predicted, in 1798, that population increase would exceed the availability of our planet to provide food and other life-support resources, and consequently people would die. He seems to have been wrong, so far.[33] Even if correct, predictive knowledge does not always make humans behave sensibly, or encourage policy-makers to make good policies.[34] On a world scale, prediction often fails, but seems vital.

Like causal analysis (above), the fundamentals of predictive analysis are often ***philosophical***.[35] Again law provides useful insights. The decision whether to hold a suspect in prison ('on remand'), before a trial has established guilt, is often on the basis of 'likelihood of further offending', and this prediction can be based on whether the suspect has committed similar crimes before. This might seem reasonable, but if you made a mistake such as burning the rice, does that mean you are more likely to do the same thing again or less likely because you have learned a lesson? If the 'likelihood of further offending' logic were used within international relations, academics should all be arguing for America to give up its nuclear weapons because it is the only country to have used them previously against civilians, twice.

Studies may be designed to be predictive, or predictive patterns may be sought during further analysis of general data. Almost all research has a predictive element, even if unstated. Every day we make predictions that permit us to plan ahead and survive productively, but predictive analysis goes beyond these everyday understandings, and explores two types of 'unknowns':

Epistemological prediction is based on assuming that the 'truth' exists in some way, but we do not know what it is – predicting the 'known unknowns' (C1.1). This often relates to predictive hypotheses about *natural systems* and *human biology* (quantum mechanics, epigenetics). *Inference* and *generalization*, from samples to populations (C9.3.3) is similar, because we do not know if the whole population is the same as the sample, but the 'truth' exists within the population. The problem is not that the truth does not exist, but that we don't know how to find out what it is.

Temporal prediction implies that the truth has not happened yet – predicting the future 'unknown unknowns' (C1.1). This might relate to *natural systems* and *biological populations* (asteroids hitting Earth, epidemics) but it is also relevant to *human populations* and *individuals* (voting,[36] customer purchasing).[37]

Predictive analysis about humans often combines the two, and becomes very complicated. For example, – could humans be cloned (*epistemological*), and if so, will humans do it (*temporal*)?[38]

Within this framework, predictive research design and analysis therefore includes:

Epistemological

- *hypothetical* – X relates to Y. "People (X) are angry about GM foods (Y)."
- *investigative* – W did Z. "The prime minister (W) deceived parliament (Z)."
- *inferential* – The population is like the sample. "If 80% of the sample does not believe in god, 80% of the population does not believe" (C9.3.3).

Temporal

- *future causation* – X in the present may cause Y in the future. "An increasing public addiction to sweet food now (X) may cause a diabetes epidemic in the future (Y)."
- *causal projection* – If A causes B in the present, then A will cause B in the future. "The death rate among heroin addicts next year will be the same as this year."
- *projected analogy* – If Q relates to T now, q will relate to t in the future. "The sales pattern of a new sports car next year should be like that of a similar model this year."
- *trends* – Trajectories and patterns from the past to present may (or may not) continue in the future. "Sales of tablet devices are overtaking sales of PCs, which is likely to continue."

In these and other forms, the underlying assumption reflects Stephen Hawking's 'time cones' and his profound but simple truth that the future is simply everything from the past, which passes through, and is mediated by, the present.[39]

But the world is ***complex***, and many factors can disrupt predictive analyses, including:

- *self-fulfilling prophecies* – the research findings "find" what they have created. If a study predicts that water shortage could cause war between two countries, a war might happen because national leaders hear about that prediction.[40]
- *pre-emptive deceit* – powerful people deploy 'an incorrect or misleading statement or process...to preclude subsequent truth and/or obscure subsequent acts or omissions', such as the British *Iraq Dossier*.[41]
- *optimism bias*[42] – we tend to believe that outcomes will always be better than the evidence suggests, and so underestimate risk. This effect can be compounded in group assessments. 'Smart' people are often 'stupid',[43] for example 'positive illusions'[44] about risk.
- *brain lag* – the human brain is essentially Stone Age, and cannot perceive the present and future clearly. We know that sugar, salt and fat were rare in a Stone Age environment, and so now we gorge on them. Despite that knowledge, our brain still cannot predict that they are harmful.[45]
- *complexity* and *chaos* – human-influenced systems rapidly become too muddled and unstable for traditional predictions to be made, for example organizations like *al-Qaeda*.[46]

Complex systems are often analysed by changing the *scale* of observation, and looking for *patterns*. There is no clear pattern when tossing a coin a few times, but observe many coins tossed many times, and the 50–50 pattern becomes evident.

So prediction is never completely ***certain***, and the likelihood of things happening is often described as ***probabilities*** – in percentages (90% certain), frequency (every century), ratios (a 1 in 5 chance), or consistent terms (high, moderate, low). ***Uncertainty*** describes factors that cannot be described or measured accurately. *Understandinguncertainty.org* provides ongoing discussions. The pattern across most forms of prediction is a paradox. In both the natural and social world it seems harder to make small-scale predictions (a child will suffer depression if its father dies) than to make large-scale predictions (20% of children will suffer depression). The broad trajectories of climate change are now well understood. But is very hard to predict how communities, nations and individuals will respond – increased war or humanitarian assistance, crime or altruism.

Certainty usually diminishes as the human aspect of the prediction becomes greater.

- Predictions about ***natural systems*** (physical, chemical, biological[47]) are *epistemological*, and so usually *more certain*, because the correct answers exist in some form (unless the laws of physics evolve[48]).
- Predictions about ***engineered systems*** (machines, buildings, infrastructure) are also more certain because we engineer on the basis of natural laws and understand how we do it. But human influence (corruption, incompetence), or *environmental* impacts (earthquakes, floods), can change the dynamics.
- Predictions about ***biological populations*** (evolution, disease) can be moderately certain, unless human behaviour (genetic modification, synthetic biology) or *environmental* factors (temperature change, land erosion) influence what happens. Prediction about ***human populations*** *is more difficult* because the dynamics are influenced by human decision-making which is affected by *social contexts*. The fact

that 20% of a population used painkillers in the past does not mean 20% will do the same in the future – a scare story about painkillers could dramatically alter that behaviour. 'Crowd behaviour' can sometimes be predicted (avoiding threats, fighting injustice), but the triggers are still not well understood.[49] Projections that view *human populations* as *biological populations* (health outcomes, birth-rates) can be quite accurate. If, in the past, 20% of a population with X severity of Y disease died within one year, it is very likely that, within a similar population, 20% with the same condition may die in the future. But that could be radically changed by a new cure, for example from pharmacogenetics, or aggravating environmental factors like new viruses.

- **Population predictions** (biological, human) are generally much better than predictions about *individual behaviour.* On an individual level *social context* becomes very significant – if you go to observe a Catholic priest leading a service in a church, you can be almost certain you will hear Catholic doctrine; if you meet him in the pub an hour later, his topic might be very unpredictable.

The distinction between non-human and human probabilities is often muddled.

thinking zone: are tossers more predictable than placers?

tossers

Toss a coin many times and record each time how it falls – heads or tails. The result will be a seemingly random pattern. But over a long period, the ratio will be about 50–50. If we did an analogous experiment using an animal, machine or natural occurrence to generate the coin tossing, the outcome would be the same. We could devise an experiment that apparently permits an (untutored) animal to exercise its independent behaviour by choosing to place a coin heads or tails, but over time there will be a 50–50 distribution.

placers

Ask a human to *place* the coin, and the result might be the same, but it might not. The outcome could reflect some form of plan resulting in a seemingly regular pattern – heads, tails, heads, tails... But this pattern could change at any time. The outcome could also be the persistent placing of one side – heads, heads, heads... A human might place the coin – tails, heads, heads, heads... This removes any element of predictability that we might have concluded in relation to the previous outcomes.

predictability

Coin *placing* is unique to humans because our behaviour stems from reason, not just reaction or cause and effect. The consequence sounds like a paradox.

Non-human behaviour creates an outcome that, although seeming random, *is* broadly predictable. Human behaviour can create an outcome that is *not* random, but therefore *not* broadly predictable.

pertinacity

Humans destroy the environment because they can be pertinacious, 'very or extremely (per) tenacious' – 'persistent or stubborn in holding to one's own opinion or design...Chiefly as a bad quality' (OED).

so

In terms of predictability, what type of human behaviour is more like that of animals or machines, and why?

[See References for further information.[50]]

14.3.1 Frameworks for predictive analyses

Predictive analysis is very popular, especially *forecasting*,[51] within economics and strategic studies. The annual *State of the Future Report* covers world issues, and journals like the *International Journal of Forecasting* discuss methods. Relevant analytical frameworks fall into two broad categories – *physical-human*, which uses physical factors that are more certain as a basis for estimating human factors that are less certain (*risk analysis*, *scenario analysis*), and *crowd* which uses 'collective intelligence' of large groups (*prediction markets*, *big data*).

Risk analysis involves predictions that something negative may happen, and usually involves *uncertainty*. Methods can be *quantitative*,[52] and *qualitative*.[53] On a world scale this reflects Ulrich Beck's concept of the *Risk Society*,[54] and the *Journal of Risk Research* provides ongoing discussions. Risk *assessments* are often expressed in terms of the *probability* (*likelihood* – *risk*) of something happening, then the *probable impact* from those *threats* or *hazards* actually causing harm, and then an estimation of the *cost* of the harm (or opportunities for business) if it occurs. Examples of quantitative risk analysis include actuarial analysis for insurance – linking claims for burglaries to postcodes can automatically change premiums on the basis of postcode. But even seemingly sophisticated statistical assessments will usually entail qualitative judgements – guesswork – somewhere in the process.

Assessments may start by *identifying* and then *categorizing* possible *threats* (acid rain, corruption) in relation to *mitigating factors* (anti-pollution technology, regulatory systems). Then ***probability assessment*** may use quantitative data (previous weather patterns), together with qualitative judgements (honesty of factory managers), and is based on factors such as:

- *threat* – "acid rain caused by pollution from a cement factory".
- *impact* – "forests dying from acid rain".
- *magnitude* – "1000 trees dying".
- *frequency* – "1000 trees in 10 years".
- *probability* (*likelihood*) – ranging from "certainly will not happen" (0) to "certainly will happen" (1, 10, or 100%).
- *when* – "while the cement factories are operating".
- *where* – "around Chengdu".
- *assumptions* – "the cement factories will not improve their pollution controls".

The above factors need to be included in research questions – "If the cement factories do not improve pollution controls, how probable is it that more than 1000 trees will die each decade, because of acid rain caused by pollution from the factories, around Chengdu?" To reduce bias from individual judgements, relevant groups (experts/locals/administrators) may be asked to rate risks numerically, and the results then averaged and presented in relevant forms.

The *impact*, and the cost of *harm* is then assessed, but this is often based on accountancy or procurement data, which may be accurate but very limited. In world contexts, assessments of harm should include intangible 'loss costs' such as biodiversity, mental decline, disability.[55] Like probability, *harm* can also be assessed by qualitative judgements.[56] Risk assessment of complex systems may use specialized flow charts – *event trees* which *map* possible problems outwards from the present, and *fault trees* which track backwards from hypothetical problems.

Scenario analysis came to public attention in the 1970s when *Shell* oil used it to survive fluctuating oil prices better than other companies[57] – *www.shell.com/scenarios* is useful. The strength of scenarios is that they accommodate uncertainties and unknowns better than linear models, because they model more than one possible future 'world', and only claim to predict what *could* happen, not what *will* happen.[58] Scenario analysis is a form of *causal projection* and is based on frameworks:

- Defining

  long-term assumptions – things that are likely to stay predictable over long periods (languages, law).

- Identifying

  drivers – influencing factors that are more certain (economic, demographics, climate change).

- Agreeing

  likely *outcomes* of drivers – factors that are less certain (floods, political stability, migration).

- Creating

  scenarios based on different *assumptions* (1. Refugees will try to migrate to the nearest safe place. 2. Governments will try to prevent immigration. 3. Some countries will accept managed immigration).

Although the *scenarios* might be very different from one another, they each have their own *internal causal logic*, and share a common *external causal logic* based on the *drivers* and *outcomes*. Common *factors* are then sought across the *scenarios*, which can permit planning *priorities* on the basis of criteria such as *scale, frequency* and *severity*.

Trend driver analysis is similar to scenario analysis, and is applied to global security problems, using analytical frameworks such as: *input data > trends and drivers > outcomes > predictions and explorations.*[59] This is often used within military training, and 'wild cards' can be identified from the frequency of unexpected or unpredictable events mentioned in relevant literature. The 'wild card' is then often introduced in training or group analysis at critical moments, to see how people respond to unexpected events. *Backcasting* inverts these methods, and works backwards from a desired or hypothesized future scenario, to identify how policies and actions might bring about that scenario.[60]

Crowd predictions use the 'collective intelligence' of large numbers of people, as advocated in James Suroweicki's *The Wisdom of Crowds,*[61] and are an aspect of *crowd-sourced research* (C6.4). Crowd assessment can work well for *epistemological predictions* ("How many sweets in that big jar?"), because the answer exists, and so the average of many guesses is likely to be more accurate than the guess of any single individual. The weakness of this approach is that if a few people have expertise (in filling bottles with sweets), their informed and probably more accurate estimates will probably disappear in the aggregation of incorrect guesses. Crowds are less likely to be useful for *temporal predictions* ("If we leave the room, will the children start stealing the sweets?"), because no one can know what the correct answer is, and the answer could be determined by group dynamics or a particularly persuasive leader.

Prediction markets ('information markets', 'event futures') are an innovative way to harness collective intelligence.[62] The *Journal of Prediction Markets* provides ongoing discussions, and interesting examples include *ideosphere.com* and *newsfutures.com.* Researchers set up online systems, similar to futures trading or online betting, to permit people to "invest" in geopolitical risk such as the outcomes of wars, terrorism, elections or resource depletion. The assumption is that if more people back a particular prediction, it is more likely to be correct, which can be expressed as means or probabilities – a €60 bid for a €1 "share" could imply 60% certainty. The criteria need to be clear and simple – what, when, where. Results can provide direct measures (that X% of a population would use euthanasia), or proxies (a probable decline in church attendance means an increase of secularism). The type of "bet" includes winner-takes-all, index ('totalizer'), or spread. Rewards can be real or virtual and those who bet correctly can be rewarded for improving the effectiveness of the systems, and *vice versa*. The "gamblers" are likely to do research to get accurate information to inform their choices, so the crowd tangibly extends the ambit of evidence gathering beyond the researcher. Prediction markets seem to compare well with other methods for accuracy.[63]

A *prediction market* could utilize *findings* presented as *scenarios*. On a small scale this can be done as a *focus group* (C8.2). Face-to-face group results might even be better than the online markets because group discussion provides feedback and modification of participants' ideas. ***Citizen Juries*** are an example.[64] Around 12 lay, local people are permitted to hear evidence from, and cross-examine, experts in relevant fields, about local decisions, such as where best to site a waste disposal centre, or how to reduce crime. The idea can also be applied to research.[65] The general conclusion about the success of these juries is that they are no worse than experts – that, "The worse possible outcome from a Citizen Jury will be the same views as the experts."

Big data also presents interesting new ways to use crowds (C9.4). Sites like *culturomics.org* provide access to tools and ideas such has searching for 'sentiment' in literature. Whereas markets and groups (above) use crowds as an extended researcher network, big data uses online crowds as a source of data. *Machine learning*[66] has led to *predictive analytics*,[67] which can be based on extracting data from social media sites, and uses patterns to suggest future trends. Big data can also be used to validate small-scale conclusions about social trends. *Google Trends* can be used to check general usage of words and phrases, and the occurrence of events, over time. *Google Books Ngram Viewer* provides evidence of the use of terms in books since 1800 (Box 3.1), but be aware of what type of books are likely to be in this database before making conclusions about the findings.

But, as a predictive method, big data is based on big assumptions. Fundamentally, it assumes that human decisions can be predicted. Can they?

- Do *you* know exactly what you will do tomorrow? If not, how can an algorithm know,[68] unless it is measuring something subconscious and biological, like behaviour during the early stages of pregnancy?
- Is the *context* of our decisions predictable? Do you know which friends will phone you tomorrow with what news and how you will respond?
- Computer programmers are assumed to be objective, but inevitably embed their beliefs and biases in the programs – would a CIA employee program in the same way as an *al-Qaeda* operative?
- Computer predictions often jump directly from the independent variable to the (apparently) dependent variable. If someone does an online search for terrorist sites, this might lead to a conclusion that this person is a potential terrorist, yet she or he could be a police officer studying terrorism for a PhD.

14.4 Creating indexes

Indexes provide a way to consolidate and compare large amounts of diverse world data. They may cover many countries, cities or other places.[69] *Rankings* (league tables), like those from the OECD,[70] attract ongoing critical discussion.[71] *Indicators* imply caution when interpreting the data – indicators *only* indicate.[72] *Indexes* usually include little descriptive analysis, but they sometimes include qualitative data.[73] *Indexes* that cover the whole world may be unreliable, because basic data from less wealthy countries is often not accurate.[74] The point of indexes is that they permit *comparisons* (C14.1) – "1278 children in Hanoi hospitals" is just a statistic, but comparing Hanoi with other city hospitals creates knowledge.

The data for indexes comes from *secondary* sources (government or commercial statistics), surveys (C9.3), or participatory methods.[75] The easiest way to determine a methodology for creating an index is to adapt the methodology from a similar index. Many explain how they are created.[76]

Most indexes start from ***concepts*** that cannot be measured because they are too abstract – health, integrity, happiness – including 'fuzzy' concepts such as 'democracy'.[77] But studies are often designed around things that are easy to measure ("death"), rather than things that are important ("pain reduction"). Concepts also mean different things to different people, and so they need to be *defined* ("Good health is...").

Concepts are then operationalized as ***proxy indicators*** that can be measured. The concept of 'state legitimacy' may be assessed through indicators such as 'political violence', 'political prisoners', 'mass emigration', 'anti-system movements'.[78]

Indicators (e.g. for the concept 'health care') might be *direct* (number of nurses) and/or *indirect* (access to fresh water). They might measure *inputs* (vaccination) and/or *outputs* (child mortality). *Longitudinal studies* (e.g. trends in commercial airline policy) might start from *baseline indicators* (miles flown by commercial airlines), to monitor and evaluate interventions (cutprice airlines). But if the baselines are not accurate, the rest of the study is useless.

Individual *indicators* do not usually, on their own, provide accurate measurements of a *concept*, and so diverse data is usually ***aggregated*** (C9.3.1). The data from many different indicators is *standardized* to give a single score to measure the whole concept and create a *composite index*. The *Human Development Index* aggregates a large amount of statistical data to assess concepts such as 'poverty' or 'health', and the *World Press Freedom Index* is similar (Figure 13.1). Aggregate data can be used to create 'constitutive' or 'substitutive' indicators, for example to compare the success of governments or other entities in relation to achieving 'latent' conceptual goals.[79] On the basis that political leaders have the responsibility to ratify international conventions and other codes, and for creating wars and environmental harm, indicators about war, corruption and environment can be aggregated to create an index and rankings about the *concept* 'global leadership responsibility'.

Creating indexes, especially indicators, usually involves many methodological compromises but, in general:

- Use as few indicators as possible, but enough to create a comprehensive, reasonably unbiased, picture of what is being assessed.

- Use indicators that:
  - clearly operationalize the concept
  - are simple but robust
  - can be easily followed over time
  - can be easily compared with other places
  - can create useful composite indexes
  - can be created and used within available resources (cash, people, expertise)
  - use existing data, if possible
  - use the best quality data.

Rankings are often based on pollicized methodologies, as with the Olympic Games (Figure 0.2). The more credible rankings are adjusted or 'weighted' for population size and other factors. *Musicmetric's Digital Music Index* (2012) *weights* 'downloads' in relation to 'country population', to provide a 'per capita' figure for rankings. The UK has the most downloads, but Australia has more per person (Figure 14.4).[80] But if a *measure* becomes a *target*, it becomes a bad measure, because the target then changes what is being measured, and the indicator becomes meaningless.

Musicmetric's **Digital Music Index (DMI) 2012** Top countries for total BitTorrent downloads during first half of 2012, per capita				
	Country name	**Total downloads**	**Approx songs**	**Country population**
1	Australia	19,232,252	154,242,661	21,766,711
2	Ireland	3,434,737	27,546,591	4,670,976
3	Slovenia	1,416,433	11,359,793	2,000,092
4	Canada	23,959,924	192,158,590	34,030,586
5	United Kingdom	43,263,582	346,973,928	62,698,362
6	Norway	2,827,508	22,676,614	4,691,849
7	Italy	33,158,943	265,934,723	61,016,804
8	Portugal	5,607,910	44,975,438	10,760,305
9	Croatia	2,305,095	18,486,862	4,483,804
10	Greece	4,933,478	39,566,494	10,760,136

Figure 14.4 File-sharing rankings

Source: Pakinkis, T. (2012) 'The state of music piracy: in-depth data from new global report', *Musicweek*, 17 September.

14.5 Generalization, theories and concepts

"So *what's the big idea?*" is the question that journalists enjoy asking, and researchers hate answering. For a study to have international or global relevance, usually some form of *generalization* or *scaling* is necessary. Generalization usually entails locating findings in broader frames of reference so that they have greater relevance and can contribute to higher level thinking.

Generalization is usually seen as ***scaling up*** the findings of a study. Using micro-data may need to inform macro-theories, for example about state crime:

> Interviewing violence perpetrators and constructing their place within state hierarchies of violence requires inserting micro-level findings into macro-level theories of State, of social organization, of framing ideologies, and of work and career...Placing micro-level findings about Brazilian torturers into a macro-level framework captures State torture's systemic nature, with its five 'actor types'—"perpetrators", "facilitators", "framing ideologies", "bureaucratic organizations", and "bystanders"...By studying only torturers perpetrators, and not theorizing State, researchers bypass torture's systemic nature and can promote State torture system longevity.[81]

But it may also be necessary to generalize by ***scaling down*** from findings about international and global systems to local and individual circumstances. This is a distinct aspect of world-scale research, and is often ignored – why did research for the *World Bank* 'structural adjustment' plans of the 1990s not consider how encouraging governments to privatize bus services would reduce school attendance in rural villages? There is also an absence of *mezzo-level* (mid-level) understanding. There is good macro-data about the Chinese economy, and quite good micro-data about household economies in China, but little about what is happening in between at city or town level.[82]

Studies about ***people*** (C8) are often qualitative and interpretative,[83] and may be generalized in terms of their 'fittingness' or 'transferability' to analogous contexts.[84] Within human biology, studies on a few individuals are thought to be universally applicable because human biology seems universal. Psychologists also assume that their work is universally applicable. But, 'we have no notion of human psychology on a global scale. Most research is carried out on Americans and Europeans – samples from just over 10 percent of the world's population'.[85] Certain small-scale studies can be scaled up by locating them within international law – girls' health within human rights frameworks, child labour within ILO standards. Interviews with a few Ministry officials may need to be theorized in relation to theories about whole bureaucracies. Cultural research might also have global relevance. Discovering better ways to interpret the music of J.S. Bach has global significance for the present-day performance of Bach's music anywhere in the world.[86]

Population studies (C9) can be scaled up statistically, including non-human populations such as documents (C13). This need not be complicated. Standardizing data immediately makes it comparable more broadly (C9.3.1). If the sample is *representative* of a specific population, the findings of the study can usually be generalized to that population, and sometimes to similar populations (C7.4). *Sampling error* describes the degree of the chance difference between a population and its probability sample, such as a different percentage of children or women, and can be assessed and often corrected during analysis. *Non-sampling error* arises from factors such as bad questions or data processing, or low response rate, and this cannot be corrected. *Non-representative* samples cannot be scaled up statistically. But, although it is wrong for a researcher to over-claim the generalizability of findings from non-representative samples, a reader can generalize from relevant findings. The way a despotic regime used torture in South America may indicate, to an African reader, how torture is used in an African country.

Missing, or ***overlapping***, ***data*** is a particular problem with population studies, particularly about issues such as human rights abuses. Innovative methods such as *Multiple Systems Estimation* (MSE) try to address this problem.[87] MSE makes use of data from probability and non-probability samples so that missing data can be inferred from existing data, much as the picture on the missing pieces of a jigsaw puzzle can be inferred from the surrounding pieces. This may entail comparing different lists of names of relevant people – hospital, NGO and press lists of victims of torture – and deleting the overlaps. Or it may use past norms to assess a new circumstance. During a war, the number of village graves dug during the year of that war (G), minus the average number of graves dug annually before that year (g/per annum), could indicate the number of war-related deaths (WD). (G – g/per annum = WD).

Places (C10) often provide data at mezzo level, which can be scaled up and down. Much data is scalable because it follows physical laws, particularly infrastructure data – all rivers flow towards the sea and so factory pollution in rivers will behave in much the same way anywhere, the earthquake-proofing of buildings in Japan can be applied to countries that experience similar types of earthquakes. ***Mapping*** (C11) also entails decisions about scaling. Scaling up loses detailed information but improves context, and scaling down improves detail but loses context, as with online maps. Thinking about how cartographers overcome this provides useful insights for other approaches. They focus on the *purpose* of the map, highlight what matters and omit what does not. A London Underground map is perfect for travelling by train, but useless for cyclists.

Systems (C12) may provide data that is intrinsically generalizable. If a new law is said to affect a few gay people in a particular way, it is likely potentially to affect most gay people in the whole jurisdiction, in the same way. But it is necessary to check that those few people understood and reported what happened accurately, and that the law was applied correctly. Most importantly, for some purposes systems data can have great impact without being generalizable. Good, non-representative data about mass killings of civilians in a war can be sufficient to evidence war crimes without knowing how many people in a whole population were affected.

Theoretical generalization (C2) entails locating a study within a particular theory or theoretical framework, and comparing findings with theory[88] – "How does government enthusiasm for a war fit with theories of 'military Keynesianism'?"[89] Stephen Jay Gould elaborates,

> Facts do not "speak for themselves"; they are read in the light of theory. Creative thought...is the motor of changing opinion. Science is a quintessentially human activity, not a mechanized, robotlike accumulation of objective information, leading by laws of logic to inescapable interpretation.[90]

Theorization includes broad *general theory, specific theory* about unique situations, and practical and *functional theory* which relates closely to practice (Figure 14.5).[91] *Meta-theory* is an overview of theories – theories of theories – and can include an assessment of the methods used to support those theories. *Theoretical research* is based on reason, logic, calculation, modelling and argument, and may address issues like bargaining and conflict, justice and equity, and legitimization processes.[92]

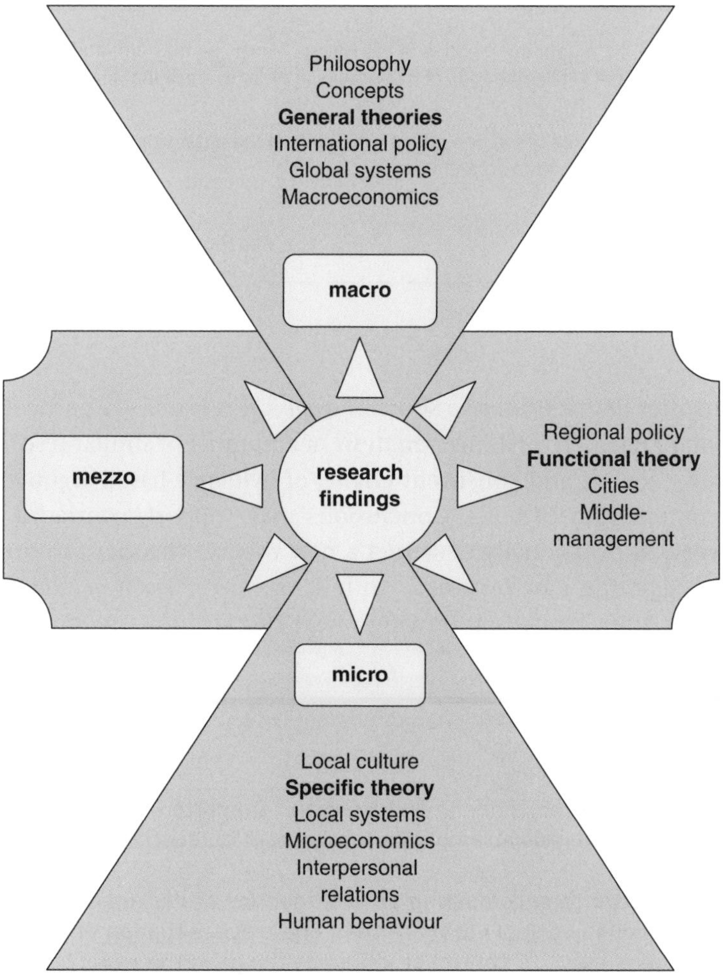

Figure 14.5 Theorizing world research

When a study is being designed (C4), decisions will be made about the use of theory. It can be *deductive* – existing theory is tested by observations and findings – or *inductive* – observations and findings are explained by existing or new theory. But in practice, research is often a mixture of both inductive and deductive analyses. A *grounded theory* approach starts, without a theory or hypothesis, from data collection. Significant data is identified and coded, and codes are grouped into concepts. From these concepts categories are built, from which new theories and hypotheses may emerge.

International theorization usually compares *others* with European-American theoretical constructs. But historically, there have been interesting attempts to understand *others*, from a less partisan viewpoint. In his book *India* (1030AD), al-Bīrūnī termed theory 'truth in the abstract', and his comparative method was based on theories *from* different cultures, not *about* different cultures (Figure 14.6).[93] It is hard to think of present-day examples of theories being compared on their own culturally distinct terms.

> I shall place before the reader the theories of the Hindus exactly as they are, and I shall mention in connection with them similar theories of the Greeks in order to show the relationship existing between them.
>
> I like to confront the theories of the one nation with those of the other simply on account of their close relationship, not in order to correct them.
>
> أبو ريحان بن محمد البيروني
>
> Abū Rayhān al-Bīrūnī, *India* (circa 1030)

Figure 14.6 Theory (al-Bīrūnī)

Formal theories derive from two sources: *empirical* research – a particularly robust piece of primary research, or a meta-analysis of a number of similar research studies, and/or *reason* – logical and consistent chains of evidence-based argument. Usually there is a combination of both. Conclusions may support, contradict or modify existing theory, or occasionally construct a new theory. Theories can inform future research by suggesting new *hypotheses* to test, or new *research questions* to address (C4.1). Johnson and Christensen provide a neat checklist for assessing theories:[94]

1. Is it logical and coherent?
2. Is it clear and parsimonious?
3. Does it fit the available data?
4. Does it provide testable claims?
5. Have theory-based predictions been tested and supported?
6. Has it survived numerous attempts by researchers to identify problems with it or to falsify it?
7. Does it work better than competing or rival theories or explanations?
8. Is it general enough to apply to more than one place, situation or person?
9. Can practitioners use it to control or influence things in the world?

In time, theories can create and elaborate ***concepts*** (terms implying a distinct idea or meaning) – 'security', 'sovereignty', 'discrimination' – and consensual *norms* or *moral values* – 'tolerance', 'international understanding' 'global justice'. Research findings, theoretical ideas and concepts may also be related to ***philosophy*** and ***ethics***.

But generalization on a world scale can go wrong, and theorization can culminate in the creation of simplistic paradigms. Karl Marx's theories were relevant to 19th century Britain, but mutated into Stalinist and Maoist ideologies which permitted the powerful to repress the powerless. In 1946, Bertrand Russell warned of the problem of 'theoretical imperialism', which continues.

> It is mainly through theorists that the maxims regulating the policy of advanced countries become known to less advanced countries. In the advanced countries, practice inspires theory; in the others, theory inspires practice. This difference is one of the reasons why transplanted ideas are seldom so successful as they were in their native soil.[95]

There are many explanations about why we distort generalizations.[96] 'Confirmation bias' means that we tend to favour information that fits our prevailing worldviews.[97] 'Pathological analysis' happens when small pieces of information are given too much importance because they fit a prevailing paradigm. 'Cherry picking and stovepiping' means selecting favoured evidence and channelling it to decision-makers.[98] But the bigger problem is that indigenous and minority group perspectives are ignored by theorists.

thinking zone: how do we create culturally-based theories?

identifying

- Which indigenous, traditional or culturally-based ideas could contribute to a theoretical framework for a present-day research study?
- Which non-European/American philosophical systems might provide ideas that can be compared with European-American theories?
- Could any religious *beliefs* (not historical events) form the basis of a theory that could be compared with non-religious theories?

applying

- How could the Confucian idea of *filial piety* (respect for family and elders) be compared with British theories of state welfare provision for older people, without trying to 'correct' either viewpoint?
- How can indigenous ideas of agriculture and forestry be compared with concepts such as 'sustainable development' or 'green growth'?
- How might different cultural ideas of gender roles be compared to inform international human rights theories?

World research often gets away with massive erroneous claims that would not be tolerated within small-scale studies.[99] Any analysis needs ongoing consideration of the ***integrity*** of conclusions, and what they will mean for the people, the research concerns and others. This is discussed further on the website.

main ideas

- ***Comparison*** is the basis of all analysis and knowledge-creation. It is also a specific approach to international research, based on *common questions. Historical natural experiments* are an example.
- ***Causation*** on a world scale is hard to demonstrate. The bases are philosophical, and differ across cultures. Causal diagrams can identify *necessary, sufficient* and *contributory* factors, and *causal loop diagrams* help to include causal factors in all directions.
- ***Predictive analysis*** can be *epistemological* (hypothetical, investigative, inferential) or/and *temporal (future causation, causal projection, projected analogy, trends).* Analytical frameworks include *risk analysis, scenario analysis, collective crowd intelligence* and big data.
- ***Indexes*** *aggregate* secondary data, in relation to *concepts*, to create rankings, *league tables* and indicators.
- ***Generalizing*** findings extends their relevance to *macro, mezzo* and *micro* levels. Analysis may include *statistical, interpretive, theoretical* and *philosophical* arguments.

key reading

Cua, A.S. (1975) 'The problems of causation: East and West', *Philosophy East and West*, 25 (1): 1–10.

Kutach, D. (2014) *Causation*. Cambridge: Polity.

Morse, S. (2004) *Indices and Indicators in Development: An Unhealthy Obsession with Numbers.* London: Earthscan.

Ragin, C.C. (1992) *The Comparative Method: Moving Beyond Qualitative and Quantitative Strategies.* Berkeley: University of California Press.

Scott, A.J. (ed.) (2001) *Principles of Forecasting: A Handbook for Researchers and Practitioners.* Norwell, MA: Kluwer Academic.

online resources

To access the resources – search on the name in italics, use the http, or search on the generic term in 'quote marks'.

Index Mundi – compares country profiles

TextCompare – finds differences in similar texts

Excel – can compare spreadsheets

culturomics.org – access to big data tools and discussion

Google Books Ngram – *"big data"* searches in books since 1800

Prediction markets – ideosphere.com – newsfutures.com

International ranking indexes – http://en.wikipedia.org/wiki/List_of_top_international_rankings_by_country

UN Statistics – http://unstats.un.org/unsd/default.htm

EC MDG Dashboard – http://esl.jrc.ec.europa.eu/envind/db_meths.htm

UNDP – Human Development Index – http://hdr.undp.org/en/statistics/hdi

World Bank Institute – governance indicators – http://info.worldbank.org/governance/wgi/index.aspx#doc

MORE ON THE WEBSITE

FIFTEEN

Reporting the research

'Be short, be simple, be human', advised a British civil servant in 1948.[1] A chapter on writing research reports could end there.

But, a world research report potentially has a world readership. This means thinking about diverse presentation styles – international and inclusive, academic and professional, expert and public, local and global. Research funders (C4.3) may want a *communications plan*, including an *open notebook* presentation of data throughout a project, interim *findings* and *briefing papers* for policy-makers and the press, *open access* papers online, the use of *social media*, and an assessment of *impact*.[2] But the most important aim is to make research accessible to those who contributed to it, and to people who it might directly concern. This all requires a wide range of presentation skills and styles.[3] This chapter outlines *international style*, the basics of *academic* and *professional* report writing, *public presentation* techniques, and how research outcomes might contribute to *social change* on a world scale.

At an organizational level, using research outcomes is no longer a one-way researcher-to-user 'dissemination' process. It is a dynamic, interactive and ongoing knowledge-creation-sharing process, as the *EU Eionet* paradigm suggests (Figure 15.1).[4] Much 'reporting' of 'research findings' is instantaneous, on platforms like

Crowdmap. Digital press agencies, such as *Citizenside*, link thousands of citizen reporters using platforms like *Reporter Kit*. A smart crowdsourced research project (C6.4), with a popular aim, simple robust methods and good freeware, could potentially evolve into a viral research project, which is taken up in different forms around the world, beyond the control of its instigators, with an infinite life. This would take the concept of 'participatory research' onto a new level.

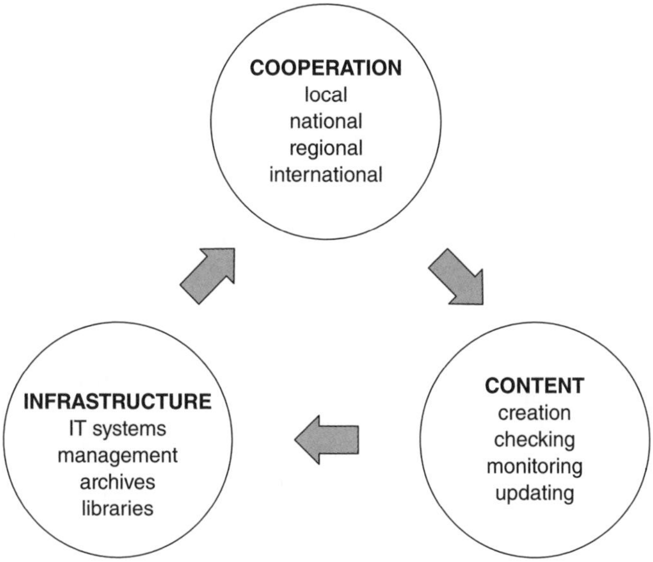

Figure 15.1 Knowledge sharing

Source: Based on *the European Environment Information and Observation Network* (*Eionet*).

15.1 International style

World research reports obviously need to be written in a way that is accessible to a world audience – in a 'plain' international style. But there is often confusion about what this means. The present-day expectation is for clear international English (or other language), not obtuse academic language or official legal language. Books like *Plain English Guide* provide sound advice;[5] and *Writing for the Internet*[6] and *Writing for the Media*[7] apply these principles. George Orwell's 'rules', from 1946, were prescient of present-day standards, and are now available on a Russian website:[8]

1. Never use a metaphor, simile, or other figure of speech which you are used to seeing in print.
2. Never use a long word where a short one will do.
3. If it is possible to cut a word out, always cut it out.
4. Never use the passive where you can use the active.
5. Never use a foreign phrase, a scientific word, or a jargon word if you can think of an everyday English equivalent.
6. Break any of these rules sooner than say anything outright barbarous.

The style used by the international media – *al Jazeera, Russia Today, BBC, China Daily* – provides good examples. These organizations use style-guides such as the *AP Stylebook*,[9] or those from national press.[10] Specialist advice is available from organizations, such as *Writing Effectively for WHO*[11] and glossaries from initiatives such as the IPCC.[12] The *Wikipedia Manual of Style* provides updates.[13] Recent academic textbooks and journals, from respectable academic publishers, are a useful guide to modern standards. When writing about other countries in another language, think carefully about when to use indigenous languages and scripts (Box 15.1).

Box 15.1 Using other languages and fonts

Tenses are confusing, especially when writing in English, and more difficult if you are Chinese.

- A research report is a *report* of something that *has* happened recently. The text is not yet widely accepted as knowledge, and so it will generally be in the *past* tense ("The study *found* that...").
- But literature and theoretical reviews usually use the *present* tense to indicate that the ideas *do* reflect accepted knowledge and remain current ("Gandhi *says* that..."). But if it seems appropriate to present an idea as clearly from a *past* era, use the past tense ("Hitler *said* that...").

Further advice is on the website.

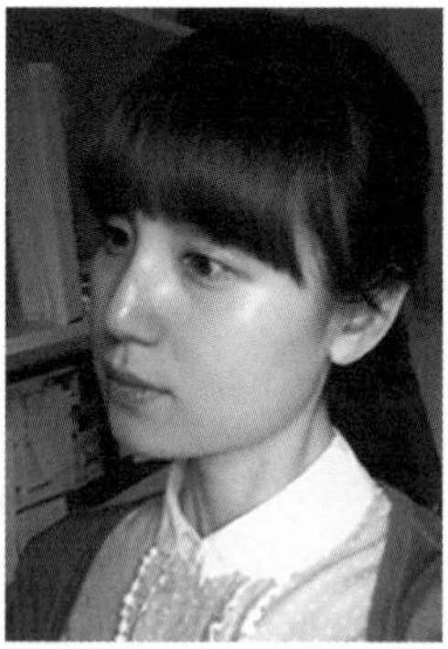

童宁 – 童甯
Tong Ning
(International Student Advisor)

In international settings, ***inappropriate terms*** can cause offence or create significant misunderstandings, and opinions are constantly changing. Terms such as the 'Third World', 'developing countries' and the economic 'South and North' are losing viable meaning. The Orientalist construct of the "Far East" is now usually termed 'East Asia', and the 'Middle East' is more sensibly described by the UN as 'West Asia'. 'The West' is also becoming meaningless – not least because from East Asia people often fly east to get to 'the West'. Culturally, 'European-American' seems more accurate. Don't repeat politicized terms unthinkingly. Why call the end of colonial rule 'independence', as if a country is like a child, and has just grown up. Isn't 'liberation' or 'withdrawal of occupying powers' more accurate? Did 5th century Britain become 'independent' from the Romans?

Obviously nationalistic, ethnocentric, paternalist or pejorative statements should be avoided – "Companies in these countries cannot reach international standards." Try not to imply that the people of a nation are all responsible for the actions of their wayward governments – not "The Ugandans are homophobic" when meaning "Ugandan politicians...". Try to use international and local norms for describing specific groups. But this can be complicated – Americans may use "people of color", but British writers would use "black", and both may include Asian people. Check styles on relevant international websites such as *UN Enable*. Listen to how particular people describe themselves, for example on national websites.

It is hard to accommodate and respect all ***cultural traditions*** and ***political views*** when producing content for a world audience. The UNESCO *Disarming History* project is evolving useful methods from diplomacy when trying to create documents about places where events are disputed. In general:

- At first, *only include things that everyone agrees about*, using basic language ("Japanese military in Nanjing", not "Nanjing Massacre").
- *Circulate initial drafts* widely for comment, in relevant languages, and discuss responses openly.
- Build *acceptance of the process*.
- Identify *international norms* as a basis for discussing contentious material (*Children's Rights Convention, ICC Statute*).
- Use *international terminology* from relevant and objective glossaries and lexicons (WHO, IPCC).
- Then *work incrementally* to agree and phrase contentious material.
- If agreement cannot be reached, *explain why*, and *present all views*.
- *Do not trade facts* politically, only use agreed material.
- Although slow, this builds support for the eventual outcomes.

So that documents can be found globally, research projects, documents, websites and other materials need clear ***international locators***, which should be tested on global search engines. This includes:

- a distinctive but informative *project title* – "Invisible Victims".
- an explanatory *subtitle* using the *keywords* – "Crime and abuse against people with learning disabilities".
- the likely *Library of Congress profile* – where bookshops and libraries might locate publications – "Criminology. Human Rights. Social Work".
- consistent *meta-data tags* – "disability", "victims", "crime" – and *hashtags* – *#InvisVict.*
- a *logo, key photos* and *images* – *Google Images* will demonstrate if image searches lead back to project materials.
- key *names* – researchers, partners, places.
- *links* to relevant organizations and projects.

If commercial publishers are likely to use the research outputs, check that they agree with this plan. Also check accessibility for people the research concerns – languages, translations of keywords, disability access.

Good international journals try to ensure that their publications are ***accessible*** and open to young researchers in less wealthy countries. The *Open Data Institute* works to make complex information accessible. Second language speakers, and people with reading difficulties, may not be able to scan-read text – they will read in 'series', every word from beginning to end. There are methods to make research accessible for the people it concerns, even if they have difficulty reading. For blind people, tactile diagrams and photos can be produced.[14] Computers can read documents aloud, but they should be checked – the word "therapist" might be read aloud as "the rapist". Creating documents with a clear international style is very similar to the methods used to make documents accessible for people with learning disabilities, such as a simplified 'parallel text'.[15]

15.2 Academic and professional reporting

Research reports use two basic forms of text to explain the outcomes of research – the new knowledge and ideas.

- *Descriptive findings,* which present the main facts of the research in a straightforward way, with clarifications but very little opinion.
- The *narrative* (story) which is based on casual chains of evidence and explanation leading to logical conclusions.

For any report be aware of copyright, libel and blasphemy laws in the relevant countries (C5.2). Check anonymity. The country where data came from will usually be identifiable, which can put people in that country at risk.

Many books explain ***academic writing***.[16] The format of an academic report usually includes: Introduction, Literature Review, Theoretical Framework, Methods, Findings and initial analysis, Discussion/Further Analysis, Conclusions and implications. The website provides an elaboration. Academic theses and dissertations usually need a full description of methods, to demonstrate to examiners that the work is robust. Journal articles require a clear but shorter description, unless the methods are innovative. Good academic style is usually objective, not personal ("The study found that..." not "My research found..."), but using the first person ("I", "my", "me") is acceptable when it is the simplest way to phrase something ("My family..." may be better than, "The family of the researcher..."). Check about plagiarism, and whether audio and video material can be included. If a report is part of an academic course, check the criteria that examiners use before writing the report (Box 15.2). These criteria should be reflected in the Abstract, perhaps in the Introduction, and certainly in the Conclusion. Examiners will use those sections to assess the whole study quickly.

Professional reports need clear evidence-based findings, and a logical discussion of the implications. The *Royal Geographical Society* provides useful advice, especially for fieldwork.[17] Professional research often demands 'problem-solving'[18] or 'solution-oriented'[19] outcomes (C4.2.1) – problems together with solutions. Conclusions go beyond discovering 'what is' to assessing critically 'what could be'.[20] The most important part is the executive summary, because this is all that most people will read. Professional reports usually minimize the discussion of the research methods, perhaps by describing them in an appendix or website. But often the same things have been said many times before, and have changed nothing. One way to deal with this is to present the history of failure as an aspect of the research, and challenge policy-makers to do better.[21]

An academic or professional report may then be the basis for ***academic papers*** or ***books***, but it is rare that a report is simply published commercially in its original form. Academic papers need to be framed in specific ways for specific journals,[22] and books need to appeal to a wide audience. Most book publishers want a structured proposal (usually explained in online 'guidance for submissions') and the most important section concerns sales and marketing. An initial research report might also be re-presented to form a funding proposal for further research.[23]

Box 15.2 The requirements for a thesis or dissertation

The dissertation/thesis should:

- be clearly written and presented, and use relevant and coherent arguments.
- take critical account of previous work on the subject.
- use, and develop, relevant methods proficiently.
- demonstrate that the study is the student's own independent work.
- make a significant contribution to learning, through the
    - discovery of new knowledge,
    - connection of previously unrelated facts,
    - development of new theory or methods,
    - revision of older views.
- be of a standard to merit publication, in whole or in part, or in a revised form.

[Based on regulations from the universities of Oxford, Cambridge and London.]

15.3 Public presentation

Presenting research to a world audience is demanding. Many 'public understanding' movements specialize in presenting complicated research in effective ways. The journal *Public Understanding of Science* hosts ongoing discussions,[24] and risk communication is a special skill.[25] Websites such as *PublicEngagement* provide useful frameworks and tools for embedding research projects in public domains. Digital data capture makes creating videos and webcasts simple, but audio soundscapes are underused and can enhance podcasts and radio programmes. Speaking at international conferences, especially with interpretation, requires planning (Figure 15.2). This includes thinking about cross-cultural aspects of *materials* (slides and videos), *technology* use (do your materials work on local systems?), *platform* position (maintaining contact with audience and media), *interpretation* (simultaneous and non-simultaneous), *fieldwork* presentations (appropriate technologies). This is explained further on the website.

Visualization entails thinking about the design, size, colour, density, emotion, and the narrative of informative images.[26] Specialists provide a wealth of ideas.[27] But don't use anything just for an effect. Do graphs provide better information if shown as 3D blocks or in colour? If not, a basic format is better. Colours and grey shades often do not copy or print well – black and white is more transferable. A smart line diagram might be better than slow online visualizations. For example, a simple Venn diagram can be used to depict and explain the complicated geopolitics of the 'British

Isles'. Matching the presentation style to the likely audience is more important than impressive graphics.[28] Many books explain specific techniques such as flow charts[29] or process *maps*,[30] and effective 'envisionings',[31] including *PowerPoint*[32] and quantitative information.[33] Infographics software includes *Adobe Illustrator*, the free *Inkscape*, and *Creately*, which allows users to work together over the internet. The *Wikipedia* page 'infographics' provides updates.

Angolan and Portuguese speaker, Alfonso Dala C. Fula presents in Russian.
(1st European Quality Education Forum, Magna Carta College, in Minsk.)

Figure 15.2 Presenting at international conferences

There is further information about presenting on the website.
Photo: Author's own

If research is to be used in a ***forensic setting*** (courts), this may involve showing persuasive technical slides,[34] and providing good audit trails for the evidence. It is necessary to select clear examples, but not to select untypical examples. Opposing lawyers can also examine the same evidence, and can challenge a biased presentation of data. The scope of court evidence is widening. The ICC has accepted children's drawings as contextual evidence of war crimes in Sudan.[35]

But smart technologies are simply the tools of presentation, not the content. Any presentation is a narrative, and, like innovations in novel writing, cinema, theatre and opera, it is still possible to do new things in old ways.

thinking zone: should narratives be presented backwards?

tradition

Historical narratives usually start from a significant date in the past, and stop at another significant later date. The dates, and remit of the narrative, reflect the historical traditions of the writer - often wars , laws, and "great men".

In contrast, archaeologists and evolutionary theorists often 'reverse engineer' their analysis from a new find or scientific discovery. Similarly, policy analysts might 'back-cast' analysis from a current event to assess how previous policies related to it.

think backwards

Map the causal chains - events, ideologies, people, science - of an international issue (gay rights, the ethics of using drones) by drawing a flow chart (or 'tree') backwards from a relevant event (a papal statement, drone attacks in Pakistan).

Stop at points when data becomes unavailable, unreliable or irrelevant. Use dotted lines for signicant gaps in data.

what's missing?

What might be missing from the chart because evidence is:

- in another language?
- not a text (statues, inscriptions, 'intangible heritage')?
- lost, destroyed or hidden?
- not accessible through Google?

narrative

Consider how you would write-up this chart as a reverse narrative.

What might be the differences between this backwards presentation and a traditional narrative text?

- Are different things included, and excluded?
- Are national historical traditions more, or less, controlling?
- Are different conclusions likely?
- Do the dotted lines suggest areas for potential research?

How might this approach contribute to the UNESCO aim of 'disarming history'?

[See: Critical Process Analysis, Figure 12.4.]

15.4 Influencing world change

World research often aims to change things. But it is not easy for individual researchers to meet powerful decision-makers and reach a world audience, and so it is usually necessary to work with campaigning or educational organizations. Consider who would be interested in the research, and why? Who would benefit from it, and how? Might the research contribute to policy, practice or advocacy, and when? Which events would help, and where? Can a website be created, and who will maintain it? Can the *International Studies Association* help?

Research-based ***arts***, created by the people the research concerns, can be vehicles for change – poetry, pictures, videos, magazines, stories, songs and plays. *Artists Against War* is a significant example. Media companies which make 'soap operas' may build the research into a story-line. Reproductive health information in Central

Asia (*Silk Road Radio*), and justice issues in Rwanda are presented in this way. Social impact computer games, such as *World Without Oil*, *Pipe Trouble* and *Desert of Real*, offer another way to influence people through interactive narratives. *Games for Change* is evolving strategies for designing effective serious games.

Educational materials can be based on research. Distance education programmes may be interested in research-based material. Issues from findings might be included in curricula and exam syllabuses. *Child-to-child* methods can implement health and related studies. But avoid exaggeration, test out materials, and remember that not everyone understands sophisticated images and symbolism. When research about malaria was first utilized, villagers took no notice of posters because they had never seen mosquitoes the size of a dog (Figure 15.3).

A Chinese malaria education poster

Figure 15.3 Massive mosquitoes

Conceptual tools are available to analyse and use power groups. The need to find 'spaces' for change is central.[36] This includes identifying the 'spaces for participation' (closed, invited, claimed/created), in relation to visible, hidden and invisible forms of power, at local, national and global levels.[37] Researchers should identify 'sources, structures, positions, relationships and mechanisms, and outcomes of power'.[38] Tools can be categorized into tools for understanding, organizing and ensuring action and sustainability.[39] These approaches recognize that bringing about change means engaging with powerful people, and therefore understanding the nature of power.[40] Similar tools are available to support grassroots organizations to achieve change.[41]

Professional campaigners try to identify ***agency*** – what or who will make the difference to a situation? Environmental campaigners might work to change how global companies behave by influencing their insurers or investors. Politicians will respond to likely media coverage. Press editors know that a newspaper can be brought down by advertisers being persuaded to pull out. Large retailers will change practice quickly if they fear consumer boycotts. Since 1995, *Transparency International* has used a methodology which has an integral social change mechanism, because those asked to contribute to the research – CEOs, politicians, experts, academics - are likely to have an interest in using it.[42]

Decision-makers, journalists and others who can influence change, are busy people who do not have the time to read long research reports – they need *summaries*. Short 'findings'[43] or 'briefings'[44] papers may present key outcomes in a few bullet points on a front page, with elaborations and sources of further information later.[45] These should contain clear, and if necessary simplified, descriptions of the research outcomes, but not political rhetoric or simplistic sound bites. Project websites can contain further information, resources and full reports. SMS texting and email alerts should only be used with permission from the recipients, or the impact can be negative.

Press and other media receive numerous press releases, and the major outlets usually respond better when these come from known press officers. The basics of creating a press release are on the website. A 'letter to the editor' in a national newspaper may be picked up by journalists on that paper or elsewhere. Investigatory journalists, such as those at India's *Tehelka*,[46] or *exaronews.com* for business stories, appreciate good evidence of relevant abuses of power, although they may take all the credit for revealing the story. To get a longer factual article accepted entails a brief email to a relevant editor, asking if she or he would be interested to see a full draft. Opportunistic media dissemination can come from using radio phone-ins or programmes that put public questions to high profile panellists, and contributing to blogs and other online discussions.

Free online ***repositories*** such as the *Social Science Research Network*[47] and *SCRIBD* can be used to provide open access to full reports.[48] The *Ranking Web of World Repositories* provides details of hundreds of similar sites.[49] *Sage OPEN* combines standard peer review and open access to create a repository-style online journal. An internet site could be the main outcome of a research project, with an archive of reports, and links to similar sites. Support and dissemination comes from sites such as *Dkosopedia*. Making appropriate contributions to *Wikipedia* and similar wikis can embed research within overall paradigms. And academics can add their own research to course reading lists to publicize their work outside their own departments, and use university data archives.

Face-to-face meetings with decision-makers can be difficult to manage. Providing a clear indication of the content of any meeting will mean they can get other relevant staff to attend, and leaving well-written briefing papers (with contact details) for possible follow-up is essential. Treat the meeting as a chance to enlighten and educate, not pressurize. Senior people are often shielded from the truth about their actions, and so a briefing from a well-informed outsider is often very welcome, particularly if it comes at an apposite moment. Government officials will appreciate good evidence if they need to attend an inquiry or international meeting on that topic, and CEOs may welcome hearing about a problem within their organization before a TV appearance. Finding the *windows of opportunity* is crucial – approaching the right person at the right time with the right information.

Another strategy is to present information to ***accountability organizations***. At an international level, this might include the ICC, and at a national level evidence might be submitted to the police or prosecution service, or to formal complaints agencies such as Trading Standards offices. Formal government inquiries also often accept evidence from experts and organizations, and may eventually present it online.[50] Shadow sites may accept other material and analysis.[51] Professional bodies will usually consider evidence in the form of complaints, and many organizations specialize in redressing specific forms of abuse of power.[52]

Social media sites are significant catalysts for change, for example through a petition on sites like *www.change.org*. But using social media to promote a research report is not always effective, unless there are 'killer facts' which also get the attention of the mainstream media. The influential sites (at present) include:

- *Facebook* (and *Weibo* and *Yandex*) (networking and information exchange, especially for organizations).
- *Twitter* (sound bites, linked to other material).
- *Tout* (micro video blogs).
- *Linkedin* (to network key researchers).
- *Google Scholar* (author profiles to track when reports are used).
- *Slideshare* (sharing presentations).
- *YouTube* (sharing video material).

Social Media for Academics provides ongoing lists, discussions and updates. Social networking has changed the style of presenting research findings. The *Stop Killer Robots* campaign is an example. To get world attention, claims need to:

- use *clear terms* – 'Killer robots', not 'autonomous unmanned armed aerial vehicles'.
- appear *new* and *significant* – They have 'dramatically changed warfare, bringing new humanitarian and legal challenges'.
- use simple *challenging questions* to engage the audience – 'Do machines have the right to decide to take the lives of human beings?'
- *appeal to normality* – 'Take off your uniform. Think of your family.'

Social network sites also provide the chance to coordinate numerous similar organizations, which increases the legitimacy of a campaign. *Avaaz* provides a platform for multidimensional campaigning. *WORLDbytes* works with citizen journalists.

Measuring the ***impact*** of research is increasingly important, and increasingly easy.[53] *Flag counter* counts the nationalities of who visits a site. Studies in *altmetrics* are developing tools that permit the measurement of web-based activity surrounding online material. This goes beyond citations, and includes usage statistics, online discussions, bookmarking and recommendations.[54] 'Uptake' entails longer term embedding of ideas through 'stakeholder involvement' and 'capacity building'.[55] The *Research for Development* (R4D) dashboard is an example.

And this all needs to be done with awareness of ***scams*** – fake conferences (Figure 15.4), phony journals and book publishers, corrupt commercial interference,[56] and countless other ways that online wrongdoers will try to extort money. Others may try to discredit research. Right-wing groups such as *American Majority* train members to manipulate ratings for books on *Amazon*, and sentiment for films, to influence keyword searches. PR companies such as the *Bivings Group* specialize in internet lobbying and attack scientific articles that challenge the companies they work for. So called fact checkers' like *Sense About Science* (SAS) often make more sense to dubious companies than to scientists.[57] Online research papers critical of the Chinese government may be attacked by thousands of individuals paid by the Chinese government.[58] The Israeli government arranges 'scholarships' for students who manipulate social media to present Israel positively.[59] And, of course, these nuisance people have their own research methodologies. Apparently, Nigerian scammers don't hide their nationality, because they need to filter out the mass of smart people at an early stage in the relationship.[60] *Scamwarners.com* can help, but common sense is essential. In cyberspace, and everywhere else, research presentation should be short, simple, human, *and smart.*

THE TRICKS	-------- Пересылаемое сообщение ------ От кого: United Nations <invitation@unwps.org> Кому: xxxxxxxxxxxx Дата: Sun, 4 May 2014 15:28:47 +0200 (CEST) Тема: Invitation: UN World Partnership Summit on Sustainable Development 24th – 27th June, 2014, London, United Kingdom. Dear Invitee, Nonprofit/NGO Colleague, On behalf of the organizing and scientific working committee, the United Nations Department for Sustainable Development (UN-DSD) invites you to a Four-day summit...	**THE MISTAKES**
Email address copies the UN style. It targets places where awareness is less, and the need for free travel is more. 'Invitee' and 'invite' makes recipient feel special.		The 'UNWPS' does not exist. There is no mention of this 'Summit' on search engines. The 'UN Department for Sustainable Development' does not exist. It is a 'division', which does not use the abbreviation 'DSD'.
Anyone who applied would probably be asked to pay a large deposit for the hotel, and hear no more. Full version on the website.		

Figure 15.4 Fake conferences

main ideas

The first aim is to reach ***research participants***, and others who have a ***direct interest*** in the research. This may mean producing reports using:

- relevant local languages.
- accessible formats for people with disabilities.

International presentation of research requires thinking about:

- the laws of *libel* and *copyright*, and the safety of researchers and others involved in a piece of research.
- a clear *style of writing*. An academic report for experts will include technical details to provide convincing testable evidence. A professional report will minimize technical details and provide good summaries.

- the criteria that *examiners* may use to assess theses and dissertations.
- effective *presentation techniques* – current trends in communications and publishing; using *online resources* – tools to create effective visualizations and assess the impact and uptake of online research, online repositories and social media.

Achieving world change entails:

- identifying the *'spaces'* for achieving change – the 'windows of opportunity'.
- using a *solution-oriented* style – problems presented together with proposals for solving them.
- being aware of *scams* and the *misuse of research* by others.

key reading

Cornwall, A. and Coehlo, V. (eds) (2006) *Spaces for Change? The Politics of Citizen Participation in New Democratic Arenas.* London: Zed Books.

Cutts, M. (1999) *Plain English Guide: How to Write Clearly and Communicate Better.* Oxford: Oxford University Press.

Denicolo, P. and Becker, L. (2011) *Success in Publishing Journal Articles.* London: Sage.

Few, S. (2004) *Show Me the Numbers: Designing Tables and Graphs to Enlighten.* Oakland, CA: Analytics Press.

McCandless, D. (2010) *Information is Beautiful.* London: Collins.

Pinker, S. (2014) *The Sense of Style: The Thinking Person's Guide to Writing in the 21st Century.* London: Allen Lane.

Richardson, L. (1990) *Writing Strategies: Reaching Diverse Audiences.* London: Sage

online resources

To access the resources – search on the name in italics, use the http, or search on the generic term in 'quote marks'.

Royal Geographical Society – recording your expedition – www.rgs.org/OurWork/Publications/EAC+publications/Expedition+Handbook/Recording+your+expedition.htm

AP Stylebook – www.apstylebook.com/?do=product

Writing Effectively for WHO – www.colelearning.net/who/

IPCC climate change glossaries – www.ipcc.ch/publications_and_data/publications_and_data_glossary.shtml

Research for Development – dashboard – http://r4d.dfid.gov.uk/UsageDashboard.aspx

Artists Against War – cultural campaigning – www.artistsagainstwar.ca/

Stop Killer Robots – campaign against automatic drone killing – www.stopkillerrobots.org/learn/

Social Media for Academics – www.andymiah.net/2012/12/30/the-a-to-z-of-social-media-for-academics/

Flag counter – http://s09.flagcounter.com/index.html

Games for Change – serious games for social justice

Glossary

abroad out of a "home" country

alien belonging to another place

anarchy 'without a ruler' – the absence of a hierarchical system of government

area study research or facts about a geographic region, structured in a way that makes comparisons possible

asymmetrical not evenly formed

big data data sets that are too big, too fast or slow, too diverse (sources and types) and/or too complex to be managed and analysed by traditional systems

bilateral between two countries

bishopric the province of a bishop

border a political boundary which requires permission to cross

citizens those who have a right to live in a particular state, nationals

city state a city that claims the status of a state

civilization a people with a shared history and culture

civilizational state a large state that claims legitimacy on the basis of a shared history and culture

collective defence an agreement that an attack on one country amounts to an attack on all

colony a settlement in a conquered or acquired place

comparative method an old and now discredited approach to comparing peoples on the basis of "race" (*Linguistics:* a method for comparing languages with the same origins)

comparative study analysis of the similarities and differences, concerning a common factor, between two or more places

continent geographical land mass

cosmopolitan an undivided view of humanity and power

country the territory or land of a people or nation

country case study a bounded study of a country or issue within a country

cross-border crosses national boundaries

crowds the masses, non-elites, 'down-system' people

cultural imperialism using the culture of a powerful group to dominate others

culture 'a design for living' (Kluckhohn and Kelly)

democracy rule by the people

development an unfolding to its potential

development assistance financial and technical aid to less developed countries

diplomacy a process that 'enables states to secure their foreign polices without resort to force, propaganda, or law' (Berridge)

donors countries that give aid to less wealthy countries

Earth the name of our planet

elites select groups, 'up-system' people

empire a large territory governed by 'emperors'

environmentalism an organized concern for the environment

ethnic nationalism the use of race to legitimize a nation or nationalist ideology

ethnicity identity, a general ancestry or cultural heritage

ethnocentric believing in the centrality and paramount importance of one's own people

ethnology the study of groups on the basis of race

eugenics the spurious "improvement" of a people on the basis of genetics

exceptionalist a belief within a group that it is different from, and better than, others

expansionism increasing the territory of a state by extending its borders

fiefdom land given by a superior to a subordinate in return for loyalty and/or military support

foreign happening, or came from, elsewhere

global relating to parts of the whole world; worldwide

global commons shared areas not part of nation states

global governance a process of regulation intending to have global reach, transnational governance

globalization a process that affects a sector of the world

glocal 'think global, act local'

governance rule that is not based on an enforceable system of laws

humanitarian assistance help for people suffering emergencies or disasters

humanity the number and nature of the people of the whole world

idealism an approach to international relations based on what ought to be – human rights, UN codes, internationalisation, etc (see realism)

ideology a system of ideas (usually about social life)

in-group insiders

insiders those who have a "we" relationship

international between nations

international community a non-specific group of state and non-state actors who share common values about human rights and global problems

international organizations formal bodies that work between nations

international relations the bilateral and multilateral interactions across national borders

lands territories

legitimate accepted or successful

location a specific point relative to other criteria

minority a group with less power

mitigating reducing the detrimental aspects

multilateral between more than two countries

multinational across many nations

nation a territorial people with a shared history, identity, culture, language and/or ethnicity

nationalistic an excessive national ideology

nationals people who belong to a nation

neocolonial a new form of colonialism

nihilism (ontology) a belief that nothing truly exists

nominalism (ontology) arguing that existence comes from an interplay of experiences and mental events

others "them" rather than "us"

out-group outsiders

outsiders those who do not have a "we" relationship

overseas abroad

pan- all

peoples a body of persons sharing a common culture, language, history or inherited condition of life

place a physical area which may imply other things such as historic significance

planet a major celestial body orbiting a star

planetary pertaining to the planet

postcolonial after being a colony

posthuman beyond a human state

principality the dominion of a prince

realism an approach to international relations based on the reality of what is (see idealism); (ontology) accepting that anything that is a noun exists

region a place defined geographically, political or culturally, often embracing smaller places

rights moral principles of human behaviour, often entitlements

scientific racism the application of spurious scientific methods to demonstrate the inferiority of other ethnic groups

security regime the rules for security arrangements

sovereign state a territory that has a permanent population, a government, and the capacity to enter into relations with other sovereign states

sovereignty ultimate authority within a defined territory

space a real or imagined area that may have political meaning

state crime abuses of power that are committed or permitted by governments

stateless peoples cultural groups without citizenship or nationality

stereotype something continued or repeated unthinkingly

supra-national above nations

supremacist claiming a right to rule "inferior" groups

system a whole composed of parts in orderly arrangement according to some scheme or plan

territory a tract of land, or district, of unidentified boundaries

transhuman spanning a human and a non-human state

transnational across nations

tribal land territory used by groups united by kinship or other close ties

universal pertaining to everything or everyone

world the Earth, together with all of its countries and peoples

worldview an outlook encompassing the whole of an individual's or group's knowledge and opinions

xenophobic a fear strangers or foreigners

References

How to use this book

1. Wilson, E.O. (1998) *Consilience: The Unity of Knowledge*. London: Little Brown.
2. Wilkinson, P. (2007) *International Relations: A Very Short Introduction*. Oxford: Oxford University Press, pp. 52–57, 65–66. Williams, C. (2012) *Researching Power, Elites and Leadership*. London: Sage.
3. Bastow, S. et al. (2014) *The Impact of the Social Sciences*. London: Sage.

Introduction

1. Abdullah Faisal. (2000) *100 Fabricated Hadiths*. Delhi: Darul Islam Publishers. Sha, I. (1999) *The Sufis*. London: Octagon Press. Daiyu Wang (2012) 'Authenticity of "Seek knowledge even as far as China" ', *Islam in China* – http://islaminchina.wordpress.com/2007/11/06/authenticity-of-seek-knowledge-even-as-far-as-china/
2. Jones, H.L. (1924) *The Geography of Strabo*. Cambridge, MA: Harvard University Press. (Strabo XI.XI.I.)
3. *Without borders* – http://en.wikipedia.org/wiki/List_of_Without_Borders_organizations
4. Proust, M. (1927/2003) *The Prisoner and the Fugitive*. London: Penguin. ['The only true voyage…would be not to visit strange lands but to possess other eyes, to see the universe through the eyes of another, of a hundred others, to see the hundred universes that each of them sees.']
5. Lorenz, C. and Tinbergen, N., reported in Nelson, M. (1992) Unpublished discussion at the *Third International Workshop on Closed Ecological Systems*, 24–27 April.
6. Bouzouggar, A. et al. (2007) '82,000-year-old shell beads from North Africa and implications for the origins of modern human behavior', *Proceedings of the National Academy of Sciences*, 104 (24): 9964–9969.
7. Vanhaeren, M. et al. (2004) 'Middle Stone Age shell beads from South Africa', *Science*, 304 (5669): 404.
8. Klein, R.G. (2000) 'Archeology and the evolution of human behavior', *Evolutionary Anthropology: Issues, News, and Reviews*, 9 (1): 7–36.
9. Leviticus 14:1–4.
10. Harari, Y.H. (2015) *Sapiens: A Brief History of Humankind*. London: Harper, pp. 24–39.

11. Hui, C.H. (2010) '*Huangming Zuxun* and Zheng He's voyages to the Western Oceans', *Journal of Chinese Studies*, 51: 67–85.
12. Assyria: Siege of Lachish (Room 10b), British Museum – www.britishmuseum.org/explore/galleries/middle_east/room_10_assyria_lion_hunts.aspx
13. Abu-Lughod, J. (1991) *Before European Hegemony: The World System A.D. 1250–1350*. Oxford: Oxford University Press.
14. Harari, Y.H. (2015) *Sapiens: A Brief History of Humankind*. London: Harper, pp. 247–274.
15. Tapper, R. (1995) 'Islamic anthropology and the anthropology of Islam', *Anthropological Quarterly*, 68 (3): 185–193.
16. Nawata Ward, H. (2009) *Women Religious Leaders in Japan's Christian Century, 1549–1650*. Ashgate: Farnham.
17. Pinto, M.H.M. (1988) *Biombos Namban* [Namban Screens]. Lisbon: Museo Nacional de Arte Antiga.
18. Qureshi, S. (2011) *Peoples on Parade: Exhibitions, Empire and Anthropology in Nineteenth-Century Britain*. Chicago: University of Chicago Press.
19. Cooper, M. (2005) *The Japanese Mission to Europe, 1582–1590: The Journey of Four Samurai Boys Through Portugal, Spain and Italy*. Kent: Global Oriental.
20. Holmes, R. (2006) *The Hottentot Venus*. London: Bloomsbury, Random House.
21. Meyer, K.E. and Brysac, S. (2008) *Kingmakers: The Invention of the Modern Middle East*. New York: W.W. Norton, p. 162.
22. Forthsyth, S. (2012) London 2012 Olympic medal tally – http://simon.forsyth.net/olympics.html
23. Wood, P. (1994) *Scientific Illustration: A Guide to Biological, Zoological, and Medical Rendering Techniques, Design, Printing, and Display*. New York: Van Nostrand Reinhold.
24. Panchenko, D.V. (1998) 'Scylax circumnavigation of India and its interpretation in early Greek geography, ethnography and cosmography', *Hyperboreus*, 4 (2): 211–242.
25. Erksine, A. (1995) 'Culture and power in Ptolemaic Egypt: the museum and library of Alexandria', *Greece and Rome*, 42 (1): 38–48.
26. Assange, J. (2013) 'People who shape our world', Oxford Union – YouTube.comOxfordUnion
27. Ukers, W.H. (1922) *All about Coffee*. New York: The Tea and Coffee Trade Journal Company.
28. Figes, O. (2010) *Crimea: The Last Crusade*. London: Allen Lane, pp. 306–309.
29. O'Connor, D. (2003) 'Egypt's view of others', in J. Tait (ed.),*'Never Had the Like Occurred': Egypt's View of its Past*. London: UCL Press, pp. 155–156, 169–171.
30. Watt, A. (1967) *The Evolution of Australian Foreign Policy: 1938–1965*. Cambridge: Cambridge University Press.
31. Chilisa, B. (2011) *Indigenous Research Methodologies*. London: Sage.
32. Smith, L.T. (2012) *Decolonizing Methodologies: Research and Indigenous Peoples*. London: Zed Books. Prior, D. (2007) 'Decolonising research: a shift toward reconciliation', *Nursing Inquiry*, 14 (2): 162–168.
33. Anthes, E. and Huber, H. (2013) *Frankenstein's Cat: Cuddling Up to Biotech's Brave New Beasts*. New York: Scientific American/Farrar, Straus and Giroux.

Chapter 1 Understanding world knowledge

1. Santayana, G. (1905/1980) *The Life of Reason: Reason in Common Sense*. New York: Dover Edition, Vol. 1, Ch. XII.
2. Tickner, A. and Blaney, D.L. (2013) *Claiming the International*. London: Routledge.

3. al-Bīrūnī, Abū al-Rayḥān (1910) (E. Sachau, ed.) *Al-Beruni's India: An Account of the Religion, Philosophy, Literature, Geography, Chronology, Astronomy, Customs, Laws and Astrology of India*. London: Kegan Paul, Trench, Trubner, Vol. 1, p. 1.
4. Bostrom, N. (2009) 'The simulation argument: some explanations', *Analysis*, 69 (3): 458–461.
5. Jacquette, D. (2003) *Ontology*. Montreal: McGill-Queen's University Press.
6. Dick, P.K. (1978) 'How to build a universe that doesn't fall apart two days later' (public speech) – http://deoxy.org/pkd_how2build.htm
7. Searle, J.R. (2006) 'Social ontology: some basic principles', *Anthropological Theory*, 6 (1): 12–29. Searle, J.R. (1995) *The Construction of Social Reality*. New York: Free Press. Searle, J.R. (2010) *Making the Social World*. Oxford: Oxford University Press.
8. Harari, Y.H. (2015) *Sapiens: A Brief History of Humankind*. London: Harper, pp. 24–39.
9. Wildman, W.J. (2010) 'An introduction to relational ontology', in J. Polkinghorne and J. Zizioulas (eds), *The Trinity and an Entangled World: Relationality in Physical Science and Theology*. Grand Rapids, MI: Eerdmans, pp. 55–73.
10. Godart, G.C. (2008) ' "Philosophy" or "religion"? The confrontation with foreign categories in late nineteenth century Japan', *Journal of the History of Ideas*, 69 (1): 71–91.
11. Poole, S. (2007) *Unspeak: Words are Weapons*. London: Abacus.
12. Schmidt, B.C. (1989) *The Political Discourse of Anarchy: A Disciplinary History of International Relations*. Albany, NY: State University of New York Press, p. 231. Odysseos, L. (2002) 'Dangerous ontologies: the ethos of survival and ethical theorizing in International Relations', *Review of International Studies*, 28(2): 403–418.
13. Rosenblatt, P.C. (1984) 'Epistemology and ontology in cross-cultural research', *Cross-Cultural Research*, 19 (1–4): 112–126.
14. Frisina, W.G. (1987) *Relational Ontology from a Cross Cultural Perspective*. Chicago: University of Chicago, Divinity School.
15. Zaharna, R.S. (1991) 'The ontological function of interpersonal communication: a cross-cultural analysis of Palestinians and Americans', *Howard Journal of Communication*, 3: 87–98.
16. BBC (2012) 'Saudi man executed for "witchcraft and sorcery" ', *BBC News Online* – www.bbc.co.uk/news/world-middle-east-18503550
17. Herdt, G. (1991) 'Representations of homosexuality: an essay on cultural ontology and historical comparison', *Journal of the History of Sexuality*, 1 (3): 481–504.
18. BBC (2002) 'Iran president in NY campus row', *BBC News Online*, 25 September. Taylor, J. (2011) 'Three men hanged for sodomy in Iran – where "gay people don't exist" ', *The Independent*, 8 September: 32.
19. Effingham, N. (2013) *An Introduction to Ontology*. Cambridge: Polity.
20. Judges 1:2–6. Numbers 25:8.
21. Deuteronomy 13:1–5, 12:30, 17:2–7, 13:6.10.
22. Deuteronomy 31:1–54.
23. Numbers 14:8.
24. Ward, B. (1966) *Spaceship Earth*. New York: Columbia University Press, p. 121.
25. Sartre, J.-P. (1958/2003) (H.E. Barnes, trans.) *Being and Nothingness*. London: Routledge.
26. Conor, C. (2002) *A Genealogy of Nihilism: Philosophies of Nothing and the Difference of Theology*. London: Routledge, pp. 251–255.
27. Sacks, J. (2008) 'Our right to Israel could not be more powerful', *Jewish Chronicle Online*, 18 January.
28. Audi, R. (1997) *Epistemology: A Contemporary Introduction to the Theory of Knowledge*. London: Routledge. Evans, I. and Smith, N.D. (2012) *Knowledge*. Cambridge: Polity.

29. Blackburn, S. (1996) *Dictionary of Philosophy*. Oxford: Oxford University Press.
30. Aikman, S. (1999) *Intercultural Education and Literacy: An Ethnographic Study of Indigenous Knowledge and Learning in the Peruvian Amazon.* Amsterdam: John Benjamins.
31. Salmon, M.H. (2006) *Introduction to Critical Reasoning.* Mason, OH: Thomson Wadsworth. pp. 118–119.
32. Nisbett, R.E. and Wilson, T.D. (1977) 'The halo effect: evidence for unconscious alteration of judgments', *Journal of Personality and Social Psychology*, 35 (4): 250–256.
33. Khaldūn, Ibn (1967/2004) (F. Rosenthal, trans.; N.J. Dawood and B. Lawrence, eds) *The Muqaddimah: An Introduction to History.* Princeton, NJ: Princeton University Press. (Bk 1: Preliminary Remarks.)
34. Williams, C. (2012) *Researching Power, Elites and Leadership*. London: Sage, p. 80.
35. Chomsky, N. (1992) 'The threat of a good example' – www.chomsky.info/books/unclesam01.htm
36. Williams, C. (2011) 'Learning to redress preemptive deceit: the Iraq Dossier', *Sage OPEN*, DOI: 10.1177/2158244011427060
37. Bhaskar, R.A. (1975/1997) *A Realist Theory of Science.* London: Version.
38. Richard, F. (2004) *Spirituality in the Land of the Noble: How Iran Shaped the World's Religions*. Oxford: Oneworld Publications.
39. Eppler, M. (2003) *The Wright Way.* New York: AMACOM.
40. Binet, A. and Simon, T. (1904) 'Méthodes nouvelles pour le diagnostic du niveau intellectuel des anormaux', *L'Année Psychologique*, 11: 191–244.
41. Bourdieu, P. (1992) *Invitation to a Reflexive Sociology.* Chicago: University of Chicago Press.
42. Woolgar, S. (1988) *Knowledge and Reflexivity: New Frontiers in the Sociology of Knowledge.* London: Sage. Steier, F. (ed.) (1991) *Research and Reflexivity.* London: Sage. Ashmore, M. (1989) *The Reflexive Thesis*. Chicago: University of Chicago Press.
43. Weick, K.E. and Sutcliffe, K.M. (2007) *Managing the Unexpected: Resilient Performance in an Age of Uncertainty*. New York: Jossey-Bass, p. 32.
44. Kuang, Ssu-ma (司馬光) (*c.* 1080) *Comprehensive Mirror for Aid in Governance* (資治通鑒). Original text – http://www.guoxue.com/shibu/zztj/zztjml.htm
45. Nagel, T. (1989) *The View from Nowhere*. New York: Oxford University Press.
46. Ahern, K. (1999) 'Ten tips for reflexive bracketing', *Qualitative Health Research*, 9 (1): 407–411.
47. Rose, G. (1997) 'Situating knowledges: positionality reflexivities and other tactics', *Progress in Human Geography*, 21 (3): 305–320.
48. Mullings, B. (1999) 'Insider or outsider, both or neither: some dilemmas of interviewing in a cross-cultural setting', *Geoforum*, 30 (4): 337–350.
49. Ganga, D. and Scott, S. (2006) 'Cultural "insiders" and the issue of positionality in qualitative migration research: moving across and moving along research participant divides', *Forum of Qualitative Social Research*, 7 (3): 7. Gallais, T. (2003) *From Native Stranger to Stranger and Back Again: Questions for Reflexive Practitioners*. BEREA Paper 10/9/2003.
50. Sultana, F. (2007) 'Reflexivity, positionality and participatory ethics: negotiating fieldwork dilemmas in international research', *ACME: An International E-Journal for Critical Geographies*, 6 (3): 374–385.
51. Ward, K. and Jones, M. (1999) 'Researching local elites: reflexivity, "situatedness" and political-temporal contingency', *Geoforum*, 30 (4): 301–312.
52. Temple, B. and Edwards, R. (2002) 'Interpreters/translators and cross-language research: reflexivity and border crossings', *International Journal of Qualitative Methods*, 1 (2): 1–12.
53. Jentsch, B. (1998) 'The "interpreter effect": rendering interpreters visible in cross-cultural research methodology', *Journal of European Social Policy*, 8 (4): 275–289.

54. Brew, A. et al. (2013) 'Reflexive deliberation in international research collaboration: minimising risk and maximising opportunity', *Higher Education*, November.
55. Easterby-Smith, M. and Malina, D. (1999) 'Cross-cultural collaborative research: toward reflexivity', *The Academy of Management Journal*, 42 (1): 76–86.
56. Eagleton, M. (2009) 'Examining the case for reflexivity in international relations: insights from Bourdieu', *Journal of Critical Globalisation Studies*, 1: 111–123.
57. Waever, O. (1998) 'The sociology of a not so international discipline: American and European developments in international relations', *International Organization*, 52 (4): 687–727.
58. Blaxter, L. et al. (2001) *How to Research*. Buckingham: Open University Press.
59. Strong, C.F. (1954) 'Education for international understanding', *Educational Review*, 6 (2): 79–102.
60. Cited in Ravi, S.S. (2011) *A Comprehensive Study of Education*. Delhi: Prentice-Hall of India, p. 700.
61. *Without borders* – http://en.wikipedia.org/wiki/List_of_Without_Borders_organizations
62. MacKenzie, D. (2010) *A World Beyond Borders: An Introduction to the History of International Organizations*. Toronto: University of Toronto Press.
63. Keck, M.E. and Sikkink, K. (1998) *Activists Beyond Borders: Advocacy Networks in International Politics*. Ithaca, NY: Cornell University Press.
64. Orwell, G. (1945) 'You and the atomic bomb', *Tribune*, 19 October.
65. *World Potato Atlas*, International Potato Centre (*Centro Internacional de la Papa*). McNeill, W.H. (1999) 'How the potato changed the world's history', *Social Research*, 66 (1): 67–83. Zuckerman, L. (1998) *The Potato: How the Humble Spud Rescued the Western World*. London: Douglas & McIntyre.

Chapter 2 Theories and concepts in world research

1. Pojman, L.P. (2008) *Philosophy: The Quest for Truth*. Oxford: Oxford University Press.
2. Deutsch, D. (2011) *The Beginning of Infinity: Explanations that Transform the World*. London: Allen Lane, pp. 1–33.
3. Cannadine, D. (2013) *The Undivided Past: History Beyond Our Differences*. London: Allen Lane.
4. Hippocrates (*c*. 400BC) *On Airs, Waters, and Places*, Part 24.
5. Brown, D.E. (1991) *Human Universals*. New York: McGraw-Hill.
6. Pinker, S. (1997) *How the Mind Works*. London: Penguin, pp. 383–385.
7. Derrida, J. (1978) 'Violence and metaphysics: an essay on the thought of Emmanuel Levinas', in (A. Bass, trans.), *Writing and Difference*. Chicago and London: University of Chicago Press, pp. 79–153.
8. Kurt, A.R. and Talbert, R.J.A (2009) *Geography and Ethnography: Perceptions of the World in Pre-Modern Societies*. London: Wiley.
9. Cannadine, D. (2013) *The Undivided Past: History Beyond Our Differences*. London: Allen Lane.
10. al-Bīrūnī, Abū al-Rayḥān (E. Sachau, ed.) (1910) *Al-Beruni's India: An Account of the Religion, Philosophy, Literature, Geography, Chronology, Astronomy, Customs, Laws and Astrology of India*. London: Kegan Paul, Trench, Trubner, Vol. 1, pp. 19–20.
11. Khaldūn, Ibn (1377/1967) (F. Rosenthal, trans.; N.J. Dawood and B. Lawrence, eds) *The Muqaddimah: An Introduction to History*. Princeton, NJ: Princeton University Press. (Second Prefactory Discussion: The First Zone.)

12. Compte de Gobineau, J.A. (1853–1855) *Essai sur l'inégalité des races humaines* [An Essay on the Inequality of the Human Races], Vol. I, Ch. 11.
13. King James Bible, Joshua 9:23.
14. Numbers 31:9, 15, 17, 18.
15. Deuteronomy 22:22.
16. Deuteronomy 22:22–24.
17. Penal Code of Iran, Art. 102, 104.
18. *United Nations Convention on the Prevention and Punishment of the Crime of Genocide* (CPPCG) (1948), Art. 2.
19. *UN Resolution 1820* (2008).
20. Leoussi, A.S. and Grosby, S. (2006) *Nationalism and Ethnosymbolism: History, Culture and Ethnicity in the Formation of Nations*. Edinburgh: Edinburgh University Press.
21. Jefferson, T. (1801) Letter, to James Monroe, November 24. *Thomas Jefferson Papers*, Library of Congress.
22. Toye, R. (2010) *Churchill's Empire*. London: Macmillan. Gilbert, M. (2009) 'Churchill and eugenics', The Churchill Centre – www.winstonchurchill.org/support/the-churchill-centre/publications/finest-hour-online/594-churchill-and-eugenics
23. Fenton, S. (2011) *Ethnicity*. Cambridge: Polity.
24. Sen, A. (2007) *Identity and Violence: The Illusion of Destiny*. London: Penguin.
25. Herrnstein, R.J. and Murray, C. (1994) *The Bell Curve*. New York: Free Press, Ch. 13.
26. Montagu, A. (ed.) (1999) *Race and IQ*. Oxford: Oxford University Press.
27. Sefa Deia, G.J. (1999) 'The denial of difference: refraining anti-racist praxis', *Race Ethnicity and Education*, 2 (1): 17–38.
28. Fernandez-Armesto, F. (2001) *Civilizations*. New York: Pan Books.
29. Glenn, H.P. (2000) *Legal Traditions of the World*. Oxford: Oxford University Press.
30. Stowasser, B. (1984) *Ibn Khaldun's Philosophy of History: The Rise and Fall of States and Civilisations*. Ankara: Ankara University. Turchin, P. (2003) *Historical Dynamics: Why States Rise and Fall*. Princeton, NJ: Princeton University Press. Diamond, J. (2011) *Collapse: How Societies Choose to Fail or Succeed*. London: Penguin. Morris, I. (2013) *The Measure of Civilisation: How Social Development Decides the Fate of Nations*. London: Profile Books.
31. Revelations 16:12.
32. Rupert, G.G. (1911) *The Yellow Peril; or, the Orient vs. the Occident*. Union Publishing, p. 9.
33. Huntington, S.P. (2011) *The Clash of Civilizations and the Remaking of World Order*. New York: Simon & Schuster.
34. Huntington, S.P. (2011) *The Clash of Civilizations and the Remaking of World Order*. New York: Simon & Schuster.
35. Marks, P. (2009) 'Video games need more diverse characters', *New Scientist*, 22 September.
36. Thorne, S. (2006) *The Language of War*. London: Routledge, pp. 79–90.
37. Kluckhohn, C. and Kelly, W.H. (1945) 'The concept of culture', in R. Linton (ed.), *The Science of Man in the World Crisis*. New York: Columbia University Press, pp. 78–105.
38. Ogburn, W.F. (1957) 'Cultural lag as theory', *Sociology and Social Research*, 41 (3): 167–174.
39. Bilimoria, P. and Irvine, A.B. (eds) (2013) *Sophia Studies in Cross-Cultural Philosophy of Traditions and Cultures*. London: Pearson.
40. Kirmayer, L.J. and Minas, H. (2000) 'The future of cultural psychiatry: an international perspective', *Canadian Journal of Psychiatry*, 45 (5): 438–446. Kirmayer, L.J. (2006) 'Beyond the "new cross-cultural psychiatry": cultural biology, discursive psychology and the ironies of globalization', *Transcultural Psychiatry*, 43 (1): 126–144.
41. Tomlinson, J. (2008) *Cultural Imperialism: A Critical Introduction*. New York: ACLS Humanities.

42. Davidann, J.T. (2007) *Cultural Diplomacy in U.S.–Japanese Relations, 1919–1941*. London: Palgrave Macmillan.
43. *The Political Arts Initiative* – www.politicalarts.org
44. Edgar, A. and Sedgwick, P. (2005) *Cultural Theory: The Key Concepts*. New York: Routledge.
45. Watson, J. and Caldwell, M.L. (eds) (2005) *The Cultural Politics of Food and Eating*. Oxford: Blackwell.
46. Nye, J.S. (2005) *Soft Power: The Means to Success in World Politics*. Washington, DC: World Affairs.
47. Williams, C. (2012) *Researching Power, Elites and Leadership*. London: Sage, pp. 63–68.
48. Bottomore, T.B. (1993) *Elites and Society*. London: Routledge.
49. Lasswell, H.D. et al. (1952) *The Comparative Study of Elites*. Stanford, CA: Stanford University Press.
50. Conniff, M.L. and McCann, F.D. (1991) *Modern Brazil: Elites and Masses in Historical Perspective*. Lincoln: University of Nebraska Press.
51. Farmer, K.C. (1992) *The Soviet Administrative Elite*. Santa Barbara, CA: Greenwood Press.
52. alden, G. (2000) *The New Elites: Making a Career in the Masses*. London: Allen Lane.
53. Kerbo, H.K. and McKinsky, J.A. (1995) *Who Rules Japan: The Inner Circles of Economic and Political Power*. Santa Barbara, CA: Greenwood Press. Scalapino, R.A. (1972) *Elites in the People's Republic of China*. Seattle: University of Washington Press.
54. Rothkopf, D. (2009) *Superclass: The Global Power Elite and the World They Are Making*. London: Abacus.
55. Mill, J.S. (1859/1995) *On Liberty*. London: Penguin Classics.
56. Mackay, C. (1841) *Extraordinary Popular Delusions and the Madness of Crowds*. London: Wordsworth Editions.
57. Le Bon, G. (1896/2002) *The Crowd: A Study of the Popular Mind*. London: Dover.
58. Oretega y Gasset, J. (1930/1994) *The Revolt of the Masses*. London: W.W. Norton.
59. Campbell, S. (1943) *The Menace of the Herd*. Milwaukee, WI: The Bruce Publishing Company.
60. Buford, B. (1991) *Among the Thugs: The Experience, and the Seduction, of Crowd Violence*. New York: W.W. Norton.
61. Rheingold, H. (2003) *Smart Mobs: The Next Social Revolution*. London: Perseus Books.
62. Surowiecki, J. (2004) *The Wisdom of Crowds: Why the Many are Smarter than the Few and How Collective Wisdom Shapes Business, Economies, Societies and Nations*. London: Doubleday.
63. Howe, J. (2009) *Crowdsourcing: Why the Power of the Crowd is Driving the Future of Business*. New York: Crown Business.
64. Williams, C. (2013) 'Crowdsourcing research: a method for investigating state crime', *State Crime*, 2 (1): 30–52.
65. Bayly, S. (1999) *Caste, Society and Politics in India from the Eighteenth Century to the Modern Age*. Cambridge: Cambridge University Press.
66. Savage, M. et al. (2013) 'A new model of social class: findings from the BBC's great British class survey experiments', *Sociology*, (Online), 2 April, DOI: 10.1177/0038038513481128 – www.bbc.co.uk/science/0/21970879
67. Held, D. (2010) *Cosmopolitanism: Ideals and Realities*. Cambridge: Polity.
68. Appiah, K.A. (2006) *Cosmopolitanism: Ethics in a World of Strangers*. New York: W.W. Norton.
69. Nussbaum, M. (1994) 'Patriotism and cosmopolitanism', *Boston Review*, October/November.
70. Andreotti, V. (2006) 'Soft versus critical global citizenship', *Policy and Practice*, 1 (3): 40–51.

71. Hutchings, K. (2009) *Global Ethics*. Cambridge: Polity.
72. Williams, C. (2010) 'Global justice and education: from nation to neuron', *Educational Review*, 62 (3): 343–356.
73. Crowder, G. and Haddock, I. (2013) *Theories of Multiculturalism*. Cambridge: Polity.
74. Held, D. and McGrew, A. (eds) (2007) *Globalization Theory: Approaches and Controversies*. Cambridge: Cambridge University Press.
75. Baldwin, T. and Rozenberg, G. (2004) 'Britain must scrap multiculturalism', *The Times*, 3 April.
76. Jacoby, T. (2004) *Reinventing the Melting Pot: The New Immigrants and What it Means to be American*. New York: Basic Books.
77. Lawler, S. (2013) *Identity: Sociological Perspectives*. Cambridge: Polity.
78. Rumford, C. (2013) *The Globalization of Strangeness*. London: Palgrave Macmillan.
79. Appadurai, A. (1996) *Modernity at Large: Cultural Dimensions of Globalization*. Minneapolis: University of Minnesota Press.
80. Williams, C. (2001) *Leaders of Integrity: Ethics and a Code for Global Leadership*. Amman: United Nations University Leadership Academy.
81. Bisaz, C. (2012) *The Concept of Group Rights in International Law: Groups as Contested Right-Holders, Subjects and Legal Persons*. Leiden: Martinus Nijhoff.
82. Williams, C. (1993) *The Right to be Known: A Global View of Human Rights and Mental Handicap*. Bristol: Norah Fry Research Centre.
83. Williams, C. (1995) *Invisible Victims: Crime and Abuse Against People with Learning Disabilities*. London: Jessica Kingsley.
84. Williams, C. (ed.) (1998) *Environmental Victims: New Risks, New Injustice*. London: Earthscan.
85. Tremmel, J.C. (2006) *Handbook of Intergenerational Justice*. Cheltenham: Edward Elgar.
86. Singer, P. (2009) *Animal Liberation: The Definitive Classic of the Animal Movement*. New York: Harper.
87. Gray, J. (2002) *Straw Dogs: Thoughts on Human and Other Animals*. London: Granta Books.
88. Mithen, S. (1996) *The Prehistory of the Mind*. London: Thames & Hudson.
89. Taylor, T. (2010) *The Artificial Ape: How Technology Changed the Course of Human Evolution*. London: Palgrave Macmillan.
90. Bloom, H. (2000) *Global Brain: The Evolution of the Mass Mind from the Big Bang to the 21st Century*. London: John Wiley.
91. Sharot, T. (2012) *The Optimism Bias*. London: Constable & Robinson.
92. Johnson, D.D.P. (2004) *Overconfidence and War: The Havoc and Glory of Positive Illusions*. Cambridge, MA: Harvard University Press.
93. Kahneman, D. (2011) *Thinking Fast and Slow*. London: Allen Lane.
94. Greenfield, S. (2003) *Tomorrow's People: How 21st-Century Technology is Changing the Way We Think and Feel*. London: Penguin.
95. Greenfield, S. (2011) *You and Me: The Neuroscience of Identity*. London: Notting Hill Editions.
96. Hsu, M. et al. (2008) 'The right and the good: distributive justice and neural encoding of equity and efficiency', *Science*, 320 (1092): 1092–1095.
97. Braidotti, R. (2013) *The Posthuman*. Cambridge: Polity.
98. Leroi, A.M. (2006) 'The future of neo-eugenics', *EMBO Reports*, 7: 1184–1187.
99. Rose, N. and Abi-Rached, M. (2014) *Neuro: The New Brain Sciences and the Management of the Mind*. Princeton, NJ: Princeton University Press.
100. Hamilton, W.D. (2000) 'A review of dysgenics: genetic deterioration in modern populations', *Annals of Human Genetics*, 64 (4): 363–374.

101. Williams, C. (1997) *Terminus Brain: The Environmental Threats to Human Intelligence*. London: Cassell. Kubo, D.R.T. et al. (2013) 'Brain size of Homo floresiensis and its evolutionary implications', *Proceedings of the Royal Society* B 280: 1760. Lynn, R. and Harvey, J. (2008) 'The decline of the world's IQ', *Intelligence*, 36: 112–120.
102. Stringer, C. and McKie, R. (1996) *African Exodus: The Origins of Modern Humanity*. London: Pimlico.
103. Rees, T. (2009) 'The shared genetic heritage of Jews and Palestinians', *Epiphenom* – www.patheos.com/blogs/epiphenom/2009/01/shared-genetic-heritage-of-jews-and.html
104. Hsu, M. et al. (2008) 'The right and the good: distributive justice and neural encoding of equity and efficiency', *Science*, 320 (1092): 1092–1095.
105. Regan, T. and Singer, P. (eds) (1976) *Animal Rights and Human Obligations*. London: Prentice-Hall.
106. Jones, S. (2002) Unpublished interview on *The Science Show*, broadcast on ABC Radio, January – www.abc.net.au/rn/science/ss/stories/s456478.htm
107. Wilson, E.O. (1998) *Consilience: The Unity of Knowledge*. New York: Little Brown, pp. 188–189.
108. Bonnett, A. (2008) *What is Geography?* London: Sage.
109. Chant, S. and McIlwaine, C. (2008) *Geographies in the 21st Century*. Cheltenham: Edward Elgar.
110. Robertson, G. (2010) *The Case of the Pope: Vatican Accountability for Human Rights Abuse*. London: Penguin.
111. Pulleyblank, E.G. (1999) 'The Roman Empire as known to Han China', *Journal of the American Oriental Society*, 119 (1): 71–79.
112. Plato. *Laws* 5:740.
113. Seth, S. (ed.) (2012) *Postcolonial Theory and International Relations: A Critical Introduction*. London: Routledge.
114. Williams, C. (2012) *Researching Power, Elites and Leadership*. London: Sage, pp. 27–29.
115. Rodriguez, J.P. (ed.) (1997) *The Historical Encyclopedia of World Slavery*. Santa Barbara, CA: ABC-CLIO.
116. Fanon, F. (2001) *The Wretched of the Earth*. London: Penguin.
117. Said, E.W. (2003) *Orientalism*. London: Penguin.
118. Carrier, J.G. (1995) *Occidentalism: Images of the West*. Oxford: Oxford University Press.
119. Sartre, J.-P. (trans.: A. Haddour) (2001) *Colonialism and Neo-Colonialism*. London: Routledge.
120. Nye, J.S. (2005) *Soft Power: The Means to Success in World Politics*. New York: Public Affairs.
121. Nolan, P. (2012) *Is China Buying the World?* Cambridge: Polity.
122. Glenn, H.P. (2000) *Legal Traditions of the World*. Oxford: Oxford University Press, pp. 282–285.
123. Leoussi, A.S. and Grosby, S. (2006) *Nationalism and Ethnosymbolism: History, Culture and Ethnicity in the Formation of Nations*. Edinburgh: Edinburgh University Press.
124. Hobsbawm, E. and Ranger, T. (eds) (1983) *The Invention of Tradition*. Cambridge: Cambridge University Press. Sand, S. (2010) *The Invention of the Jewish People*. London: Verso.
125. Anderson, B. (2006) *Imagined Communities: Reflections on the Origin and Spread of Nationalism*. New York: Verso.
126. Masuzawa, T. (2005) *The Invention of World Religions*. Chicago: University of Chicago Press. Sand, S. (2012) *The Invention of the Land of Israel: From Holy Land to Homeland*. London: Verso.
127. Zhang, W. (2012) *The China Wave: Rise of a Civilizational State*. Hackensack, NJ: World Century.

128. Osiander, A. (2001) 'Sovereignty, international relations, and the Westphalian myth', *International Organization*, 55 (2): 251–287.
129. Wickeri, E. and Kalhan, A. (2009) *Lands Rights Issues in International Human Rights Laws*. London: Institute of Human Rights and Business.
130. Lipton, M. (2009) *Land Reform in Developing Countries: Property Rights and Property Wrongs*. London: Routledge.
131. Gray, K. (1993) 'The ambivalence of property', in G. Prins (ed.), *Threats without Enemies*. London: Earthscan.
132. Jessop, B. (2013) *The State*. Cambridge: Polity. Lachmann, R. (2009) *States and Power*. Cambridge: Polity. Malesevic, S. (2013) *Nation-States and Nationalisms*. Cambridge: Polity.
133. Thomas, D. and Grant, T.D. (1999) *The Recognition of States: Law and Practice in Debate and Evolution*. Westport, CT: Praeger.
134. Troianiello, A. (1999) *Raison d'État et droit public*, Thèse dactylographiée. Havre: Université du Havre.
135. Kupchan, C.A. (2012) *No One's World: The West, the Rising Rest, and the Coming Global Turn*. Oxford: Oxford University Press.
136. Ryan, J. et al. (2006) *Micronations*. London: Lonely Planet.
137. Williams, C. (2009) 'Should Korea return to three kingdoms?', *The Korea Herald*, 28 August: 4.
138. Zartman, W.I. (1995) *Collapsed States: The Disintegration and Restoration of Legitimate Authority*. New York: Lynne Rienner.
139. Brock, L. et al. (2011) *Fragile States*. Cambridge: Polity.
140. Nath, S. et al. (2010) *Saving Small Island Developing States*. London: Commonwealth Secretariat. Connell, J. (2013) *Islands at Risk: Environments, Economies and Contemporary Change*. Cheltenham: Edward Elgar.
141. *Index of Possessions and Colonies* – http://worldstatesmen.org/COLONIES.html
142. Goodwin-Gill, G.G. (2010) *Convention Relating to the Status of Stateless Persons (1954)*. New York: United Nations Audiovisual Library of International Law.
143. Black, R. (2001) *Environmental Refugees: Myth or Reality?* UNHCR Working Paper No. 34 – www.unhcr.org/3ae6a0d00.html
144. Caspersen, N. (2011) *Unrecognised States*. Cambridge: Polity. Minahan, J. (ed.) (2002) *Encyclopedia of the Stateless Nations: Ethnic and National Groups Around the World*. Westport, CT: Greenwood Press.
145. UNSTATS – http://unstats.un.org/unsd/methods/m49/m49regin.htm
146. *Euroregions* – http://en.wikipedia.org/wiki/List_of_Euroregions
147. Graham, K. and Felicio, T. (n.d.) *Regional Security and Global Governance: A Proposal for a Regional-Global Security Mechanism*. Ghent: Academia Press.
148. Sands, P. (2003) *Principles of International Environment Law*. Cambridge: Cambridge University Press.
149. Kranich, N. (2004) *The Information Commons: A Public Policy Report*. New York: Free Expression Policy Project.
150. Rincon, P. (2013) 'New venture "to mine asteroids" ', *BBC News Online*, 22 January.
151. *Big Think* editors (2010) 'Stephen Hawking's warning: Abandon Earth – or face extinction', *Big Think*, 6 August.
152. Herren, M. (2009) *Internationale Organisationen seit 1865. Eine Globalgeschichte der inter-nationalen Ordnung* [International Organizations since 1865. A Global History of International Order]. Darmstadt: Wissenschaftliche Buchgesellschaft.
153. Franklin, B. (2008) *The Autobiography of Benjamin Franklin*. Rockville, MD: ARC Manor, p. 30.
154. Reinalda, B. (2009) *Routledge History of International Organizations: From 1815 to the Present Day*. London: Routledge.

155. Burritt, E. (1869) *Lectures and Speeches by Elihu Burritt*. London: Sampson Low.
156. Reinalda, B. (2013) *Routledge Handbook of International Organization*. London: Routledge.
157. Shaw, M.N. (1997) *International Law*. Cambridge: Cambridge University Press.
158. Williams, C. (2006) *Leadership Accountability in a Globalizing World*. London: Palgrave Macmillan, pp. 21–24.
159. Glenn, H.P. (2000) *Legal Traditions of the World*. Oxford: Oxford University Press.
160. Köchler, H. (2006) 'The United Nations Organization and global power politics: the antagonism between power and law and the future of world order', *Chinese Journal of International Law*, 5 (2): 323–340.
161. Green, P. and Ward, T. (2004) *State Crime*. London: Pluto Press.
162. Weiss, T.G. (2012) *What's Wrong with the United Nations and How to Fix It*. Cambridge: Polity.
163. Baylis, J. and Smith, S. (2001) *The Globalization of World Politics*. Oxford: Oxford University Press.
164. Mathews, G. (2011) *Ghetto at the Center of the World: ChungKkng Mansions, Hong Kong*. London: University of Chicago Press.
165. Held, D. (2013) *Global Governance in Crisis*. Cambridge: Polity.
166. Held, D. et al. (1999) *Global Transformations*. Cambridge: Polity Press.
167. MacLeod, S. (ed.) (2006) *Global Governance and the Quest for Justice*. New York: Hart Publishing.
168. Sharma, M.R. and Banerjee, A.M. (2010) *United Nations International Civil Service: Perceptions, Realities and Career Prospects*. New Delhi: Academic Foundation.
169. Sen, A. (1999) 'Global justice: beyond international equity', in I. Kaul (ed.), *Global Public Goods: International Cooperation in the 21st Century*. Oxford: Oxford University Press.
170. Krut, R. (1997) *Globalization and Civil Society: NGO Influence in International Decision-Making*. Geneva: UNRISD.
171. West, D. (2013) *Social Movement in Global Politics*. Cambridge: Polity.
172. Colás, A. (2002) *International Civil Society: Social Movements in World Politics*. Cambridge: Polity.
173. Kaldor, M. (2003) *Global Civil Society: An Answer to War*. Cambridge: Polity.
174. JCIE (1998) *Globalisation, Governance and Civil Society*. Tokyo: Japan Center for International Exchange.
175. Shapcott, R. (2010) *International Ethics*. Cambridge: Polity.
176. Hutchings, K. (2010) *Global Ethics*. Cambridge: Polity.
177. Stares, P.B. (1998) *The New Security Agenda: A Global Survey*. New York: Japan Center for International Exchange. Hough, P. (2013) *Understanding Global Security*. London: Routledge.
178. Williams, C. (1996) 'Environment and global security in the context of developing countries', in R.K. Nayak (ed.), *The Environmental and Consumer Protection Foundation*. New Delhi: ECPFO, pp. 129–133.
179. Jørgensen, K.E. (2010) *International Relations Theory: A New Introduction*. London: Palgrave Macmillan. Lawson, S. (2012) *International Relations*. Cambridge: Polity.
180. Chahin, M. (1987) *The Kingdom of Armenia*. New York: Dorset Press, Preface.
181. Wilkinson, P. (2007) *International Relations: A Very Short Introduction*. Oxford: Oxford University Press, p. 2.
182. Jackson, P.T. (2010) *The Conduct of Inquiry in International Relations*. London: Routledge.
183. Archibugi, D. et al. (eds) (2011) *Global Democracy: Normative and Empirical Perspectives*. Cambridge: Cambridge University Press.
184. Shapcott, R. (2009) *International Ethics*. Cambridge: Polity.

185. Beardsworth, R. (2011) *Cosmopolitanism and International Relations Theory*. Cambridge: Polity.
186. McInnes, C. and Lee, K. (2011) *Global Health and International Relations*. Cambridge: Polity.
187. Steans, J. (2013) *Gender and International Relations*. Cambridge: Polity.
188. Eagleton, M. (2009) 'Examining the case for reflexivity in international relations: insights from Bourdieu', *Journal of Critical Globalisation Studies*, 1: 111–123.
189. Waever, O. (1998) 'The sociology of a not so international discipline: American and European developments in international relations', *International Organization*, 52 (4): 687–727.
190. Richardson, L.F. (1939) 'Generalized foreign politics', *The British Journal of Psychology*, (monograph supplement), 23. Richardson, L.F. (1960) *Statistics of Deadly Quarrels*. Pacific Grove, CA: Boxwood Press. Richardson, L.F. (1993) *The Collected Papers of Lewis Fry Richardson*. Cambridge: Cambridge University Press. (Vol. 2: *Quantitative Psychology and Studies of Conflict*.)
191. Lamont, C. (2015) *Research Methods in International Relations*. New York: Sage.
192. Boesche, R. (2002) *The First Great Political Realist: Kautilya and his Arthashastra*. Lanham, MD: Lexington Books.
193. Waltz, K.N. (1979) *Theory of International Politics*. New York: McGraw-Hill.
194. Keohane, R.O. (1984) *After Hegemony: Cooperation and Discord in the World Political Economy*. Princeton, NJ: Princeton University Press.
195. Schmidt, B.C. (1989) *The Political Discourse of Anarchy: A Disciplinary History of International Relations*. Albany, NY: State University of New York Press.
196. Odysseos, L. (2002) 'Dangerous ontologies: the ethos of survival and ethical theorizing in international relations', *Review of International Studies*, 28(2): 403–418.
197. Todorov, T. (2910) *The Fear of Barbarians*. Cambridge: Polity.
198. Evans, B. (2013) *Liberal Terror*. Cambridge: Polity.
199. Custers, P. (2010) 'Military Keynesianism today: an innovative discourse', *Race and Class*, 51 (4): 79–94.
200. Orwell, G. (1949) *Nineteen Eighty-Four. A Novel*. London: Secker & Warburg.
201. Orwell, G. (1945) 'You and the atomic bomb', *Tribune*, 19 October.
202. Piquet, H.S. (1945) 'Functional international organization', *American Academy of Political and Social Science*, 240: 43–50.
203. Wolf, P. (1973) 'International organization and attitude change: a re-examination of the functionalist approach', *International Organization*, 27 (3): 347–371.
204. Jameson, F. and Larsen, N. (1988) *The Ideologies of Theory: Essays 1971–1986*. London: Routledge.
205. Krasner, S.D. (ed.) (1983) *International Regimes*. Ithaca, NY: Cornell University Press.
206. Baldwin, D.A. (1993) *Neorealism and Neoliberalism: The Contemporary Debate*. New York: Basic Books.
207. Berridge, G.R. (2010) *Diplomacy: Theory and Practice*. London: Palgrave Macmillan.
208. Greig, J.M. and Diehl, P.F. (2012) *International Mediation*. Cambridge: Polity.
209. Boyd-Judson, L. (2011) *Strategic Moral Diplomacy: Understanding the Enemy's Moral Universe*. Sterling, VA: Kumarian Press.
210. Power, M. et al. (2012) *China's Resource Diplomacy in Africa: Powering Development?* London: Palgrave Macmillan.
211. Beckett, C. and Ball, J. (2012) *Wikileaks: News in a Networked Era*. Cambridge: Polity.
212 Amitav, A. (2009) *Constructing a security community in Southeast Asia: ASEAN and the problem of Regional Order*. London: Routledge.

213. Orwell, G. (1945) 'You and the atomic bomb', *Tribune*, 19 October.
214. BBC (2011) 'LulSec hackers claim CIA website shutdown', *BBC News Online*, 16 June.
215. Nye, J. (2011) *The Future of Power.* New York: Public Affairs.
216. Singer, P. (2009) *Wired for War*. London: Penguin.
217. US Army research contracts – www.dodsbir.net/selections/abs2011-1/armyabs111.htm
218. Weinberger, S. (2011) 'Terrorist "pre-crime" detector field tested in United States screening system aims to pinpoint passengers with malicious intentions', *Nature News* – www.nature.com/news/2011/110527/full/news.2011.323.html
219. Weiss, T.G. (2012) *Humanitarian Intervention*. Cambridge: Polity.
220. Minear, L. (1999) 'The theory and practice of neutrality: some thoughts on the tensions', *International Review of the Red Cross*, 833.
221. Keen, D. (2007) *Complex Emergencies*. Cambridge: Polity.
222. Hannigan, J. (2012) *Disasters Without Borders*. Cambridge: Polity.
223. Davies, L. et al. (2004) *Education in Emergencies in South Asia*. Kathmandu: UNICEF, pp. 33–34.
224. Aldrich, D. (2012) *Building Resilience: Social Capital in Post-Disaster Recovery.* Chicago: University of Chicago Press.
225. Williams, C. and Yazdani, F. (2009) 'The rehabilitation paradox: street working children in Afghanistan', *Diaspora, Indigenous, and Minority Education*, 3 (1): 4–20.
226. Weiss, T.G. (2013) *Humanitarian Business*. Cambridge: Polity.
227. Singer, P. (1972) 'Famine, affluence, and morality', *Philosophy and Public Affairs*, 1(1): 229–243.
228. Alesina, A. and Weder, B. (2002) 'Do corrupt governments receive less foreign aid?', *American Economic Review*, 92 (4): 1126–1137.
229. Williams, C. (2006) *Leadership Accountability in a Globalizing World.* London: Palgrave Macmillan.
230. Truman, H.S. (1949) Inaugural address, January 20 – www.trumanlibrary.org/calendar/viewpapers.php?pid=1030
231. Robinson, P. and Dixon, J. (2013) *Aiding Afghanistan: A History of Soviet Assistance to a Developing Country*. London: Hurst & Co.
232. Foreign Affairs paper 'Russia's participation in international development assistance' – www.minfin.ru/common/img/uploaded/library/2007/06/concept_eng.pdf
233. Brautigam, D. (2011) 'Chinese development aid in Africa', in J. Golley and L. Song (eds), *Rising China: Global Challenges and Opportunities*. Canberra: Australian National University Press.
234. Xinhua News Agency (2011) *China's Foreign Aid* – http://news.xinhuanet.com/english2010/china/2011-04/21/c_13839683.htm
235. AidData – www.aiddata.org/content/index/data-search
236. Official Development Assistance. OECD – http://stats.oecd.org/Index.aspx?DatasetCode=TABLE1
237. Global Humanitarian Assistance. Aid donors – www.globalhumanitarianassistance.org/report/gha-report-2010
238. Calgar, G. et al. (2012) *Feminist Strategy in International Governance*. London: Routledge.
239. Stone, E. (ed.) (1999) *Disability and Development: Learning from Action and Research on Disability in the Majority World*. London: Disability Press.
240. Williams, C. (2000) 'Education and human survival: the relevance of global security to international education', *International Review of Education*, 46 (3–4): 183–203.
241. Davies, L. (2004) *Education and Conflict: Complexity and Chaos*. London: Routledge.
242. Davies, L. (2008) *Educating Against Extremism*. Sterling, VA: Trentham.
243. Harber, C. (2004) *Schooling as Violence: How Schools Harm Pupils and Societies*. London: Routledge.

244. Merson, M.H. et al. (2005) *International Public Health: Diseases, Programs, Systems, and Policies*. New York: Jones and Bartlett.
245. Elbe, S. (2010) *Security and Global Health*. Cambridge: Polity.
246. Beaglehole, R. and Bonita, R. (2009) *Global Public Health: A New Era*. Oxford: Oxford University Press.
247. Dyson, S.M. and Atkin, K. (2012) *Genetics and Global Public Health: Sickle Cell and Thalassaemia*. London: Routledge.
248. McMichael, A.J. (1993) *Planetary Overload: Global Environmental Change and the Health of the Human Species*. Cambridge: Cambridge University Press.
249. Matthews, D. (2011) *Intellectual Property, Human Rights and Development*. Cheltenham: Edward Elgar. Correa, C.M. (2010) *Research Handbook on the Protection of Intellectual Property Under WTO Rules*. Cheltenham: Edward Elgar.
250. Shadlen, K.C. (2011) *Intellectual Property, Pharmaceuticals and Public Health*. Cheltenham: Edward Elgar.
251. Bubela, T. and Gold, E.R. (2012) *Genetic Resources and Traditional Knowledge*. Cheltenham: Edward Elgar. Chiarolla, C. (2011) *Intellectual Property, Agriculture and Global Food Security*. Cheltenham: Edward Elgar.
252. Bridge, G. and le Billon, P. (2012) *Oil*. Cambridge: Polity.
253. Hall, D. (2012) *Land*. Cambridge: Polity.
254. Clapp, J. (2011) *Food*. Cambridge: Polity
255. UNIDO (2012) *World Statistics on Mining and Utilities*. Cheltenham: Edward Elgar.
256. Chatham House (2013) *Resources Futures: Methodology for the Chatham House Resource Trade Database*. London: Chatham House.
257. Williams, C. (2006) *Leadership Accountability in a Globalizing World*. London: Palgrave Macmillan.
258. Yamashita, H. and Williams, C. (2002) 'A vote for consensus: democracy and difference in Japan', *Comparative Education*, 38 (3): 277–289.
259. British Council (2013) 'Pakistan's youth vote explained', *The Nation*, 7 April.
260. Power, M. et al. (2012) *China's Resource Diplomacy in Africa: Powering Development?* London: Palgrave Macmillan.
261. Todaro, M. and Smith, S. (2006) *Economic Development*. New York: Addison-Wesley.
262. Rostow, W.W. (2003) 'The five stages of growth', in M. Seligson and J. Passe-Smith (eds), *Development and Underdevelopment: The Political Economy of Global Inequality*. Boulder, CO: Lynne Rienner, pp. 123–131.
263. Sachs, J. (2005) *The End of Poverty*. London: Penguin.
264. William, E. (2007) *The White Man's Burden*. Oxford: Oxford University Press.
265. Kaufman, Z.D. (2012) *Social Entrepreneurship in the Age of Atrocities*. Cheltenham: Edward Elgar.
266. Acs, Z.J. et al. (2013) *Global Entrepreneurship and Development Index*. Cheltenham: Edward Elgar.
267. Leys, C. (1996) *The Rise and Fall of Development Theory*. Bloomington: Indiana University Press.
268. Dichter, T.W. (2003) *Despite Good Intentions: Why Development Assistance to the Third World Has Failed*. Cambridge, MA: University of Massachusetts Press. Moyo, D. (2010) *Dead Aid: Why Aid is Not Working and How There is Another Way for Africa*. London: Penguin.
269. Sen, A. (2001) *Development as Freedom*. Oxford: Oxford University Press.
270. Wilkinson, R. and Hulme, D. (eds) (2012) *The Millennium Development Goals and Beyond: Global Development after 2015*. London: Routledge.

271. Higgins, K. et al. (2010) *Economic Growth and the MDGs*. ODI Briefing Papers 60.
272. Willis, K. (2011) *Theories and Practices of Development*. London: Routledge. Hopper, P. (2012) *Understanding Development*. Cambridge: Polity.
273. Lin, J.Y. (2003) *The China Miracle: Development Strategy and Economic Reform*. Beijing: Chinese University Press.
274. Power, M. et al. (2012) *China's Resource Diplomacy in Africa: Powering Development?* London: Palgrave Macmillan.
275. Selwyn, B. (2013) *The Global Development Process*. Cambridge: Polity.
276. Schenk, C.R. (2011) *International Economic Relations since 1945*. London: Routledge.
277. Jackson, J.H. and Davey, W.J. (1999) *Legal Problems of International Economic Relations*. Eagan, MN: West Publications.
278. Edelman, J. et al. (2009) *The Politics of International Economic Relations*. Boston, MA: Wadsworth.
279. Waring, M. (2003) 'Counting for something! Recognising women's contribution to the global economy through alternative accounting systems', *Gender and Development*, 11 (1): 35–43.
280. Bastiat, F. (1850) 'That which is seen and that which is unseen' –https://sites.google.com/site/theamiaelibrary/browse-authors/frederic-bastiat/that-which-is-seen-and-that-which-is-unseen
281. Vreeland, J.R. (2003) *The IMF and Economic Development*. Cambridge: Cambridge University Press.
282. Thomas, J. (2000) *The Battle in Seattle: The Story Behind and Beyond the WTO Demonstrations*. London: Fulcrum.
283. Harvey, D. (2005) *A Brief History of Neoliberalism*. Oxford: Oxford University Press. Crouch, C. (2011) *The Strange Non-Death of Neo-Liberalism*. Cambridge: Polity.
284. Centeno, M.A. and Cohen, J.C. (2010) *Global Capitalism: A Sociological Perspective*. Cambridge: Polity. Hutton, W. and Giddens, A. (eds) (2001) *Global Capitalism*. London: New Press.
285. Haley, U.C.V. and Haley, G.T. (2013) *Subsidies to Chinese Industry: State Capitalism, Business Strategy, and Trade Policy*. New York: Oxford University Press.
286. de Soto, H. (2000) *The Mystery of Capital: Why Capitalism Triumphs in the West and Fails Everywhere Else*. London: Bantam Press.
287. Fukuyama, F. (2006) *The End of History and the Last Man*. New York: Free Press.
288. Mulgan, G. (2013) *The Locust and the Bee: Predators and Creators in Capitalism's Future*. Princeton, NJ: Princeton University Press.
289. Moulier Boutang, Y. (2012) *Cognitive Capitalism*. Cambridge: Polity.
290. Ilinski, K. (2001) *Physics of Finance: Gauge Modelling in Non-Equilibrium Pricing*. London: Wiley.
291. Kirilenko, A.M. et al. (2011) *The Flash Crash: The Impact of High Frequency Trading on an Electronic Market*. Working paper – http://papers.ssrn.com/sol3/papers.cfm?abstract_id=1686004
292. Davies, H. (2010) *The Financial Crisis*. Cambridge: Polity.
293. Keen, S. (2011) *Debunking Economics*. London: Zed Books. Cooper, G. (2008) *The Origin of Financial Crises*. London: Vintage. Feil, M. (2010) *The Failure of Free Market Economics*. London: Scribe. Touraine, A. (2013) *After the Crisis*. Cambridge: Polity.
294. Loungani, P. (2002) *How Accurate Are Private Sector Forecasts? Cross-Country Evidence from Consensus Forecasts of Output Growth*. IMF Working Paper No. 00/77 – http://ssrn.com/abstract=227868; http://dx.doi.org/10.2139/ssrn.227868
295. Gray, J. (1998) *False Dawn: The Delusions of Global Capitalism*. London: Granta Books.
296. Amato, M. and Fantacci, L. (2011) *The End of Finance*. Cambridge: Polity.

297. Acemoglu, D. and Robinson, J. (2012) *Why Nations Fail: The Origins of Power, Prosperity, and Poverty*. London: Crown Business.
298. Davis, G.A. (2009) 'Extractive economies, growth, and the poor', *Mining, Society and a Sustainable World*, DOI: 10.1007/978-3-642-01 103-0_2
299. Keen, S. (2012) 'Ignoring the role of private debt in an economy is like driving without accounting for your blind-spot' – http://blogs.lse.ac.uk/politicsandpolicy/archives/21465
300. King, S.D. (2013) *When the Money Runs Out: The End of Western Affluence*. New Haven, CT: Yale University Press. King, S.D. (2011) *Losing Control: The Emerging Threats to Western Prosperity*. New Haven, CT: Yale University Press.
301. Hilton, A. (2013) 'The stealth raid on our wealth', *Evening Standard*, 26 March: 50.
302. Ryan-Collins, J. et al. (2012) *Where Does Money Come From?* London: Positive Money.
303. E-money systems – http://projects.exeter.ac.uk/RDavies/arian/emoney.html
304. Jackson, T. (2009) *Prosperity without Growth*. London: Earthscan. Victor, P. (2008) *Managing without Growth*. London: Edward Elgar.
305. Meadows, D.H. et al. (1974) *The Limits to Growth: A Report for the Club of Rome's Project on the Predicament of Mankind*. New York: Universe Books.
306. Patel, R. (2009) *The Value of Nothing*. London: Portobello Books. Simms, A. et al. (2010) *Growth Isn't Possible: Why We Need a New Economic Direction*. London: New Economics Foundation.
307. Platt, L. (2011) *Understanding Inequalities*. Cambridge: Polity.
308. Wilkinson, R. and Pickett, K. (2009) *The Spirit Level: Why Equality is Better for Everyone*. London: Penguin.
309. Stiglitz, J.E. (2012) *The Price of Inequality*. London: Penguin.
310. Byrne, J. (ed.) (2012) *The Occupy Handbook*. New York: Back Bay Books.
311. Colchester, N. (1981) 'Mars bar', *Financial Times*, 24 November.
312. UNESCO World Water Portal – World Water Assessment Programme (WWAP).]
313. Zelco, F. (2004) 'Making Greenpeace: direct action environmentalism in British Columbia', *BC Studies*, 142/143: 197–240.
314. Ward, B. (1966) *Spaceship Earth*. New York: Columbia University Press.
315. Ward, B. and Dubos, R. (1972) *Only One Earth: The Care and Maintenance of a Small Planet*. London: Andre Deutsch.
316. Barry, R. et al. (1971) *Balance and Biosphere (A Radio Symposium on the Environmental Crisis)*. Toronto: Canadian Broadcasting Corporation.
317. Club of Rome (1972) *The Limits to Growth: A Report for the Club of Rome's Project on the Predicament of Mankind*. London: Macmillan.
318. Carson, R. (1962) *Silent Spring*. Boston: Houghton Mifflin.
319. Lifton, R.J. (1967) *Death in Life: Survivors of Hiroshima*. New York: Random House.
320. Schumacher, E.F. (1973) *Small is Beautiful: A Study of Economics as if People Mattered*. London: Blond & Briggs.
321. Lovelock, J. (1979) *Gaia: A New Look at Life on Earth*. Oxford: Oxford University Press.
322. Williams, C. (ed.) (1998) *Environmental Victims: New Risks, New Injustice*. London: Earthscan.
323. George, S.T. (2001) *Minamata: Pollution and the Struggle for Democracy in Postwar Japan*. Cambridge, MA: Harvard University Press.
324. Beder, S. (1997) *Global Spin: The Corporate Assault on Environmentalism*. Totnes: Green Books.
325. Dauverge, P. and Lister, J. (2011) *Timber*. Cambridge: Polity.

326. DeSombre, E.R. and Barkin, S. (2011) *Fish*. Cambridge: Polity.
327. Vallely, P. (2012) 'The planet looked to Rio again, and Rio looked away', *The Independent*, 24 June.
328. Urry, J. (2011) *Climate Change and Society*. Cambridge: Polity.
329. Williams, C. (2006) *Leadership Accountability in a Globalizing World*. London: Palgrave Macmillan, p. 211.
330. Prins, G. and Rayner, S. (2007) 'Time to ditch Kyoto', *Nature*, 449 (25 Oct.): 973–975.
331. Sands, P. (2003) *Principles of International Environmental Law*. Cambridge: Cambridge University Press.
332. Beder, S. (2006) *Environmental Principles and Policies: An Interdisciplinary Approach*. London: Earthscan.
333. Birnie, P.W. and Boyle, A.E. (1992) *International Law and the Environment*. Oxford: Clarendon.
334. Malcolm, R.A. (1994) *Guidebook to Environmental Law*. London: Sweet & Maxwell.
335. Graham, K. (1999) *The Planetary Interest: A New Concept for the Global Age*. London: Rutgers University Press.
336. Schlosberg, D. (2007) *Defining Environmental Justice: Theories, Movements, and Nature*. Oxford: Oxford University Press.
337. Bosselmann, K. (1999) *Environmental Justice and Market Mechanisms: Key Challenges for Environmental Law and Policy*. London: Kluwer Law.
338. South, N. and Beirne, P. (2006) *Green Criminology*. Farnham: Ashgate.
339. Williams, C. (ed.) (1998) *Environmental Victims: New Risks, New Injustice*. London: Earthscan.
340. Hall, M. (2013) *Victims of Environmental Harm: Rights, Recognition and Redress Under National and International Law*. London: Routledge.
341. Hanley, N. et al. (2007) *Environmental Economics in Theory and Practice*. London: Palgrave.
342. Bi Jun et al. (2000) 'Circular economy: an industrial ecology practice under the new development strategy in China', unpublished paper, Canter for Environmental Management and Policy, Nanjing University.
343. Sachs, J. (2008) *Common Wealth: Economics for a Crowded Planet*. London: Penguin.
344. Holder, J. (2004) *Environmental Assessment: The Regulation of Decision Making*. New York: Oxford University Press.
345. Harris, J. (2006) *Environmental and Natural Resource Economics: A Contemporary Approach*. New York: Houghton Mifflin.
346. Heller, W.P. and Starrett, D.A. (1976) 'On the nature of externalities', in S.A.Y. Lin (ed.), *Theory and Measurement of Economic Externalities*. New York: Academic Press, p. 10.
347. Williams, C. (1997) 'Environmental victims: arguing the costs', *Environmental Values*, 6 (1): 3–30.
348. BBC (2012) 'Climate talks: UN forum extends Kyoto Protocol to 2020', *BBC News Online*, 8 December.
349. Curry, P. (2011) *Ecological Ethics*. Cambridge: Polity.
350. van den Bergh, J. (2001) 'Ecological economics: themes, approaches, and differences with environmental economics', *Regional Environmental Change*, 2 (1): 13–23.
351. Wackernagel, M. and Rees, W. (1996) *Our Ecological Footprint*. New York: New Society Press.
352. Williams, C. (2007) 'Environment protection is a shared responsibility', *China Daily*, 12 July: 11 – www.chinadaily.com.cn/cndy/2007-07/12/content_5433311.htm
353. Beck, U. (1992) *Risk Society: Towards a New Modernity*. London: Sage.
354. Kasperson, J.X. and Kasperson, R.E. (eds) (2001) *Global Environmental Risk*. Tokyo: United Nations University Press.

355. Prins, G. (ed.) (1993) *Threats Without Enemies: Facing Environmental Insecurity*. London: Earthscan, pp. 171–191.
356. LSE Mackinder Programme for the Study of Long Wave Events – www2.lse.ac.uk/researchAndExpertise/units/mackinder/Home.aspx
357. Seidel, P. (1998) *Invisible Walls: Why We Ignore the Damage We Inflict on the Planet and Ourselves*. New York: Prometheus Books.
358. Williams, C. (2002) 'New security risks and public educating: the relevance of recent evolutionary brain science', *Journal of Risk Research*, 5 (3): 225–248.
359. Bostrom, N. (2013) 'Existential risk prevention as global priority', *Global Policy*, 4(1): 15–31.
360. Laszlo, E. and Seidel, P. (eds) (2006) *Global Survival*. New York: Select Books.
361. May, R.M. (1972) 'Will a large complex system be stable?', *Nature*, 238: 413–414, DOI: 10.1038/238413a0
362. Brickner, P. (2013) *The Fanaticism of the Apocalypse: Save the Earth. Punish Human Beings*. Cambridge: Polity.
363. eslie, J. (1996) *The End of the World: The Science and Ethics of Human Extinction*. London: Routledge.
364. Wilson, E.O. (2002) *The Future of Life*. London: Little Brown.
365. Rees, M. (2003) *Our Final Century: Will Civilisation Survive the Twenty-First Century?* London: Heinemann.
366. Hamilton, C. (2010) *Requiem for a Species: Why We Resist the Truth about Climate Change*. London: Routledge.
367. Lovelock, J. (2009) *The Vanishing Face of Gaia: A Final Warning*. London: Allen Lane.
368. Dukes, P. (2011) *Minutes to Midnight: History and the Anthropocene Era from 1763*. London: Anthem Press.
369. Jha, A. (2012) *The Doomsday Handbook*. London: Quercus.
370. Williams, C. (2009) 'Sometimes information poses a global threat', *Korea Herald*, 3 November: 4. (Based on 'Understanding omnicide', lecture, Trinity College Oxford, 27 February 2001.)
371. Conway, E. and Oreskes, N. (2010) *Merchants of Doubt: How a Handful of Scientists Obscured the Truth on Issues from Tobacco Smoke to Global Warming*. London: Bloomsbury.
372. Lomborg, B. (2001) *The Skeptical Environmentalist: Measuring the Real State of the World*. Cambridge: Cambridge University Press.
373. Lynus, M. (2011) *The God Species: Saving the Planet in the Age of Humans*. Margate: National Geographic.
374. Fox, T. (2009) *Climate Change: Have We Lost the Battle?* London: Institution of Mechanical Engineers.
375. Hamilton, C. (2013) *Earth Masters: Playing God with the Climate*. London: Allen & Unwin.
376. Gray, J. (2004) *Heresies: Against Progress and Other Illusions*. London: Granta, pp. 20, 22.
377. Kuhn, T.S. (1962) *The Structure of Scientific Revolutions*. Chicago: University of Chicago Press.
378. Revkin, A.C. (2008) 'Ecuador constitution grants rights to nature', *New York Times*, 29 September (Opinion).
379. Higgins, P. (2010) *Eradicating Ecocide: Laws and Governance to Prevent the Destruction of our Planet*. London: Shepheard-Walwyn.
380. Turner, D. (1991) *Escape from God: The Use of Religion and Philosophy to Evade Responsibility*. Carol Stream, IL: Hope Publishing, p. 120.

Chapter 3 Searching and reviewing world literature

1. Source: al-Bīrūnī, Abū al-Rayḥān (1910) (E. Sachau, ed.) *Al-Beruni's India: An Account of the Religion, Philosophy, Literature, Geography, Chronology, Astronomy, Customs, Laws and Astrology of India*. London: Kegan Paul, Trench, Trubner, Vol. 1, p. 18.
2. Rocco, T.S. and Plakhotnik, M.S. (2009) 'Literature reviews: conceptual and theoretical frameworks', *Human Resource Development Review*, 8 (1): 120–130.
3. Fouchard, G. and Young, R. (2001) *A Simple Guide to Searching the Internet*. Upper Saddle River, NJ: Prentice-Hall.
4. UN Web TV – http://webtv.un.org
5. Access to university libraries – http://dir.yahoo.com/reference/libraries/academic_libraries/. Surrey University: Doing online searches – www.surrey.ac.uk/library/subject/onlinelitsearch/
6. Rocco, T.S. and Plakhotnik, M.S. (2009) 'Literature reviews: conceptual and theoretical frameworks', *Human Resource Development Review*, 8 (1): 120–130.
7. Booth, C. (2010) *Did Bach Really Mean That? Deceptive Notation in Baroque Keyboard Music*. Wells: Soundboard.
8. Hart, C. (1998) *Doing a Literature Review: Releasing the Social Science Research Imagination*. London: Sage.
9. Schirmer, J. (2011) 'Elite perpetrators', unpublished paper presented at the *International State Crime Initiative (ISCI) Research Methods Workshop: 'The State of State Crime Research'*, ISCI, King's College, London. (Based on *The Guatemalan Military Project: A Violence called Democracy*. Philadelphia: University of Pennsylvania Press, 1999.)
10. Arens, W. (1979) *The Man-Eating Myth: Anthropology and Anthropophagy*. Oxford: Oxford University Press.
11. Heng, G. (1998) 'Cannibalism, The First Crusade and the Genesis of Medieval Romance', *Differences*, 10(1): 98–174. Arens, W. (1979) *The Man-Eating Myth: Anthropology and Anthropophagy*. Oxford: Oxford University Press. Fisher, M. (2013) 'The cannibals of North Korea', *The Washington Post*.
12. Miller, V. (2010) 'How much legislation comes from Europe?', Reserach Paper, 10/62. London House of Commons Library – file:///C:/Users/Admin/AppData/Local/Temp/RP10-62.pdf
13. Howden, D. (2010) 'I'll close down Twitter, says ridiculed ANC leader', *The Independent*, 5 November: 35.
14. Howard, M. (2005) *We Know What You Want: How They Change Your Mind*. New York: The Disinformation Company.
15. Fake news – www.prwatch.org/fakenews3/summary
16. Smith, H. (2004) 'Improving intelligence on North Korea', *Jane's Intelligence Review*, April: 48–51.
17. Calacanis, J. – www.Mahalo.com

Chapter 4 Research design and logistics

1. Ahrens, T. (2004) 'Refining research questions in the course of negotiating access for fieldwork', in C. Humphrey (ed.), *The Real Life Guide to Accounting Research*. Oxford: Elsevier, pp. 295–307.

2. Fumoto, E. (2014) Polaris project management, Geneva – www.pm-polaris.ch
3. Blaikie, N. (2009) *Designing Social Research*. London: Sage. de Vaus, D. (2001) *Research Design in Social Research*. London: Sage. Maxwell, J.A. (2005) *Qualitative Research Design: An Interactive Approach*. London: Sage. Gorard, S. (2013) *Research Design: Creating Robust Approaches for the Social Sciences*. London: Sage.
4. Cresswell, J.W. (2009) *Research Design: Qualitative, Quantitative, and Mixed Methods Approaches*. London: Sage.
5. Types of research designs – www.experiment-resources.com/research-designs.html
6. Halai, A. and William, D. (eds) (2012) *Research Methodologies in the 'South'*. Karachi: Oxford University Press Pakistan.
7. Shively, W.P. (1980) *The Craft of Political Research*. Upper Saddle River, NJ: Prentice-Hall, p. 21.
8. Ragin, C.C. (1987) *The Comparative Method: Moving Beyond Qualitative and Quantitative Strategies*. Berkeley: University of California Press.
9. Ragin, C.C. (1992) *Comparative Method: Moving Beyond Qualitative and Quantitative Strategies*. Berkeley: University of California Press. Rihoux, B. and Grimm, H. (2006) *Innovative Comparative Methods for Policy Analysis: Beyond the Quantitative–Qualitative Divide*. London: Springer.
10. Cresswell, J.W. (2009) *Research Design: Qualitative, Quantitative, and Mixed Methods Approaches*. London: Sage.
11. Charlier, P. (2010) 'Multidisciplinary medical identification of a French king's head (Henry IV)', *British Medical Journal*, 341:c6805 14 December.
12. Williams, C. (2012) *Researching Power, Elites and Leadership*. London: Sage, pp. 144, 204–207.
13. Nielsen, J. (1993) 'Iterative user interface design', *IEEE Computer*, 26 (11): 32–41.
14. *Google Books Ngram Viewer* – http://books.google.com/ngrams
15. Robertson, G. (2013) *Stephen Ward Was Innocent, OK: The Case for Overturning his Conviction*. London: Biteback. Davenport-Hines, R. (2013) *An English Affair: Sex, Class and Power in the Age of Profumo*. London: Harper Press.
16. Crotty, M.J. (1998) *Foundations of Social Research: Meaning and Perspective in the Research Process*. London: Sage.
17. Collier, D. and Mahoney, J. (1996) 'Insights and pitfalls: selection bias in qualitative research', *World Politics*, 49: 1.
18. Thomas, R.M. (1990) *International Comparative Education: Practices Issues and Prospects*. Oxford: Pergamon.
19. Yeager, P.C. and Kram, K.E. (1995) 'Fielding hot topics in cool settings', in R. Hertz and J.B. Imber (eds), *Studying Elites Using Qualitative Methods*. London: Sage, p. 42.
20. *Wordle* – www.wordle.net
21. Crotty, M.J. (1998) *Foundations of Social Research: Meaning and Perspective in the Research Process*. London: Sage.
22. Holmes, B. (1985) 'The problem (solving) approach', in A. Watson and R. Wilson (eds), *Contemporary Issues in Comparative Education*. London: Croom Helm.
23. Parkin, S. (2010) *The Positive Deviant: Sustainability Leadership in a Perverse World*. London: Earthscan.
24. Club of Rome (1991) *The First Global Revolution*. London: Pantheon.
25. Holmes, B. (1985) 'The problem (solving) approach', in A. Watson and R. Wilson (eds), *Contemporary Issues in Comparative Education*. London: Croom Helm.
26. Prins, G. et al. (2010) *The Hartwell Paper: A New Direction for Climate Policy After the Crash of 2009*. London: LSE/McKinder Programme, pp. 16–17.

27. Bedell-Avers, K.E. et al. (2008) 'Conditions of problem-solving and the performance of charismatic, ideological, and pragmatic leaders: a comparative experimental study', *Leadership Quarterly*, 19: 89–106.
28. Onwuegbuzie, A.J. (2006) 'Linking research questions to mixed methods data analysis procedures', *The Qualitative Report*, 11 (3): 474–498.
29. Bostrom, N. & R. Roache (2008) 'Ethical Issues in Human Enhancement', in Ryberg, J. et al. (ed.) *New Waves in Applied Ethics*. London: Palgrave Macmillan, pp.120–152.
30. Lee-Treweek, G. and Linkogle, S. (eds) (2000) *Danger in the Field: Risk and Ethics in Social Research*. New York: Routledge.

Chapter 5 Research ethics and integrity

1. Hammersley, M. and Traianou, A. (2011) *Ethics in Qualitative Research*. London: Sage.
2. Denscombe, M. (2002) *Ground Rules for Social Research*. Milton Keynes: Open University Press.
3. Israel, M. and Hay, I. (2006) *Research Ethics for Social Scientists*. London: Sage. Iphofen, R. (2011) *Ethical Decision Making in Social Research*. London: Palgrave Macmillan.
4. Halai, A. and William, D. (2012) *Research Methodologies in the 'South'*. Karachi: Oxford University Press Pakistan. Barrett, B. and Cason, J.W. (2010) *Overseas Research Practice: A Practical Guide*. London: Routledge.
5. International research. Yale University –www.yale.edu/hrpp/resources/docs/450GD1Internationalresearch_000.pdf
6. Ferreira, W.F. (2008) 'Conducting research and sponsored programs overseas', *Medical Research Law and Policy Report*, 7 (14): 441–449.
7. Ward, S.J.A. (2010) *Global Journalism Ethics*. Quebec: McGill-Queen's University Press.
8. Barendt, E. (2010) *Academic Freedom and the Law: A Comparative Study*. Oxford: Hart Publishing.
9. Dalton, M. (1959) *Men who Manage*. New York: John Wiley & Sons.
10. Milmo, C. (2011) 'Lloyd's insurer sues Saudi Arabia for funding 9/11 attacks', *The Independent*, 19 September: 25.
11. Dehn, G. and Calland, R. (2010) *Whistle Blowing Around the World: Law Culture and Practice*. London: ODAC/PCAW .
12. Alston, P. (1994) *The Best Interests of the Child: Reconciling Culture and Human Rights*. London: Clarendon Press.
13. Emanuel, E. and Emanuel, L. (1992) 'Proxy decision making for incompetent patients: an ethical and empirical analysis', *Journal of the American Medical Association*, 267 (15): 2067–2071.
14. Dawson, J. and Peart, N.S. (2003) *The Law of Research: A Guide*. Dunedin: University of Otago Press.
15. Williams, C. (1995) *Invisible Victims: Crime and Abuse Against People with Learning Disabilities*. London: Jessica Kingsley, pp. 60–64.
16. Pratt, B. and Loizos, P. (1992) *Choosing Research Methods*. Oxford: Oxfam, p. 13.
17. Schlebusch, C. (2010) 'Issues raised by use of ethnic-group names in genome study', *Nature*, 464 (7288): 487.
18. Washington, H.A. (2007) *Medical Apartheid: The Dark History of Medical Experimentation on Black Americans from Colonial Times to the Present*. New York: Doubleday.

19. Williams, C. (1997) *Terminus Brain: The Environmental Threats to Human Intelligence.* London: Cassell, p. 208.
20. Corry, S. (2013) 'Savaging primitives: why Jared Diamond's "The World Until Yesterday" is completely wrong', *The Daily Beast,* 30 January.
21. The Society for Ethnomusicology (1998) Ethics statement – www.ethnomusicology.org/?EthicsStatement
22. Baxter, C. et al. (1990) *Double Discrimination: Issues and Services for People with Learning Difficulties from Black and Ethnic Minority Communities.* London: King's Fund.
23. Alderson, P. and Morrow, V. (2011) *The Ethics of Research with Children and Young People: A Practical Handbook.* London: Sage.
24. Bendor, A. et al. (1993) 'Insanity and war: the Gulf War and a psychiatric institution', *American Journal of Psychotherapy,* 47 (3): 424–442.
25. Williams, C. (2012) *Researching Power, Elites, and Leadership.* London: Sage, pp. 128–135.
26. Walmsley, J. (2008) *Inclusive Research with People with Learning Disabilities: Past, Present and Futures.* London: Jessica Kingsley. Williams, C. (1995) *Invisible Victims: Crime and Abuse Against People with Learning Disabilities.* London: Jessica Kingsley.
27. Williams, C. (1992) '"Is it for them or us?" – the inclusion of people with learning difficulties at conferences', *Community Care,* 2 July: 15.
28. Brock, K. and McGee, R. (2002) *Knowing Poverty: Critical Reflections on Participatory Research and Policy.* London: Routledge.
29. Elgesem, D. (2001) 'What is special about the ethical issues in online research?', *Internet Research Ethics* – www.nyu.edu/projects/nissenbaum/ethics_elgesem.html
30. Mann, C. and Stewart, F. (2000) *Online Communication and Qualitative Research: A Handbook for Researching Online.* London: Sage. (Ch. 3: 'An ethical framework'.)
31. Frankel, M.S. and Siang, S. (1999) *Ethical and Legal Aspects of Human Subjects Research on the Internet.* Washington, DC: Scientific Freedom, American Association for the Advancement of Science – www.aaas.org/spp/sfrl/projects/intres/report.pdf
32. Whitehouse, G. (2010) 'Expanding ethics codes to reflect change in the digital media age', *Journal of Mass Media Ethics,* 25 (4): 310–327.
33. Bruckman, A. (2001) 'Studying the amateur artist: a perspective on disguising data collected in human subjects research on the internet', *Internet Research Ethics* – www.nyu.edu/projects/nissenbaum/ethics_bruckman.html
34. Williams, C. (2013) 'Crowdsourcing research: a methodology for investigating state crime', *State Crime,* 2 (1): 30–51.
35. Asimov. I (1950) *I Robot.* New York: Doubleplay & Company.
36. Engineering and Physical Sciences Research Council (2011) 'Ethical principles for robot design'.
37. Swan, N. et al. (2011) *Ethics Protocols and Research Ethics Committees.* Sonning Common: Academic Publishing International.
38. Hammersley, M. and Atkinson, P. (1995) *Ethnography: Principles in Practice.* London: Routledge, pp. 263–287.
39. Eckstein, S. (ed.) (2003) *Manual for Research Ethics Committees: Centre of Medical Law and Ethics, King's College London.* Cambridge: Cambridge University Press.
40. Harvard Humanitarian Initiative (2012) 'Monitoring humanitarian crises in a digital age' – www.hpcrresearch.org/events/live-web-seminar-49-monitoring-humanitarian-crises-digital-age-crisis-mapping-crowdsourcing-4
41. Williams, C. (2011) 'Learning to redress preemptive deceit: the "Iraq Dossier" ', *Sage OPEN,* DOI: 10.1177/2158244011427060
42. Gazzaniga, M.S. (2005) *The Ethical Brain.* New York: Harper Perennial.Pfaff, D.W. (2007) *The Neuroscience of Fair Play: Why We (Usually) Follow the Golden Rule.* Chicago: University og Chicago Press.

Chapter 6 Choosing research frameworks

1. Beissel-Durrant, G. (2004) 'A typology of research methods within the social sciences', unpublished working paper, ESRC National Centre for Research Methods – http://eprints.ncrm.ac.uk/115/
2. Denscombe, M. (1998) *The Good Research Guide*. Buckingham: The Open University Press.
3. Cresswell, J.W. (2009) *Research Design: Qualitative, Quantitative, and Mixed Methods Approaches*. London: Sage.
4. Bryman, A. (2008) *Social Research Methods*. Oxford: Oxford University Press, p. 35.
5. Salkind, N. (ed.) (2007) *Encyclopedia of Measurement and Statistics*. Thousand Oaks, CA: Sage.
6. Conti, J.A. and O'Neil, M. (2007) 'Studying power: qualitative methods and the global elite', *Qualitative Research*, 7 (1): 70.
7. Yanow, D. and Schwartz-Shea, P. (2006) *Interpretation and Method: Empirical Research Methods and the Interpretive Turn*. New York: M.E. Sharpe.
8. Cresswell, J.W. (2009) *Research Design: Qualitative, Quantitative, and Mixed Methods Approaches*. London: Sage, p. 13.
9. Denscombe, M. (1998) *The Good Research Guide*. Buckingham: The Open University Press.
10. Warren, C.A.B. and Karner, T.X. (2009) *Discovering Qualitative Methods: Field Research, Interviews, and Analysis*. New York: Oxford University Press.
11. Trauth, E.M. (2001) *Interpretive Methods: Qualitative Research in International Settings: Issues and Trends*. Hershey, PA: Idea Group Publishing.
12. Lynch, C. (2013) *Interpreting International Politics*. London: Routledge.
13. Jackson, P.T. (2010) *The Conduct of Inquiry in International Relations*. London: Routledge.
14. Environmental Protection Agency (2000) *Developing Country Case-Studies: Integrated Strategies for Air Pollution and Greenhouse Gas Mitigation*. Oak Ridge, TN: U.S. Department of Energy.
15. Yin, R.K. (2002) *Case Study Research: Design and Methods*. Thousand Oaks, CA: Sage.
16. Sooryamoorthy, R. and Gangrade, K.D. (2001) *NGOs in India: A Cross-Sectional Study*. Westport, CT: Greenwood Press.
17. Epstein, M. (1969) *Transcultural Experiments: Russian and American Models of Creative Communication*. New York: St. Martin's Press. (Ch. 1: 'From culturology to transculture'.)
18. Hammersley, M. and Alkinson, P. (2007) *Ethnography: Principles in Practice*. London: Routledge.
19. DeWalt, K.M. and DeWalt, B.R. (2002) *Participant Observation: A Guide for Fieldworkers*. Lanham, MD: AltaMira Press.
20. Thomas, J. (1993) *Doing Critical Ethnography*. London: Sage.
21. Davies, C.A. (2007) *Reflexive Ethnography: A Guide to Researching Selves and Others*. London: Routledge.
22. Mead, M. and Metraux, R. (eds) (1953) *The Study of Culture at a Distance*. Chicago: University of Chicago Press.
23. Burns, K.R. (2006) *The Forensic Anthropology Training Manual*. London: Pearson Education.
24. Myers, H. (ed.) (1992) *Ethnomusicology: An Introduction*. New York: W.W. Norton.
25. Comprehensive table of musical instrument classifications – www.music.vt.edu/music-dictionary/appendix/instruments/instrumentmain.html
26. Kodály, Z. (1971) *Folk Music of Hungary*. New York: Praeger.
27. Bartók, B. (1976) 'The influence of peasant music on modern music (1931)', in B. Suchoff (ed.), *Béla Bartók Essays*. London: Faber & Faber, pp. 340–344.

28. Merriam, A.P. (1975) 'Ethnomusicology today', *Current Musicology*, 20: 50–66.
29. Wiseman, R.L. (ed.) (1995) *Intercultural Communication Theory*. Thousand Oaks, CA: Sage.
30. Beekes, R.S.P. (1995) *Comparative Indo-European Linguistics*. Amsterdam: John Benjamins.
31. Khairullina-Valieva, A.G. (2011) *Linguistics and Culture of Ancient Migrants to Europe in a Broad Historical Context*. Sofia: National Library of St Cyril and Methodius.
32. Harper, E.B. (1964) 'Ritual pollution as an integrator of caste and religion', *Journal of Asian Studies*, 23: 151–197, DOI: http://dx.doi.org/10.2307/2050627
33. Pugh, C. and Day, M. (1992) *Toxic Torts*. London: UK Environmental Law Association.
34. Dellapenna, J. (2003) *Suing Foreign Governments and their Corporations*. Leiden: Martinus Nijhoff. Anderson, D. (2005) *Histories of the Hanged, Britain's Dirty War in Kenya and the End of Empire*. London: Weidenfeld & Nicolson. Elkins, C. (2005) *Imperial Reckoning: The Untold Story of Britain's Gulag in Kenya*. London: Henry Holt/Jonathan Cape.
35. Skinnera, M. et al. (2003) 'Guidelines for international forensic bio-archaeology monitors of mass grave exhumations', *Forensic Science International*, 134: 81–92.
36. Núñez, A.C. (2012) *Admissibility of Remote Sensing Evidence before International and Regional Tribunals*. Innovations in Human Rights Monitoring, Working Paper. New York: Amnesty International USA.
37. Beers, D.A. (2011) *Practical Methods for Legal Investigations: Concepts and Protocols in Civil and Criminal Cases*. New York: CRC Press.
38. Nissan, E. (2010) *Computer Applications for Handling Legal Evidence, Police Investigation and Case Argumentation*. New York: Springer.
39. Daniel, L. (2011) *Digital Forensics for Legal Professionals: Understanding Digital Evidence from the Warrant to the Courtroom*. New York: Syngress.
40. MSHP (2003) *Forensic Evidence Handbook*. (SHP-145 B 8/2003). Missouri State Highway Patrol – www.crime-scene-investigator.net/forensic_evidence_manual_MO.pdf
41. BBC (2009) 'Child drawings of Darfur', *BBC News Online*, 4 March. Draw and tell methodology – www.statecrime.org/testimonyproject/drawandtell#references
42. Ward, J. and Peppard, J. (2002) 'Situation analysis', *Strategic Planning for Information Technology*. London: Wiley.
43. Pahl, N. and Richter, A. (2009) *SWOT Analysis – Idea, Methodology and a Practical Approach*. Munich: GRIN Verlag oHG.
44. Rossi, P.H. et al. (2004) *Evaluation: A Systematic Approach*. Thousand Oaks, CA: Sage.
45. White, H. (2006) *Impact Evaluation: The Experience of the Independent Evaluation Group at the World Bank*. Washington, DC: World Bank.
46. Chambers, R. (1983) *Rural Development: Putting the Last First*. London: Longmans. McCracken, J.A. et al. (1988) *An Introduction to Rapid Rural Appraisal for Agricultural Development*. London: International Institute for Environment and Development.
47. Chambers, R. (1992) *Rural Appraisal: Rapid, Relaxed, and Participatory*. Discussion Paper 311. Brighton: Institute of Development Studies. Theis, J. and Grady, H. (1991) *Participatory Rapid Appraisal for Community Development. A Training Manual Based on Experiences in the Middle East and North Africa*. London: International Institute for Environment and Development.
48. Rifkin, S.B. and Pridmore, P. (2001) *Partners in Planning: Information, Participation and Empowerment*. London: Longman.
49. Coicaud, J.-M. and Warner, D. (2013) *Ethics and International Affairs: Extent and Limits*. Tokyo: United Nations University Press.
50. Sidgwick, H. (1907/1981) *The Methods of Ethics*. Indianapolis: Hackett.
51. Williams, C. (2001) *Leaders of Integrity: Ethics and a Code for Global Leadership*. Amman: United Nations University Leadership Academy.
52. Hutchings, K. (2009) *Global Ethics*. Cambridge: Polity.

53. Nagel, T. (2005) 'The problem of global justice', *Philosophy and Public Affairs*, 33 (2): 113–147.
54. Williams, C. (2010) 'Global justice and education: from nation to neuron', *Educational Review*, 62 (3): 343–356
55. Davidann, J.T. (2007) *Cultural Diplomacy in U.S.–Japanese Relations, 1919–1941*. London: Palgrave Macmillan.
56. UNESCO. Culture and development – www.unesco.org/new/en/culture/themes/culture-and-development/
57. Tomlinson, J. (2008) *Cultural Imperialism: A Critical Introduction*. New York: ACLS Humanities.
58. CPANDA. Cultural Policy and the Arts National Data Archive – www.cpanda.org/stage/about
59. al-Bīrūnī, Abū al-Rayḥān (1910) (E. Sachau, ed.) *Al-Beruni's India: An Account of the Religion, Philosophy, Literature, Geography, Chronology, Astronomy, Customs, Laws and Astrology of India*. London: Kegan Paul, Trench, Trubner.
60. Kandel, I.L. (1933) *Comparative Education*. Houghton Mifflin.
61. Tessler, M. and Nachtwey, J. (1999) *Area Studies and Social Science: Strategies for Understanding Middle East Politics*. Bloomington: Indiana University Press.
62. Okabe, A. (ed.) (2011) *Islamic Area Studies with Geographical Information Systems*. London: Routledge.
63. Szanton, D.L. (2004) 'The origin, nature and challenges of area studies in the United States', in D.L. Szanton (ed.), *The Politics of Knowledge: Area Studies and the Disciplines*. Berkeley: University of California Press.
64. Schäfer, W. (2010) 'Reconfiguring area studies for the global age', *Globality Studies Journal*, 22 – https://gsj.stonybrook.edu/article/reconfiguring-area-studies-for-the-global-age
65. Shrinking Cities International Research Network (SCIRN) – www.ru.uni-kl.de/en/ips/research/networks-and-cooperations/shrinking-cities-international-research-network-scirn
66. Monmonier, M. (1991) *How to Lie with Maps*. Chicago: University of Chicago Press.
67. Wiechmann, T. (2008) 'Errors expected – aligning urban strategy with demographic uncertainty in shrinking cities', *International Planning Studies*, Special Issue on Demographic Changes and the New Landscapes for Planning, 13 (4): 431–446.
68. Faist, T. et al. (2013) *Transnational Migration*. Cambridge: Polity.
69. Livi Bacci, M. (2012) *A Short History of Migration*. Cambridge: Polity.
70. Adams, J. (1999) *The Social Implications of Hypermobility*. Paris: OECD.
71. Ender, M. (ed.) (2002) *Military Brats and Other Global Nomads*. Portland, OR: Greenwood.
72. Pollock, D.C. and Van Reken, R.E. (2009) *Third Culture Kids: Growing Up Among Worlds*. London: Nicholas Brealey.
73. Hantrais, L. (2008) *International Comparative Research: Theory, Methods and Practice*. London: Palgrave Macmillan.
74. Inkeles, A. and Sasaki, M. (1995) *Comparing Societies and Cultures: Readings in a Cross-Disciplinary Perspective*. London: Pearson.
75. Williams, C. (1990) 'Street children and education: a comparative study of European and third world approaches'. PhD thesis, University of Birmingham – http://etheses.bham.ac.uk/698/
76. Hantrais, L. (2008) *International Comparative Research: Theory, Methods and Practice*. London: Palgrave Macmillan.
77. Landman, T. (2008) *Issues and Methods in Comparative Politics: An Introduction*. London: Routledge. Pennings, P. et al. (2005) *Doing Research in Political Science: An Introduction to Comparative Methods and Statistics*. London: Sage.
78. Clarke, B.S. (1998) *Political Economy: A Comparative Approach*. London: Praeger.

79. Steinberg, P.F. and Vandeveer, S.D. (2012) *Comparative Environmental Politics: Theory, Practice, and Prospects*. Cambridge, MA: MIT Press.
80. Phillips, D. and Schweisfurth, M. (2008) *Comparative and International Education: An Introduction to Theory, Method and Practice*. London: Continuum. Bray, M. (2007) *Comparative Education Research: Approaches and Methods*. Hong Kong: Comparative Education Research Centre, Hong Kong University.
81. Clasen, J. (1998) *Comparative Social Policy, Theories and Methods*. Oxford: Wiley-Blackwell.
82. Reimann, M. and Zimmermann, R. (2008) *The Oxford Handbook of Comparative Law*. Oxford: Oxford University Press.
83. Chodosh, H.E. (2005) *Global Justice Reform: A Comparative Methodology*. New York: NYU Press.
84. Blank, R.A. and Burau, V. (2010) *Comparative Health Policy*. London: Palgrave Macmillan.
85. Hallin, D.C. and Mancini, P. (2004) *Comparing Media Systems: Three Models of Media and Politics*. Cambridge: Cambridge University Press. Livingstone, S. (2003) 'On the challenges of cross-national comparative media research', *European Journal of Communication*, 18 (4): 477–500.
86. Lange, M. (2012) *Comparative-Historical Methods*. London: Sage.
87. Livingstone, S. and Lemish, D. (2001) 'Doing comparative research with children and young people', in S. Livingstone and M. Bovill (eds), *Children and their Changing Media Environment: A European Comparative Study*. London: Lawrence Erlbaum.
88. *BBC News Online*. 'Have your say' – www.bbc.co.uk/news/
89. Diamond, J. and Robinson, J.A. (eds) (2010) *Natural Experiments of History*. Cambridge, MA: Belknap Press of Harvard University Press.
90. Diamond, J. (2005) *Collapse: How Societies Choose to Fail or Survive*. London: Allen Lane.
91. Radin, B. (2000) *Beyond Machiavelli: Policy Analysis Comes of Age*. Washington, DC: Georgetown University Press.
92. Babones, S. and Chase-Dunn, C. (2012) *Handbook of World Systems Analysis*. London: Routledge.
93. Wallerstein, I. (1974) *The Modern World-System: Capitalist Agriculture and the Origins of the European World-Economy in the Sixteenth Century*. New York: Academic Press.
94. Chase-Dunn, C. et al. (2000) 'Trade globalization since 1795: waves of integration in the world-system', *American Sociological Review*, 65 (1): 77–95.
95. Wellman, B. and Berkowitz, S.D. (eds) (1988) *Social Structures: A Network Approach*. Cambridge: Cambridge University Press. Brandes, U. and Erlebah, T. (eds) (2005) *Network Analysis: Methodological Foundations*. Berlin: Springer-Verlag. Freeman, L. (2006) *The Development of Social Network Analysis*. Vancouver: Empirical Press.
96. *Nature* (2013) 'Complex networks in finance', *Nature Physics*, 9 (3): 119–197.
97. Savage, M. (2010) 'The story so far: a blame game with one politician in the frame', *The Independent*, 23 January: 13.
98. Buchana, D. and Bryman, A. (2009) *The Sage Handbook of Organizational Research Methods*. London: Sage.
99. Punnett, B.J. and Shenkar, O. (2004) *Handbook for International Management Research*. London: Wiley. (Part 2: 'Designing effective research'.)
100. Merrill, J. et al. (2006) 'Description of a method to support public health information management: organizational network analysis', *Journal of Biomedical Informatics*, 40 (4): 422–428.
101. Nagel, S.S. (1999) *Policy Analysis Methods*. New York: New Science Publishers. Fischer, F. and Miller, G.J. (2006) *Handbook of Policy Analysis: Theory, Politics and Methods*. London: CRC Press/Taylor & Francis. Fischer, F. et al. (eds) (2006) *Handbook of Public Policy Analysis: Theory, Methods, and Politics*. New York: Marcel Dekker.
102. Starr, H. (2006) *Approaches, Levels and Methods of Analysis in International Politics: Crossing Boundaries*. Basingstoke: Palgrave.

103. Alden, C. (2011) *Foreign Policy Analysis: New Approaches: Understanding the Diplomacy of War, Profit and Justice*. London: Routledge.
104. Dutta, P.K. (1999) *Strategies and Games: Theory and Practice*. Cambridge, MA: MIT Press.
105. Jackson, P. (2013) *Intelligence Studies*. London: Sage.
106. *International Journal of Intelligence and Counterintelligence*.
107. Ross, C. – www.carneross.com/writings
108. MoD (2009) *Security and Stabilisation: The Military Contribution*. Joint Doctrine Publications 3–40: Ch. 9, 'Political and social analysis' – www.mod.uk/DefenceInternet/microsite/dcdc
109. De Smith, M.J. et al. (2006) *Geospatial Analysis: A Comprehensive Guide to Principles, Techniques and Software Tools*. London: Matador.
110. Judd, T. (2011) 'Police and military trial 3D tracking technology', *The Independent*, 12 May: 9.
111. BBC (2010) 'White house welcomes: state dinner to cold shoulder', *BBC News Online* – www.bbc.co.uk/news/world-us-canada-10470615
112. International Association of Protocol Consultants and Officers – www.protocolconsultants.org/; www.ediplomat.com/nd/protocol/diplomatic_protocol.htm; www.dev.diplomacy.edu/edu/protocol.old/protocol_b.htm
113. McCaffree, M.J. et al. (2002) *Protocol: The Complete Handbook of Diplomatic, Official and Social Usage*. Dallas: Durban House Press.
114. Northmore, D. (1996) *Lifting the Lid: A Guide to Investigative Research*. London: Continuum.
115. Douglas, J.D. (1976) *Investigative Social Research*. Beverly Hills, CA: Sage.
116. Morgan, J.B. (1990) *The Police Function and the Investigation of Crime*. London: Avebury.
117. Innes, M. (1985) *Investigating Murder*. London: Police Foundation.
118. Fredrickson, D.D. (2004) *Street Drug Investigation: A Practical Guide for Plainclothes and Uniformed Personnel*. New York: Charles C. Thomas.
119. Viaene, S. et al. (2002) 'A comparison of state-of-the-art classification techniques for expert automobile insurance claim fraud detection', *Journal of Risk and Insurance*, 69 (3): 373–421.
120. Bolton, R.J. and Hand, D.J. (2002) 'Statistical fraud detection: a review', *Statistical Science*, 17 (3): 235–249.
121. Ohr, B.C. (n.d.) *Effective Methods to Combat Transnational Organised Crime in Criminal Justice Processes*. Chief, Organized Crime and Racketeering Section, Criminal Division, United States Department of Justice, United States of America – www.unafei.or.jp/english/pdf/PDF_rms/no58/58-05.pdf
122. Buckwalter, A. (1983) *Surveillance and Undercover Investigation*. London: Butterworth-Heinemann. Volkman, E. (2007) *The History of Espionage*. London: Carlton.
123. Dalton, M. (1959) *Men Who Manage*. New York: Wiley. Ho, K. (2010) *Liquidated: An Ethnography of Wall Street*. Durham, NC: Duke University Press.
124. De Burgh, H. (2008) *Investigative Journalism*. London: Routledge.
125. Tweedale, G. (2003) 'Researching corporate crime: a business historian's perspective', in S. Tombs and D. Whyte (eds), *Unmasking the Crimes of the Powerful: Scrutinizing States and Corporations*. New York: Peter Lang.
126. Hunter, M.L. (2011) *Story-Based Inquiry: A Manual for Investigative Journalists*. Paris: UNESCO, p. 31.
127. Mitchell, J. (2013) 'Agent Orange evidence mounts, U.S. still denies', *Japan Times*, 4 June: 12–13. Young, A.L. (2013) *Investigations into Allegations of Herbicide Orange on Okinawa, Japan*. For the Office of the Deputy Under Secretary of Defense (I&E), US Army Public Health Command.
128. Williams, C. (2013) 'Crowdsourcing research: a methodology for investigating state crime', *State Crime*, 2 (1): 30–51.
129. Schiller, B. (2012) 'Can citizen scientists be our first line of defense in environmental disasters?', Fast Company – www.fastcoexist.com/1681099/can-citizen-scientists-be-our-first-line-of-defense-in-environmental-disasters

130. Williams, C. (2013) 'Crowdsourcing research: a methodology for investigating state crime', *State Crime*, 2 (1): 30–51.
131. *Ushahidi* crowdsourcing tools – www.ushahidi.com/
132. Meier, P. (2012) 'The role of Ushahidi as a liberation technology in Egypt and Beyond', in L. Diamond and M. Plattner (eds), *Liberation Technology: Social Media and the Struggle for Democracy*. Baltimore, MD: Johns Hopkins University Press.
133. Meier, P. (2011) 'New information technologies and their impact on the humanitarian sector', *International Review of the Red Cross*, 93 (884).
134. Pisano, F. (2005) 'Using satellite imagery to improve emergency relief', *Humanitarian Exchange Magazine*, 32.
135. Harvard Humanitarian Initiative (2012) 'Monitoring humanitarian crises in a digital age' – www.hpcrresearch.org/events/live-web-seminar-49-monitoring-humanitarian-crises-digital-age-crisis-mapping-crowdsourcing-4
136. Ford, N. (2011) *The Essential Guide to Using the Web for Research*. London: Sage.
137. Donelan, B. (2004) 'Extremist Groups of the Midwest: A Content Analysis of Internet Websites' *Great Plains Sociologist,* 16(1): 1–27.
138. Lobe, B. et al. (2008) *Best Practice Research Guide: How to Research Children and Online Technologies in Comparative Perspective*. The EC Safer Internet Plus Programme. London: LSE.
139. Openshaw, S. et al. (1987) 'A Mark I Geographical Analysis Machine for the automated analysis of point data sets', *International Journal of Geographical Information Systems*, 1(4): 335–358.
140. Villasenor, J. (2011) *Recording Everything: Digital Storage as an Enabler of Authoritarian Governments*. Washington, DC: Center for Innovation Technology at Brookings.
141. Reshef, D.N. et al. (2011) 'Detecting novel associations in large data sets', *Science*, 334 (6062): 1518–1524.
142. Shah, S. et al. (2012) 'Good data won't guarantee good decisions', *Harvard Business Review*, April.
143. WEF (2012) *Big Data, Big Impact: New Possibilities for International Development*. Geneva: World Economic Forum, p. 4.

Chapter 7 Data management

1. Rose, S. (2010) *For All the Tea in China: How England Stole the World's Favourite Drink and Changed History*. London: Penguin.
2. BBC (2014) 'Robot writes LA Times earthquake breaking news article', *BBC News Online*, 18 March.
3. Proust, M. (2003) *The Prisoner and The Fugitive*. London: Penguin.
4. Campbell, D. (n.d.) 'How embassy eavesdropping works' – www.duncancampbell.org/embassy-bugging
5. 'How to detect hidden cameras and microphones' – www.wikihow.com/Detect-Hidden-Cameras-and-Microphones
6. Van den Eynden, V. et al. (2011) *Managing and Sharing Data*. Colchester: UK Data Archive.
7. MIT data security requirements – http//libraries.mit.edu/guides/subjects/data-management/plans.html
8. Hildebrandt, M. and Gutwirth, S. (2008) *Profiling the European Citizen: Cross Disciplinary Perspectives*. Dordrecht: Springer.

9. Steinbock, D. (2005) 'Data matching, data mining, and due process', *Georgia Law Review*, 40 (1):1–84.
10. Saldana, J. (2009) *The Coding Manual for Qualitative Researchers*. London: Sage.
11. Robson, C. (1993) *Real World Research*. Oxford: Blackwell, (Observation).
12. Bryant, A. and Charmaz, K. (eds) (2010) *The Sage Handbook of Grounded Theory*. London: Sage.
13. Blasius, J. and Thiessen, V. (2011) *A Guide to Using and Understanding Secondary Data*. London: Sage.
14. George, A.L. and Bennett, A. (2005) *Case Studies and Theory Development in the Social Sciences*. Cambridge, MA: MIT Press, p. 32.
15. Dexter, L.A. (1970) *Elite and Specialized Interviewing*. Evanston, IL: Northwestern University Press, p. 7.
16. Davies, P.H.J. (2001) 'Spies as informants: triangulation and the interpretation of elite interview data in the study of the intelligence and security services', *Politics*, 21 (1): 73–80.
17. Slawner, K. (2006) 'Interpreting victim testimony: survivor discourse and the narration of history' – www.yendor.com/vanished/karenhead.html
18. Godin, M. et al. (2006) *The Medium of Testimony: Testimony as Re-presentation*. Oxford: Refugee Studies Centre.
19. Denzin, N. (2006) *Sociological Methods: A Sourcebook*. Piscataway, NJ: Aldine Transaction.
20. Campbell, D.T. and Fiske, D.W. (1959) 'Convergent and discriminant validation by the multitrait-multimethod matrix', *Psychological Bulletin*, 56 (2): 465–476.
21. Berry, J.M. (2002) 'Validity and reliability issues in elite interviewing', *Political Science and Politics*, 35 (4):679–82.
22. Cole, R.L. (1980) *Introduction to Political Inquiry*. New York: Macmillan, p. 83.
23. Stigler, S. (2008) 'Fisher and the 5% level', *Chance*, 21 (4): 12.
24. Murray, A. (2011) 'BBC processes for verifying social media content' – www.bbc.co.uk/blogs/blogcollegeofjournalism/posts/bbcsms_bbc_procedures_for_veri
25. Prohibited goods – www.royalmail.com/prohibitedgoods
26. WHO. Transporting hazardous materials and infectious substances – www.who.int/ihr/infectious_substances/en/
27. IATA. Dangerous goods classifications/manual – www2.umdnj.edu/eohssweb/publications/dangerousgoods.htm; www.iata.org/whatwedo/dangerous_goods
28. Avoiding IP-address tracking – www.techsono.com/usenet/faq/avoid-ip-address-tracking
29. Burrell, I. (2013) 'Point and clicks: how Dolphin-cam will help BBC capture secrets of life in the pod', *The Independent*, 24 September: 13.
30. Nicholson, H. (2012) 'A facsimile fit for a Pharaoh: replica of Tutankhamun's tomb unveiled in Egypt', *Mail Online* – www.dailymail.co.uk/travel/article-2232766/Replica-Tutankhamuns-tomb-unveiled-Egypt.html
31. Bowdler, N. (2013) 'Live robot art created in three cities', *BBC News Online*, 27 September – www.bbc.co.uk/news/technology-24299869
32. Campbell, D. (n.d.) 'How embassy eavesdropping works' – www.duncancampbell.org/embassy-bugging

Chapter 8 Researching people

1. Engramelle, M.D.J. (1775) *La Tonotechnie: ou l'art de noter sur les cylindres et tout ce qui est susceptible de notage dans les instruments de concerts méchaniques*. New York: Minkoff Reprints.

2. Booth, C. (2010) *Did Bach Really Mean That? Deceptive Notation in Baroque Keyboard Music*. Wells: Soundboard.
3. Davidov, E. et al. (2011) *Cross-Cultural Analysis: Methods and Applications*. London: Sage.
4. Lange, M. (2012) *Comparative-Historical Methods*. London: Sage.
5. Hammersley, M. and Atkinson, P. (2007) *Ethnography: Principles in Practice*. London: Routledge.
6. Epstein, M. (1969) *Transcultural Experiments: Russian and American Models of Creative Communication*. New York: St. Martin's Press. (Ch. 1: 'From culturology to transculture'.)
7. Miller, R.L. (2005) *Biographical Research Methods*. London: Sage. Lee, H. (2009) *Biography: A Very Short Introduction*. Oxford: Oxford University Press.
8. Seldon, A. and Pappworth, J. (1983) *By Word of Mouth: Elite Oral History*. London: Methuen.
9. Gardner, H. (1995) *Leading Minds*. New York: Basic Books.
10. Alaszewski, A. (2006) *Using Diaries for Social Research*. London: Sage, pp. 24–25: 'Researching diaries'.
11. Mumford, M. et al. (2007) 'The sources of leader violence: a comparison of ideological and non-ideological leaders', *The Leadership Quarterly*, 18: 217–235.
12. Shafer, R.J. (1974) *A Guide to Historical Method*. Homewood, IL: The Dorsey Press.
13. Redi, J.A. et al (2011) 'Digital image forensics: a booklet for beginners', *Multimedia Tools and Applications*, 51 (1): 133–162.
14. Weiss, R.S. (1995) *Learning from Strangers: The Art and Method of Qualitative Interview Studies*. New York: The Free Press.
15. Welch, C. (2007) *Interviewing Elites in International Organisations*. Sydney: University of Western Sydney.
16. Peabody, R.L. et al. (1990) 'Interviewing political elites', *Political Science and Politics*, 23: 451–455.
17. Rivera, S.W. et al. (2002) 'Interviewing political elites: lessons from Russia', *Political Science and Politics*, 35 (4): 683–688. Czudnowski, M.M. (1987) 'Interviewing political elites in Taiwan', in G. Moyser and M. Wagstaffe (eds), *Research Methods for Elite Studies*.Winchester, Mass.: Allen and Unwin, pp. 232–263.
18. Suh, D.-s. and Lee, C.-j. (eds) (1976) *Political Leadership in Korea*. Seattle: University of Washington Press.
19. Cross-cultural interview/focus groups – www.qualitative-researcher.com/focus-group/cross-cultural-qualitative-interviewing/
20. Davies, P.H.J. (2001) 'Spies as informants: triangulation and the interpretation of elite interview data in the study of the intelligence and security services', *Politics*, 21 (1): 73–80.
21. Davies, P.H.J. (2000) 'MI6's requirements directorate: integrating intelligence into the machinery of government', *Public Administration*, 78 (1): 29–49. Eftimiades, N. (1994) *Chinese Intelligence Operations*. London: Frank Cass.
22. Denitch, B. (1972) 'Elite interviewing and social structure: an example from Yugoslavia', *Public Opinion Quarterly*, 36: 143–158.
23. Scheyvens, R. et al. (2003) 'Working with marginalised, vulnerable or privileged groups', in R. Scheyvens and D. Storey (eds), *Development Fieldwork*. London: Sage, pp. 168–192.
24. Nind, M. (2008) 'Conducting qualitative research with people with learning, communication and other disabilities: methodological challenges', National Centre for Research Methods (NCRM/012) – http://eprints.ncrm.ac.uk/491/1/MethodsReviewPaperNCRM-012.pdf
25. Leech, B. (2002) 'Interview methods in political science', *Political Science and Politics*, 35 (4): 665–668.
26. Undheim, T.A. (2006) 'Getting connected: how sociologists can access the high tech elite', in S. Nagy et al. (eds), *Emergent Methods in Social Research*. London: Sage, pp. 13–36.

27. Kinkaid, H.V. and Bright, M. (1957) 'The tandem interview: a trial of the two-interviewer team', *Public Opinion Quarterly*, 21 (2): 304–312.
28. *How I Cross Examine a Cop* – www.youtube.com/watch?v=-oQOdV21d6M
29. Memon, A. and Bull, R. (eds) (1999) *Handbook of the Psychology of Interviewing*. Chichester: Wiley. Milne, R. and Bull, R. (1999) *Investigative Interviewing: Psychology and Practice*. London: Wiley. Campos, I. (1999) 'The cognitive interview', *Psychology, Crime and Law*, 5: 1–2.
30. Raskin, D.C. (1989) *Psychological Methods in Criminal Investigation and Evidence*. New York: Springer. (Ch. 6: 'The cognitive interview'.)
31. Stewart, D.W. and Shamdasani, N. (1990) *Focus Groups: Theory and Practice*. London: Sage. Barbour, R. (2007) *Doing Focus Groups*. Thousand Oaks, CA: Sage.
32. Gaiser, T.J. (1997) 'Conducting on-line focus groups: a methodological discussion', *Social Science Computer Review*, 15 (2): 135–144. Schneider, S.J. et al. (2002) 'Characteristics of the discussion in online and face-to-face focus groups', *Social Science Computer Review*, 20 (1): 31–42.
33. Morgan, D.L. and Lobe, B. (2013) 'Online focus groups', and Moyle, K. (2013) 'Using emerging technologies in focus group interviews', in S.N. Hesse-Biber (ed.), *The Handbook of Emergent Technologies in Social Research*. Oxford: Oxford University Press.
34. Hennink, M.M. (2007) *International Focus Group Research: A Handbook for the Health and Social Sciences*. Cambridge: Cambridge University Press.
35. Lunt, P. and Livingstone, S. (1996) 'Rethinking the focus group in media and communications research', *Journal of Communication*, 46 (2): 79–98.
36. Morgan, D. and Krueger, R.A. (1997) *The Focus Group Kit*. London: Sage.
37. National Association of the Deaf (2013) 'Video remote interpreting' – www.nad.org/issues/technology/vri
38. al-Bīrūnī, Abū al-Rayḥān (1910) (E. Sachau, ed.) *Al-Beruni's India: An Account of the Religion, Philosophy, Literature, Geography, Chronology, Astronomy, Customs, Laws and Astrology of India*. London: Kegan Paul, Trench, Trubner.
39. Richards, D. (1996) 'Elite interviewing: approaches and pitfalls', *Politics*, 16 (3): 199–204.
40. Conti, J.A. and O'Neil, M. (2007) 'Studying power: qualitative methods and the global elite', *Qualitative Research*, 7 (1): 63–82.
41. Williams, C. (2012) *Researching Power, Elites and Leadership*. London: Sage, pp. 124–127, 161–170.
42. Gamble, A. (1994) 'Political memories', *Politics*, 14(1): 35–41.
43. Tisdall, K. et al (2009) *Researching with Children and Young People: Research Design, Methods and Analysis*. New York: Sage.
44. Swart, J. (1990) *Malunde: The Street Children of Hillbrow*. Johannesburg: Witwatersrand University Press.
45. Ellis, K. (2008) *Arretez-vous et reflechissez: employant les marionettes educatives*. London TALC.
46. Waldman, M. (2010) *The Sun in the Sky: The Relationship Between Pakistan's ISI and Afghan Insurgents*. Discussion Paper 18. London: LSE/DESTIN, p. 3.
47. Stephens, N. (2007) 'Collecting data from elites and ultra elites: telephone and face-to-face interviews with macroeconomists', *Qualitative Research*, 7 (2): 203–216.
48. Miller, T.W. and Walkowski, J. (2003) 'Virtual ethnography: interactive interviewing online as method', *Canadian Journal of Learning and Technology*, 29(2): 15–27.
49. Acton, Q.A. (2013) *Robotics: Advances in Research and Application*. Atlanta, GA: Scholarly Editions.
50. Kozima, H. et al. (2009) 'Keepom: a playful robot for research, therapy and entertainment', *Robitics*, 1 (3): 3–18.

51. BBC (2013) 'Japanese robot astronaut can talk to crew', *BBC New Online,* 27 June – www.bbc.co.uk/news/world-asia-23076297
52. Wood, L.J. et al. (2013) 'Robot-mediated interviews – how effective is a humanoid robot as a tool for interviewing young children?', *Plos One*, 8 (3): e59448.
53. Gillham, B. (2008) *Observation Techniques: Structured and Unstructured Approaches*. London: Continuum.
54. Atkinson, J.M. (1984) *Our Masters' Voices: The Language and Body Language of Politics*. London: Methuen.
55. Winter, D.G. and Stewart, A.J. (1977) 'Content analysis', in M.G. Hermann (ed.), *A Psychological Examination of Political Leaders*. New York: The Free Press, pp. 27–62.
56. Winter, D.G. and Stewart, A.J. (1977) 'Non-verbal and paralinguistic analysis', in M.G. Hermann (ed.), *A Psychological Examination of Political Leaders*. New York: The Free Press, pp. 62–79.
57. Browne, C.G. and Thomas, S.C. (1958) 'Observation and evaluation methods', *The Study of Leadership*, Danvill, Ill.: The Interstate Printers and Publishers, pp. 87–122.
58. Millen, D. (2000) 'Rapid ethnography: a time deepening strategy for HCI field research', in *Proceedings of the 3rd Conference on Designing Interactive Systems: Processes, Practices, Methods, and Techniques*. New York: ACM, pp. 280–286 – http://dl.acm.org/citation.cfm?id=347763
59. Emerson, R.M. et al. (1995) *Writing Ethnographic Fieldnotes*. Chicago: University of Chicago Press.
60. Jorgensen, D.L. (1989) *Participant Observation: A Methodology for Human Studies*. London: Sage.
61. Geertz, C. (1973) *The Interpretation of Cultures*. New York: Basic Books.
62. Lee, R.M. (2000) *Unobtrusive Methods in Social Research*. Buckingham: Open University Press.
63. Margolis, E. and Pauwels, L. (2011) *The Sage Handbook of Visual Research Methods*. London: Sage.
64. Emotion analytics – www.beyondverbal.com
65. Ford, N. (2011) *The Essential Guide to Using the Web for Research*. London: Sage.
66. Horst, H.A. and Miller, D. (eds) (2012) *Digital Anthropology*. London: Berg Publishers.
67. Hine, C.M. (2000) *Virtual Ethnography*. London: Sage. Garcia, A.C. (2009) 'Ethnographic approaches to the internet and computer-mediated communication', *Journal of Contemporary Ethnography*, 38 (1): 52–84.
68. Miller, D. and Slater, D. (2001) *The Internet: An Ethnographic Approach*. London: Berg Publishers.
69. Kozinets, R.V. (2009) *Netnography: Doing Ethnographic Research Online*. London: Sage.
70. Marcus, G.E. (1998) 'Ethnography in/of the world system: the emergence of multi-sited ethnography', in *Ethnography through Thick and Thin*. Princeton, NJ: Princeton University Press, pp. 79–104.
71. Vis, F. and Thelwall, M. (2014) *Researching Social Media*. London: Sage.
72. *The European Online Grooming Project* – www.europeanonlinegroomingproject.com
73. Reips, U.D. (2007) 'The methodology of Internet-based experiments', in A. Joinson et al. (eds), *The Oxford Handbook of Internet Psychology*. Oxford: Oxford University Press.
74. Sowe, S.K. et al. (eds) (2012) *Free and Open Source Software and Technology for Sustainable Development*. Tokyo: UNU Press.
75. *Wikileaks* – www.wikileaks.org
76. White, D. (2008) 'Obama's speech on patriotism and love of America' – http://usliberals.about.com/od/electionreform/a/ObamaPatriotism_3.htm. President Obama's speech to the nation, 10 September 2013. Factor, M. (2010) 'American exceptionalism – and an "exceptional" president' – www.forbes.com/2010/08/31/barack-obama-exceptionalism-america-opinions-columnists-mallory-factor.html.

77. Jay, H. (2013) 'South Korean internet war goes on as conservative website grows', *Korea Bang*, 16 January – www.koreabang.com/2013/stories/south-korean-internet-war-goes-on-as-conservative-website-grows.html

Chapter 9 Researching populations

1. Holdsworth, C. et al. (2013) *Population and Society*. London: Sage.
2. Meyer, H.-D. and Benavot, A. (2013) *PISA, Power, and Policy: The Emergence of Global Educational Governance*. Oxford: Symposium.
3. Office for National Statistics. Methods guidance – www.ons.gov.uk/ons/guide-method/index.html
4. Campbell, P.C. (1923) *Chinese Coolie Emigration to Countries within the British Empire*. London: P.S. King.
5. Madge, C. and Jennings, H. (eds) (1937) *May the Twelfth, Mass-Observation Day-Surveys 1937, by over Two Hundred Observers*. London: Faber & Faber.
6. Mass-Observation (1943) *The Pub and the People*. London: Gollancz.
7. Mass-Observation (1943) *War Factory*. London: Gollancz.
8. Harrisson, T. (1976) *Living through the Blitz*. London: Collins.
9. *One Day in History* – www.webarchive.org.uk/wayback/archive/20061212120000/http://www.historymatters.org.uk/output/Page96.html
10. International ranking – http://en.wikipedia.org/wiki/List_of_top_international_rankings_by_country
11. BBC (2010) 'National census in 2011 could be last of its kind', *BBC News Online*, 10 July.
12. Marchetti, C. et al. (1996) 'Human population dynamics revisited with the logistic model: how much can be modeled and predicted?', *Technological Forecasting and Social Change*, 52: 1–30.
13. Morgan, M.S. (2012) *The World in the Model: How Economists Work and Think*. Cambridge: Cambridge University Press.
14. Cohen, J. (1995) *How Many People Can the Earth Support?* New York: W.W. Norton.
15. Trochim, W.M. (2006) 'Likert scaling', Research Methods Knowledge Base – www.socialresearchmethods.net/kb/scallik.php
16. 'What is the Corruption Perceptions Index?' – http://cpi.transparency.org/cpi2012/in_detail/
17. Camerer, M. (2006) 'Measuring public integrity', *Journal of Democracy*, 17 (1): 152–165. Sik, E. (2002) 'The bad, the worse and the worst: guesstimating the level of corruption', in S. Kotkin and A. Sajo (eds), *Political Corruption in Transition: A Skeptic's Handbook*. Budapest: Central European University Press, pp. 91–113.
18. *Crime Survey for England and Wales* – www.crimesurvey.co.uk
19. *Pew Research Center's Global Attitudes Project* – www.pewglobal.org/about
20. McQuarrie, E. (2005) *The Market Research Toolbox: A Concise Guide for Beginners*. London: Sage.
21. Bradley, N. (2010) *Marketing Research: Tools and Techniques*. Oxford: Oxford University Press.
22. Kozinets, R.V. (2009) *Netnography: Doing Ethnographic Research Online*. London: Sage.
23. Siegel, E. (2013) *Predictive Analytics: The Power to Predict Who Will Click, Buy, Lie, or Die*. London: Wiley.
24. Lefebvre, R.C. (2013) *Social Marketing and Social Change: Strategies and Tools for Improving Health, Well-Being and the Environment*. London: Wiley.

25. Walpole, S.C. et al. (2012) 'The weight of nations: an estimation of adult biomass', *BMC Public Health*, 12: 439. (Quotes – Ian Roberts). McGrath, M. (2012) 'Global weight gain more damaging than rising numbers', *BBC News Online*, 20 June. Boss, P. (2013) 'Cow farts have "larger greenhouse gas impact" than previously thought; methane pushes climate change', *International Business Times*, 26 November.
26. Ennew, J. (2000) *Street and Working Children: A Guide to Planning*. London: Save the Children.
27. Shipman, M.D. (1972) *The Limitations of Social Research*. London: Longman, p. 50.
28. Dillman, D.A. et al. (2009) *Internet, Mail, and Mixed-Mode Surveys: The Tailored Design Method*. London: Wiley.
29. Saporitti, A. (1994) 'A methodology for making children count', in J. Qvortrup et al. (eds), *Childhood Matters: Social Theory, Practice and Politics*. Aldershot: Avebury.
30. Sharot, T. (2012) *The Optimism Bias*. London: Constable & Robinson, p. 14.
31. Blair, J. et al. (2014) *Designing Surveys*. London: Sage. Fowler, F.J. (2008) *Survey Research Methods*. Thousand Oaks, CA: Sage.
32. Argyrous, G. (2011) *Statistics for Research*. London: Sage.
33. Argyrous, G. (2011) pp. 80–100.
34. Argyrous, G. (2011) pp. 17, 55–99.
35. Argyrous, G. (2011) pp. 101–114.
36. Stigler, S. (2008) 'Fisher and the 5% level', *Chance*, 21 (4): 12.
37. Barakso, M. et al. (2013) *Understanding Political Science Research Methods: The Challenge of Inference*. London: Routledge.
38. Scheuch, E.K. (1968) 'The cross-cultural use of sample survey: problems of comparability', in S. Rokkan (ed.), *Comparative Research Across Cultures and Nations*. The Hague: Mouton. Frey, F.W. (1970) 'Cross-cultural survey research in political science', in R.T. Holt and J.E. Turner (eds), *The Methodology of Comparative Research*. London: The Free Press, pp. 173–294.
39. Scheuch, E.K. (1989) 'Theoretical implications of comparative survey research: why the wheel of cross-cultural methodology keeps on being reinvented', *International Sociology*, 4 (2): 147–167.
40. Poynter, R. (2010) *The Handbook of Online and Social Media Research: Tools and Techniques for Market Researchers*. London: Wiley.
41. Manyika, J. et al. (2011) *Big Data: The Next Frontier for Innovation, Competition, and Productivity*. Boston: McKinsey Global Institute.
42. Barbarena, M.A. and León, M. (2010) *Webnography: A New Market Survey Technique*. Amsterdam: ESOMA World Research. Puri, A. (2007) 'The web of insights – the art and practice of webnography', *International Journal of Market Research*, 49(3): 387–408.
43. Mayer-Schonberger, V. and Cukier, K.N. (2013) *Big Data: A Revolution That Will Transform How We Live, Work, and Think*. London: John Murray.
44. Siegel, E. (2013) *Predictive Analytics: The Power to Predict Who Will Click, Buy, Lie, or Die*. London: Wiley.
45. WEF (2012) *Big Data, Big Impact: New Possibilities for International Development*. Geneva: World Economic Forum.
46. Office for National Statistics (2012) *What Insights Can Google Trends Provide About Tourism in Specific Destinations?* – www.ons.gov.uk/ons/guide-method/method-quality/specific/economy/economic-value-of-tourism/google-trends/index.html. Office for National Statistics (2012) Economic Value of Tourism – www.ons.gov.uk/ons/guide-method/method-quality/specific/economy/economic-value-of-tourism/index.html

Chapter 10 Researching places

1. Flowerdew, R. and David, M. (2005) *Methods in Human Geography: A Guide for Students Doing a Research Project.* Harlow: Prentice Hall.
2. Michael, S.R. (2010) *Archaeology: Basic Field Methods.* Dubuque, IA: Kendall Hunt Publishing.
3. Hammersley, M. and Atkinson, P. (2007) *Ethnography: Principles in Practice.* London: Routledge.
4. Epstein, M. (1969) *Transcultural Experiments: Russian and American Models of Creative Communication.* New York: St. Martin's Press. (Ch. 1: 'From culturology to transculture'.)
5. Sinton, D. and Lund, J. (eds) (2006) *Understanding Place.* Redlands, CA: ESRI Press.
6. Makagon, D. and Neumean, M. (2009) *Recording Culture: Audio Documentary and the Ethnographic Experience.* New York: Sage. Bauer, M.W. and Gaskell, G. (eds) (2000) *Qualitative Researching with Text, Image and Sound: A Practical Handbook.* New York: Sage.
7. al-Bīrūnī, Abū al-Rayḥān (1910) (E. Sachau, ed.) *Al-Beruni's India: An Account of the Religion, Philosophy, Literature, Geography, Chronology, Astronomy, Customs, Laws and Astrology of India.* London: Kegan Paul, Trench, Trubner, Vol. 1, p. 3.
8. Mayhew, H. (1850/2008) *London Labour and the London Poor.* London: Wordsworth.
9. 'Street ethnography' – http://blogs.ubc.ca/qualresearch/2012/11/12/street-ethnography/
10. Williams, C. (2012) *Researching Power, Elites and Leadership.* London: Sage, pp. 77–81.
11. McNamara, R.P. (ed.) (1995) *Sex, Scams, and Street Life: The Sociology of New York City's Times Square.* Westport, CT: Greenwood Press.
12. Klein, M.W. (2005) 'The value of comparisons in street gang research', *Journal of Contemporary Criminal Justice,* 21 (2): 135–152.
13. Trussell, R.P (1999) The children's streets: an ethnographic study of street children in Ciudad Juárez, Mexico', *International Social Work,* 42 (2): 189–199.
14. Butchinsky, C. (2013) 'Sources of stigma: researching street homelessness – interviews and participant observation' – www.academia.edu
15. Strickland, D.A. and Schlesinger, L.E. (1969) 'Lurking as a research method', *Journal of Human Organization,* 28 (3): 9.
16. Kusenbach, M. (2003) 'Street phenomenology: the Go-Along as ethnographic research tool', *Ethnography,* 4 (3): 455–485. Williams, C. (2012) *Draw and Tell: Street Children in Apartheid South Africa* – www.statecrime.org/testimonyproject/drawandtell
17. Pamela, E.O. and Myers, D.J. (2002) 'Formal models in studying collective action and social movements', in B. Klandermans and S. Staggenborg (eds), *Methods of Research in Social Movements.* Minneapolis: University of Minnesota Press.
18. ESRC (2012) 'Riots: the research evidence' – www.esrc.ac.uk/research/research-topics/security/conflict/riots-research-evidence.aspx
19. Audiences London (2011) *Researching Audiences at Outdoor Events and Festivals.* London: Audiences London.
20. *International Journal of Event Management Research* – www.ijemr.org/
21. Yip, S.F.P. et al. (2010) 'Estimation of the number of people in a demonstration', *Australian and New Zealand Journal of Statistics,* 52 (1): 17–26.
22. King, R. (2013) 'Homeland Security to test BOSS facial recognition at junior hockey game', *Biometric Update* – www.biometricupdate.com/201309/u-s-testing-crowd-scanning-facial-recognition-system
23. *Daily Mail* (2011) 'Festival crush disasters could be prevented with software that detects dangerous crowd build-up', *Daily Mail Online,* 4 August.

24. Gibbs, J.P. (1961) *Urban Research Methods*. Princeton, NJ: Van Nostrand. Andranovich, G.D. and Riposa, G. (eds) (1993) *Doing Urban Research*. New York: Sage.
25. Duneier, M. et al. (eds) (2014) *The Urban Ethnography Reader*. New York: Oxford University Press.
26. Basham, R. (1978) *Urban Anthropology: The Cross-Cultural Study of Complex Societies*. Houston: Mayfield Publishing. Fox, R.G. (1977) *Urban Anthropology: Cities in their Cultural Settings*. New York: Prentice-Hall. Hannerz, U. (1980) *Exploring the City: Inquiries Toward an Urban Anthropology*. New York: Columbia University Press. Guldin, G.E and Southall, A.W. (eds) (1993) *Urban Anthropology in China*. Leiden: Brill. Eames, E. (1977) *Anthropology of the City: An Introduction to Urban Anthropology*. Englewood Cliffs, NJ: Prentice-Hall.
27. Silva, C.N. (2012) *Online Research Methods in Urban and Planning Studies: Design and Outcomes*. Hershey, PA: IGI Global.
28. Kresl, P.K. and Ietri, D. (eds) (2012) *European Cities and Global Competitiveness*. Cheltenham: Edward Elgar. Bradley, J. and Katz, B. (2013) *The Metropolitan Revolution*. Washington, DC: Brookings Institution.
29. UN-HABITAT (2008) *State of the World's Cities*. London: Earthscan. Brinkhoff, T. (2011) *The Principal Agglomerations of the World* – www.cirypopulation.de
30. Centre for Urban Conflict – www.conflictincities.org
31. Hoornbeek, J. (2009) *Literature Review: Sustainable Infrastructure in Shrinking Cities*. Kent, OH: Kent State University, Center for Public Administration and Public Policy and the Cleveland Urban Design Collaborative.
32. Smith, S. (2005) *Underground London: Travels Beneath the City Streets*. London: Abacus.
33. Abandoned Mine Research – www.undergroundminers.com/amr.html
34. McCamley, N. (2013) *Cold War Secret Nuclear Bunkers*. Barnsley: Pen & Sword Military.
35. Laurie, P. (1979) *Beneath the City Streets*. London: HarperCollins.
36. Garber, A. and Turner, R.S. (1994) *Gender in Urban Research*. New York: Sage.
37. Xerez, R. and Fonseca, J. (2011) *Mixing Methods in Urban Research: Exploring City and Community Social Capital*. Amsterdam: CAPP.
38. Aguettant, J.L. (1996) 'Impact of population registration on hilltribe development in Thailand', *Asia Pacific Population Journal*, 11 (4): 47–72.
39. Buadaeng, K. (2006) 'The rise and fall of the Tribal Research Institute (TRI): "Hill Tribe" policy and studies in Thailand', *Southeast Asian Studies*, 44(3) 359–384.
40. Yang, G. (2009) 'Investigating the agricultural techniques used by the Hmong in Chiang Mai Province, Thailand', *UW-L Journal of Undergraduate Research*, XII:1–4
41. Rock, F. (ed.) (2001) *Participatory Land Use Planning (PLUP) in Rural Cambodia. Annex 11*. Cambodia, Phnom Penh: Ministry of Land Management, Urban Planning and Construction (MLMUPC).
42. Adugna, A. (n.d.) *Combined Methods Case study. Zambia (PSIA: Land Reform)*. London: DFID/World Bank – http://go.worldbank.org/DUKPM9RSM0
43. Haynie, D.L. and Gorman, B.K. (1999) 'A gendered context of opportunity: determinants of poverty across urban and rural labor markets', *The Sociological Quarterly*, 40 (2): 177–197.
44. Buller, H. (2003) *The Demography of Rural Areas: A Literature Review*. London: DEFRA.
45. Australian Institute of Health and Welfare (2008) *Rural, Regional and Remote Health: Indicators of Health Status and Determinants of Health*. Canberra: AIHW.
46. Sontheimer, S. et al. (1999) *Conducting a PRA Training and Modifying PRA Tools to Your Needs: An Example from a Participatory Household Food Security and Nutrition Project in Ethiopia*. Rome: FAO.
47. Fritz, S. (2009) 'Geo-Wiki.Org: the use of crowdsourcing to improve global land cover', *Remote Sensing*, 1 (3): 345–354.

48. Lwasa, I. (2012) *The Role of Urban and Peri-Urban Agriculture in Enhancing Food Security and Climate Change Resilience in East and West African Cities*. Ibadan: START.
49. Kruger, J. (2011) *Bolokang Metsire Iploloke* [Save Water, Save Ourselves]. Ifafi: Jill Kruger Research.
50. Hughes, A. et al. (2000) *Ethnography and Rural Research*. Gloucester: The Countryside & Community Press.
51. Twumasi, P.A. (2001) *Social Research in Rural Communities*. Accra: Ghana University Press. Chambers, R. (2008) *Revolutions in Development Inquiry*. London: Earthscan.
52. Chitere, O. et al. (eds) (1991) *Working with Rural Communities: Participatory Action Research in Kenya*. Nairobi: Nairobi University Press.
53. Rifkin, S.B. and Pridmore, P. (2001) *Partners in Planning: Information, Participation and Empowerment*. London: Macmillan.
54. Kruger, J. (2011) *Bolokang Metsire Iploloke* [Save Water, Save Ourselves). Ifafi: Jill Kruger Research.
55. Chambers, R. (1983) *Rural Development: Putting the Last First*. London: Longmans. Cracken, J. et al. (1988) *An Introduction to Rapid Rural Appraisal for Agricultural Development*. London: IIED. Chambers, R. (1992) *Rural Appraisal: Rapid, Relaxed, and Participatory*. Discussion Paper 311. Brighton: Institute of Development Studies.
56. World Bank. 'Participatory tools for micro-level poverty and social impact analysis' – http://go.worldbank.org/ZGZHJEDBZ0
57. Nagao, T. (2001) *Higata no Minsyusyugi* [Democracy in Tidal Areas]. Tokyo: Gendai Syokan, p. 193.
58. Mandelbrot, B.B. (1982) *The Fractal Geometry of Nature*. London: Macmillan, pp. 25–33.
59. Oxfam (2005) *The Tsunami's Impact on Women*. Briefing note. Oxford: Oxfam.
60. Van Ginkel, R. (2008) *Coastal Cultures: An Anthropology of Fishing and Whaling*. Amsterdam: Het Pinhuis. Halls, A.S. and Mustafa, M.G. (2006) *Final Assessment of the Impact of the CBFM Project on Community-Managed Fisheries in Bangladesh*. London: DFID.
61. Kay, R. and Alder, J. (2005) *Coastal Planning and Management*. Abingdon: Taylor & Francis.
62. Zsamboky, M. (2011) *Impacts of Climate Change on Disadvantaged UK Coastal Communities*. York: Joseph Rowntree Foundation.
63. Burke, L.A. et al. (2001) *Coastal ecosystems*. Washington, DC: World Resources Institute.
64. Yamashita, H. (2009) 'Making invisible risks visible: education, environmental risk information and coastal development', *Ocean and Coastal Management*, 52 (7): 327–335.
65. Singh, H. et al. (2000) 'Imaging underwater for archaeology', *Journal of Field Archaeology*, 27 (3): 319–328.
66. Masazumi, H. (1972/2004) (T. Sachie and T.S. George, trans.) *Minamata Disease*. Kumamoto: Kumamoto Nichinchi Shinbun.
67. Hardin, G. (1968) 'The tragedy of the commons', *Science*, 162 (3859): 1243–1248.
68. Jasper, S. (2012) *Conflict and Cooperation in the Global Commons: A Comprehensive Approach for International Security*. Washington, DC: Georgetown University Press.
69. Thompson, J. (1996) 'Space for rent: the International Telecommunications Union, space law, and orbit/spectrum leasing', *Journal of Air Law and Commerce*, 62: 279–311.
70. Morris, L. and Cox, K. (2010) *Space Commerce: The Inside Story*. Washington, DC: ATWG/NASA.
71. Stimson. *Space Security Project* – www.stimson.org/programs/space-security/
72. Environmental Protection Agency (2013) 'Climate impacts on agriculture and food supply' – www.epa.gov/climatechange/impacts-adaptation/agriculture.html
73. McMichael, A.J. et al. (2006) 'Climate change and human health: present and future risks', *Lancet*, 367 (9513): 859–869.
74. IISD (2003) *Livelihoods and Climate Change*. Stockholm: International Institute for Sustainable Development.

75. Myers, N. (1993) 'Environmental refugees in a globally warmed world', *BioScience*, 43 (11): 752–761.
76. UNEP/GLOBIO. *Mapping Human Impacts on the Biosphere* – www.globio.info
77. Matheson, C. et al. (2001) 'The health of fishermen in the catching sector of the fishing industry: a gap analysis', *Occupational Medicine*, 51 (5): 305–311.
78. Sheavly, S.B. and Register, K.M. (2007) 'Marine debris and plastics: environmental concerns, sources, impacts and solutions', *Journal of Polymers and the Environment*, 15 (4): 301–305. Raloff, J. (2008) 'Marine pollution spawns "wonky babies" ', *Science News*, 26 November.
79. Heffernan, P.H. (1981) 'Conflict over marine resources', *Proceedings of the Academy of Political Science*, 34 (1): 168–180.
80. The Ship Safety Research Centre (SSRC), University of Strathclyde.
81. Coppens, F. et al. (2007) *Economic Impact of Port Activity: A Disaggregate Analysis. The Case of Antwerp*. Brussels: National Bank of Belgium.
82. Heller-Roazen, D. (2009) *The Enemy of All: Piracy and the Law of Nations*. Cambridge: Zone Books.
83. Nicholls, R.J. and Mimura, N. (1998) 'Regional issues raised by sea-level rise and their policy implications', *Climate Research*, 11: 5–18.
84. Abdullah, M.H. (2003) 'Optimization analysis for groundwater extraction in a sandy aquifer of an island [in Malay]', *Borneo Science*, 13: 34–43.
85. Victor, P.-É. (1963) (S. Sullivan, trans.) *Man and the Conquest of the Poles*. New York: Simon & Schuster.
86. National Aeronautics and Space Administration (2007) 'Sea ice remote sensing' – http://polynya.gsfc.nasa.gov/seaice_projects.html
87. UNEP/GLOBIO. *Mapping Human Impacts on the Biosphere (Polar Regions)* – www.grida.no/geo/GEO/Geo-2-421.htm
88. Loader, B.D. (2004) *The Governance of Cyberspace: Politics, Technology and Global Restructuring*. London: Routledge.
89. *Cyber Warfare* – www.icrc.org/eng/war-and-law/conduct-hostilities/information-warfare/index.jsp
90. Ostrom, E. et al. (2002) *The Drama of the Commons*. Committee on the Human Dimensions of Global Change. Washington, DC: National Academies of Science.
91. Zürn, M. (1998) 'The rise of international environmental politics: a review of current research', *World Politics*, 50 (4): 617–649.
92. Kaul, I. et al. (1999) *Global Public Goods: International Cooperation in the 21st Century*. New York: Oxford University Press.
93. Hardison, P. (2006) 'Indigenous peoples and the commons', *On the Commons*, 20 November – http://onthecommons.org/indigenous-peoples-and-commons
94. Bruggeman, D. (2013) 'A more, and less, powerful crowdsourcing for emissions modelling', *Pasco Phronesis*, 17 May.
95. Ball, M. (2011) 'Australian scientists win grant to develop mobile GHG sensors', *Spatial Sustain*, 28 June – www.sensysmag.com/spatialsustain/australian-scientists-win-grant-to-develop-mobile-ghg-sensors.html
96. Tcktcktck (2013) 'Track the spill: NGO aims to crowdsource information on oil leaks' – http://tcktcktck.org/2013/10/57567/57567
97. Kress, G. and van Leeuwen, T. (1996) *Reading Images: The Grammar of Visual Design*. London: Routledge.
98. Margolis, E. and Pauwels, L. (eds) (2011) *The Sage Handbook of Visual Research Methods*. London: Sage.

99. Noble, I. and Bestley, R. (2009) *Visual Research: An Introduction to Research Methodologies in Graphic Design*. London: AVA Publishing.
100. Ball, M.S. and Smith, G.W.H. (1992) *Analyzing Visual Data*. Newbury Park, CA: Sage.
101. Williams, C. (2012) *Researching Power, Elites and Leadership*. London: Sage, pp. 1–2.
102. Emmison, M. and Smith, P.D. (2000) *Researching the Visual: Images, Objects, Contexts and Interactions in Social and Cultural Inquiry*. London: Sage.
103. BAJR (2006) *Short Guide to Digital Photography in Archaeology* – www.bajr.org/documents/digitalphotography.pdf
104. Michael, S.R. (2010) *Archaeology: Basic Field Methods*. Dubuque, IA: Kendall Hunt Publishing.
105. Baxter, J.E. (2005) *The Archaeology of Childhood: Children, Gender, and Material Culture*. Blue Ridge Summit, PA: AltaMira Press.
106. Burns, K.R. (2006) *The Forensic Anthropology Training Manual*. London: Pearson Education.
107. MSHP (2003) *Forensic Evidence Handbook*. (SHP-145 B 8/2003). Missouri State Highway Patrol – www.crime-scene-investigator.net/forensic_evidence_manual_MO.pdf
108. Fisk, R. (2001) 'Death in Bethlehem, made in America', *The Independent*, 15 April.
109. Dee, M. et al. (2013) 'An absolute chronology for early Egypt using radiocarbon dating and Bayesian statistical modelling', *Proceedings of the Royal Society*, 469 (2159) – http://rspa.royalsocietypublishing.org/content/469/2159/20130395
110. Cowen, R. (2009) 'Earliest known sound recordings revealed: Researchers unveil imprints made 20 years before Edison invented phonograph', *Science News*, 26 June.
111. *Researching Historic Buildings* – www.buildinghistory.org
112. Cragoe, C.D. (2008) *How to Read Buildings*. London: Herbert Press.
113. De Jonge, K. and Van Balen, K. (eds) (2002) *Preparatory Architectural Investigation in the Restoration of Historical Buildings*. Ithaca, NY: Cornell University Press.
114. Roppola, T. (2013) *Designing for the Museum Visitor Experience*. London: Routledge.
115. Maass, P. (2003) 'The toppling: how the media inflated a minor moment in a long war', *The New Yorker*, 10 January.
116. Ternes, T.A. (1998) 'Occurrence of drugs in German sewage treatment plants and rivers', *Water Research*, 32 (11): 3245–3260.
117. Greenpeace (2012) *Clean our Cloud* – www.greenpeace.org/international/en/campaigns/climate-change/cleanourcloud/
118. Watkins, A. (1988) *The Old Straight Track: Its Mounds, Beacons, Moats, Sites and Mark Stones*. London: Abacus.
119. Foucault, M. (1979/1991) *Discipline and Punish*. (Theories of 'surveillance'.) London: Penguin. Campbell, D. (n.d.) 'How embassy eavesdropping works' – www.duncan-campbell.org/embassy-bugging. Interception of communications – www.lamont.me.uk/capenhurst/followup.html
120. Louv, R. et al. (2012) *Citizen Science: Public Participation in Environmental Research*. Sacramento, CA: Comstock.
121. Williams, C. (ed.) (1998) *Environmental Victims: New Risks, New Injustice*. London: Earthscan.
122. PubLab (2010) Gulf Coast. Deepwater Horizon oil spill mapping 2010–2011 – http://publiclab.org/wiki/gulf-coast
123. Warren, J. (2010) 'DIY mappers offer remarkable images of Gulf Coast oil spill', *IdeaLab* – www.pbs.org/idealab/2010/05/diy-mappers-offer-remarkable-images-of-gulf-coast-oil-spill132/
124. Hernandez, J. et al. (2013) 'Moisture measurement in crops using spherical robots', *Industrial Robot: An International Journal*, 40: 59–66, 2013. Read more at http://phys.org/news/2013-06-rosphere-spherical-robot-exploration-missions.html#jCp

125. Lifton, R.J. (1969) *Death in Life: Survivors of Hiroshima*. New York: Random House, pp. 33–34.
126. Nakamoto, T. (2005) 'Study of odor recorder for dynamical change of odor', *Chemical Senses* 30 (suppl. 1): i254–i255.
127. Henshaw, V. (2014) *Urban Smellscapes: Understanding and Designing City Smell Environments*. London: Sage.
128. Makagon, D. and Neumean, M. (2009) *Recording Culture: Audio Documentary and the Ethnographic Experience*. Thousand Oaks, CA: Sage.

Chapter 11 Mapping places

1. Monmonier, M. (1993) *Mapping it Out*. Chicago: University of Chicago Press.
2. Slocum, T. (2003) *Thematic Cartography and Geographic Visualization*. Upper Saddle River, NJ: Prentice-Hall.
3. Brotton, J. (2012) *A History of the World in Twelve Maps*. London: Allen Lane.
4. Sinton, D. and Lund, J. (2007) 'What is GIS? A very brief description for the newly curious', in D. Sinton and J. Lund (eds), *Understanding Place*. Redlands, CA: ESRI Press.
5. Monmonier, M. (1996) *How to Lie with Maps*. Chicago: University of Chicago Press.
6. Dymaxion Map. Buckmister Fuller Institute – www.bfi.org/about-bucky/buckys-big-ideas/dymaxion-world/dymaxion-map
7. www.japantimes.co.jp/culture/2013/05/21/arts/outsider-art-that-comes-from-within
8. 'Where commuters run over black children' – http://civic.mit.edu/blog/kanarinka/the-detroit-geographic-expedition-and-institute-a-case-study-in-civic-mapping
9. Genz, J. et al. (2009) 'Wave navigation in the Marshall Islands', *Oceanography*, 22 (2): 234–245.
10. Zlatanova, S. and Li, J. (eds) (2008) *Geospatial Information Technology for Emergency Response*. London: Taylor & Francis.
11. USGS. Real time earthquake maps – http://earthquake.usgs.gov/earthquakes/map/
12. Li, J. and Chapman, M.A. (2008) 'Terrestrial mobile mapping towards real-time geospatial data collection', in S. Zlatanova and J. Li (eds), *Geospatial Information Technology for Emergency Response*. London: Taylor & Francis.
13. Fritz, S. (2009) 'Geo-Wiki.Org: the use of crowdsourcing to improve global land cover', *Remote Sensing*, 1 (3): 345–354.
14. Weng, Q. (2009) *Remote Sensing and GIS Integration: Theories, Methods, and Applications*. New York: McGraw–Hill. Chuvieco, E. and Chuvieco, E. (eds) (2009) *The Fundamentals of Satellite Remote Sensing*. Boca Raton, FL: CRC Press. Campbell, J.B. (2002) *Introduction to Remote Sensing*. London: The Guilford Press.
15. Gao, J. (2009) *Digital Analysis of Remotely Sensed Imagery*. New York: McGraw-Hill.
16. Pigeon remote sensing – http://beatrizdacosta.net/Pigeonblog/index.php
17. Goodchild, M.F. (2007) 'Citizens as sensors: the world of volunteered geography', *GeoJournal*, 69: 211–221.
18. Eagle, N. (2013) 'Mobile phones as sensors for social research', in S.N. Hesse-Biber (ed.), *The Handbook of Emergent Technologies in Social Research*. Oxford: Oxford University Press, Ch. 22.
19. van Oosterom, P. (2008) *Advances in 3D Geoinformation Systems: Lecture Notes in Geoinformation and Cartography*. New York: Springer.
20. Yamashita, H. (2009) 'Making invisible risks visible: education, environmental risk information and coastal development', *Ocean and Coastal Management*, 52 (7): 327–335.

21. Easter Island, drone mappers – www.eisp.org/
22. Wall, M. (2013) 'The maps transforming how we interact with the world', *BBC News Online*, 13 September – www.bbc.co.uk/news/business-24067745
23. Slocum, T. (2003) *Thematic Cartography and Geographic Visualization*. Upper Saddle River, NJ: Prentice-Hall.
24. Hellenthal, G. et al. (2014) 'A genetic atlas of human admixture history', *Science*, 14 February. Interactive map – www.admixturemap.paintmychromosomes.com/
25. El Nadeem Centre (2006) *Torture in Egypt: A State Policy*. Cairo: El Nadeem Centre.
26. Masami, N. (2004) 'Bikini: 50 years of nuclear exposure', *Japan Focus* – http://japanfocus.org/-Sadamatsu-Shinjiro/2121
27. Driskell, D. (2002) *Creating Better Cities with Children and Youth: A Manual for Participation*. London: Earthscan/UNESCO.
28. Tao, C.V. (2007) *Advances in Mobile Mapping Technology*. London: Taylor & Francis.
29. Bankoff, G. et al. (2004) *Mapping Vulnerability: Disasters, Development, and People*. London: Earthscan.
30. Meier, P. and Leaning, J. (2009) *Applied Technology to Crisis Mapping and Early Warning in Humanitarian Settings*. Cambridge, MA: Harvard Humanitarian Initiative.
31. Terrain surface mapping, discussion group – www.diydrones.com/group/terrain-surface-mapping
32. Meier, P. (2013) 'Crowdsourcing to map conflict, crises and humanitarian response', in D. Backer et al. (eds), *Peace and Conflict*. Bethesda: University of Maryland Press.
33. Steffen, F. et al. (2009) 'Geo-Wiki.Org: the use of crowdsourcing to improve global land cover', *Remote Sensing*, 1 (3): 345–354.
34. World Bank. 'Participatory tools for micro-level poverty and social impact analysis' – http://go.worldbank.org/ZGZHJEDBZ0
35. IFAD (2009) *Enabling Poor Rural People to Overcome Poverty: Good Practices in Participatory Mapping*. Rome: International Fund for Agricultural Development – www.ifad.org/pub/map/pm_web.pdf
36. Goodchild, M.F. (2007) 'Citizens as sensors: the world of volunteered geography', *GeoJournal*, 69 (4): 211–221.
37. *North Korean Economy Watch* (2009) 'North Korea uncovered' – www.nkeconwatch.com/north-korea-uncovered-google-earth/
38. Moses, A. (2009) 'Amateur spies put North Korea on the Map', *Brisbane Times* – www.brisbanetimes.com.au/technology/amateur-spies-put-north-korea-on-the-map-20090602-bttj.html
39. Tactile maps for blind and partially sighted people – www.tactileview.com/mapmaker

Chapter 12 Analysing world systems

1. *Airline Route Maps* – www.airlineroutemaps.com
2. Bastow, S. et al. (2014) *The Impact of the Social Sciences*. London: Sage.
3. Hsiang, S.M (2013) 'Quantifying the influence of climate on human conflict', *Science*, 341 (6151), DOI: 10.1126/science.1235367
4. Reinalda, B. (ed.) (2013) *Routledge Handbook of International Organization*. London: Routledge.
5. Guide to the UN – http://library.law.columbia.edu/guides/United_Nations
6. Model UN Research – http://bestdelegate.com/research/

7. Researching the WTO/GATT – http://nyulaw.libguides.com/content.php?pid=55653&sid=424226
8. Researching the World Bank – http://econ.worldbank.org/external/default/main?menuPK=577939&pagePK=64165265&piPK=64165423&theSitePK=469382
9. Researching the IMF – www.lib.berkeley.edu/doemoff/govinfo/intl/gov_imf.html
10. Model UN Research – http://bestdelegate.com/research/
11. *United Nations System* – www.unsceb.org
12. Directory of United Nations System organizations index – www.un.org/en/index.shtml
13. *Protocol and Liaison Service Blue Book* – www.un.int/protocol/bluebook.html
14. UN Web TV – http://webtv.un.org
15. Bloodgood, E. and Schmitz, H.P. (2006) 'Researching INGOs: innovations in data collection and methods of analysis' – http://faculty.maxwell.syr.edu/hpschmitz/Papers/ResearchingINGOs_February6.pdf
16. Wallerstein, I. (1974) *The Modern World-System: Capitalist Agriculture and the Origins of the European World-Economy in the Sixteenth Century*. New York: Academic Press.
17. Babones, S. and Chase-Dunn, C. (2012) *Handbook of World Systems Analysis*. London: Routledge.
18. Williams, C. (2012) *Researching Power, Elites and Leadership*. London: Sage.
19. Brandes, U. and Erlebah, T. (eds) (2005) *Network Analysis: Methodological Foundations*. Berlin: Springer-Verlag. Freeman, L. (2006) *The Development of Social Network Analysis*. Vancouver: Empirical Press.
20. Boje, D.M. (2001) *Narrative Methods for Organizational and Communication Research*. London: Sage.
21. Czarniawska-Joerges, B. (2004) *Narratives in Social Science Research*. Thousand Oaks, CA: Sage. Boje, D.M. (2001) *Narrative Methods for Organizational and Communication Research*. London: Sage. Yorozu, C. (2010) 'Narrative management by a celebrity CEO', unpublished paper presented at the *ESRC Seminar 'Studying Elites'*, CRESC, Manchester University.
22. Merrill, J. et al. (2006) 'Description of a method to support public health information management: organizational network analysis', *Journal of Biomedical Informatics*, 40 (4): 422–428.
23. Corporate Watch (2010) *How to Research Companies* – www.corporatewatch.org.uk
24. Checkland, P. and Scholes, J. (1990) *Soft Systems Methodology in Action*. Chichester: Wiley.
25. Checkland, P. (1981) *Systems Thinking, Systems Practice*. New York: Wiley.
26. Buchana, D. and Bryman, A. (2009) *The Sage Handbook of Organizational Research Methods*. London: Sage. Punnett, B.J. and Shenkar, O. (2004) *Handbook for International Management Research*. London: Wiley.
27. Buchana, D. and Bryman, A. (2009) *The Sage Handbook of Organizational Research Methods*. London: Sage.
28. Brandes, U. and Erlebah, T. (eds) (2005) *Network Analysis: Methodological Foundations*. Berlin: Springer-Verlag. Freeman, L. (2006) *The Development of Social Network Analysis*. Vancouver: Empirical Press.
29. Burris, V. (1991) 'Director interlocks and the political behaviour of corporations and corporate elites', *Social Science Quarterly*, 72 (3): 637–651.
30. Pahl, N. and Richter, A. (2009) *SWOT Analysis – Idea, Methodology and a Practical Approach*. Munich: GRIN Verlag oHG.
31. Jackson, P. (2013) *Intelligence Studies*. London: Sage.
32. *International Journal of Intelligence and Counterintelligence*.
33. Williams, C. (2012) *Researching Power, Elites and Leadership*. London: Sage.
34. de Garzia, A. (1954) *Discovering National Elites: A Manual of Methods for Discovering the Leadership of a Society and its Vulnerabilities to Propaganda*. Stanford, CA: Institute for

Journalistic Studies, Stanford University – www.grazian-archive.com/governing/Elite/Table%20of%20Contents.html
35. *Manual of Protocol* – www.un.int/protocol/manual_toc.html
36. Smith, H. (2004) 'Improving intelligence on North Korea', *Jane's Intelligence Review*, April: 48–51.
37. Bresler, F. (1993) *Interpol*. London: Mandarin.
38. Vlassis, D. and Williams, P. (eds) (2001) *Combating Transnational Crime: Concepts, Activities and Responses*. Abingdon: Frank Cass.
39. Shelley, L.I. et al. (2005) *Methods and Motives: Exploring Links Between Transnational Organized Crime and International Terrorism*. Washington, DC: National Institute of Justice, U.S. Department of Justice, Office of Justice Programs – www.ncjrs.gov/pdffiles1/nij/grants/211207.pdf
40. Fuchs, C. (2009) *Social Networking Sites and the Surveillance Society: A Critical Case Study of the Usage of studiVZ, Facebook, and MySpace by Students in Salzburg in the Context of Electronic Surveillance*. Salzburg and Vienna: Verein zur Förderung der Integration der Informationswissenschaften.
41. Cheung, Y. and Bal, J. (1998) 'Process analysis techniques and tools for business improvements', *Business Process Management Journal*, 4 (4): 274–290. Biazzo, S. (2002) 'Process mapping techniques and organisational analysis: lessons from sociotechnical system theory', *Business Process Management Journal*, 8 (1): 42–52.
42. Johnson, J.A. et al. (2013) 'Social network analysis: a systematic approach for investigating', *FBI Law Enforcement Bulletin* – www.fbi.gov/stats-services/publications/law-enforcement-bulletin/2013/March/social-network-analysis
43. For updated lists, see *Wiki*, 'Social network analysis software' and 'Comparison of network diagram software'.
44. Wilson, B. (2001) *Soft Systems Methodology, Conceptual Model Building and its Contribution*. London: Wiley.
45. Williams, C. (2012) *Researching Power, Elites and Leadership*. London: Sage, pp. 161–170.
46. Eagle, N. (2013) 'Mobile phones as sensors for social research', in S.N. Hesse-Biber (ed.), *The Handbook of Emergent Technologies in Social Research*. Oxford: Oxford University Press.
47. Sibert, J.R. and Nielsen, J.L. (2010) *Electronic Tagging and Tracking in Marine Fisheries*. Amsterdam: Kluwer.
48. BBC (2008) 'The box', *BBC News Online* – http://news.bbc.co.uk/1/hi/in_depth/business/2008/the_box/default.stm
49. Aksoy, Y. and Derbez, A (2003) 'Software survey: supply chain management' – www.orms-today.org/orms-6-03/frscm.html
50. Laczko, F. and Gozdziak, E. (eds) (2005) *Data and Research on Human Trafficking: A Global Survey*. Geneva: United Nations/International Organization for Migration (IOM).
51. Mackenzie, S. (2006) 'Systematic crimes of the powerful: criminal aspects of the global economy', *Social Justice*, 33 (1): 162–182.
52. Williams, C. (2013) 'Crowdsourcing research: a methodology for researching state crime', *State Crime*, 2 (1): 30–51.
53. Fulmer, J. (2009) 'What in the world is infrastructure?', *PEI Infrastructure Investor*, July/August: 30–32.
54. ITO infrastructure maps – www.itoworld.com
55. *Business Insider* (2013) 'The 15 oil and gas pipelines that are changing the world's strategic map' – www.businessinsider.com/the-15-oil-and-gas-pipelines-changing-the-worlds-strategic-map-2010-3#us-influence-tapi-pipeline-1
56. Bookbinder, J.H. (2012) *Handbook of Global Logistics: Transportation in International Supply Chains*. London: Springer.

57. Helpman, E. (2011) *Understanding Global Trade*. Cambridge, MA: University of Harvard Press.
58. Gillett, J. and Gillett, M. (2011) *Transport Networks*. London: Wayland.
59. Mowlana, H. (1997) *Global Information and World Communication: New Frontiers in International Relations*. London: Sage.
60. *Net World Map* – www.networldmap.com
61. *Submarine Cable Map* – www.submarinecablemap.com
62. ITO world pipeline maps – www.itoworld.com/map/220?lon=7.49215&lat=33.56617&zoom=2
63. Banks, F.E. (2006) *Political Economy of World Energy*. Uppsala: WSPC.
64. Vaughn, J. (2009) *Waste Management: A Reference Handbook*. Brussels: ABC/CLIO.
65. UN-ESCAP. *Asian Highway Agreement* – www.unescap.org/TTDW/index.asp?MenuName=AsianHighway
66. Darnton, G. and Darnton, M. (1997) *Business Process Analysis*. Andover: Thomson Business Press.
67. Lynch, F. (1994) *Reengineering Business Processes and People Systems*. Pagosa Springs, CO: QualTeam, Inc.
68. Tansey, O. (2007) 'Process tracing and elite interviewing: a case for non-probability sampling', *Political Science and Politics*, 40 (4): 1–23.
69. George, A.L. and Bennett, A. (2005) *Case Studies and Theory Development in the Social Sciences*. Cambridge, MA: MIT Press, pp. 6, 206.
70. Levine, H.L. (2007) 'The use of critical process analysis to reduce risk and increase biologics product quality', unpublished presentation at the FIP Quality International 2007 Conference, Acton, MA, BioProcess Technology Consultants.
71. Guzzetti, B.J. et al. (1993) 'Promoting conceptual change in science: a comparative meta-analysis of instructional interventions from reading education and science education', *Reading Research Quarterly*, 28 (2): 116–159.

Chapter 13 Analysing official documents

1. BBC (2012) 'Vietnam refuses to stamp new Chinese passports over map', *BBC News Online*, 26 November – www.bbc.co.uk/news/world-asia-20491426
2. Ford, N. (2011) *The Essential Guide to Using the Web for Research*. London: Sage.
3. UN documentation: overview – http://research.un.org/en/docs
4. *UN History Project* – http://unhistoryproject.org/research/research_guides.html
5. *UN History Project* archives – http://unhistoryproject.org/research/online_archives.html
6. National constitutions – www.constituteproject.org/#/
7. *UN Treaty Collection* – https://treaties.un.org/
8. *Iraq Inquiry Digest* (2011) 'New early drafts of Iraq Dossier published' – www.iraqinquiry-digest.org/?p=11636
9. Hill, M.R. (1993) *Archival Strategies and Techniques*. Thousand Oaks, CA: Sage.
10. Glynn, S. and Booth, A. (1979) 'The public records office and recent British economic historiography', *The Economic History Review*, 23 (3): 303–315.
11. CIA. Freedom of Information – www.foia.cia.gov
12. National Archive (UK). Military resources: classified/declassified records – www.archives.gov/research/alic/reference/military/records-declassification.html
13. Dikotter, F. (2005) *Mao's Great Famine: The Story of Mao's Most Devastating Catastrophe, 1958–62*. London: Bloomsbury.

14. UCB libraries – http://ucblibraries.colorado.edu/govpubs/us/declassified.htm.
15. Reporters Without Borders – http://en.rsf.org/press-freedom-index-2013,1054.html
16. Chapman, R.A. and Hunt, M. (2010) *Freedom of Information: Local Government and Accountability*. Abingdon: Ashgate.
17. Canada FOI resource website – www3.telus.net/index100/indextorulings.
18. *Open Government: A Journal on Freedom of Information* – www.opengovjournal.org
19. MRS (2006) *Freedom of Information Act 2000: Guidance*. London: Market Research Society. CIA. Freedom of Information – www.foia.cia.gov
20. Prior, L. (2003) *Using Documents in Social Research*. London: Sage.
21. Scott, J.C. (1990) *A Matter of Record: Documentary Sources in Social Research*. Cambridge: Polity.
22. Hansen, A. (2009) *Mass Communication Research Methods*. London: Sage.
23. Bazeley, P. (2007) *Qualitative Data Analysis with NVivo*. London: Sage.
24. *QDA Miner* – http://provalisresearch.com/products/qualitative-data-analysis-software/
25. Scott, J.P. (2006) *Documentary Research*. London: Sage. Prior, L. (2003) *Using Documents in Social Research*. Thousand Oaks, CA: Sage.
26. *Wikileaks* – www.wikileaks.org
27. Saldana, J. (2009) *The Coding Manual for Qualitative Researchers*. London: Sage.
28. Krippendorff, K. (2004) *Content Analysis: An Introduction to its Methodology*. Thousand Oaks, CA: Sage.
29. Krippendorff, K. (2004) *Content Analysis: An Introduction to its Methodology*. Thousand Oaks, CA: Sage. Winter, D.G. and Stewart, A.J. (1977) 'Content analysis as a technique for assessing political leaders', in M.G. Hermann (ed.), *A Psychological Examination of Political Leaders*. London: The Free Press. Bligh, M.C. et al. (2004) 'Charisma under crisis: presidential leadership, rhetoric and media responses before and after the September 11th terrorist attacks', *Leadership Quarterly*, 15 (2): 211–239. Insch, G.S. et al. (2002) 'Content analysis in leadership research: examples, procedures, and suggestions for future use', *Leadership Quarterly*, 8 (1): 1–25.
30. Shafer, R.J. (1974) *A Guide to Historical Method*. Homewood, IL: The Dorsey Press.
31. Morrell, K. (2010) 'Leadership, rhetoric, and formalist literary theory', *Journal of Leadership Studies*, 3 (4): 86–90.
32. Gee, J.P. (2005) *An Introduction to Discourse Analysis: Theory and Method*. London: Routledge. van Dijk, T.A. (ed.) (1997) *Discourse Studies*. London: Sage.
33. General discussion - www.discourseanalysis.net. Discourse analysis software – http://sourceforge.net/projects/datool/
34. Cookson, P.W. (1994) 'The power discourse: elite narratives and educational policy formation', in G. Walford (ed.), *Researching the Powerful in Education*. London: UCL Press, pp. 127–128.
35. Fowler, R. (1979) *Language and Control*. London: Routledge. Holes, C. (1995) *Critical Discourse Analysis: The Critical Study of Language*. London: Longman. Bloor, M. and Bloor, T.B. (2007) *The Practice of Critical Discourse Analysis*. London: Hodder Arnold. van Dijk, T.A. (1998) *Ideology: A Multidisciplinary Approach*. London: Sage.
36. Fairclough, N. (2001) *Language and Power*. London: Longman.
37. van Dijk, T.A. (2008) 'Discourse, knowledge, power and politics: towards critical epistemic discourse analysis', lecture CADAAD, Hertfordshire, 10–12 July – www.discourses.org/UnpublishedArticles/Discourse,%20knowledge,%20power%20and%20politics.pdf
38. Williams, C. (2012) *Researching Power, Elites and Leadership*. London: Sage, pp. 195–200.
39. UNEP (2006) *Consistency in Laws and Regulations (46), Manual on Compliance with and Enforcement of Multilateral Environmental Agreements*. Nairobi: United Nations Environment Programme.

40. Thornton, G.C. (1996) *Legislative Drafting*. London: LexisNexis, pp. 72, 113.
41. Atheist Ireland (2010) Freedom of speech campaign. 'Is this blasphemy?' – http://blasphemy.ie/2010/01/01/atheist-ireland-publishes-25-blasphemous-quotes
42. Gospel According to John 8:44.
43. *Hadith of Bukhari*, Vol. 1, Book 8, Hadith 427.
44. Monmonier, M. (1996) *How to Lie with Maps*. Chicago: University of Chicago Press.
45. *Palestinian Maps Omitting Israel* – www.jewishvirtuallibrary.org/jsource/History/palmatoc1.html
46. Ellen, D. (1989) *The Scientific Examination of Documents*. New York: Wiley.
47. Michel, L. and Baier, P.E. (1985) 'The diaries of Adolf Hitler: implications for document examination', *Journal of the Forensic Science Society*, 25: 167.
48. Heingartner, D. (2003) 'Back together again', *New York Times*, 17 July – www.nytimes.com/2003/07/17/technology/back-together-again.html
49. Alden, C. (2011) *Foreign Policy Analysis: New Approaches: Understanding the Diplomacy of War, Profit and Justice*. London: Routledge. Starr, H. (2006) *Approaches, Levels and Methods of Analysis in International Politics: Crossing Boundaries*. Basingstoke: Palgrave.
50. Nagel, S.S. (1999) *Policy Analysis Methods*. New York: New Science Publishers. Fischer, F. et al. (eds) (2006) *Handbook of Public Policy Analysis: Theory, Methods, and Politics*. New York: Marcel Dekker.
51. Williams, C. (2012) *Researching Power, Elites and Leadership*. London: Sage, pp. 204–207.
52. International Institute for Democracy and Electoral Assistance (IDEA) – www.idea.int/resources
53. Grayling, A.C. (2007) *Among the Dead Cities: The History and Moral Legacy of the WWII Bombing of Civilians in Germany and Japan*. New York: Walker & Company.Chomsky, N. and Vltchek, A. (2013) *On Western Terrorism: From Hiroshima to Drone Warfare*. London: Pluto Press.

Chapter 14 Further analysis

1. Nelson, M. (1992) Unpublished discussion at the *Third International Workshop on Closed Ecological Systems*, 24–27 April – www.biospherics.org/hist3rdwkshopintro.html
2. Bronner, S.E. (2011) *Critical Theory: A Very Short Introduction*. Oxford: Oxford University Press.
3. Gould, S.J. (1998) *Full House: The Spread of Excellence from Plato to Darwin*. New York: Random House.
4. Locke, J. (1690) *Essay Concerning Human Understanding*. London.
5. Ragin, C.C. (1992) *The Comparative Method: Moving Beyond Qualitative and Quantitative Strategies*. Berkeley: University of California Press.
6. Friendly, M. (1991) *SAS System for Statistical Graphics*. Cary, NC: SAS Institute, p. 414.
7. *Index Mundi* – www.indexmundi.com/
8. *Country Reports* – compare and contrast – www.countryreports.org
9. *If It Were My Home* – www.ifitweremyhome.com/
10. Diamond, J. and Robinson, J.A. (eds) (2010) *Natural Experiments of History*. Cambridge, MA: Belknap Press of Harvard University Press.
11. Deutsch, D. (2011) *The Beginning of Infinity: Explanations that Transform the World*. London: Allen Lane, pp. 1–33.
12. Shively, W.P. (1980) *The Craft of Political Research*. Upper Saddle River, NJ: Prentice-Hall, pp. 14–15.

13. White, H. (2009) *Theory-Based Impact Evaluation: Principles and Practice.* Working Paper 3. New Delhi: International Initiative for Impact Evaluation.
14. Kutach, D. (2014) *Causation.* Cambridge: Polity.
15. Dasgupta, S. (1927) *A History of Indian Philosophy.* Cambridge: Cambridge University Press, pp. 517–518.
16. Cua, A.S. (1975) 'The problems of causation: East and West', *Philosophy East and West,* 25 (1): 1–10.
17. Ozzie Saffa (2014) 'South Africa: Zuma stirs up ghosts at ANC poll-rouser', 27 January – http://ozziesaffa.blogspot.co.uk/2014/01/south-africa-zuma-stirs-up-ghosts-at.html
18. Williams, C. (ed.) (1998) *Environmental Victims: New Risks, New Injustice.* London: Earthscan, pp. 8–9.
19. Hart, H.L.A. and Honore, A.M. (1985) *Causation in Law.* Oxford: Oxford University Press.
20. Williams, C. (2001) *Leaders of Integrity: Ethics and a Code for Global Leadership.* Amman: United Nation University Leadership Academy.
21. Williams, C. (2006) *Leadership Accountability in a Globalizing World.* London: Palgrave Macmillan.
22. Williams, C. (ed.) (1998) *Environmental Victims: New Risks, New Injustice.* London: Earthscan, pp. 8–9.
23. Boaduo, N.A.-P. (2010) 'Epistemological analysis: conflict and resolution in Africa', *The Journal of Pan African Studies,* 3 (10): 34–45.
24. Lindley, T.F. (1987) 'David Hume and necessary connections', *Philosophy,* 62 (239): 49–58.
25. Wildman, W.J. (2010) 'An introduction to relational ontology', in J. Polkinghorne and J. Zizioulas (eds), *The Trinity and an Entangled World: Relationality in Physical Science and Theology.* Grand Rapids, MI: Eerdmans, pp. 55–73.
26. Barker, C. (2005) *Cultural Studies: Theory and Practice.* London: Sage, p. 448. Giddens, A. (1984) *The Constitution of Society.* Cambridge: Polity.
27. Lewis, D.K. (1973) *Counterfactuals.* Cambridge, MA: Harvard University Press.
28. Rossi, P.H. et al. (2004) *Evaluation: A Systematic Approach.* Thousand Oaks, CA: Sage.
29. Lewin, K. et al. (1939) 'Patterns of aggressive behaviour in experimentally created "social climates"', *Journal of Social Psychology,* 10: 271–299.
30. Ishikawa, K. (1976) *Guide to Quality Control.* Tokyo: Asian Productivity Organization. HCi: Cause and effect diagrams – www.hci.com.au/cause-and-effect-diagrams/
31. Ladkin, P. and Loer, K. (1998) 'Analysing aviation accidents using WB-Analysis – an application of multimodal reasoning', *Spring Symposium,* AAAI, Palo Alto, CA.
32. Sterman, J.D. (2000) *Business Dynamics: Systems Thinking and Modeling for a Complex World.* New York: McGraw-Hill.
33. Mayhew, R.J. (2014) *Malthus: The Life and Legacies of an Untimely Prophet.* Cambridge, MA: Belknap Press.
34. EEA (2013) *Late Lessons from Early Warnings: Science, Precaution, Innovation.* Copenhagen: European Environment Agency.
35. Bostrom, N. (1998) 'Predictions from philosophy? How philosophers could make themselves useful', Department of Philosophy, Logic and Scientific Method, London School of Economics and Political Sciences – http://www.nickbostrom.com/old/predict.html
36. Alverson, C. (2012) 'Polling and statistical models can't predict the future' – www.cameronalverson.com/2012/09/polling-and-statistical-models-cant.html
37. Barrett, J. and Kyle, P. (2006) 'Prediction', in J. Pfeifer and S. Sarkar (eds), *The Philosophy of Science: An Encyclopedia.* New York: Routledge.
38. Williams, M.B. (1982) 'The importance of prediction testing in evolutionary biology', *Erkenntnis,* 17: 291–306.

39. Hawking, S. (1988) *A Brief History of Time: From the Big Bang to Black Holes*. London: Bantam Press, pp. 26–27.
40. Allport, G. (1950) 'The role of expectancy', in H. Cantrill (ed.), *The Tensions that Cause Wars*. Urbana: University of Illinois, pp. 43–78.
41. Williams, C. (2011) 'Learning to redress pre-emptive deceit: the Iraq Dossier', *Sage OPEN* – http://sgo.sagepub.com/content/1/3/2158244011427060.full.print
42. Sharot, T. (2012) *The Optimism Bias: Why We're Wired to Look on the Bright Side*. London: Robinson.
43. Sternberg, R.J. (2002) *Why Smart People Can Be So Stupid*. New Haven, CT: Yale University Press.
44. Johnson, D.D.P. (2004) *Overconfidence and War: The Havoc and Glory of Positive Illusions*. Cambridge, MA: Harvard University Press.
45. Williams, C. (2002) 'New security risks and public educating: the relevance of recent evolutionary brain science', *Journal of Risk Research*, 5 (3): 225–248.
46. Davies, L. (2004) *Education and Conflict; Complexity and Chaos*. London: Routledge Falmer, pp. 34–37.
47. Renshaw, E. (1991) *Modelling Biological Populations in Space and Time*. Cambridge: Cambridge University Press.
48. Smolin, L. (2013) *Time Reborn: From the Crisis in Physics to the Future of the Universe*. London: Houghton Mifflin Harcourt.
49. Williams, C. (2012) *Researching Power, Elites and Leadership*. London: Sage, pp. 78–79.
50. Williams, C. (1997) Terminus Brain: The Environmental Threats to Human Intelligence. London: Cassell, pp. 174–180.
51. Scott, A.J. (ed.) (2001) *Principles of Forecasting: A Handbook for Researchers and Practitioners*. Norwell, MA: Kluwer Academic.
52. Vose, D. (2008) *Risk Analysis: A Quantitative Guide*. London: Wiley.
53. Segudovic, H. (2006) *Qualitative Risk Analysis Method Comparison*. Zagreb: Infigo.
54. Beck, U. (1992) *Risk Society: Towards a New Modernity*. London: Sage.
55. Williams, C. (1997) 'Environmental victims: arguing the costs', *Environmental Values*, 6 (1): 3–30.
56. Segudovic, H. (2006) *Qualitative Risk Analysis Method Comparison*. Zagreb: Infigo.
57. Cornelius, P. et al. (2005) 'Three decades of scenario planning at Shell', *California Management Review*, 98 (1): 92–109.
58. Fahey, L. and Randall, R.M. (1997) *Learning from the Future: Competitive Foresight Scenarios*. London: Wiley. Schwartz, P. (1991) *The Art of the Long View*. London: Doubleday.
59. Davies, S. et al. (2001) *Strategic Futures Thinking: Meta-Analysis of Published Material on Drivers and Trends*. Farnborough: DERA.
60. Holmberg, J. and Robèrt, K.H. (2000) 'Backcasting from non-overlapping sustainability principles: a framework for strategic planning', *International Journal of Sustainable Development and World Ecology*, 7: 291–308.
61. Surowiecki, J. (2005) *The Wisdom of Crowds*. London: Anchor.
62. Wolfers, J. and Zitzewitz, E. (2004) 'Prediction markets', *Journal of Economic Perspectives*, 18 (2): 107–126.
63. Graefe, A. and Armstrong, J.S. (2011) 'Comparing face-to-face meetings, nominal groups, Delphi and prediction markets on an estimation task', *International Journal of Forecasting*, 27 (1): 183–195.
64. Coote, A. and Lenhaglan, J. (1997) *Citizens' Juries: From Theory to Practice*. London: IPPR.
65. Wakeford, T. (2002) 'Citizens juries: a radical alternative for social research', *Social Research Update*, 37 (Summer).
66. Mitchell, T. (1997) *Machine Learning*. New York: McGraw-Hill.

67. Siegel, E. (2013) *Predictive Analytics: The Power to Predict Who Will Click, Buy, Lie, or Die*. London: Wiley.
68. Temple-Raston, D. (2012) 'Predicting the future: fantasy or a good algorithm?' – www.npr.org/2012/10/08/162397787/predicting-the-future-fantasy-or-a-good-algorithm
69. UN Statistics – http://unstats.un.org/unsd/default.htm
70. OECD Data Lab – www.oecd.org/statistics/datalab/
71. Meyer, H.-D. and Benavot, A. (2013) *PISA, Power, and Policy: The Emergence of Global Educational Governance*. Oxford: Symposium. Arndt, C. and Oman, C. (2006) *Uses and Abuses of Governance Indicators*. Paris: OECD Development Centre.
72. Ennew, J. (1996) *Indicators for Children's Rights: A Resource File*. Oslo: UNICEF International Child Development Centre, Childwatch International.
73. Duncan, N. (2006) 'The non-perception based measurement of corruption: a review of issues and methods from a policy perspective', in C. Sampford et al. (eds), *Measuring Corruption*. Burlington, VT: Ashgate, pp. 131–161.
74. Morse, S. (2004) *Indices and Indicators in Development: An Unhealthy Obsession with Numbers*. London: Earthscan.
75. Reed, M.S. et al. (2008) 'Participatory indicator development: what can ecologists and local communities learn from each other?', *Ecological Applications*, 18 (5): 1253–1269.
76. World Bank Institute. Governance indicators. Methods – http://info.worldbank.org/governance/wgi/index.aspx#doc. 'What is the Corruption Perceptions Index?' – http://cpi.transparency.org/cpi2012/in_detail/
77. Munck, G.L. (2009) *Measuring Democracy: A Bridge Between Scholarship and Politics*. Baltimore, MD: Johns Hopkins University Press.
78. Gilley, B. (2006) 'The meaning and measure of state legitimacy: results for 72 countries', *European Journal of Political Research*, 45 (3): 499–525.
79. Bollen, K.A. and Lennox, R. (1991) 'Conventional wisdom on measurement: a structural equation perspective', *Psychological Bulletin*, 110 (2): 305–314.
80. Pakinkis, T. (2012) 'The state of music piracy: in-depth data from new global report', *Musicweek*, 17 September – www.musicweek.com/news/read/musicmetric-s-global-file-sharing-data-in-full/051817. See: http://static.semetric.com/dmi/Musicmetric_DMI_Extended_Summary_2012.pdf
81. Huggins, M. (2011) 'Interviewing perpetrators – theorizing State' (Research on Brazilian police torturers, 1964–1985), unpublished paper, *Research Methods Workshop: 'The State of State Crime Research'*, International State Crime Initiative (ISCI), King's College, London, April.
82. Yueh, L. (2013) *China's Growth: The Making of an Economic Superpower*. Oxford: Oxford University Press.
83. Falk, I. and Guenther, J. (2006) 'Generalising from qualitative research: case studies from VET in contexts', *15th NCVER Conference*, Mooloolaba, Queensland. Williams, M. (2000) 'Interpretivism and generalisation', *Sociology*, 34 (2): 209–224.
84. Lincoln, Y. and Guba, E. (1985) *Naturalistic Inquiry*. Newbury Park, CA: Sage, pp. 124, 217.
85. Haun, D. (2011) 'How odd I am!', in M. Brockman (ed.), *Future Science*. Oxford: Oxford University Press, pp. 224–235.
86. Booth, C. (2010) *Did Bach Really Mean That? Deceptive Notation in Baroque Keyboard Music*. Wells: Soundboard.
87. Green, A.H. (2013) 'Multiple systems estimation: the basics' – https://hrdag.org/mse-the-basics/
88. Somekh, B. (2011) *Theory and Methods in Social Research*. London: Sage. Woodiwiss, A. (2005) *Scoping the Social*. London: Open University Press.
89. Custers, P. (2010) 'Military Keynesianism today: an innovative discourse', *Race and Class*, 51 (4): 79–94.

90. Gould, S.J. (1979) *Ever Since Darwin*. New York: W.W. Norton, pp. 161–162.
91. Chemers, M.M. (2000) 'Leadership research and theory: a functional integration', *Group Dynamics: Theory, Research, and Practice*, 4 (1): 27–43.
92. Berger, J. and Zelditch, M. (1993) *Theoretical Research Programs: Studies in Theory Growth*. Stanford, CA: Stanford University Press.
93. al-Bīrūnī, Abū al-Rayḥān (1910) (E. Sachau, ed.) *Al-Beruni's India: An Account of the Religion, Philosophy, Literature, Geography, Chronology, Astronomy, Customs, Laws and Astrology of India*. London: Kegan Paul, Trench, Trubner, Vol. 1, pp. 8, 17, 24.
94. Johnson, B. and Christensen, L. (2004) *Educational Research: Quantitative, Qualitative, and Mixed Approaches, Research Edition*. Boston: Allyn & Bacon, p. 19.
95. Russell, B. (1946/2004) *A History of Western Philosophy*. London: Routledge, p. 548.
96. Baron, J. (2000) *Thinking and Deciding*. New York: Cambridge University Press.
97. Oswald, M.E. et al. (2004) 'Confirmation bias', in R.F. Pohl (ed.), *Cognitive Illusions: A Handbook on Fallacies and Biases in Thinking, Judgement and Memory*. Hove: Psychology Press, pp. 79–96.
98. Williams, C. (2006) *Leadership Accountability in a Globalizing World*. London: Palgrave Macmillan, pp. 110–119.
99. Odysseos, L. (2002) 'Dangerous ontologies: the ethos of survival and ethical theorizing in International Relations', *Review of International Studies*, 28 (2): 403–418.

Chapter 15 Reporting the research

1. Gowers, E. (1948) *Plain Words: A Guide to the Use of English*. London: His Majesty's Stationery Office.
2. Bastow, S. et al. (2014) *The Impact of the Social Sciences: How Academics Make a Difference*. London: Sage.
3. Richardson, L. (1990) *Writing Strategies*. London: Sage.
4. Corti, L. et al. (2014) *Managing and Sharing Research Data: A Guide to Good Practice*. London: Sage.
5. Cutts, M. (1999) *Plain English Guide: How to Write Clearly and Communicate Better*. Oxford: Oxford University Press.
6. Dorner, J. (2002) *Writing for the Internet*. Oxford: Oxford University Press.
7. Nel, F. (2001) *Writing for the Media*. Oxford: Oxford University Press.
8. Orwell, G. (1946) 'Politics and the English language', *Horizon*, April. George Orwell Web Ring – www.orwell.ru/library/essays/politics/english/e_polit
9. Associated Press. *AP Stylebook* – www.apstylebook.com/?do=product
10. British English media style guide – www.theguardian.com/guardian-observer-style-guide-a
11. *Writing Effectively for WHO* – www.colelearning.net/who
12. IPCC climate change glossaries – www.ipcc.ch/publications_and_data/publications_and_data_glossary.shtml
13. *Wikipedia: Manual of Style* – http://en.wikipedia.org/wiki/Wikipedia:Manual_of_Style
14. Tactile documents for blind and partially sighted people – www.tactilePhoto.com www.tactileview.com
15. Bashford, L. et al. (1995) 'Parallel text: making research accessible to people with learning difficulties', *International Journal of Disability, Development and Education*, 42 (3): 211–220.

16. Day, R.A. and Gastel, B. (2006) *How to Write and Publish a Scientific Paper.* Cambridge: Cambridge University Press.
17. Royal Geographical Society. 'Recording your expedition' – www.rgs.org/OurWork/Publications/EAC+publications/Expedition+Handbook/Recording+your+expedition.htm
18. Holmes, B. (1985) 'The problem (solving) approach', in A. Watson and R. Wilson (eds), *Contemporary Issues in Comparative Education.* London: Croom Helm.
19. Parkin, S. (2010) *The Positive Deviant: Sustainability Leadership in a Perverse World.* London: Earthscan.
20. Bronner, S.E. (2011) *Critical Theory: A Very Short Introduction.* Oxford: Oxford University Press.
21. EEA (2002/2012) *Late Lessons from Early Warnings: The Precautionary Principle 1896–2000.* Copenhagen: European Environment Agency.
22. Denicolo, P. and Becker, L. (2011) *Success in Publishing Journal Articles.* London: Sage.
23. Denicolo, P. and Becker, L. (2011) *Success in Research Proposals.* London: Sage.
24. Knight, D. (2006) *Public Understanding of Science: A History of Communicating Scientific Ideas.* London: Routledge.
25. David Spiegelhalter's personal home page – www.statslab.cam.ac.uk/Dept/People/Spiegelhalter/davids.html
26. McCandless, D. (2010) *Information is Beautiful.* London: Collins.
27. Visualizations – www.cleverfranke.com/
28. Few, S. (2004) *Show Me the Numbers: Designing Tables and Graphs to Enlighten.* Oakland, CA: Analytics Press.
29. Joiner Associates Staff (1995) *Flowcharts: Plain and Simple Learning and Application Guide.* Greenwood: Oriel Inc.
30. Damelio, R. (1996) *The Basics of Process Mapping.* New York: Productivity Press.
31. Tufte, E.R. (1990) *Envisioning Information.* Cheshire: Graphics Press.
32. Tufte, E.R. (2003) *The Cognitive Style of Power Point.* Cheshire: Graphics Press.
33. Tufte, E.R. (2001) *The Visual Display of Quantitative Information.* Cheshire: Graphics Press.
34. Ellen, D. (1989) *The Scientific Examination of Documents.* New York: Wiley. (Ch. 11: 'Document examination in court'.)
35. Williams, C. (2012) *Draw and Tell: Street Children in Apartheid South Africa, ISCI* – www.statecrime.org/testimonyproject/drawandtell
36. Cornwall, A. and Coehlo, V. (eds) (2006) *Spaces for Change? The Politics of Citizen Participation in New Democratic Arenas.* London: Zed Books.
37. Gavanta, J. (2006) 'Finding the spaces for change: a power analysis', *IDS Bulletin*, 37 (6): 23–33.
38. Vermeulen, S. (2005) *Power Tools: Handbook to Tools and Resources for Policy Influence in Natural Resource Management.* London: IIED.
39. Keophilavong, S. (2008) *The Democracy Initiative: Researching Power and Influence.* London: Carnegie Trust.
40. Hunjan, R. and Keophilavong, S. (2010) *Power and Making Change Happen.* Dunfermline: Carnegie UK Trust. Williams, C. (2012) *Researching Power, Elites and Leadership.* London: Sage.
41. Nkloma, S.H. (2003) *Encouraging Change.* London: TALC.
42. Transparency International. Policy and research – www.transparency.org/policy_research_surveys_indices/cpi/2008
43. Williams, C. (1995) 'Crime and abuse against people with learning disabilities'. Findings – www.jrf.org.uk/sites/files/jrf/sc70.pdf
44. ESRC. 'Evidence briefings' – www.esrc.ac.uk/publications/evidence-briefings/default.aspx
45. Stephens, C. et al. (2001) *Environmental Justice.* ESRC Global Environmental Change Programme – www.foe.co.uk/resource/reports/environmental_justice.pdf

46. Tehelka – www.tehelka.com
47. Social Science Research Network – www.ssrn.com
48. SCRIBD – www.scribd.com
49. *Ranking Web of World Repositories* – http://repositories.webometrics.info
50. *Hutton Inquiry* – www.the-hutton-inquiry.org.uk/content/evidence.htm#full
51. *Iraq Inquiry Digest* – www.iraqinquirydigest.org/?p=5355
52. Abuse of power organizations – www.datehookup.com/content-organizations-dedicated-to-fighting-abuse.htm
53. Bastow, S. et al. (2013) *The Impact of the Social Sciences*. London: Sage.
54. Altmetrics Collection (2012) *PLOS Collections* – www.ploscollections.org/altmetrics
55. DFID (2013) *Research Uptake*. London: DFID.
56. Robinson, C. and Latham, J. (2012) 'The Goodman affair: Monsanto targets the heart of science' – www.earthopensource.org/index.php/news/147-the-goodman-affair-monsanto-targets-the-heart-of-science
57. Goldsmith, Z. (2010) 'So much for "sense" about science', *The Guardian*, 5 January – www.theguardian.com/commentisfree/2010/jan/05/sense-about-science-celebrity-observations
58. Monbiot, G. (2010) 'These Astroturf libertarians are the real threat to democracy', *The Guardian*, 14 December: 29.
59. Hoffman, G. (2013) 'Government to use citizens as army in social media war', *The Jerusalem Post*, 14 August – www.jpost.com/Diplomacy-and-Politics/Government-to-use-citizens-as-army-in-social-media-war-322972
60. Herley, C. (2012) 'Why do Nigerian scammers say they are from Nigeria?', Microsoft Research – http://research.microsoft.com/pubs/167719/WhyFromNigeria.pdf

Index